# From Theory of Knowledge Management to Practice

*Edited by Fausto Pedro García Márquez and René Vinicio Sánchez Loja*

Published in London, United Kingdom

From Theory of Knowledge Management to Practice
http://dx.doi.org/10.5772/intechopen.1000367
Edited by Fausto Pedro García Márquez and René Vinicio Sánchez Loja

Contributors
Jan Kazmierczak, Leila Halawi, Kei Aoki, Seyyed Mohammad Kashef, Steven T. Buccola, Dora Gelo Čolić, Massimo Vaccarini, Alessandro Carbonari, Francesco Spegni, Alberto Giretti, Saba Qadhi, Hakem Sharari, Stéphane Goria, Audrey Sanctorum, Jan Maushagen, Sara Sepehri, Guillaume Vrijens, Joery De Kock, Tamara Vanhaecke, Olga De Troyer, Christophe Debruyne, Jonathan Whiting, Cesar Ricardo Castillo, Jon Weers, Katie Peterson, Will Peplinski, Kelley Ruehl, Andrea Copping, Megan Anderson, Fadia Ticona Rollano, Nicholas Gilroy, Paul Susmarski, Lysel Garavelli, Hanna Fields, Hayley Farr, Sean Morris, Yuichi Matsumoto



First published in London, United Kingdom, 2024 by IntechOpen
IntechOpen is the global imprint of INTECHOPEN LIMITED, registered in England and Wales, registration number: 11086078, 5 Princes Gate Court, London, SW7 2QJ, United Kingdom

British Library Cataloguing-in-Publication Data
A catalogue record for this book is available from the British Library

Additional hard and PDF copies can be obtained from orders@intechopen.com

From Theory of Knowledge Management to Practice
Edited by Fausto Pedro García Márquez and René Vinicio Sánchez Loja
p. cm.
Print ISBN 978-1-83769-422-8
Online ISBN 978-1-83769-421-1
eBook (PDF) ISBN 978-1-83769-423-5

For EU product safety concerns:
IN TECH d.o.o., Prolaz Marije Krucifikse Kozulić 3, 51000 Rijeka, Croatia,
info@intechopen.com or visit our website at intechopen.com.

# Meet the editors

Fausto Pedro García Márquez is a full Professor at the University of Castilla-La Mancha (UCLM), Spain, an honorary senior research fellow at Birmingham University, UK, a lecturer at the Postgraduate European Institute, and a research fellow at INTI International University & Colleges, Malaysia. Previously, he was a senior manager at Accenture. He obtained his European Ph.D. with maximum distinction. He is recipient of numerous awards and prizes, including Runner Prize (2023), Nominate Prize (2022), Gran Maestre (2022), Grand Prize (2021), Runner Prize (2020) and Advancement Prize (2018), Runner (2015), Advancement (2013) and Silver (2012) by the International Society of Management Science and Engineering Management (ICMSEM), First International Business Ideas Competition 2017 Award (2017), and more. He has published more than 257 papers and more than 53 books,100 book chapters, and 6 patents. He is the editor of five international journals and a committee member of more than seventy conferences. He has been the principal investigator in four European projects, eight national projects, and more than 150 projects for universities, companies, and so on. His main interests include artificial intelligence, maintenance, management, renewable energy, transport, advanced analytics, and data science. Dr. Márquez is an expert for AI4People (European Institute for Science, Media and Democracy) and the European Science Foundation. He is also the director of the INGENIUM group, a senior member of the Institute of Electrical and Electronics Engineers (IEEE), an honorary member of the Research Council of the Indian Institute of Finance, and a committee chair of the International Society for Management Science and Engineering Management (ISMSEM).

René Vinicio Sánchez Loja is a full professor at the Universidad Politécnica Salesiana (UPS), Ecuador. He obtained his master's degree and Ph.D. in Industrial Technologies Research at the Universidad Nacional de Educación a Distancia (UNED), Spain, as well as a Ph.D. in Engineering at the Universidad Pontificia Bolivariana, Colombia. He has been a professor at UPS since 2004, mainly in areas related to sequential process automation. In 2014, Dr. Loja founded the Industrial Technologies Research and Development Group (GIDTEC) and completed a guest Ph.D. abroad at Chongqing University of Technology and Business, China. He has been a senior member of the Institute of Electrical and Electronics Engineers (IEEE) since 2022. He has extensive experience in conference organization, technology project implementation, and research project management and execution. He has more than sixty scientific publications to his credit and is a reviewer for several high-impact journals. His current interests include project management, condition-based maintenance, engineering education, and Industry 4.0, especially for small- and medium-sized enterprises (SMEs).

# Contents

# Preface

This book is a comprehensive guide that bridges the gap between theory and practical application in knowledge management. Its interdisciplinary approach, integrating engineering/technology with organizational and planning aspects, is crucial in today's complex business landscape.

The diverse array of contributors sharing their expertise through different chapters enriches the content by offering varied perspectives and case studies across sectors. It is particularly valuable that the book covers various sub-disciplines such as economics, finance, marketing, and decision and risk analysis, illustrating the broad relevance of knowledge management principles.

The emphasis on demonstrating theory through real-world case studies provides a tangible understanding of how these principles are applied in different scenarios. Moreover, the progression from fundamental theories to more intricate decision-making processes, especially when dealing with extensive data sets like big data, is commendable. The inclusion of computational techniques, dynamic analysis, probabilistic methods, and optimization strategies is crucial in addressing multifaceted decision-making challenges within defined constraints.

Overall, this book offers a holistic view of knowledge management by combining theoretical foundations with practical insights and advanced analysis techniques, making it a valuable resource for professionals seeking to navigate the complexities of modern business environments.

**Fausto Pedro García Márquez**
Ingenium Research Group,
University of Castilla-La Mancha,
Ciudad Real, Spain

**René Vinicio Sánchez Loja**
Research and Development Group in Industrial Technologies,
Salesian Polytechnic University,
Cuenca, Ecuador

Chapter 1

# How to Manage Knowledge Supporting Stakeholders of Smart Cities?

*Jan Kazmierczak*


## Abstract

The chapter discusses a proposal to use a process approach to describe the transformation of urban space into smart space. Such an approach was used as a basis for discussing the need for knowledge resources and the availability of such resources in Smart City knowledge management. Using the classical management model, a methodology for carrying out the tasks of planning, organizing, and utilizing the knowledge resources of various stakeholders in Smart City creation processes is shown. The final section presents practical examples of complex problems in the area under discussion. The sub-statement shows a subjective overview of the problems that need to be addressed in further research work.


**Keywords:** Smart City, Smart City creation process, knowledge resources, knowledge management, stakeholders of Smart City processes

## 1. Introduction

Since relatively recently, there has been a very intense, even exponential increase in the number of publications appearing in various search engines after typing in the keywords "Smart City" or "Smart Cities" (S.C.). For example, in the Mendeley® search engine, the use of the aforementioned keywords resulted in finding 2579 items in 2015, but in 2022 there are already 8827 items. Research devoted to the idea of a Smart City has previously appeared in various research centers [1–3], while the authorship of the aforementioned concept itself is quite commonly attributed to scientists from the Massachusetts Institute of Technology [4, 5]. The idea of a functional comparison of information flow networks in the city with similar flows in the human body has sometimes been criticized for the excessive anthropomorphization of such an approach, but at the same time, it has been correlated with the approach, appearing in studies, dealing with the "urban organism" [6, 7]. The work published in 2001 [8], representing the current research on the problems of managing an intelligent society in an urban e-environment is also worth mentioning.

Today, the term Smart City has moved beyond its original IT-related framework. Perhaps the best way to convey the meaning of the term is to say that smart urban space is the result of transforming an existing urbanized space (or the result of building such a space from scratch), in which users live better. The term "quality of life improvement" is also used. However, the above statements contain a fair amount of ambiguity, especially in defining the beneficiaries of such a better life.

The approach of the authors of many publications to this issue is, in a sense, the fault of B. Cohen, who proposed [9] the following classification of Smart City creation processes (referred to in this chapter as "S.C. processes") using the "fashionable" notation: Smart City 1.0, Smart City 2.0, and Smart City 3.0.

Cohen takes as the basis of his, perhaps oversimplified, proposal the assumption that the participants in the processes of creating a better living space in cities are: (1) providers of information systems that potentially give a city an intelligence value, (2) the authorities of the cities where such systems will be implemented, and (3) the residents of those cities. It further assumes that in successive classes of S.C. processes (with increasing value of the index), individual groups of beneficiaries cease to be objective and become subjective participants in activities aimed at creating Smart City space and become leaders of S.C. processes. Such leaders in the Smart City 1.0 class are system providers (group 1) and in the Smart City 2.0 class, the functions of project leaders are taken over by city authorities (group 2). In the Smart City 3.0 class, there is the involvement and active participation of group participants (3). Linking Cohen's proposal to one of the emerging approaches in the literature of the Smart City as a "city of happy people" [10, 11] one can somewhat sarcastically conclude that in the S.C. 1.0 process group, happy are the system providers (because they do good business); in the S.C. 2.0 group, happy are city officials (because they get a good theme for self-promotion); while in the S.C. 3.0 group, theoretically happy should be all participants in the process, including, most importantly, city residents. However, it is not known what it will be like in reality, as the level of S.C. 3.0 remains so far - in the opinion of the author of this chapter - a futuristic entity.

B. Cohen, moreover, with his proposal, caused a certain limitation in the attention of many researchers, especially on such issues as the categorization of knowledge needed to manage a city (not only an intelligent one!) or the available and usable sources of such knowledge (along with an assessment of the possibility of obtaining it). Using Cohen's concept, one should probably automatically assume that the leader of the S.C. process from a particular group automatically has the knowledge necessary to effectively manage the implementation of that process. This means that it is assumed that, for example, the IT system provider who won the tender for the IT equipment for the S.C. process in city X, just by virtue of that decision, has the knowledge necessary to carry out the implementation. Similarly, the newly elected mayor of a city has such knowledge as a result of the majority (voters) decision. Problems such as the source or sources of this knowledge remain unknown. Moreover, Cohen's proposed uniformity does not facilitate consideration of the particularly high level of diversity of potential sources of knowledge relating to any unique urban organism and its unique environment when considering urban knowledge.

It is, of course, possible to identify repetitive areas in the functioning of urban organisms (e.g., the organization of traffic, the organization of public transportation, or systems for providing useful information). However, the effectiveness of such an approach depletes with the increasing complexity, and at the same time with individualization of the knowledge necessary for managing a specific sphere of public services in a specific city, as well as in managing the city as a whole.

It is worth adding at this point that those ideas of "higher categories" (i.e., 4.0, 5.0, etc.) of S.C. processes have already appeared in the described studies, usually linking such processes to Industry 4.0 and Society 5.0 concepts (e.g., [12] or Green Economy [13]).

However, in this study, the author, in accordance with Ockham's prohibition of multiplying entities, decided to limit his considerations to "existing entities," i.e., Smart City 1.0, Smart City 2.0, and (if successful) Smart City 3.0 processes.

Referring to the search results of the studies cited above, it can be pointed out here that for the set of keywords "Smart cities knowledge manager" in 2015, 86 items were found in the Mendeley® search engine, and in 2022–183 items, so a very small percentage of publications on smart cities. Only very recently have cross-cutting studies appeared in the subject area, such as [14] or [15]. However, there are no known works presenting a unified methodological approach to the management of knowledge about (and for) a Smart City. Therefore, the author of this study decided to offer the methodological proposals presented below, which assume that any action or activities undertaken (including those related to urban knowledge) should correspond to a previously identified need or needs.

Let us try, as a kind of guide for identifying the needs and determining the means and ways of managing knowledge of an intelligent urbanized space, as well as managing knowledge in such a space, to use the well-known and long-used (since ancient times?) 5 W + H model [16], in which the starting point for solving the problem are the questions: What?, Why?, Where?, When?, Who? and finally How?

According to this model, let us next attempt to clarify the content (elaboration) of the above questions, relating them to the problems of knowledge management in a Smart City. In particular, let us ask:

1. What (what - resulting from the identified needs - goal do we intend to achieve)?

2. Why (why do we feel we need to achieve the identified goal)?

3. Where (where are we going to implement the planned project)?

4. When (when do we plan to start and complete this project)?

5. Who (who will implement and/or participate in this project)?

6. How (with what means and ways will the venture be implemented?

Since the order in which the individual questions are asked is not, from the point of view of the applicability of the methodology described above, *important as* an element that determines the plan for the implementation of the task, when planning the research intention described in this chapter, it was assumed that the question *Q1* i.e., the question about the purpose of the activity, requires an answer. The simplest answer to this question is that the goal is to identify the body of knowledge necessary for the transformation of a selected urbanized space (city) into a smart space.

Let us then try to answer question *Q3* i.e., the question about the place whose purpose is formulated above. The simplest answer to the question, stating that such a place is a city, is trivial. In contrast, an answer that includes the name of a specific city also leads nowhere. Each city is, for obvious reasons, unique and unrepeatable, so creating a methodology for such a unique object also seems pointless. However, by analyzing any city as a complex organism performing various functions, we can find repetitive elements in the ways these functions are performed. This can provide a basis for developing certain patterns that can be used for various specific situations. Thus, the author made an attempt, described in this chapter, to propose a certain model approach to the consideration of urban knowledge, usable not only in one specific case of an urban organism.

Before moving on to the next section, let us further assume that the answer to question *Q4* is now and in the near future. The term "near future" here refers to the practice of the processes of investment planning and implementation carried out by city governments. In other words, the author assumes that the considerations in this study do not refer to futuristic processes.

Concluding the introduction to this chapter, it is still necessary to point out that the term "management" will be understood as the process of planning and organizing the resources and activities of an entity in order to achieve certain goals in the most effective and efficient manner possible. In this approach, efficiency in management refers to the proper performance of tasks at minimum cost. In practical terms, we will try to show a sequence of activities, including (A) planning, (B) organizing, (C) motivating, and (D) monitoring the process of creating a Smart City. This chapter highlights the first and second management task areas.

## 2. Identification of stakeholder groups as the basis of the city knowledge acquisition plan

The next question that should be answered at this point is question *Q5*, or "Who?". It was decided to use the concept of "stakeholders" as the basis for formulating this answer. The most popular definition of a stakeholder, by R. E. Freeman [17, 18] says that a stakeholder is any person or group that can influence or is influenced by the achievement of an organization's goals.

It seems natural to assume that the undertakings discussed in this chapter must involve as many stakeholders as possible in the processes of creating and using smart urban space (Smart City). Thus, the author decided, as a first step, to identify the groups of stakeholders participating realistically or potentially in the processes of transforming urbanized space into smart space.

This study intentionally (see the above reference to question *Q4*) omits the theme of creating smart urban space from scratch. Such a theme results in visualizations available on the web, where we can see beautiful space and urban solutions, beautiful buildings, and lots of greenery, while there are usually no "down-to-earth" (or even "underground") elements, not to mention the presence in this space, the so-called normal (not idealized) residents. We do not see there, for example, internal and external logistic routes, the problem of waste generated by the urbanized area, the presence of sources of environmental pollution in the urban space (dust, sewage, and noise), and many other, less pleasant effects of any space inhabited by humans. We also usually do not see the presence of inhabitants in such a space, treated not as an averaged population of a given size, but as a very complex social group, whose - perhaps - only common distinguishing feature is residence in one area. Above all, we do not see actual human behavior, both individual and group behavior, with the group generally representing only a part of the city's population.

In addition, it is worth noting that not only residents can be perceived as users of the urban space which is intended to be transformed into a smart one. Such a space is, after all, an area of various activities of newcomers from outside the city, so they cannot be perceived as a homogeneous group. These include, in particular, people associated with the education system at various levels (from kindergartens to universities), i.e., teachers and students living outside the city, people conducting business in the city but living outside it, people employed in production and service companies, including, for example, stores or restaurants, also living outside the city, people visiting relatives and friends living in the city, and, finally, management entities of a regional and national nature with delegations (representative offices, offices, etc.) in the city, together with some of the staff coming from outside the city to their place of work. In some of the cities included in the S.C. processes, a significant group of public space users may also be tourists or pilgrims visiting places of worship. This should also include individuals or groups of individuals managing, respectively, facilities visited by tourists and places of worship with their infrastructure (e.g., temples). It is justified to ask whether these groups should also be treated as equal stakeholders in the above-mentioned processes.

For the purposes of this study, it was decided to consider the following as stakeholders in the process of transforming the city into a Smart City:

1. City authorities, empowered to make strategic planning decisions and budgetary decisions, including usually:

    a. Decision-making body: City Council.

    b. Executive body: the Mayor of the City and his deputy or deputies, together with the clerical structures that support him (City Hall).

    c. Other entities whose participation in decision-making regarding the operation of the city is conditioned by existing solutions of a legislative nature.

2. Managers of entities responsible for carrying out tasks in the area of broadly defined municipal management and the so-called own tasks of the city (e.g., in Poland such a task is the organization of education at the level of kindergartens and elementary schools) and managers of other public facilities (e.g., health care facilities or facilities of a cultural and sports or recreational nature).

3. City residents, both participating in the processes in question individually and through appropriate structures of a representative nature (residents' associations, NGOs, neighborhood councils, etc.).

4. Providers of technical solutions that can be used in S.C. processes (primarily, but not exclusively, solutions from the ICT area).

5. Experts, supporting the activities of primarily the city government, but also stakeholders from other groups. The term "experts" is used here to describe all providers of knowledge complementing the stock of such knowledge possessed by the internal stakeholders indicated above to the extent necessary for effective city management.

The author decided not to include persons and entities "structurally external" to the analyzed urban organism in the list of stakeholders of S.C. processes presented above. Such a nature can be attributed, for example, to legislative bodies, creating the legal framework for the implementation of S.C. processes, or to control bodies, authorized by law to check the correctness of the implementation of these processes, both formally (e.g., compliance with the obligation to spend public funds in a tender formula) and financially. However, it was deemed necessary to take into account the participation of stakeholders from "external" groups (4) and (5) each time in the S.C. process, whose knowledge should, by definition, fill in the gaps in the body of knowledge held by internal stakeholders.

Each of the above-mentioned stakeholder groups has (potentially and realistically) a certain amount of knowledge, concerning the functioning of "its" urban organism. At the same time, it is reasonable to assume that such knowledge may not be sufficient to initiate and carry out the tasks of this particular group in transforming this organism into a smart urban space.

In the considerations presented here, it is important to perceive such transformation not as a project, but as a process. The project approach seems unjustified here insofar as activities aimed at transforming urban space into smart space cannot be closed in a specific time frame. After all, we are observing the constant development of all kinds of solutions, already used or possible to be used in space, defined by the term "Smart City." The assumption that the possibilities of such development will be exhausted at some point seems unfounded.

Let us further assume that, in practical terms, the process of building a smart urbanized space can be perceived in a discrete manner, that is, as a sequence of discrete states of the process that follow one another, with a specific time step [19]. In this approach, we can conceive of the process as a film, and the instantaneous state of this process as a single frame of the film. Consequently, this chapter uses the term "S.C. process" in reference to the transformation of urban space into a smart space (Smart City) in the sense presented above. The tasks carried out as part of the process are sections of the film, in which the first frame shows the initial state and the last frame – the assumed target state.

The initial classification of tasks, also in the process of transforming urban space into smart space, should include:

I. To identify and describe a sequence of past states (the history of the process under study),

II. Identify and describe the current state of the process,

III. Determine, to the extent possible, the future of the process, e.g., using appropriate forecasting methods [20–22].

Transferring the above set of tasks to the field of research on knowledge in and about the Smart City, it is necessary to repeat the statement that the development of science and technology offers more and more opportunities to apply innovative solutions in making urban space more user-friendly (smarter?). The above statement determines the necessity for stakeholders, especially decision makers of S.C. processes, to keep up with such developments, also in terms of managing the knowledge necessary for their tasks. Therefore, the task plan, aimed at managing such a body of knowledge, should take into account, in addition to the need to initially identify the body of available knowledge and determine the means and ways of acquiring, collecting, and sharing it, the need to plan and organize adequate means and ways of supplementing such knowledge.

## 3. Knowledge of the city in the process of transforming this city into a smart space

Now let us ask how the concept of a "Smart City" relates to any existing and inhabited, larger or smaller city that has the ambition to be smart but is in a particular "existing (current) state."

As indicated above, three groups of stakeholders from those indicated above naturally exist and function in any urban body: groups (1), (2), and (3). These are the groups that make up the "social infrastructure" of a given city and have, through the functioning of "structural" mechanisms, so to speak, for acquiring and collecting data, processing this data to obtain useful information and, as a result, creating a certain body of knowledge about that city.

Such knowledge primarily includes the history (in discrete process terms: a sequence of previous states over a pre-approved time horizon) and the current state of the city, identifiable in particular by:

A. Specific territorial conditions, such as the location of the city (region, country, continent, and climate zone) and specific neighborhoods affect, for example, the way municipal tasks are carried out. Nowadays, the formula of metropolises as peculiar communities of local government units, established by a group of neighboring units to jointly carry out specific tasks, is widespread. In the author's place of residence (the region of Upper Silesia in Poland) there is a metropolitan structure (the Metropolis GZM), which unites 41 cities and municipalities with a total area of 2.5 thousand square kilometers, in which 2.3 million residents live. Within the GZM, most of its entities are in contact with each other's borders, with the result that many cities border only cities (and not rural areas). Such a structure of neighborhoods has led to the decision of the Metropolitan Cities and Municipalities to delegate to the Metropolitan Management Board to carry out its own tasks of organizing public transportation in the entire area of the GZM.

B. Specific geographic, climatic, and geological conditions, that determine the manner of land development. We are talking, for example, about the need for specific solutions in the construction of buildings in earthquake zones, zones threatened by frequent river flooding, or, finally, zones in which existing and planned urban infrastructure may be threatened by the effects of such human activities as underground mining (surface damage caused by ground movements forced by mine operations) or open-pit mining (significantly affecting the state of groundwater).

C. Urban conditions, i.e., existing residential and non-residential buildings, historical monuments, green, recreational, and sports areas with their own infrastructure, places of religious worship, industrial areas with production facilities, etc.

D. Municipal infrastructure, i.e., road network, bridges, and viaducts, above- and underground rail networks (streetcar, subway, and railroad), electrical networks, gas pipelines, water pipelines, and sewage networks together with their own instrumentation (transformer stations, switching stations, pumping stations, and treatment plants)

E. The social profile of the city's residents (number of residents, age profile, education, and property status).

F. Other historical and cultural conditions, such as the presence among the city's residents of adherents of different religions, national minorities, or clusters of immigrants.

Such an existing reality conditions, on the one hand, an identified or identifiable, to a greater or lesser extent, specificity of knowledge needed in managing such an "urban reality" and, on the other hand, a specific set of end users, using such knowledge to a different extent and in different ways. In particular, such knowledge should be the basis for the initial decision to undertake the implementation of the process of transforming a city space into a smart space.

It should be borne in mind, of course, that first of all, the body of knowledge of a particular stakeholder group in a particular area is not, by definition, the same as that of another group. This is primarily due to the dissimilarity of knowledge acquisition channels. Secondly, on the other hand, the extent of knowledge collected and stored by stakeholders is strongly related to the ways in which such knowledge is used. Slightly generalizing, we can assume that stakeholders from the first group most often and most willingly use knowledge based on statistical data, the individual city resident is not interested in being an "average resident." Instead, it is important for him to have detailed knowledge about his immediate environment: family, neighbors, and local community.

According to the author of this chapter, the factors differentiating the process of creating a Smart City "from scratch" and the process of transforming an existing and functioning urban organism into a Smart City are worth discussing at this point. Here we can notice key differences, conditioning the possibilities of knowledge acquisition and utilization.

In the first option, internal stakeholders - at least at the time of planning, organizing, and starting the process of building the target structure in practice do not exist. The city, which is just beginning to emerge or is still in the planning and design phase, has no residents, authorities, or municipal services, or has authorities in a seed state. Without fear of making a big mistake, it can be assumed that the people employed by the entity creating such a new structure will, for the vast majority, not be associated with it ultimately. This brings on a moral hazard to treat the target stakeholders in a maximally simplified and idealized way. This is evident in a great many studies dealing with S.C. The authors of the process usually devote only limited attention to the issue of the presence of residents in such a newly emerging urban organism. For example, it is assumed that all residents will be equally well educated and heavily involved in the S.C. process and that this involvement will be based on altruistic attitudes [23, 24]. It can be somewhat maliciously stated that the creators of such concepts most often wish that all residents of the newly created smart urbanized space will be young, beautiful, healthy, and at least tolerate (and perhaps love?) each other.

However, in option two, when attempting to transform existing urban space into smart space, we must face a much more difficult and complex problem. In particular, we cannot arbitrarily make simplifying (and usually facilitating) assumptions, but must take into account the "existing state," both the state of the city's inanimate matter and the state of its population, along with all the factors that impede - potentially and usually realistically - the S.C. process.

It is worth formulating a few more detailed questions at this point, such as:

- Can the characteristics of smart space be obtained by existing urban space and under what conditions?

- What means and ways can enable a city to achieve “smart” characteristics if such a process starts from “found” conditions?

Sometimes it is also worth asking (which can be extremely important in practice, especially for financial reasons):

- Can the process of a city acquiring the characteristics of “intelligence” be subject to staging?

- Whether the implementation and possible staging of Smart solutions can and should apply only to selected “sectoral” tasks (e.g., only the organization of public transportation or the system of supplying residents with water linked to the disposal of municipal wastewater)?

- What sectors of the city’s operations should and can be included in the transformation first?

- What order of implementation (rank of importance/relevance) should be adopted for each stage of the S.C. process?

An inquiry may also be warranted:

- What is the end goal of a given task in the S.C. process (what instantaneous state do we intend to achieve)?

- What resources are needed to achieve this goal?

- What preparatory activities are required to start the implementation of the task (e.g., change of the spatial development plan for part of the city, public consultations, obtaining external funding)?

- What is the deadline for achieving the end goal for this task?

It seems obvious that, just as the structures of any existing and functioning urban organism are created and developed in stages, the city’s intelligence is also worth building in a similar way. Since the S.C. process is multi-faceted, i.e., it involves many different aspects of the city’s functioning (e.g., communications, security, and waste management), the process stages oriented to these aspects can be implemented in parallel or partially overlap in time. However, it must be remembered that each aspect goal is part of an overarching goal: building a smart urban space. It is therefore necessary to ensure that the sub-tasks are properly coordinated. It is unacceptable, for example, if the implementation of a task from the area of implementing new transportation solutions significantly impedes the implementation of a task from the area of restructuring the system of water and sewage networks. In addition, if we have grounds for predicting that the results of the implementation of a particular stage of the S.C. process may change the rationale for the implementation of another “sectoral” stage, we should rather use a serial arrangement of such stages. For example, if we make changes to the road system, it is worth waiting until the completion of the implementation of this work to take measures aimed at reorganizing the public transportation system.

Let us also remember that the introduction of Smart solutions in the second of the considered variants of the S.C. process is carried out on the "living urban tissue," which raises the necessity to take into account certain attitudes and behaviors of residents (sometimes resistance of some residents). It is worth for decision-makers to give all stakeholders time to get acquainted with and "get used to" the implemented solutions. Again, it is worth remembering that altruistic attitudes in the real world are the exception rather than the rule. City residents tend to consider proposals for change according to the criterion of their own benefit from the solution proposed under the S. C. project. Actions aimed at S.C. should therefore include, for example, specific actions to convince unconvinced residents of the transformed urban space of the benefits resulting from the introduction of new solutions, and then educate these residents in the use of the introduced solutions.

Reports of S.C. deployments in various parts of the world abound in the literature bases, such as [25–27], but the social dimension of such implementations is perhaps not sufficiently appreciated (and studied and then described) by their authors. A kind of fascination with technologies, especially ICT technologies, dominates the available studies, while - in the opinion of the author of this study - too little attention is paid to such factors as customs and culture at the place of implementation (taking into account the size of the "cultural leap" needed to achieve the assumed level of Smart), as well as the level of willingness of local residents to accept Smart solutions. Anyway, the latter factor is related to elements of behavior and attitudes that are "beyond geography" and "beyond culture," such as fears stemming from technophobia, observed especially in older people [28].

Education needs appear to be crucial to the success of implementations of the type in question. It is still worth noting that while the available studies talk about educating the population [29, 30], educating decision-makers at various levels is extremely rarely mentioned. Similarly, an issue that is not very popular among researchers is the identification of the sources of knowledge about a particular city that may be available to the experts involved in the S.C. process (especially: external experts).

Another important issue, and unfortunately overlooked by many authors, is economic issues, for example, the amount of expenses required for the introduced solutions or the sources of funding for such expenses [31, 32]. In particular, a theme such as the ability of a city's budget to bear the expenses needed for a given implementation is practically not addressed.

It is now necessary to consider how to manage the city, and ultimately how to manage the knowledge of the city:

A. Plan and organize activities aimed at inventorying the existing body of knowledge about the city, which is assumed to be the subject of the S.C. process, with identification of the gestors of such knowledge.

B. Plan and organize channels for acquiring missing knowledge before and during the tasks that make up the S.C. process,

C. Create an entity (or entities) authorized to use the knowledge it has in implementing the S.C. process,

D. Provide means and ways to replenish one's knowledge base.

In particular, the above summary was conceived as a starting point for creating a list of knowledge resource needs necessary for effective Smart City management and associating such a list of needs with knowledge resources that are or should be held by participants in S.C. processes.

The matrix shown in **Table 1** should:

a. Identify a specific knowledge resource or resources under the responsibility of only one of the stakeholders considered at a given stage of the analysis.

b. Recognize a detailed knowledge resource or resources under the responsibility of more than one stakeholder.

c. Identify such a body of knowledge among those deemed necessary at a given stage of analysis, which is not currently available to the process stakeholders being considered.

The last of the situations indicated above requires looking for managers of the required knowledge resources outside the organization implementing the process in question. Adding such managers in terms as in **Table 1** will mean adding more rows to the table, labeled "external participant (EP)." We will finish the procedure of expanding the matrix when all the required detailed knowledge resources that we have decided to include have a manager indicated in the first column. It should also be assumed that external participants can contribute knowledge in areas already "developed" by stakeholders.

In particular, the analysis of the matrix shown in **Table 1** can provide a basis for deciding whether it is possible and reasonable to modify the plan for the creation of a knowledge resource (e.g., for the S.C. process) in such a way that the missing elements of the resource, initially recognized as needed, may not be used at a given (e.g., initial) stage of the activity with the assumption that they will be obtained and used in subsequent stages of the process, if necessary. A negative answer to the above question means, of course, that experts or other external participants with the needed knowledge should be sought immediately.

| | Resource 1 | Resource 2 | Resource 3 | Resource 4 | Resource 5 |
|---|---|---|---|---|---|
| Stakeholder 1 | x | x | x | | |
| Stakeholder 2 | | x | | | x |
| Stakeholder 3 | | | x | | |
| Stakeholder 4 | | | | | x |
| External Participants (EP) | | | | | |
| EP 1 | | | | x | |
| EP 2 | | x | | x | |
| EP 3 | | | x | | |

**Table 1.**
*Diagram of the matrix linking knowledge gestors to their area knowledge resources (own elaboration).*

If the process of acquiring detailed knowledge resources is complex and multi-threaded, it may be reasonable to use a solution that combines both paths indicated above. In particular, we can rank the needs [33] in terms of searching for managers of knowledge that we do not have at a given stage of the process and abandon a given resource at the current stage, at the same time launching a search for external participants according to the adopted hierarchy of needs.

Let us apply the above approach to the process of transforming urban space into smart space, i.e., to the S.C. process. Having made, described in this chapter, a preliminary analysis of the needs, concerning the use of detailed knowledge resources in the implementation of the process, and using the initially indicated set of participants (stakeholders) of the process, an attempt can and should be made to present how to create an adequate knowledge resource and use such knowledge in the management of the S.C. process.

In presenting a proposal for such a way below, the author of this chapter has primarily used his own experience related to:

- Many years of scientific and research work at the Silesian University of Technology, associated with the implementation of numerous research projects, including projects related to S.C. issues, as well as the development of publications, original expert reports, and evaluation of project funding applications, including those related to the broad topic of Smart Cities,

- Serving as a councilman and chairman of the City Council, and also as the deputy mayor of his City,

- Serving as a member of the executive body in the regional representation of local governments,

- Serving two four-year terms as a member of the Sejm of the Republic of Poland,

- Performing duties as a member of the Polish Parliament's delegation to the Parliamentary Assembly of the Council of Europe during the aforementioned period.

## 4. Knowledge management in the process of transforming city space into smart space

Let us take the following assumption as the basis for the considerations presented below: knowledge about a particular city is the *sum of the knowledge resources of* stakeholders operating in that city and its environment (closer and further). This assumption is often repeated in scientific studies, the authors of which propose different approaches to how to integrate such knowledge. In the available literature, there are often works dealing with this issue and embedded in the medical field. There have also been studies of a review nature, such as [34]. Quite popular, for example, is the ontological approach [35, 36]. However, in the opinion of the author of this chapter, such proposals, although methodologically correct, have - in the perspective of participants in S.C. processes - the nature of a contrived intellectual experiment. It can be assumed that the vast majority of participants in such processes, in order to understand, for example, the meaning of the term "ontology," must reach for a dictionary. Therefore, in this study, an attempt was made to take maximum account of practical aspects in the preparation and implementation of a specific S.C. process, with particular attention to the difficulties and problems in knowledge management, usually showing the gap between theory and practice.

Very often in the practice of S.C. processes, the starting point for the planning, preparation, and "launch" of the process is the implementation of a project aimed at developing a "Smart Strategy" for a given city. In order to organize further considerations, let us assume here that we will consider only S.C. projects falling within the group of Smart City 2.0 according to the proposal by B. Cohen, i.e., projects that are conducted (coordinated) by the authorities of a given city, and their implementation involves - to a greater or lesser extent - internal stakeholders of S.C. processes. However, experts or institutions employing experts (e.g., scientific and research entities) are often involved in the implementation of projects of the type in question, i.e., participants usually coming from outside a given urban body.

Smart Strategies are usually prepared for a specific time horizon and related to higher-level strategic documents, such as a city development strategy or spatial development plan. The Smart Strategy or related documents generally indicate the objective(s) to be achieved, which are then broken down into tasks to which contractors are assigned.

Let us further assume that the Smart Strategy was developed and - most often - adopted by resolution by the decision-making body (the City Council). Such a Strategy should include guidelines for practical considerations for the implementation of tasks, as indicated in the previous section.

In task *(A)*, it is crucial to identify the city's knowledge managers, which can be facilitated if such managers participate in the preparation of the Smart Strategy for the city. The next step is to assess the willingness of these managers to share their knowledge. This issue is raised in available studies, such as [37, 38] Although - in the opinion of the author of this study - the assumption that altruistic attitudes are the basis for the readiness for such sharing is not fully justified. It can be assumed that attempts to share knowledge, for example, by managers of municipal entities carrying out tasks in the area of municipal management, may be enforced by an official order issued by the governing body of the city. However, since employees with specific knowledge may find it difficult to articulate it, especially in the required form of, for example, rules, it may be reasonable, especially in the initial phase of the S.C. process, to try to implement a "meta-knowledge" formula (e.g. [39–41]). In such an approach, we take an inventory of knowledge managers while recording what knowledge assets these managers possess. Such an inventory should also be aimed at identifying such task areas for which the involvement of external experts is needed or will be necessary. An example of the use of the matrix notation, proposed previously (**Table 1**), to achieve such a goal is shown in **Table 2**.

The assignment of stakeholders to knowledge areas as in **Table 2** undoubtedly has a number of weaknesses. Undoubtedly, a major disadvantage of such an assignment is its static nature, so that, for example, it is not possible to take into account the impact of changes over time, affecting individual stakeholders, on the knowledge base held. The most obvious reason for such changes may be the tenure of the city government, and thus the impact of the emergence of new people in key decision-making positions (city councilors, mayor) as a result of elections. Another factor potentially affecting the knowledge resource of the stakeholder(s) of the S.C. processes in Group 2 is the mobility of employees, in this case, employees of the units implementing the city's own tasks.

| | "Daily functioning" of the urban organism | Development strategies, investment projects | Public transport | Waste management | ... |
|---|---|---|---|---|---|
| Internal Stakeholders (IS) | | | | | |
| City authorities and City Hall structures | x | x | x | x | |
| Managers of entities, implementing tasks in the area of municipal management and the so-called own tasks of the city | | x | x | x | |
| City residents | x | x (?) | x (?) | x | |
| External Stakeholders (ES) | | | | | |
| Municipal (metropolitan) association | | x | x | | |
| Regional authorities | | x | | | |

**Table 2.**
*Diagram of the matrix linking participants in the S.C. process to their area knowledge resources about the city (own elaboration).*

The departure of an employee with a certain amount of useful, including for the S.C. process, knowledge may result in the loss of this resource. Therefore, a decision to create a formalized knowledge base, combining a description in the formula of "meta-knowledge" (knowledge about knowledge) combinedwith a record of a set of formulable rules, drawn up using knowledge engineering methods to assist the manager of the knowledge resource in its articulation and recording in a form, adopted as the basis for the knowledge base being created, may be justified.

Another problem, worth noting and considering, is the potential reluctance or inability of individuals (from different stakeholder groups) to share knowledge, especially to articulate the knowledge they have (e.g., in the form of rules). The author of this chapter, while appreciating the competence of knowledge engineers, does not believe in their omnipotence. Also, the supporting role of the knowledge engineer has limitations, if only due to the classic principle of "Garbage in, garbage out." This problem, in the author's opinion, also requires the implementation and execution of appropriate educational measures.

Finally, it is important to consider the nature of individual internal stakeholders' knowledge about the city and the individual purposes for which this knowledge is acquired and collected. A city resident accumulates individual knowledge, such as facilitating his or her movement around the city area and the offer of different types of transportation, knowledge of places for good shopping or successful recreation but also knowledge of effective ways to break through various administrative barriers to deal with day-to-day matters, especially administrative ones.

A body of knowledge is being created, which should also be available to city managers and allow them to improve "office-citizen" contacts. These are often no-cost or low-cost measures, and their successful implementation can significantly improve residents' assessment of the quality of life in their city.

In summary, in planning the S.C. process, one should:

I. Plan and organize activities aimed at inventorying the existing body of knowledge about the city, which is assumed to be the subject of the S.C. process, with identification of the gestors of such knowledge.

II. Plan and organize channels for acquiring missing knowledge before and during the tasks that make up the S.C. process,

III. Create an entity (or entities) authorized to collect and share, as well as protect the knowledge held in the implementation of the S.C. process,

IV. Provide means and ways to replenish one's knowledge base.

Composed of the above-mentioned elements, the action plan should lead to a state in which the implementers of the S.C. process have a body of knowledge, recorded and accessible according to knowledge management theory. However, at this point, it is worth referring to practice, which often contradicts theoretical assumptions.

## 5. Subjective review of problems in the practice of urban knowledge management

In the previous sections of this chapter, the main attention was devoted to the analysis of conditions which, in matrix terms presented in **Table 1** and **Table 2**, can be described by the term "horizontal" (described by the rows of this matrix). Let us now try to consider the problems, described in the columns of this matrix. In particular, these are the problems shown in those columns where the body of "sectoral" knowledge is held by more than one manager of such knowledge.

Consider, for example, the column of the matrix shown in **Table 2**, described as "Daily functioning of the urban organism." This column identifies the city government as knowledge managers, supported by clerical structures (the City Hall) and residents. Let us try to describe the peculiarities of the knowledge base of the two mentioned managers.

The body of knowledge about the functioning of the urban organism, which is the responsibility of the city authorities, includes knowledge about the history and current image of this organism, generated both by numerous channels of information of a statistical nature and by the recording of individual residents' matters processed by the City Hall structures. It is worth noting that information, generating the knowledge resource of city decision-makers, should, as a rule, be open and accessible to city residents (with exceptions defined by relevant legal regulations). The body of knowledge of the city authorities is used in the procedure of individual matters of residents, but first of all, it is the basis for activities related to the adoption of decisions of a strategic nature by these authorities, such as budget decisions or decisions of a planning nature (e.g., regarding the city's spatial development plan), as well as the basis for the preparation of strategic documents.

Knowledge, which remains the responsibility of each resident, is of a completely different nature. The body of this knowledge consists primarily of personal experience acquired during the period of residence in a given space, combined with knowledge derived from the social relations existing in the space. It is also worth noting that such "individual knowledge" usually contains a significant base of tacit knowledge and -

especially in some cultural and political systems - a component of the base which the author proposes to call "covered knowledge." This term describes, in particular, knowledge of relationships and dependencies, including family and social relationships, allowing for faster and more efficient handling of official matters.

Comparing the descriptions of the knowledge resources of the two "city stakeholders" presented above, one can come to the conclusion that these resources are completely incompatible and cannot form the basis for joint action. However, in the author's opinion, attempting to find solutions (perhaps of an organizational and formal nature) that would, for example, limit the needs of city residents to own and use the above-mentioned "covered knowledge resource" would contribute significantly to the overall goal of the Smart City, that is, broadly understood, to improve the quality of life in the city. It needs to be noted that this is an example of improving the level of intelligence of the city without the need to purchase and implement advanced ICT solutions. Since the recommendation to make an attempt should be correlated with an indication of who should make the attempt, the author is of the opinion that in the search for an agreement between city authorities and residents, the initiating party should be the first mentioned stakeholder of the S.C. process.

Another example to consider is described in the column of the matrix shown in **Table 2** "Development strategies, investment projects." Since decisions of a strategic nature obviously affect all stakeholders in S.C. processes, they should participate as actively as possible in the preparation of the relevant documents. In addition, since every urban organism functions in a certain environment, the need to take into account knowledge of similar decisions in neighboring entities and at the superordinate level (the city's development strategy cannot be completely disconnected from the development strategy of the region in which the city is located) seems obvious when preparing the strategies and development plans. Hence, the demand for the participation of external stakeholders (in **Table 2** "municipal (metropolitan) association" and "regional authorities," respectively). Let us skip the description of the detailed knowledge requirements, which are the responsibility of all the entities included in this column, and focus on the postulate for the participation of residents in the preparation of development strategies (in particular: Smart strategies). Such a postulate seems obvious, but - as the author's practical experience shows - it is extremely difficult to implement. Hence, the question mark in the corresponding box of the matrix shown in **Table 2**. In the literature we can find numerous studies devoted to the implementation of the model of public participation in the activities of public administration (e.g., [42] or [43]). However, practice usually looks different from theory. In such practice, the participation of residents in all forms of public consultations, the carrying out of which is often, for example, in the development of strategies or changes to spatial development plans, a legal requirement, attracts a small group of residents (in a city with a population of about 200,000 such consultations usually involve at most a few dozen people), usually belonging to one of two categories:

a. Persons directly concerned, such as owners of land covered by the development plan amendment under preparation,

b. Skeptics, that is, people who contest every solution according to the principle: "No because no, we are attached to what is, we do not want novelty."

When preparing and implementing S.C. processes, we should also take into account not only the lack of interest of the general public but also various forms of resistance to change by some residents or groups of residents. It therefore becomes a necessity to implement all possible ways of educating Smart Cities stakeholders, both to involve them in the process of shaping their place of life and its surroundings and to make proper use of its "smart" capabilities obtained in the S.C. process. Once again, the city government should be the natural initiator of such activities.

Yet another type of problem is described in the matrix, shown in **Table 2**, by the "Public Transportation". At the intersection of this column and the "City residents" row, a question mark also appears next to an indication of knowledge possessed by city residents, useful in solving problems from the indicated area (an "x"). By analyzing the sample competencies and knowledge resources of individual stakeholders:

- City authorities: issuing location decisions for public transportation infrastructure elements and, most often, financing this infrastructure.

- Managers the aforementioned infrastructure: purchase and maintenance of rolling stock.

- Metropolitan union: coordination of route network, timetables, passenger information

We come across the problem of locating the routes of transportation lines and the location of bus stops. Agreeing in principle with the need to implement public participation in all activities affecting a city resident, the author believes that it will usually be justified to adopt the use of solutions adopted arbitrarily in this case. Because, most often, when discussing the location of the transportation line and stops, it turns out that everyone involved wants the line to run not directly next to their property (because of noise, vibration, and increased traffic) but very close (because then you do not have to walk far). The same applies to the location of stops. Since it is impossible to meet all such expectations, it may be worth limiting residents' influence on decisions until residents develop the right pro-community attitudes.

## 6. Conclusions

Research on the possibilities and needs for transforming urban space in such a way as to make the space as friendly as possible to its users (city residents, but not exclusively) covers more and more new problem areas.

In addition to problems such as the impact of large built-up areas on the local climate (so-called urban heat islands [44]), research is being undertaken on socially motivated phenomena, such as the occurrence of "exclusion" phenomena in cities [45]. Quite a few studies are described, showing a view of the intentions to create a Smart City from the side of communities, variously excluded or isolated (as well as self-excluded and self-isolated) in the functioning urban organism. One can sadly state that city authority, and, unfortunately, some researchers behind them, are eager to show, for example, smart traffic light management, downtown parking space management, or a Smart City information system. Hidden away, or perhaps only in the realm of understatement, are the possible expectations and needs of residents of parts of the city inhabited by ethnic minorities, or parts of the city where there is a phenomenon that can be enigmatically described as an "area with a reduced standard of living space" remain hidden, or perhaps only understated. On the other hand, in many cities, we are dealing with the phenomenon of creating enclaves of substandard living, referred to by the term "gentrification" [46].

Therefore, the author of this chapter wants to clearly emphasize that the thoughts presented herein are an attempt to describe the current state. Undoubtedly, however, the problems of knowledge of the urban organism, the construction and management of the resources of such knowledge, and the making of decisions based on this knowledge are and will remain both the subject of research by scientists and the subject of the practice of the stakeholders of the processes taking place in the urban organism, such as S.C. processes.

## Abbreviations

S.C.: Smart City
S.C. process: process focused on creating intelligent urban space
IT: informatic techniques/informatic tools
ICT: information and communication technologies
5 W + H model: model based on answering the questions: What?, Why?, Where?, When?, Who? and How? (to do something, to solve some problem)
NGO: Non-Governmental Organization

## Author details

Jan Kazmierczak
Faculty of Organization and Management, Silesian University of Technology, Zabrze, Poland

*Address all correspondence to: jan.kazmierczak@polsl.pl

## References

[1] Komninos N. Intelligent cities: Towards interactive and global innovation environments. International Journal of Innovation and Regional Development. 2009;**1**(4):337-355

[2] Batty M. Intelligent cities, virtual cities. In: Encyclopedia of Digital Government. Vol. 5. Issue 5. IGI Global. 2009. pp. 110-1104

[3] Hollands RG. Will the real smart city please stand up? Smart, progressive or entrepreneurial? City. 2008;**12**(3)303-320. DOI: 10.1080/13604810802479126

[4] Mitchell WJ. When two worlds collide. New Scientist. 2006;**192**(2582):45. DOI: 10.1016/S0262-4079(06)61403-6

[5] Ribera-fumaz R, Vivas P. Ciudades en la sociedad de la información, una introducción. UOC Papers. 2007;**5**:31-37

[6] Webb R. The urban organism. Nature. 2007;**44**:869

[7] McDonnell MJ, Hahs AK. Adaptation and adaptedness of organisms to urban environments. Annual Review of Ecology, Evolution, and Systematics. 2015;**46**:261-280. DOI: 10.1146/annurev-ecolsys-112414-054258

[8] Coe A, Paquet G, Roy J. E-governance and smart communities: A social learning challenge. Social Science Computer Review. 2001;**19**(1):80-93. DOI: 10.1177/089443930101900107

[9] Cohen B. What Exactly is a Smart City? In: Co.Exist. Fast Company. 2012. pp. 1-9

[10] Parham S. Happy city: Transforming our lives through urban design. Journal of Urbanism: International Research on Placemaking and Urban Sustainability. 2014;**7**(2):213-215. DOI: 10.1080/17549175.2014.907521

[11] Jain TK. Concept of happy city: The smart cities of the future. SSRN Electronic Journal. 2019. DOI: 10.2139/ssrn.3314531

[12] Mishra P, Thakur P, Singh G. Sustainable smart city to society 5.0: State-of-the-art and research challenges. SAIEE Africa Research Journal. 2022;**113**(4)152-164. DOI: 10.23919/SAIEE.2022.9945865

[13] Guallart V. From digital cities to biocities: Harnessing the power of the digital revolution to reinvent the urban ecology model. Architectural Design. 2020;**90**:72-75. DOI: 10.1002/ad.2571

[14] Laurini R. A primer of knowledge management for smart city governance. Land Use Policy. Elsevier. 2021;**111**. DOI: 10.1016/j.landusepol.2020.104832

[15] Israilidis J, Odusanya K, Mazhar M. Knowledge management in smart city development: A systematic review. In: Proceedings of the European Conference on Knowledge Management. ECKM. 2019. pp. 1231-1233. DOI: 10.34190/KM.19.050

[16] Hart G. The five Ws: An old tool for the new task of audience analysis. Technical Communication. 1996;**43**(2). ISSN: 00493155

[17] Freeman ER, Evan WM. Corporate governance: A stakeholder interpretation. The Journal of Behavioural Economics. 1990;**19**(4):337-359

[18] Fassin Y. The stakeholder model refined. Journal of Business Ethics. 2009; **84**(1):113-135. DOI: 10.1007/s10551-008-9677-4

[19] Cholewa W, Kazmierczak J. Data processing and reasoning in technical diagnostics. Warsaw: Wydawnictwo Naukowo-Techniczne; 1995

[20] Song H, Li G. Tourism demand modelling and forecasting - A review of recent research. Tourism Management. Elsevier. 2008;**29**(2):203-220. DOI: 10.1016/j.tourman.2007.07.016

[21] Jiang R, Kleer R, Piller FT. Predicting the future of additive manufacturing: A Delphi study on economic and societal implications of 3D printing for 2030. Technological Forecasting and Social Change. Elsevier. 2017;**117**:84-97. DOI: 10.1016/j.techfore.2017.01.006

[22] Mohamed N, Al-Jaroodi J, Jawhar I, Idries A, Mohammed F. Unmanned aerial vehicle applications in future smart cities. Technological Forecast and Social Change. 2020;**153**:119293. DOI: 10.1016/j.techfore.2018.05.004

[23] Bibri SE, Krogstie J. On the social shaping dimensions of smart sustainable cities: A study in science, technology, and society. Sustainable Cities and Society. 2017;**29**:219-246. DOI: 10.1016/j.scs.2016.11.004

[24] Xiaoping P, Xizhou T, Xiaodong G. Prosocial behavior in organizations: A literature review and prospects. Foreign Economics & Management. 2019;**41**(05):114-127

[25] Capdevila I, Zarlenga MI. Smart cities or smart citizens? The Barcelona case. Journal of Strategy and Management. 2015;**8**(3):266-282. DOI: 10.1108/JSMA-03-2015-0030

[26] Praharaj S, Han JH, Hawken S. Towards the right model of smart city governance in India. International Journal of Sustainable Development and Planning. 2018;**13**(2):171-186WIT Press. DOI: 10.2495/SDP-V13-N2-171-186

[27] Shen L, Huang Z, Wong SW, Liao S, Lou Y. A holistic evaluation of smart city performance in the context of China. Journal of Cleaner Production. 2018;**200**:667-679. DOI: 10.1016/j.jclepro.2018.07.281

[28] Nimrod G. Technophobia among older Internet users. Educational Gerontology. 2018;**44**(2-3):148-162. DOI: 10.1080/03601277.2018.1428145

[29] Williamson B. Educating the smart city: Schooling smart citizens through computational urbanism. Big Data & Society - Sage Journals. 2015;**2**(2):1-13. DOI: 10.1177/2053951715617783

[30] Wolff A, Kortuem G, Cavero J. Towards smart city education. In: 2015 Sustainable Internet and ICT for Sustainability (SustainIT). Madrid, Spain. 2015. pp. 1-3. DOI: 10.1109/SustainIT.2015.7101381

[31] Voda AI, Radu L-D. Investigating economic factors of sustainability in European smart cities. European Journal of Sustainable Development. 2018;**7**(1):107. DOI: 10.14207/ejsd.2018.v7n1p107

[32] Jonek-Kowalska I, Kazmierczak J. Environmental expenses in municipal budgets in Poland in the context of aspiring to becoming a smart, sustainable city. In: International Conference on Geolinks, Plovdiv, Bulgaria, 23–25 March 2020. Book 2 Ecology and Environmental Studies. Saima Consult Ltd. 2020. pp. 35-46. DOI: 10.32008/GEOLINKS2020/B2/V2/03

[33] Majee W, Conteh N, Jacobs J, Wegner L. Needs ranking: A qualitative study using a participatory approach. Health & Social Care in the Community.

2022;**30**(6):i-iv, 2025-2430. DOI: 10.1111/hsc.13924

[34] Wiig KM, De Hoog R, Van Der Spek R. Supporting knowledge management: A selection of methods and techniques. Expert Systems with Applications. Elsevier. 1997;**13**(1):15-27. DOI: 10.1016/S0957-4174(97)00019-5

[35] Přibyl P, Přibyl O, Svítek M, Janota A. Smart city design based on an ontological knowledge system. In: Research and the Future of Telematics: 20th International Conference on Transport Systems Telematics, TST 2020, Kraków, Poland, 27-30 October 2020. Springer International Publishing. 2020. pp. 152-164. Selected Papers 20. DOI: 10.1007/978-3-030-59270-7_12

[36] Ramaprasad A, Sánchez-ortiz A, Syn T. Ontological review of smart city research. In: Proceedings of the 23rd Americas Conference on Information Systems. Boston. 2017. pp. 1-10

[37] Ahmad F, Karim M. Impacts of knowledge sharing: A review and directions for future research. Journal of Workplace Learning. 2019;**31**(3):207-230. DOI: 10.1108/JWL-07-2018-0096

[38] Nguyen TM, Siri NS, Malik A. Multilevel influences on individual knowledge sharing behaviors: The moderating effects of knowledge sharing opportunity and collectivism. Journal of Knowledge Management. 2022;**26**(1):70-87. DOI: 10.1108/JKM-01-2021-0009

[39] Nov O, Ye C, Kumar N. A social capital perspective on meta-knowledge contribution and social computing. Decision Support Systems. 2012;**53**(1):118-126. DOI: 10.1016/j.dss.2011.12.009

[40] Engelbrecht A, Gerlach JP, Benlian A, Buxmann P. How employees gain meta-knowledge using enterprise social networks: A validation and extension of communication visibility theory. Journal of Strategic Information Systems. 2019;**28**(3):292-309. DOI: 10.1016/j.jsis.2019.04.001

[41] Lan Y, Xu X, Fang Q, Zeng Y, Liu X, Zhang X. Transfer reinforcement learning via meta-knowledge extraction using auto-pruned decision trees. Knowledge Based Systems. 2022;**242**:108221. DOI: 10.1016/j.knosys.2022.108221

[42] Grundel I, Dahlström M. A quadruple and quintuple helix approach to regional innovation systems in the transformation to a forestry-based bioeconomy. Journal of the Knowledge Economy. 2016;7:963-983. DOI: 10.1007/s13132-016-0411-7

[43] Sisto R, Cappelletti GM, Bianchi P, Sica E. Sustainable and accessible tourism in natural areas: A participatory approach. Current Issues in Tourism. 2022;**25**(8):1307-1324. DOI: 10.1080/13683500.2021.1920002

[44] Mirzaei PA. Recent challenges in modeling of urban heat island. Sustainable Cities and Society. 2015;**19**:200-206. DOI: 10.1016/j.scs.2015.04.001

[45] Engelbert J, van Zoonen L, Hirzalla F. Excluding citizens from the European smart city: The discourse practices of pursuing and granting smartness. Technological Forecasting and Social Change. 2019;**142**:347-353. DOI: 10.1016/j.techfore.2018.08.020

[46] Cole HVS, Mehdipanah R, Gullón P, Triguero-Mas M. Breaking down and building up: Gentrification, its drivers, and urban health inequality. Current Environmental Health Reports. 2021;**8**(2):157-166. DOI: 10.1007/s40572-021-00309-5

Chapter 2

# Harnessing the Power of Culture and Cultural Intelligence within Knowledge Management

*Leila Halawi*

## Abstract

As smart machines and artificial intelligence become more prevalent in the workplace, organizations must prioritize building a culture that supports knowledge management initiatives. However, cultural diversity may hinder effective knowledge sharing, transfer, and collaboration. Organizations must cultivate cultural intelligence to overcome these challenges and fully utilize the potential of culture. This chapter investigates the role of culture and cultural intelligence. It examines the significance of culture in knowledge management. It offers practical examples and best practices from organizations such as IBM and Unilever for utilizing culture to improve knowledge management practices. The chapter examines the relationship between culture and KM and discusses cultural intelligence, its importance, and its application. Additionally, the chapter delves into strategies employed by IBM and Unilever to cultivate a culture that supports knowledge management. By examining their success stories, valuable insights and best practices can be derived.

**Keywords:** knowledge management, cultural intelligence, culture, IBM, Unilever

## 1. Introduction

Competing in the twenty-first century represents a paradigm shift compared to the past [1, 2]. Markets have become increasingly dynamic, fluid, and uncertain, while consumers exhibit higher levels of demand and discernment. Competitors now possess enhanced agility and display predatory tendencies, while employees are characterized by greater intelligence and transience. Consequently, competition on a global scale has undergone dramatic changes, especially post-COVID-19, and intensified over the last two decades. The dynamic forces of the globalization age have forced organizations to search within for their full main capabilities to meet the challenges of their imminent obligations. Nations around the globe reacted differently to the dynamic changes that are impacting their economies. The economic language has also changed from seeking economies of scale based purely on productivity and return on investment to managing the "Age of Thinking and Resilience" [3, 4] or, for some, the "Creative Age" [5] "Third Industrial Revolution" [3] or still the "Knowledge Age."

The continuous advancements in computing power, the Internet, information technology (IT) infrastructure, and the integration of technologies from IoT to big data revolution and production advancements that could potentially lead to a future without work have resulted in widespread recognition of the power of information and connectivity. The accounts envisioning a future without work in the coming years draw inspiration from a body of research that argues that advanced technologies such as smart machines (e.g., algorithms, artificial intelligence, and the Internet of things) are progressively eliminating the concept of work, including knowledge-based task; nevertheless, Karakilic [6] emphasizes the ongoing importance of human involvement in knowledge work.

Multinational organizations face considerable challenges in managing knowledge across different cultural contexts. An organization's culture shapes employees' attitudes and behaviors toward knowledge sharing and collaboration [7]. It significantly influences how individuals and organizations create, share, and apply knowledge. Cultural differences pose communication barriers; divergent norms and values affect knowledge perception and collaboration; trust and relationship building are influenced by cultural nuances; power dynamics hinder knowledge sharing; contextual differences impact knowledge application; and resistance to change arises from cultural factors, emphasizing the importance of cultural Intelligence (CQ) in overcoming these challenges and promoting effective knowledge sharing and collaboration across cultural boundaries [8]. CQ represents the person's capability to understand and effectively network with individuals from diverse cultural backgrounds [8]. In knowledge management (KM), CQ enables employees to navigate cultural differences, adapt communication styles, and build cross-border relationships [9]. By possessing CQ, employees are better equipped to comprehend and appreciate different perspectives, leading to improved knowledge sharing and collaboration within multinational organizations [10]. CQ also facilitates the development of cross-cultural communities of practice, where employees from various cultural backgrounds can collaborate and exchange knowledge [11].

Therefore, understanding the impact of culture and CQ on KM is crucial for developing effective strategies that promote knowledge sharing, learning, and innovation.

## 2. Knowledge management (KM)

Over the years, organizations such as Amazon, Microsoft, Apple, Nike, Siemens, Unilever, IBM, Intel, Procter & Gamble, Boeing, Ernst & Young, Honeywell, Miter, KPMG, and Ford Motor Company have undertaken many KM initiatives, developed a knowledge base, developed training materials and offered training sessions on KM, implemented knowledge management systems (KMS), created knowledge networks, and created knowledge-sharing cultures to tackle the loss of explicit and implicit knowledge. These initiatives can yield several advantages, including enhanced efficiency, productivity, and customer service. KM is crucial in stimulating individuals' thinking and influencing their actions.

KM is a main competitive advantage in the era of the knowledge economy or the Third Industrial Revolution. KM encompasses a range of technological, cultural, and procedural approaches that organizations employ to enhance the value derived from knowledge [12]. This involves improving, identifying, collecting, sharing, and utilizing existing organizational knowledge and accessing or developing new knowledge through partnerships or ventures [13]. KM goes beyond the scope of information systems and technology, heavily drawing from social and cultural elements. It also intersects with organizational development, innovation, and competitive intelligence [14–16].

### 2.1 Knowledge management process

Knowledge management processes exhibit diverse forms and can be implemented in various configurations. Nissen [17] proposed a life cycle model that illustrates an organization's seamless knowledge flow, encompassing six phases. Wiig [18] pioneered a knowledge management process consisting of eight activities. Whitmore & Albers [19] also identified a nine-step comprehensive framework.

Implementing KM within a business is undoubtedly a multifaceted process. Nevertheless, its potential benefits make it a valuable tool for businesses of all sizes. By diligently following these steps, organizations can embark on the path to successful KM implementation and reap its rewards (**Figure 1**).

1. Identification of knowledge needs: First and foremost, it is crucial to identify the knowledge needs specific to the organization. This encompasses customer information, product details, employee data, and other pertinent information relevant to the business's operations.

**Figure 1.**
*Knowledge management process.*

2. Knowledge capture: The captured knowledge needs to be effectively stored and organized. This can be accomplished by establishing a comprehensive knowledge base, developing training materials, or utilizing alternative methodologies designed to capture and retain knowledge.

3. Knowledge sharing: Once the knowledge has been captured, the next step involves sharing it with employees. Cultivating a knowledge-sharing culture within the organization is essential, as it encourages employees to disseminate knowledge actively. Employing KMS or utilizing other appropriate channels facilitates the efficient and widespread distribution of knowledge among employees.

4. Knowledge management: Finally, managing shared knowledge is critical to ensure its relevance and accuracy. This includes regularly updating the knowledge base, providing training sessions to address new knowledge, and implementing appropriate methodologies to manage the knowledge repository effectively.

### 2.2 Knowledge management success factors

Within the established frameworks of KM implementation, several factors emerge as crucial elements demanding focused attention for the success of KM initiatives. However, if these factors are not properly and adequately addressed, they can transition from facilitators of KM into significant barriers that hinder the realization of KM's benefits [20].

The crucial factors encompass organizational structure, strategy, leadership, technological infrastructure, culture, organizational processes, and measurement [21]. When these factors are appropriately addressed and aligned with the goals and direction of the organization, the likelihood of achieving KM success significantly increases.

## 3. Culture

An organization's culture emerges from its members' shared fundamental assumptions and beliefs. It operates unconsciously, shaping the organization's self-perception and perception of the surrounding environment [22]. Hofstede [23] introduced a comprehensive definition of culture as the shared mental programming that sets one group apart from another. He posited that culture finds expression through symbols, heroes, rituals, and values, which manifest across multiple dimensions: power distance, individualism versus collectivism, femininity versus masculinity, uncertainty avoidance, long-term versus short-term orientation, and indulgence versus restraint. Culture encompasses the values, principles, unwritten rules, norms, and procedures that guide organizational behavior. Culture building is a slow process [24].

Culture acts as the binding force that unifies an organization and enacts a decisive part in shaping the utilization of an organization's knowledge assets. It dictates both the capabilities and limitations of what can be achieved. As organizational theorists acknowledge, culture plays a significant role in organizational performance and long-term effectiveness [25]. Successful organizations embody a cohesive organizational culture, forming a harmoniously integrated entity where everyone's contributions complement one another. Rather than solely relying on hard work, effective organizations emphasize working smarter. Within the organizational context, culture becomes the determining factor that defines the realm of possibilities.

### 3.1 Culture and knowledge management

In the context of an organization, culture influences and is influenced by infrastructure, strategy, and the organization's mission, vision, objectives, and goals. Malhotra [26] emphasizes the critical role of a healthy corporate culture in the success of KM. KM is a critical organizational process that aims to create, share, and apply knowledge to achieve corporate objectives. Culture is pivotal in KM as it shapes employees' beliefs, values, and behaviors related to knowledge sharing and collaboration.

Organizations must cultivate a culture and environment that align with KM objectives. Enhancing organizational culture should be a primary focus in strategic planning efforts [27]. Innovation and knowledge creation processes are deeply rooted in society and intricately tied to its culture. Culture significantly influences the methodologies, philosophies, and individuals within organizations. However, cultural variations can obstruct the effective transfer of knowledge [28].

By harnessing KM, competing and cooperating companies can effectively navigate cultural differences and establish fruitful business relationships with individuals from diverse countries. Achieving this objective entails understanding the intricate interplay between KM and culture and recognizing the inherent value each brings to the table [29].

To successfully implement KM processes, organizations must consider adopting a new cultural model or adapting their existing culture to foster sharing and collaboration. However, it is crucial to ensure that this cultural change is seen as an enhancement to employees' professional and personal lives rather than an imposition. Developing a knowledge-sharing culture primarily relies on establishing a solid foundation of trust among individuals. KM-enabling culture is a trusting knowledge culture that actively encourages and rewards innovation, learning, experimentation, critical analysis, and reflection [30]. Trust is vital in facilitating knowledge sharing among organization members.

### 3.2 Cultural intelligence (CQ)

Cultural intelligence (CQ) is a complex framework encompassing knowledge and understanding of effective interactions across diverse cultures [8]. The acronym for cultural intelligence (CQ), short for cultural quotient, encompasses four dimensions: "behavioral CQ, motivational CQ, cognitive CQ, and meta-cognitive CQ" [8]. Behavioral CQ pertains to the verbal and nonverbal behaviors employed to interact with colleagues in multicultural environments, focusing on actions rather than emotional or psychological factors. Motivational CQ reflects the interest and drives to engage with and understand other cultures, encompassing intrinsic and extrinsic motivation. Cognitive CQ encompasses systematic knowledge of practices and norms in different cultures, which can be acquired through education or practice. Lastly, meta-cognitive CQ involves advanced thinking skills [31] that enable abstract cognitive strategies in diverse cultural settings [32].

CQ focuses on developing diverse skills applicable to various cultural contexts rather than solely acquiring knowledge about a single culture [33]. CI plays a crucial role in KM, with a positive association between CI and KM processes

[34]. Meta-cognitive CI helps establish cultural commonalities, while cognitive CI enhances understanding of the international environment. Motivational CI promotes enjoyment during cross-cultural interactions and facilitates knowledge sharing, while behavioral CI enables effective cross-cultural communication and knowledge acquisition [35, 36].

Several studies have confirmed the positive impact of CI on knowledge sharing and standard and reverse knowledge transfer [37, 38]. Additionally, CI helps mitigate the negative effects of language barring on knowledge obscuring and collecting, leading to improved knowledge practices [39].

## 4. IBM

IBM, short for "International Business Machines," is a globally recognized American multinational information technology corporation based in Armonk, New York. With over 175 countries, IBM has established itself as a prominent figure in the information technology industry for over a century. In recent years, the company has emerged as a global leader in cloud computing, data analytics, and artificial intelligence (AI) [40]. Presently, IBM places great importance on the ability of AI to deliver tangible value through collaboration with human interaction. This philosophy underpins developing an AI-enriched knowledge management system (KMS) designed explicitly for market and competitive intelligence. This system serves as a tool that empowers business professionals across the organization to make informed decisions based on available research assets. It is worth noting that this system is not intended to replace human expertise but rather to complement and enhance human capabilities.

IBM embarked on its knowledge management (KM) journey in the early 1990s and introduced its initial KM initiative, Asset Management, from the Business Unit Perspective, in 1994 [41]. The main purpose of this initiative was to create a repository of knowledge and work-related information contributed by colleagues. This knowledge base facilitated the reuse of assets and intellectual capital, enabling IBM to deliver client solutions with improved quality and efficiency. In 2000, the company established its KM Center of Excellence, which provides guidance and support to IBM employees regarding effective knowledge management practices. Additionally, IBM has developed various KM tools and products, such as Lotus Notes, IBM Connections, and IBM Watson. IBM encompasses a range of KM initiatives, including social learning through the internal sharing and collaboration tool Yammer and diverse communities of practice and knowledge repositories. IBM's efforts in KM have garnered recognition from industry experts, with KMWorld honoring IBM as the "Knowledge Management Leader of the Year" in 2002 [41].

IBM has long recognized the significance of KM in driving organizational success. Operating in culturally diverse settings worldwide, IBM faces considerable challenges in effectively managing knowledge across borders. Acknowledging the pivotal role of culture in KM, IBM has fostered a knowledge-sharing and collaborative culture that is key to the company's success. This culture of knowledge sharing and collaboration has contributed to several business benefits for IBM, including improved customer satisfaction, increased employee productivity, reduced costs, enhanced decision-making, and increased innovation [42].

IBM has implemented various strategies to cultivate a knowledge-sharing and collaboration culture. The company upholds an organizational culture of "THINK," which emphasizes thinking and creating solutions. IBM's cognitive quotient (CQ) measures the company's ability to acquire, process, and apply knowledge. To overcome cultural barriers and promote knowledge sharing, IBM has established global communities of practice that bring together employees from diverse regions and backgrounds. These communities are platforms for sharing best practices, exchanging insights, and collaborating on projects [42]. By facilitating cross-cultural knowledge exchange, IBM encourages the development of innovative ideas and solutions that cater to diverse market needs.

Furthermore, IBM leverages technology to facilitate knowledge management across its global operations. Collaborative platforms and digital tools enable employees from different cultural backgrounds to access and share information easily, irrespective of geographical boundaries [42]. This technology-driven approach streamlines the flow of knowledge and fosters collaboration and collective learning within the organization.

Additionally, IBM has implemented training programs and initiatives to raise awareness about cultural differences and their impact on knowledge management. With a strong knowledge-sharing and collaboration culture and substantial investments in KM initiatives, IBM maintains a high CQ. The company's continuous approach to measuring CQ involves data collection, analysis, and action to improve [43]. This approach has helped IBM maintain its leadership position in the IT industry. By promoting cultural sensitivity and understanding, IBM equips its employees with the skills necessary to navigate diverse cultural contexts and effectively collaborate with colleagues across the globe.

## 5. Unilever

Unilever, a global consumer goods company established in 1930, has a rich history of innovation and has played a leading role in developing various product categories, such as detergents, shampoos, and foods. Unilever, a global corporation with operations spanning over 190 countries, boasts a diverse workforce comprising employees from more than 100 nations. The company fosters a culture of diversity, inclusion, and respect, actively encouraging employees to share their ideas and perspectives. Recognizing the significance of cultural Intelligence (CQ) in a globalized environment, Unilever prioritizes the development of this essential skill among its employees.

Unilever's leadership team plays a pivotal role in promoting the culture of CQ. Their commitment to cultivating cultural intelligence cascades throughout the organization, which reinforces its importance and influences employees at all levels. Unilever's endeavors to promote CQ have earned recognition from various organizations. In 2019, Unilever was recognized as one of the top 15 companies for diversity and as a leading Inclusion Index company with inclusive culture as an integral part of growing a sustainable organization [44]. The Human Rights Campaign also acknowledged Unilever as one of the best places to work for LGBTQ employees in 2017 [45]. Unilever's dedication to fostering CQ aligns with its strategy for success in the global marketplace. By cultivating a culture that embraces CQ, Unilever can attract and retain top talent, cultivate strong relationships with customers and partners worldwide, and effectively drive innovation. By prioritizing KM and CQ, Unilever is forging an agile and adaptable organizational culture that is better positioned to thrive in the global marketplace.

Unilever's approach to KM is grounded in the belief that knowledge is a valuable asset that can enhance the company's performance, while curiosity is seen as a core value. To effectively capture, share, and utilize knowledge, Unilever has implemented several initiatives, including:

a. A knowledge-sharing portal: This platform enables employees to access and exchange information, fostering a collaborative environment.

b. Communities of practice: Unilever facilitates the formation of communities where employees with shared interests can come together to share insights, experiences, and best practices; for example, within the culinary Category, and through effective knowledge-leveraging strategies, Unilever has made documentation, handbooks, and recognized professionals available, reducing time and improving efficiency in designing, planning, and commissioning new construction projects. Additionally, Unilever has adopted a common flavor language to facilitate seamless communication across regions, cultures, backgrounds, and experiences [46].

c. Mentoring program: Unilever's mentoring initiative pairs less experienced employees with seasoned colleagues, providing an avenue for knowledge transfer and skills development.

Unilever's organizational culture is characterized by open communication and collaboration, which nurture an environment conducive to knowledge sharing. Additionally, the company emphasizes training and development programs, enabling employees to expand their knowledge and enhance their skills.

Cultural intelligence (CQ), the ability to understand and adapt to different cultures, is a critical competency for employees working in multinational organizations like Unilever. To cultivate CQ among its workforce, Unilever employs various strategies, including:

1. Training and development programs: Unilever offers comprehensive training initiatives to enhance employees' cultural understanding and sensitivity.

2. Cross-cultural assignments: Encouraging employees to work in diverse cultural contexts helps broaden their perspectives and develop their CQ.

3. Exposure to different cultures: Unilever promotes travel and exposure to different parts of the world, enabling employees to gain firsthand experience and understanding of diverse cultural practices.

CQ equips employees with several benefits, including:

Effective communication: CQ enables individuals to communicate more proficiently with people from diverse cultural backgrounds.

Relationship building: CQ facilitates positive relationships with individuals from different cultures, fostering collaboration and teamwork.

Cross-cultural collaboration: Employees with high CQ can work effectively in cross-cultural teams, leveraging the diversity of perspectives and experiences to drive innovation and problem-solving.

Unilever is committed to cultivating a culture of CQ within the organization. The company invests in comprehensive training and development programs to develop employees' CQ and encourages cross-cultural assignments and international travel opportunities.

## 6. Insights and best practices

Organizations are intricate and dynamic systems that constantly evolve. They must navigate various elements such as profitability, culture, politics, social networks, communities, individuals, values, ethics, and goals within their environment. Knowledge databases become susceptible to rapid decay when sharing embedded knowledge is not ingrained within a specific culture [47].

Both IBM and Unilever share similarities in harnessing the power of culture and CQ within KM. To begin with, both organizations acknowledged the value of cultural diversity in their workforce, actively seeking talent from various backgrounds and promoting inclusivity. Next, they invested in CQ training programs to equip their employees with the necessary skills to navigate and adapt to diverse cultural contexts. Lastly, both companies instigated robust KMS systems and platforms to facilitate collaboration, knowledge sharing, and innovation.

Despite these similarities, there are notable differences between the two cases. As a technology company, IBM greatly emphasizes leveraging digital tools and platforms for KM. They developed AI-enriched systems for market and competitive intelligence, complementing human expertise. On the other hand, as a consumer goods company, Unilever focused on aligning its organizational culture with KM goals and driving innovation through curiosity and openness. They emphasized forming communities of practice and adopting common language and practices to facilitate knowledge sharing.

To harness the power of culture and CQ within KM, organizations can follow a series of best practices: embrace cultural diversity and inclusivity; invest in CQ training; leverage technology and AI; establish communities of practice; promote curiosity and openness; encourage cross-cultural assignments and exposure; invest in comprehensive training and development programs.

These practices collectively will drive innovation, collaboration, and organizational success.

## 7. Conclusions

The chapter unfolds structured, beginning with an introduction that sets the stage for subsequent discussions. This is followed by an in-depth examination of knowledge management, encompassing the knowledge management process and its critical success factors. Part 2 of the chapter provides an overview of culture, including its relevance to knowledge management culture and the significance of cultural intelligence [CQ] within the realm of knowledge management.

Sections 4 and 5 focus on the practical application of knowledge management, exemplified through the strategies employed by IBM and Unilever. Furthermore, these sections shed light on the pivotal role played by culture and cultural intelligence in the success of these organizations.

Drawing from these insights, the chapter closes by highlighting the implications and presenting best practices for leveraging culture and cultural intelligence in the context of knowledge management. Furthermore, the chapter is supported by a robust reference section, ensuring interested readers can delve deeper into the subject matter.

## Conflict of interest

The authors declare no conflict of interest.

## Appendices and nomenclature

| | |
|---|---|
| AI | Artificial intelligence—a broad term that suggests smart actions performed by a computer without requiring explicit human programming. |
| CQ | The acronym for cultural intelligence (CQ), short for cultural quotient—a complex framework encompassing knowledge and understanding of effective interactions across diverse cultures. |
| IT | Information technology—a set of tools that help work with information and perform tasks related to information processing. |
| KM | Knowledge management—creating, storing, arranging, retrieving, and distributing an organization's knowledge. |
| KMS | Knowledge management system—refers to using modern information technologies to systematize, enhance, and expedite intra- and inter-firm knowledge management. |

## Author details

Leila Halawi
Embry Riddle Aeronautical University, Daytona Beach, Florida, USA

*Address all correspondence to: halawil@erau.edu

## References

[1] Mische M, Marshall R. Reengineering Systems Integration Success. 98th ed Averbach. New York: Taylor & Francis; 1998

[2] Wessner C. Best Practices in State and Regional Innovation Initiatives: Competing in the 21st Century. Washington, D. C: National Academies Press; 2013. DOI: 10.17226/18364

[3] Rifkin J. The Third Industrial Revolution: How Lateral Power Is Transforming Energy, the Economy, and the World. New York: Macmillan Publishers; 2013. p. 304

[4] Davenport T. Thinking for a Living: How to Get Better Performances and Results from Knowledge Workers. Boston, Massachusetts: Harvard Business School Press; 2005. p. 240

[5] Florida R. The Rise of the Creative Class: And How It's Transforming Work, Leisure, Community, and Everyday Life. 29th ed. New York, NY: Basic Books; 2002. DOI: 10.2307/3552294

[6] Karakilic E. Why do humans remain central to knowledge work in the age of robots? Marx's fragment on machines and beyond. Work, Employment, and Society. 2022;**36**(1):179-118. DOI: 10.1177/095001702958901

[7] Al-Haddad S, Kotnour T. Integrating organizational change literature: A model for successful change. Journal of Organizational Change Management. 2015;**28**(2):234-262. DOI: 10/11008/11-2013-0215

[8] Earley C, Soon A. Cultural Intelligence: Individual Interactions across Cultures/Working across Cultures. Stanford, CA: Stanford University Press; 2003. p. 424

[9] Turner J, Kristin P. Creating self-generating knowledge sharing spirals: Improving motivation in a knowledge economy. International Society for Performance Improvement. 2015;**54**(7):20-25. DOI: 10.1002/21489

[10] Zhang Y. Exploring the longitudinal effects of emotional intelligence and cultural intelligence on knowledge management processes. Asia Pacific Journal of Management. 2022. p. 24. DOI: 10.1007/s10490-022-09825

[11] Thomas D, Inkson K. Cultural Intelligence; Living and Working Globally. 2nd ed. Oakland, CA: Berrett-Koehler Publishers; 2009. p. 222

[12] Murray J, Durcikova A. Integrating IS security with knowledge management: Are we doing enough? International Journal of Knowledge Management. 2014;**10**(2):1-12. DOI: 10.4018/201303101

[13] Staff U. An Interview with Peter Denning: Building a Culture of Innovation. Ubiquity - Association for Computing Machinery; 2004. p. 1. DOI: 10.1145/991108.991107. Available from: https://ubiquity.acm.org/article.cfm?id=991107

[14] Baddi A, Sharif A. Information management and knowledge integration for Enterprise innovation. Logistics Information Management. 2003;**16**(2):145-155. DOI: 10.1108/09576050310467287

[15] Chiucchi M. Measuring and reporting intellectual capital: Lessons learnt from some interventionist research projects. Journal of Intellectual Capital. 2013;**14**(3):395-413. DOI: 10.1108/03-2013-0036

[16] Harkema S. A complex adaptive perspective on learning within

innovation projects. The Learning Organization. 2003;**10**(6):340-346. DOI: 10.1108/09696470310497177

[17] Nissen M. Integrated analysis and Design of Knowledge Systems and Processes. Information Resources Management Journal. 2000;**13**(1):24-43. DOI: 10.4018/2000010103

[18] Wiig K. Supporting knowledge management: A selection of methods and techniques. Expert Systems with Applications. 1997;**13**(1):15-27. DOI: 10.1016/S)957-4174(97)00019-5

[19] Whitmore B, Albers J. Knowledge Management in an Accounting organization. Journal of Knowledge Management Practice. 2006;**7**(4). Available from: http://www.tlainc.com/articl123.htm

[20] Malhotra Y. Why knowledge management systems fail: Enablers and constraints of knowledge Management in Human Enterprises. In: Handbook on Knowledge Management. Berlin, Heidelberg: Springer; 2004;**1**:577-599. DOI: 10.1007/978-3-540-24746-3_30

[21] Halawi L, McCarthy R, Aronson J. Success stories in knowledge management systems. Issues in Information Systems. 2017;**18**(1):64-77

[22] Schein E. Organizational Culture and Leadership. Washington: Jossey-Bass; 1985. p. 429

[23] Hofstede G. Cultures and Organizations: Software of the Mind. New York: McGraw Hill; 2010

[24] Martin B. Knowledge management within the context of management: An evolving relationship. Singapore Management Review. 2000;**22**(2):17-27

[25] Cameron K, Quinn R. Diagnosing and Changing Organizational Culture: Based on the Competing Values Framework. 3rd ed. San Francisco, CA: Jossey-Bass; 2011. p. 288

[26] Malhotra Y. Integrating knowledge Management Technologies in Organizational Business Processes: Getting real time enterprises to deliver real business performance. Journal of Knowledge Management. 2005;**9**(1):7-28. DOI: 10.1108/13673270510582938

[27] Halawi L. Knowledge management and the competitive strategy of the firm. The Learning Organization. 2006;**13**(4):384-397. DOI: 10.1108/09696470610667751

[28] Parathrathi B, Frank-Jurgen R. Intangibles in Competition and Cooperation: Euro-Asian Perspectives. New York: Palgrave, St. Martin's Press; 2001. p. 243

[29] Konstadakopulos D. Intangibles in competition and cooperation: Euro-Asian perspectives. ASEAN Economic Bulletin. 2002;**19**(2):224-226

[30] Allee V. 12 principles of knowledge management. Training & Development. 1997;**51**(11):71-74

[31] Presbitero A. Task performance in global virtual team: Examining the roles of perceived cultural dissimilarity and cultural intelligence of member and leader. Personnel Review. 2020;**49**(5):1091-1105. DOI: 10.1108/PR-10-2018-0415

[32] Eisenberg J. Can business schools make students culturally competent? Effects of cross-cultural management courses on cultural intelligence. Academy of Management Learning & Education. 2013;**12**(4):603-621. DOI: 10.5465/2012/0022

[33] Janssens M, Cappellen T. Conceptualizing cultural intelligence:

The case of global managers. In: Handbook on Cultural Intelligence: Theory, Measurement, and Applications. Armonk, New York: M.E. Sharp; 2008. p. 371

[34] Chin T. Cross-cultural metacognition as a prior for humanitarian knowledge: When cultures collide in Global Health emergencies. Journal of Knowledge Management. 2022;**26**(1):88-101. DOI: 10.1108/10-2020-0787

[35] Ang S. Cultural intelligence: Its measurement and effects on cultural judgment and decision making, cultural adaptation, and task performance. Management and Organization Review. 2007;**3**(3):335-371. DOI: 10.1111/1740-8784

[36] Charoensukmongkol P. Cultural intelligence and export performance of small and medium Enterprises in Thailand: Mediating roles of organizational capabilities. International Small Business Journal. 2016;**34**(1):105-122. DOI: 10.1177/0266242614539364

[37] Li J. Belt and road initiative, globalization, and institutional changes: Implications for firms in Asia. Asia Pacific Journal of Management. 2022;**39**(3):843-856. DOI: 10.1007/s10490-021-09770

[38] Stoermer S. The influence of expatriate cultural intelligence on organizational embeddedness and knowledge sharing: The moderating effects of host country context. Journal of International Business Studies. 2021;**52**(3):432-453. DOI: 10.1057/s41267

[39] Albana J, Mehmet Y. Impact of linguistic ostracism on knowledge sharing, hiding and hoarding and the moderating role of cultural intelligence. Kybernetes. 2022;**51**(3):1180-1198. DOI: 10.1108/0906

[40] IBM. 2022 Annual Report [Internet]. 2022. Available from: https://www.ibm.com/investor/att/pdf/IBM_Annual_Report_2022.pdf [Accessed: June 12, 2023]

[41] IBM. What is Knowledgeable Management? [Internet]. 2022. Available from: https://www.ibm.com/topics/knowledge-management [Accessed: June 11, 2023]

[42] Salesforce. How IBM's Collaborative Communities Build a More Vibrant Work Culture [Internet]. 2023. Available from: https://www.salesforce.com/resources/customer-stories/ibm-collaborative-communities-work-culture/ [Accessed: June 12, 2023]

[43] IBM. Transforming the Workplace through Employee Experiences, Cultural Leadership and Sustainable Diversity [Internet]. 2020. Available from: https://www.ibm.com/blog/transforming-the-workplace-through-employee-experiences-cultural-leadership-and-sustainable-diversity/ [Accessed: June 11, 2023]

[44] Unilever. Unilever U.S. Named as a Leading Company on the Diversity Best Practices Inclusion Index [Internet]. 2019. Available from: https://www.unileverusa.com/news/press-releases/2019/unilever-us-named-as-a-leading-company-on-the-diversity-best-practices-inclusion/ [Accessed: June 14, 2023]

[45] Businesswire. Unilever United States Earns Top Marks in 2017 Corporate Equality Index [Internet]. 2016. Available from: https://www.businesswire.com/news/home/20161205005918/en/Unilever-United-States-Earns-Top-Marks-in-2017-Corporate-Equality-Index [Accessed: June 15, 2023]

[46] Von Krogh G. Making the Most of your Company's knowledge: A strategic

framework. Long Range Planning. 2001;**34**(4):421-439. DOI: 10.1016/S0024-6301(01)00059-0

[47] Huysman M, Dirk W. Practices of managing knowledge sharing: Towards a second wave of knowledge management. Knowledge and Process Management. 2004;**11**(2):81-92. DOI: 10.1002/kpm.192

Chapter 3

# Enhancing Well-Being through Knowledge Sharing: Participants' Paths

*Kei Aoki*


## Abstract

This study aimed to explore the mechanism of knowledge sharing as a solution to utilizing individual knowledge that is still untapped, such as user innovation. Prior research has indicated a positive relationship between knowledge sharing and well-being. This study examined participants' motivation and well-being and compared two types of participants: income-oriented individuals (workers) and hobby-oriented individuals (hobbyists). A questionnaire survey investigated the differences between these two groups in terms of their motivation to engage in knowledge sharing (RQ1) and whether there were disparities in their levels of well-being (RQ2). I found that workers exhibited significantly higher altruism levels as motivation for participating in knowledge sharing, in addition to monetary rewards, compared to hobbyists. Moreover, there was no significant difference in the levels of well-being between the two groups. Overall, this study demonstrates that individuals can improve their well-being by using their knowledge and experience to support others, regardless of whether it is related to income, hobbies, or personal enjoyment.


**Keywords:** sharing economy, knowledge sharing, user innovation, well-being, PERMA

## 1. Introduction

With the rise of the sharing economy and the increasing diversity of work styles, there are now more opportunities than ever for individuals to leverage their knowledge and experience. However, the potential of individual knowledge and ideas remains largely untapped. For example, user innovations could increase social welfare, but there is currently no adequate mechanism in society to make use of them [1]. This study fills this gap by highlighting the additional social benefits that can be achieved by utilizing individual knowledge, specifically—that is, improving the well-being of those involved.

This study focuses on knowledge sharing as a mechanism for leveraging individual knowledge. While previous research has examined knowledge sharing between consumers and firms/public sector organizations [2–6], this study specifically explores consumer-to-consumer (C-to-C) knowledge sharing. Moreover, this study investigates knowledge sharing in both face-to-face interactions and through online platforms. In C-to-C knowledge sharing, not only explicit formal knowledge is exchanged, but also tacit knowledge inherent in individuals is shared through the exchange of experience sharing. In this study, "experience" is defined as tacit knowledge and included in the scope of knowledge sharing.

Innovation by private individuals, referred to as user innovation [7] or household sector innovation [1, 8–10] in recent studies, is the convergence of personal knowledge. People try to solve some problems using their own knowledge and experience. As users, they possess a deep understanding of the problems at hand and how best to address them [9, 11, 12]. Consistent with previous literature, this study defines innovation as problem-solving.

### 1.1 Market failure in diffusion of user innovation

User innovation research has long discussed how to elicit innovative ideas that adhere to individuals [7, 13–16]. This is because most user innovators do not actively disseminate their ideas, since they do not expect incentives appropriate to their effort. Previous studies have indicated that this as a "market failure" [17, 18]. It has been suggested that user innovators create financial value by using their time beyond labor time [19, 20]. It is a great loss for society that even though user innovation could increase social welfare, these are not functioning optimally in real terms.

One effective way to diffuse user innovation is through participation in a community of user innovators [7, 13, 14], and participants' motivations have been studied. Although financial incentives have been shown to be partially effective [21, 22], the main motivations of community participants have been the fulfillment of personal needs, feedback from others, and enjoyment [21–24].

Based on the self-determination theory [25–27], Füller [21] described 10 categories of motivation for those participating in online co-creation projects. The 10 categories are divided into three subcategories: intrinsic, internalized intrinsic, and extrinsic (see details in **Table 1**). It is revealed that motivation is dependent on the characteristics of the consumer [14].

### 1.2 Knowledge sharing as a solution for diffusion of user innovation

Belk [28] has defined sharing as "the act and process of distributing what is ours to others for their use and/or the act and process of receiving or taking something from others for our use" and has demonstrated its effectiveness [29, 30]. Previously, it was noted that knowledge sharing has contributed to the development of education, culture, computing, and so on [31, 32]. With the development of the sharing economy, various platforms have been established, making it easier for individuals to disseminate and monetize their ideas. The same is true for user innovation, which can be regarded as the accumulation of individual knowledge.

Aoki [33] found that knowledge sharing is a solution to the market's failure in diffusing user innovation. It seems that through knowledge sharing, participants may be able to satisfy all the motivations Füller [21] indicated, including extrinsic motivation of reward, as well as intrinsic motivation, such as enjoyment, and internalized extrinsic motivation, such as interacting with others and gaining recognition. This study empirically confirms this through a survey of knowledge-sharing participants.

### 1.3 Relationship between knowledge sharing and well-being

Aoki [33] numerically demonstrated that knowledge-sharing participants do not only receive rewards but also improve their well-being, using the concept of "flourishing" in positive psychology [34]. Well-being has been distinguished from happiness in that it does not only deal with satisfaction with life or positive feelings, but it is also comprehensive in terms of relationships with others, autonomy, and achievement [34–37]. The process of knowledge acquisition and utilization by individuals is a continuous process and could be highly congruent with the concept of well-being. Aoki [33] visualized the nonmonetary incentives gained by knowledge-sharing participants with various motivations, in terms of improved well-being.

Flourishing is a criterion for measuring well-being and consists of the following five elements: positive emotion, engagement, relationships, meaning, and accomplishment (PERMA) [34]. Positive emotion is the degree of happiness and enjoyment [34] and is relative to enjoyment, which has been considered an important motivation for user innovators [21–24]. Engagement is the degree of absorption in something [34], or "flow," as proposed by Csikszentmihalyi [38] and Nakamura and Csikszentmihalyi [39]. When people acquire new knowledge or try to create something with it, they may be absorbed in the act. Relationships refer to positive relationships with others [34]. Interaction with others has been identified as an important motivation for people to participate in innovation communities [21–24]. Furthermore, participation in knowledge sharing inevitably leads to interaction with others. Meaning is the degree of satisfaction with one's life, and accomplishment is the degree of achievement of goals set by oneself. If their knowledge and ideas are utilized or recognized by someone else, people may find meaning in it and feel a sense of accomplishment. Thus, knowledge sharing in the form of diffusion of user innovation and PERMA are considered to have a deep relationship.

Although it is generally difficult to measure nonmonetary incentives, Butler and Kern [40] developed a PERMA measurement consisting of 15 questions (3 for each element of PERMA) in which respondents provide ratings on an 11-point scale from 0 to 10 (for details, see Appendix **Table A1**). Aoki [33] showed that knowledge-sharing participants were significantly higher than nonparticipants in four of the five PERMA elements.

Why, then, do knowledge-sharing participants have higher levels of well-being? Aoki [41] investigated this question through in-depth interviews with 10 knowledge-sharing participants who were transferring their knowledge and experience through activities using Lego bricks. She concluded that participants' well-being was enhanced through the following process:

1. Sharing knowledge.

2. Deepening the knowledge and experience they have cultivated over the years.

3. Finding meaning in passing on this knowledge and experience to the next generation.

### 1.4 Knowledge-sharing positioning and research question

Knowledge-sharing participants include those who do so through work and as an extension of hobbies. This study examines whether there is a difference in the paths that the participants followed in either case. Prior research has indicated that monetary incentives and social reputation are conflicting sources of motivation for sharing [31]. Benkler [31] introduced a study comparing paid and free blood donation programs, and the result was that the free blood donation campaign received more cooperation from the public [42]. In the field of psychology, extrinsic and intrinsic motivations have been discussed as contradictory concepts since Deci [43], who stated that monetary incentives could delegitimize intrinsic motivation. Behavioral economics research has pointed out that when monetary incentives are introduced into a market where social incentives function, the former ceases to function [44, 45].

Aoki's [41] study included a mixture of those who were involved in Lego as a hobby and those who became involved in Lego as a job after their hobby developed into a career. She found no differences between the two groups in the process of improving their well-being, such as satisfying their own intellectual curiosity and a sense of mission to pass on to the next generation. It is necessary to confirm whether this result is due to Lego or whether generalization is possible. This study examines the differences between the two groups: "workers," who are income-oriented participants, and "hobbyists," who are motivated by something other than monetary rewards such as a hobby, in terms of motivation and well-being (**Figure 1**). This study focuses on addressing the following research questions.

RQ1: What are the differences in terms of motivation to participate in knowledge sharing between "workers" and "hobbyists"?

RQ2: Are there any differences in the level of well-being between "workers" and "hobbyists" in knowledge sharing?

### 1.5 Hypotheses

With respect to "workers," who function for income purposes, the following hypothesis is derived for RQ1.

H1: In knowledge sharing, while "workers" are more extrinsically motivated, "hobbyists" are more intrinsically motivated.

As noted earlier, intrinsic and extrinsic motivation have been shown to conflict in psychology and behavioral economics [31, 42–45]. However, it is necessary to carefully examine whether any difference exists in the resulting improvement in well-being obtained by those who participate in knowledge sharing with their individual motivations. Studies on the relationship between wealth and happiness have commonly shown that the more wealth one has, the higher the level of life satisfaction, but at a certain level, a point of diminishing returns is reached [34]. The knowledge sharing addressed in this study is focused on what takes place during nonlabor time, and that income, if any, is an additional entity; therefore, the impact on well-being is likely to be limited. This leads to the following hypothesis for RQ2.

H2: There are no significant differences in the level of well-being between "workers" and "hobbyists."

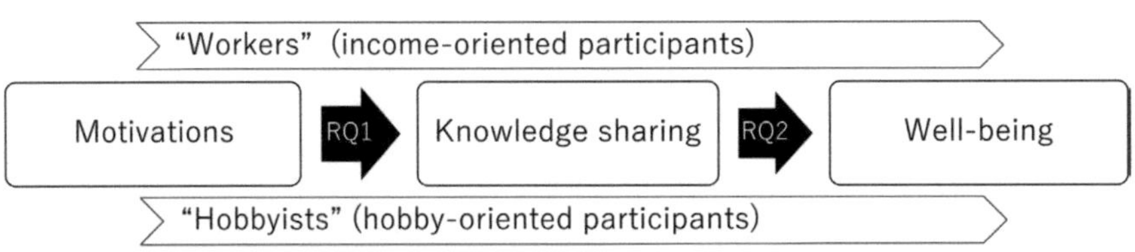


**Figure 1.**
*Research framework.*

## 2. Materials and methods

1. To answer the research questions, a questionnaire survey was conducted with knowledge-sharing participants using the following procedures: Comparative analysis of knowledge participants and a control group (nonparticipants).

2. Comparative analysis of "workers" who participate for remuneration purposes and other knowledge-sharing participants, the "hobbyists."

### 2.1 Sample

The sample of knowledge sharing participants was collected through a research agency via the proceeding steps. First, with the goal of securing a total of 1,000 participants, the following screening questions were asked to 50,000 participants between the ages of 18 and 65 years (age, sex, and residential area in this age group were in line with the population ratio of Japan).

1. Do you have experience in knowledge sharing within the last 12 months? Knowledge sharing refers to using your knowledge, experience, and skills to earn remuneration, primarily money, whenever you want, such as during your spare time. This includes even selling handmade works and so on using your knowledge and skills.

2. Please select the closest match to your knowledge-sharing position.

    a. Secondary occupation or necessary source of income

    b. As a hobby or for fun

    c. Volunteer work

    d. Other

Those who answered "yes" to the first question proceeded to the second question; those who chose a) for the second question were classified as "workers" and those who chose otherwise as "hobbyists."

Simultaneously, a control group of 1,000 men and women aged 18 to 65 years (age, sex, and residential area in this age group were in line with the population ratio in Japan) was selected.

### 2.2 Variables and measurement

#### *2.2.1 Motivation to participate in knowledge sharing*

To examine the difference in terms of motivation between "workers" and "hobbyists" (RQ1), the data was collected using the motivation items presented by Füller [21]. Füller [21] extracted these categories covering intrinsic and extrinsic motivation from diverse literature, including psychology, research on open-source software communities, word-of-mouth, and so on. Although participant motivations or incentives have been presented in knowledge-sharing studies [4–6], primarily extrinsic motivations or incentives have been discussed. This study refers to Füller [21] in order to focus on intrinsic motivation in addition to extrinsic motivation.

The motivation items were presented to the respondents in a manner consistent with those of knowledge sharing, as follows (**Table 1**). Respondents evaluated each item using a 7-point Likert scale.

| Motive categories (Füller [21]) | | Description of this survey |
|---|---|---|
| Intrinsic | Intrinsic playful | For fun |
| | Curiosity | Satisfaction of intellectual curiosity |
| Internalized extrinsic | Altruism | Own knowledge is useful for someone else |
| | Make friends | Interaction with others who share common interests |
| | Self-efficacy | Opportunity to test own knowledge and skill |
| | Information seeking | Obtaining useful information |
| | Skill development | Improvement of one's skills |
| | Recognition | Visualization of evaluations from others |
| Extrinsic | Needed | Requested, unique to me, and so on |
| | Reward | Income generation |

**Table 1.**
*Motivation items.*

### 2.2.2 PERMA

To examine the difference in terms of well-being between "workers" and "hobbyists," (RQ2) the level of well-being was based on the concept of flourishing comprising the five PERMA elements, as presented by Seligman [34].

Prior research has suggested that measures of well-being should be multidimensional [35–37] and universal in their global applicability [37]. The scale of Butler and Kern [40] has been validated through 11 quantitative surveys covering the Americas, Europe, Asia, Africa, and Oceania; Aoki [33] used a Japanese translation of the scale in her study after a back-translation process. In this study, a Japanese translation of the questions was used in the same manner.

Respondents evaluated each item from 0 to 10 (see details in Appendix **Table A1**). As recommended, the level of PERMA should be measured by the average of three responses for each element [40], and this was followed here.

### 2.2.3 Control variables

As control variables, this study collected data on age; sex (male: 1, female: 0); marital status (married: 1, never married: 0); employment status (1: unemployed, 2: part-time, 3: full-time); educational background (1: junior high school, 2: high school, 3: junior college, 4: university, 5: graduate school, and 7: high school); ordinal measure of the length of education (1: junior college/university, 3: university); and personal annual income (ordinal scale; 1: 0 yen, 2: less than 1 million yen, 3: less than 2 million yen, 11: less than 10 million yen, 12: less than 12 million yen, 13: less than 15 million yen, 14: less than 20 million yen, 15: more than 20 million yen).

### 2.3 Analysis

To test H1, a mean comparison is made between workers and hobbyists for each of the 10 motivation items. If the results show that workers exhibit higher levels of extrinsic motivation while hobbyists demonstrate higher levels of intrinsic motivation, H1 would be supported.

To test H2, a mean comparison is made between workers and hobbyists for each PERMA element. Prior to this analysis, a comparison of means is performed between knowledge-sharing participants and nonparticipants for each PERMA element. This step is necessary to ensure that knowledge-sharing participants have higher levels of well-being [33]. If a significant difference is found, a multiple regression analysis is conducted. The group dummy variable (participation to knowledge sharing; yes: 1, no: 0) is included as an independent variable along with control variables, and each PERMA element is treated as a dependent variable. This analysis aims to determine if the significant difference persists even after excluding the effects of control variables. If the results indicate no significant difference in any of the PERMA elements between workers and hobbyists, H2 would be supported.

## 3. Results

### 3.1 Sample

As a result of screening, data were obtained for 1,025 knowledge-sharing participants and 1,042 in the control group. Since the latter group included 59 knowledge-sharing participants, the analyses included them in the former group. After carefully reviewing the responses and omitting those that were unreliable or did not meet the definition of knowledge sharing for the purpose of this study, data from 1,031 knowledge-sharing participants ($M_{age}$ = 41.8 years, 58.9% male participants) and 983 nonparticipants ($M_{age}$ = 43.9 years, 49.5% male participants) was finally used for the analysis. **Table 2** breaks down the positioning of knowledge sharing among the participants (n = 1031) as a result of the screening questions. Those who chose a) in **Table 2** were classified as "workers" (n = 419), and those who chose otherwise as "hobbyists" (n = 612).

The participants' knowledge ranged from creative works to languages and child-related, etc. (**Table 3**).

| | n | % |
|---|---|---|
| **a.** Secondary occupation or necessary source of income | 419 | 40.6% |
| **b.** As a hobby or for fun | 495 | 48.0% |
| **c.** Volunteer work | 110 | 10.7% |
| **d.** Other | 7 | 0.7% |
| Total | 1031 | 100.0% |

**Table 2.**
*Positioning of knowledge sharing.*

| | n | % |
|---|---|---|
| Creative works; videos, photos, handmade works, etc. | 307 | 29.8% |
| Lifestyle; housework, cleaning, cooking, etc. | 250 | 24.2% |
| Information technology | 226 | 21.9% |
| Languages | 187 | 18.1% |
| Design | 168 | 16.3% |
| Child-related: childcare, education, etc. | 158 | 15.3% |
| Others | 133 | 12.9% |

*Note. Multiple answers.*

**Table 3.**
*Participants' knowledge-sharing categories.*

| | α | Knowledge-sharing participants (n = 1031) | | Nonparticipants (n = 983) | | t-value | |
|---|---|---|---|---|---|---|---|
| | | M | SD | M | SD | | |
| PERMA | | | | | | | |
| Positive emotion | 0.85 | 6.23 | 1.77 | 5.57 | 1.75 | 8.45 | *** |
| Engagement | 0.85 | 6.46 | 1.62 | 5.63 | 1.61 | 11.57 | *** |
| Relationship | 0.79 | 6.04 | 1.82 | 5.66 | 1.87 | 4.68 | *** |
| Meaning | 0.82 | 6.03 | 1.83 | 5.18 | 1.91 | 10.16 | *** |
| Accomplishment | 0.89 | 6.34 | 1.68 | 5.52 | 1.67 | 11.00 | *** |

$^{***}p < .001$.

**Table 4.**
*PERMA of the respondents.*

### 3.2 Comparison of knowledge-sharing participants and nonparticipants

First, I compare the PERMA levels of knowledge-sharing participants and nonparticipants: for the PERMA scale, it includes a Cronbach's alpha slightly below 0.8, which is an acceptable level consistent with previous research; and the 15 items of Butler and Kern's scale [40] were used in the analysis. The results showed that knowledge-sharing participants were significantly higher at the 0.1% level in all five PERMA elements (**Table 4**).

Next, to verify the validity, multiple regression analysis was conducted with the knowledge-sharing participation (yes: 1, no: 0) and the control variable as independent variables and each element of PERMA as a dependent variable. Prior to the analysis, the normality of the residuals for each variable was verified. Missing values were also excluded for each pair. To avoid multicollinearity, "employment status" with a variance inflation factor (VIF) greater than 10 was excluded from the independent variables. The results of the analysis show that participation in knowledge sharing significantly affects each of the PERMA components at the 0.1% level, even after excluding the effects of control variables, for all PERMA components, including Relationship, which did not reach significance in Aoki's [33] study (**Table 5**).

*DOI: http://dx.doi.org/10.5772/intechopen.1001936*

| Dependent variable | Positive emotion | | Engagement | | Relationship | | Meaning | | Accomplishment | | VIF |
|---|---|---|---|---|---|---|---|---|---|---|---|
| | β | | β | | β | | β | | β | | |
| Independent variable | | | | | | | | | | | |
| Knowledge sharing | 0.12 | *** | 0.14 | *** | 0.09 | *** | 0.14 | *** | 0.13 | *** | 2.04 |
| Sex | −0.01 | | 0.02 | | −0.02 | | 0.00 | | 0.02 | | 3.01 |
| Age | 0.40 | *** | 0.41 | *** | 0.36 | *** | 0.31 | *** | 0.39 | *** | 7.56 |
| Marital status | 0.02 | * | −0.03 | * | 0.03 | | 0.04 | * | −0.01 | | 2.56 |
| Educational background | 0.46 | *** | 0.49 | *** | 0.53 | *** | 0.47 | *** | 0.46 | *** | 7.69 |
| Personal income | 0.01 | | −0.03 | | −0.01 | | 0.05 | * | 0.01 | | 5.43 |
| $R^2$ | 0.89 | | 0.90 | | 0.88 | | 0.88 | | 0.91 | | |
| F | 2213.44 | *** | 2463.70 | *** | 1909.52 | | 1916.45 | *** | 2543.65 | *** | |

*** $p < 0.01$; *** $p < 0.001$.*

**Table 5.**
*Results of regression analysis (PERMA and knowledge sharing).*

### 3.3 Comparison of workers and hobbyists in PERMA (H2)

To examine H2, I compared the two groups on the level of PERMA, and there were no significant differences between workers and hobbyists for all elements (**Table 6**). Therefore, H2 is supported.

### 3.4 Comparison of workers and hobbyists in motivations (H1)

To examine H1, I compared the motivations for participating in knowledge sharing between two groups and found that "altruism" ($p < 0.05$) and "reward" ($p < 0.001$) were significantly higher for the workers than for the hobbyists (**Table 7**). While the result for "reward" is in line with the hypothesis, the result for "altruism" is contrary to the hypothesis. Therefore, H1 is not supported. The important implications of this result are discussed in detail in the discussion section.

| | α | Workers (n = 419) | | Hobbyists (n = 612) | | t-value |
|---|---|---|---|---|---|---|
| | | M | SD | M | SD | |
| **PERMA** | | | | | | |
| Positive emotion | 0.85 | 6.27 | 1.84 | 6.20 | 1.72 | 0.61 |
| Engagement | 0.79 | 6.47 | 1.69 | 6.45 | 1.58 | 0.14 |
| Relationship | 0.81 | 6.02 | 1.96 | 6.05 | 1.72 | 0.26 |
| Meaning | 0.87 | 6.04 | 1.98 | 6.03 | 1.71 | 0.06 |
| Accomplishment | 0.84 | 6.42 | 1.73 | 6.28 | 1.63 | 1.29 |

**Table 6.**
*PERMA of the knowledge-sharing participants.*

| | Workers (n = 419) | | Hobbyists (n = 612) | | t-value | |
|---|---|---|---|---|---|---|
| | M | SD | M | SD | | |
| Intrinsic playful | 4.96 | 1.50 | 4.87 | 1.53 | 0.95 | |
| Curiosity | 4.78 | 1.47 | 4.66 | 1.43 | 1.31 | |
| Altruism | 5.04 | 1.50 | 4.83 | 1.42 | 2.16 | * |
| Make friends | 4.57 | 1.50 | 4.51 | 1.46 | 0.59 | |
| Self-efficacy | 4.87 | 1.44 | 4.75 | 1.40 | 1.32 | |
| Information seeking | 4.63 | 1.45 | 4.54 | 1.45 | 1.05 | |
| Skill development | 4.98 | 1.46 | 4.82 | 1.46 | 1.72 | |
| Recognition | 4.63 | 1.42 | 4.48 | 1.37 | 1.70 | |
| Needed | 4.75 | 1.50 | 4.64 | 1.41 | 1.15 | |
| Reward | 5.08 | 1.57 | 4.27 | 1.55 | 8.19 | *** |

*$^{*}p < .05$; $^{***}p < .001$.*

**Table 7.**
*Motivations of the knowledge-sharing participants.*

### 3.5 Motivations influencing well-being

The findings indicate that the level of well-being of knowledge-sharing participants is significantly higher than that of nonparticipants, and there is no significant difference in the level of well-being whether knowledge sharing is positioned as a secondary job or hobby, volunteer activity, and so on. In addition, there are no other significant differences in the motivation to participate in knowledge sharing between workers and hobbyists, except for rewards and altruism.

Which motivations for participation in knowledge sharing will influence the level of well-being? Ultimately, multiple regression analysis was conducted with each element of PERMA as the dependent variable and motivation to participate in knowledge sharing and the control variables as independent variables. The results showed that altruism significantly influenced all the PERMA elements; intrinsic playful significantly influenced the four elements except accomplishment; Information seeking significantly influenced positive emotion and accomplishment; and curiosity significantly influenced engagement (**Table 8**). The motivational items demonstrated by Füller [21] are ordered from intrinsic to extrinsic. The four items that were significant in this analysis are concentrated in the first half of the motivational items. These results suggest that intrinsic motivations influence well-being.

## 4. Discussion

### 4.1 Findings

This study aimed to explore the utilization of untapped individual knowledge, such as user innovation, by investigating the mechanism of knowledge sharing as a solution. Specifically, the study examined the differences in motivation and well-being between two groups: "workers" and "hobbyists." The study yielded significant findings, which are summarized as follows:

Contrary to hypothesis H1, the "altruism" motivation was significantly higher in the worker group (whose main objective should be rewards), than in the hobbyist group, including those who engage in knowledge sharing as volunteer work. This finding suggests that factors such as a stronger sense of responsibility or mission, or a recognition of the value of one's own knowledge and experience as a result of the rewards. Notably, rewards serve as an objective evaluation of the value of personal knowledge, in addition to their monetary value.

Hypothesis H2 was supported, as no significant differences were found in any of the PERMA elements related to the level of well-being between workers and hobbyists. This study extends the findings of Aoki [33], indicating that participation in knowledge sharing enhances the well-being of participants across all five PERMA elements, even when the primary motivation is monetary compensation.

Furthermore, an additional analysis of the relationship between participants' motivation and PERMA revealed that knowledge-sharing participants enhance their well-being by contributing to others while simultaneously acquiring valuable information and satisfying their intellectual curiosity, in addition to personal enjoyment. This result aligns with and quantitatively verifies Aoki's [41] finding that knowledge-sharing participants experience increased well-being when they find meaning in deepening their own knowledge and passing it on to others, including future generations.

| Dependent variable | Positive emotion | | Engagement | | Relationship | | Meaning | | Accomplishment | | VIF |
|---|---|---|---|---|---|---|---|---|---|---|---|
| | β | | β | | β | | β | | β | | |
| **Independent variable** | | | | | | | | | | | |
| Motivations | | | | | | | | | | | |
| Intrinsic playful | 0.12 | * | 0.10 | * | 0.12 | * | 0.11 | * | 0.02 | | 2.53 |
| Curiosity | 0.05 | | 0.10 | * | 0.03 | | 0.08 | | 0.07 | | 2.49 |
| Altruism | 0.12 | * | 0.16 | *** | 0.10 | * | 0.16 | *** | 0.21 | *** | 2.53 |
| Make friends | 0.08 | | 0.00 | | 0.08 | | 0.04 | | 0.02 | | 1.79 |
| Self-efficacy | 0.07 | | 0.08 | | 0.07 | | 0.08 | | 0.08 | | 2.74 |
| Information seeking | 0.09 | * | 0.06 | | 0.06 | | 0.07 | | 0.08 | * | 1.98 |
| Skill development | −0.02 | | 0.01 | | −0.02 | | −0.02 | | 0.00 | | 2.91 |
| Recognition | −0.03 | | 0.04 | | −0.04 | | 0.00 | | 0.02 | | 2.08 |
| Needed | 0.02 | | 0.02 | | −0.03 | | −0.06 | | 0.07 | | 2.45 |
| Reward | 0.00 | | 0.02 | | −0.03 | | −0.06 | | 0.04 | | 1.35 |
| **Control variables** | | | | | | | | | | | |
| Sex | −0.01 | | 0.00 | | −0.01 | | 0.03 | | −0.01 | | 1.39 |
| Age | −0.08 | * | −0.09 | ** | −0.15 | *** | −0.14 | *** | −0.08 | * | 1.34 |
| Marital Status | 0.09 | * | 0.00 | | 0.13 | *** | 0.12 | *** | 0.03 | | 1.27 |
| Educational background | 0.04 | | 0.04 | | 0.08 | * | 0.07 | * | 0.09 | ** | 1.15 |
| Employment status | −0.04 | | −0.07 | | −0.05 | | −0.06 | | −0.03 | | 1.63 |
| Personal income | 0.09 | * | 0.05 | | 0.05 | | 0.14 | *** | 0.10 | * | 2.00 |
| $R^2$ | 0.17 | | 0.23 | | 0.10 | | 0.15 | | 0.24 | | |
| F | 11.51 | *** | 16.44 | *** | 7.16 | *** | 10.13 | *** | 17.88 | *** | |

*$^*p < .05$; $^{***}p < .001$.*

**Table 8.**
*Results of regression analysis (PERMA and motivations).*

In summary, this study demonstrates that individuals can enhance their well-being by utilizing their knowledge and experience to support others, regardless of whether it is for income, hobbies, or enjoyment.

### 4.2 Implications

This study makes several contributions to the existing research on user innovation. First, while user innovation has been recognized as a means to enhance overall social welfare [19, 20], the lack of appropriate incentives has hindered its widespread implementation [17, 18]. Although public support has been suggested as a solution [1], this study highlights the effectiveness of C-to-C knowledge sharing as an alternative solution. Individual ideas often possess niche appeal to specific target audiences, and in the initial stages, C-to-C knowledge sharing, which directly matches supply and demand, can prove more effective. Therefore, this study not only demonstrates a pathway for the application of user innovation to enhance social welfare but also identifies the nonmonetary value perceived by user-innovators. While prior research has suggested enjoyment, learning, and interaction with others as important motivations [21–24], this study provides quantitative evidence using the PERMA scale.

Note that the additional analysis in this study identifies a significant relationship between certain motivational factors and the elements of PERMA, but it does not reveal the pathway. Further research is needed.

In the context of knowledge sharing research, this study diverges from previous studies that have primarily focused on knowledge sharing between firms and consumers, instead emphasizing C-to-C knowledge sharing. While prior research has highlighted extrinsic motivation and incentives as driving factors [4–6], this study suggests intrinsic motivation among participants. However, further investigation is required to determine if the effects observed in C-to-C knowledge sharing can be applied to knowledge sharing between firms and consumers.

The COVID-19 pandemic has significantly impacted people's well-being [46–48] and altered their work patterns. From a practical perspective, this study suggests that knowledge sharing can serve as a secondary job, allowing individuals to contribute to others while earning income. With the rise of remote work and the gig economy, many employees face restrictions on engaging in secondary business activities. Concerns about interference with company operations, intellectual property leakage, and trust issues exist. However, considering the improvement of employee well-being, it is crucial for companies to be open to leveraging their employees' individual knowledge.

The pandemic has also damaged the sharing economy [49, 50], which has been growing at an accelerated pace. Movement restrictions, logistics challenges, and the need for social distancing have contributed to this decline. Knowledge sharing, by contrast, has been minimally affected by these factors, with increased interest observed in freelance work during lockdown periods [50].

Finally, the study discusses the results from a sustainability perspective. It emphasizes that acquiring knowledge alone does not bring fulfillment; rather, the true value lies in the application and utilization of knowledge. Using knowledge for the benefit of others, whether through paid or unpaid means, not only deepens one's own knowledge but also enhances well-being. This study established a sustainable flow of knowledge acquisition and utilization within individuals, applicable at any stage in life, including work, leaves of absence, and retirement. The accumulated knowledge within individuals is truly diverse. The study concludes with the hope that it will facilitate the transfer of individuals' knowledge to society, fostering greater diversity in sustainable knowledge resources.

## Acknowledgements

This work was supported by JSPS Grants-in-Aid for Scientific Research (Grant Number 20 K13631, 22 K01759).

## Nomenclature

| | |
|---|---|
| Innovation | value creation for problem-solving |
| User innovation | innovation by users involving general individuals |
| Knowledge sharing | providing knowledge and experience from those who own it to those who need it |
| Well-being | being in good health both mentally and physically |

## Appendix

| Label | Question | Response Anchors |
|---|---|---|
| A1 | How many times do you feel you are making progress toward accomplishing your goals? | 0 = never, 10 = always |
| E1 | How often do you become absorbed in what you are doing? | |
| P1 | In general, how often do you feel joyful? | |
| N1 | In general, how often do you feel anxious? | |
| A2 | How often do you achieve the important goals you have set for yourself? | |
| H1 | In general, how is your health? | 0 = terrible, 10 = excellent |
| M1 | In general, to what extent do you lead a purposeful and meaningful life? | 0 = not at all, 10 = completely |
| R1 | To what extent do you receive help and support from others when you need it? | |
| M2 | In general, to what extent do you feel that what you do in your life is valuable and worthwhile? | |
| E2 | In general, to what extent do you feel excited and interested in things? | |
| Lon | How lonely do you feel in your daily life? | |
| H2 | How satisfied are you with your current physical health? | 0 = not at all, 10 = completely |
| P2 | In general, how often do you feel positive? | 0 = never, 10 = always |
| N2 | In general, how often do you feel angry? | |
| A3 | How often are you able to handle your responsibilities? | |
| N3 | In general, how often do you feel sad? | |
| E3 | How often do you lose track of time while doing something you enjoy? | |
| H3 | Compared to others of your same age and sex, how is your health? | 0 = terrible, 10 = excellent |
| R2 | To what extent do you feel loved? | 0 = not at all, 10 = completely |

| Label | Question | Response Anchors |
|---|---|---|
| M3 | To what extent do you generally feel you have a sense of direction in your life? | |
| R3 | How satisfied are you with your personal relationships? | |
| P3 | In general, to what extent do you feel contented? | |
| Hap | Taking all things together, how happy would you say you are? | 0 = not at all,<br>10 = completely |

*Note. Of the 23 questions in this study, 15 were used in the analysis.*

**Table A1.**
*23-item PERMA profiler measure [40].*

## Author details

Kei Aoki
Hirao School of Management, Konan University, Japan

*Address all correspondence to: aoki@konan-u.ac.jp

## References

[1] Potts J, Harhoff D, Torrance AW, von Hippel EA. Social welfare gains from innovation commons: Theory, evidence, and policy implications. 2 Sep 2021. DOI: 10.2139/ssrn.3915997

[2] Ferreira J, Mueller J, Papa A. Strategic knowledge management: Theory, practice and future challenges. Journal of Knowledge Management. 2018;**24**:121-126. DOI: 10.1108/JKM-07-2018-0461

[3] López-Cabarcos MÁ, Srinivasan S, Vázquez-Rodríguez P. The role of product innovation and customer centricity in transforming tacit and explicit knowledge into profitability. Journal of Knowledge Management. 2020;**24**:1037-1057. DOI: 10.1108/JKM-02-2020-0087

[4] Eisenbardt M. ICT as a tool for gaining and sharing knowledge. Procedia Computers Science. 2021;**192**:1839-1847. DOI: 10.1016/j.procs.2021.08.189

[5] Eisenbardt M. Incentives as a trigger for consumer knowledge sharing with enterprises and public sector organizations. In: Garcia-Perez A, Simkin L, editors. Proceedings of the 21st European Conference on Knowledge Management ECKM 2020. UK: Coventry University; 2020. pp. 222-232

[6] Mullins R, Dettmer S, Eisenbardt M, Ziemba E. Using knowledge exchange between prosumers and enterprises to implement circular economy activities in businesses. Online Journal of Applications Knowledge Management. 2020;**8**:71-90

[7] von Hippel E. Democratizing Innovation. Cambridge, MA, USA: MIT Press; 2005

[8] von Hippel E. Free Innovation. Cambridge, MA, USA: MIT Press; 2017

[9] Stock-Homburg RM, Heald SL, Holthaus C, Gillert NL, von Hippel E. Need-solution pair recognition by household sector individuals: Evidence, and a cognitive mechanism explanation. Research Policy. 2021;**50**:104068

[10] Sichel D, von Hippel E. Household innovation and R&D: Bigger than you think. Review of Income and Wealth. 2021;**67**:639-658

[11] von Hippel E, Kaulartz S. Next-generation consumer innovation search: Identifying early-stage need-solution pairs on the web. Research Policy. 2021;**50**:104-156

[12] Demonaco H, Oliveira P, Torrance A, von Hippel C, von Hippel E. When patients become innovators. In: Tiwari R, Buse S, editors. Managing Innovation in a Global and Digital World: Meeting Societal Challenges and Enhancing Competitiveness. Wiesbaden, Germany: Springer Gabler; 2020. pp. 121-129

[13] Baldwin C, Hienerth C, von Hippel E. How user innovations become commercial products: A theoretical investigation and case study. Research Policy. 2006;**35**:1291-1313. DOI: 10.1016/j.respol.2006.04.012

[14] Ogawa S, Pongtanalert K. Exploring characteristics and motives of consumer innovators: Community innovators vs. independent innovators. Research-Technology Management. 2013;**56**:41-48. DOI: 10.5437/08956308X5603088

[15] Halbinger MA. The role of makerspaces in supporting consumer innovation and diffusion: An empirical analysis. Research Policy. 2018;**47**:2028-2036. DOI: 10.1016/j.respol.2018.07.008

[16] Brem A, Bilgram V, Marchuk A. How crowdfunding platforms change the nature of user innovation—From problem solving to entrepreneurship. Technological Forecasting and Social Change. 2019;**144**:348-360. DOI: 10.1016/j.techfore.2017.11.020

[17] De Jong JPJ, von Hippel E, Gault F, Kuusisto J, Raasch C. Market failure in the diffusion of consumer-developed innovations: Patterns in Finland. Research Policy. 2015;**44**:1856-1865. DOI: 10.1016/j.respol.2015.06.015

[18] von Hippel E, DeMonaco HJ, De Jong JPJ. Market failure in the diffusion of user innovations: The case of "off-label" innovations by medical clinicians. Science and Public Policy. 2017;**44**:121-131. DOI: 10.1093/scipol/scw042

[19] Raasch C, von Hippel E. Amplifying user and producer innovation: The power of participation motives. In: Herstatt C, Ehls D, editors. Open Source Innovation. London, UK: Routledge; 2015. pp. 284-309

[20] Gambardella A, Raasch C, von Hippel E. The user innovation paradigm: Impacts on markets and welfare. Management Science. 2017;**63**:1450-1468. DOI: 10.1287/mnsc.2015.2393

[21] Füller J. Refining virtual co-creation from a consumer perspective. California Management Review. 2010;**52**:98-122. DOI: 10.1525/cmr.2010.52.2.98

[22] Antorini YM, Muñiz AM Jr, Askildsen T. Collaborating with customer communities: Lessons from the LEGO group. MIT Sloan Management Review. 2012;**53**:73-79

[23] Shah SK. Motivation, governance, and the viability of hybrid forms in open source software development. Management Science. 2006;**52**:1000-1014. DOI: 10.1287/mnsc.1060.0553

[24] Janzik L, Raasch C. Online communities in mature markets: Why join, why innovate, why share? International Journal of Innovation Management. 2011;**15**:797-836. DOI: 10.1142/S1363919611003568

[25] Deci EL, Ryan RM, editors. Handbook of Self-Determination Research. Rochester, NY, USA: University Rochester Press; 2004

[26] Deci EL, Ryan RM. Intrinsic Motivation and Self-Determination in Human Behavior. New York, NY, USA: Springer Science & Business Media; 1985

[27] De Charms R. Personal Causation: The Internal Affective Determinants of Behavior. New York, USA: Routledge; 1983

[28] Belk R. Why not share rather than own? The Annals of the American Academy of Political and Social Science. 2007;**611**:126-140. DOI: 10.1177/0002716206298483

[29] Belk R. Sharing. Journal of Consumer Research. 2009;**36**:715-734

[30] Belk R. You are what you can access: Sharing and collaborative consumption online. Journal of Business Research. 2014;**67**:1595-1600. DOI: 10.1016/j.jbusres.2013.10.001

[31] Benkler Y. Sharing nicely: On shareable goods and the emergence of sharing as a modality of economic production. Yale Law Journal. 2004;**114**:273. DOI: 10.2307/4135731

[32] Benkler Y. Coase's penguin, or, Linux and the nature of the firm. In: Ghosh R, editor. Code: Collaborative Ownership

and the Digital Economy. Cambridge, MA: MIT Press; 2005

[33] Aoki K. The relationship between well-being and knowledge sharing. Sustainability. 2021;**13**(9):4978. DOI: 10.3390/su13094978

[34] Seligman MEP. Flourish: A Visionary New Understanding of Happiness and Well-Being. New York, NY, USA: Free Press; 2011

[35] Ryff CD. Happiness is everything, or is it? Explorations on the meaning of psychological well-being. Journal of Personality and Social Psychology. 1989;**57**:1069-1081. DOI: 10.1037/0022-3514.57.6.1069

[36] Medvedev ON, Landhuis CE. Exploring constructs of well-being, happiness and quality of life. PeerJ. 2018;**6**:e4903. DOI: 10.7717/peerj.4903

[37] Ruggeri K, Garcia-Garzon E, Maguire Á, Matz S, Huppert FA. Well-being is more than happiness and life satisfaction: A multidimensional analysis of 21 countries. Health and Quality of Life Outcomes. 2020;**18**:192. DOI: 10.1186/s12955-020-01423-y

[38] Csikszentmihalhi M. Finding Flow: The Psychology of Engagement with Everyday Life. UK: Hachette; 2020

[39] Nakamura J, Csikszentmihalyi M. The concept of flow. In: Snyder C, Lopez S, editors. Handbook of Positive Psychology. New York, NY, USA: Oxford University Press; 2002. pp. 89-105

[40] Butler J, Kern ML. The PERMA-profiler: A brief multidimensional measure of flourishing. International Journal of Wellbeing. 2016;**6**:1-48. DOI: 10.5502/ijw.v6i3.526

[41] Aoki K. Why knowledge sharing increases well-being—The case of adult fans of LEGO. In: Sánchez-García JC, editor. Psychosocial, Educational, and Economic Impacts of COVID-19. London, UK, London, UK: InTech Open; 2022. DOI: 10.5772/intechopen.104556

[42] Richard HM. The origin, development, and regulation of norms Mich. Law Review. 1997;**96**:338-433

[43] Deci EL. The Intrinsic Motivation of Behavior Intrinsic Motivation. Boston, MA, USA: Springer; 1975. pp. 93-125

[44] Ariely D, Bracha A, Meier S. Doing good or doing well? Image motivation and monetary incentives in behaving prosocially. The American Economic Review. 2009;**99**:544-555. DOI: 10.1257/aer.99.1.544

[45] Heyman J, Ariely D. Effort for payment. A tale of two markets. Psychological Science. 2004;**15**:787-793. DOI: 10.1111/j.0956-7976.2004.00757.x

[46] Prime H, Wade M, Browne DT. Risk and resilience in family well-being during the COVID-19 pandemic. The American Psychologist. 2020;**75**:631-643. DOI: 10.1037/amp0000660

[47] Sibley CG, Greaves LM, Satherley N, Wilson MS, Overall NC, Lee CH, et al. Effects of the COVID-19 pandemic and nationwide lockdown on trust, attitudes toward government, and well-being. The American Psychologist. 2020;**75**:618-630. DOI: 10.1037/amp0000662

[48] Brodeur A, Clark AE, Fleche S, Powdthavee N. COVID-19, lockdowns and well-being: Evidence from Google trends. Journal of Public Economics. 2021;**193**:104346. DOI: 10.1016/j.jpubeco.2020.104346

[49] Hossain M. The effect of the Covid-19 on sharing economy activities. Journal

of Cleaner Production. 2021;**280**:124782. DOI: 10.1016/j.jclepro.2020.124782

[50] Batool M, Ghulam H, Hayat MA, Naeem MZ, Ejaz A, Imran ZA, et al. How COVID-19 has shaken the sharing economy? An analysis using Google trends data. Economic Research-Ekonomska Istraživanja. 2021;**34**:2374-2386. DOI: 10.1080/1331677X.2020.1863830

Chapter 4

# A Scrutiny of the Role of Knowledge Management in Employees' Organizational Culture, Motivation, and Success

*Seyyed Mohammad Kashef*


## Abstract

Advances in information technology have swayed all of the aspects of human life in contemporary societies. Organizations constitute one of the major groups of the social entities, which have been influenced by technological developments. As a result, they have made an endeavor to acclimatize themselves to the above-mentioned advances in order to survive and to protect their competitive advantages. Among the technology-induced measures which have been taken by the organizations, strategic thinking has attracted considerable attention. This approach to manager empowerment focuses on the organization managers' ability to integrate their creativity into their intuition in order to manage their organizations strategically. Nonetheless, the formulation and implementation of strategies depends on the managers' ability to manage the knowledge of their organization. Consequently, the concept of knowledge management has been developed and has been characterized as the pivotal asset of the modern organizations. Considering the significant role of knowledge management in the amelioration of organizational performance, this chapter makes an attempt to expound on the relationship between knowledge management and employees' organizational culture, motivation, and success.


**Keywords:** employee motivation, knowledge management, organizational performance, strategic thinking, technological advancements

## 1. Introduction

At the present time, all of the modern and urbanized societies are making an endeavor to acclimatize themselves to the advancements in the field of information technology. Among the various entities of the societies, *organizations* are considered to be the entities that have been extensively affected by the above-mentioned technological advances [1]. In general, organizations constitute the unified groups of people who make an attempt to achieve a specific set of predetermined objectives including the business-oriented objectives [2].

A close examination of the behavior of various organizations in the past decades highlights the fact that they have strived to take advantage of the most efficient technology-based *management* methods and techniques for ensuring their survival, dealing with the market-oriented challenges, and gaining competitive advantage [2]. The perusal of these methods shows that, most of them have focused on the stakeholders' (e.g., managers and employees) insight into the factors in the success of the organizations [3]. More specifically, the organizations have given priority to their managers and staff members' proper understanding of the determining factors in the survival and success of their developed and implemented plans [2]. Accordingly, they have informed these stakeholders about *strategic thinking* as one of the most efficacious techniques of organizational management in the era of information technology [3].

The concept of strategic thinking has been characterized in different ways. Mintzberg [2] provided a practical definition of this concept and argued that this kind of thinking refers to the process of integrating intuition into creativity for developing a unified and thorough understanding of the pertinent business. Likewise, Kashef et al. [4] noted that strategic thinking comprises the managers' capability to predict the future on the basis of their background information and the dynamics of the environment and to formulate and implement efficient strategies for ensuring the survival and success of their organization in the market over the course of time. Accordingly, Kashef et al. [4] noted that strategic thinking has to be considered as the essential and functional prerequisite to *strategic management*.

Similar to the concept of strategic thinking, the construct of strategic management has been delineated in various ways. Rigby and Bilodeau [1] averred that strategic management encompasses the ongoing process of formulating plans, monitoring the implementation of the developed plans, and evaluating the effectiveness of the plans for ensuring the success of the organization. As they explained, in general, the organizations in different parts of the world have made an attempt to take advantage of the techniques of strategic management due mainly to their privatization and their intention to join the World Trade Organization. Likewise, Kashef et al. [4] pointed out that the above-mentioned reasons have prompted Iranian organizations to focus on the concept of strategic management in recent years. According to them, the organizations in Iran have realized that their access to organizational knowledge constitutes the essential prerequisite to effective strategic management.

The significant role of organizational knowledge in strategic management has been emphasized in the relevant studies in recent years (e.g., [5–11]). Kalseth [12] noted that managers need to have access to useful and up-to-date organizational knowledge in order to be able to develop a thorough understanding of their own responsibilities and to make and implement important and major decisions in an effective way. Considering this issue, he stated that the organizations have to consider *knowledge management* as the most integral aspect of their strategic management and have to apprise their managers of its critical role in the process of decision making.

A number of researchers (e.g., [13–17]) have made an endeavor to provide a clear and precise definition of the concept of knowledge management. Among these definitions, Kalseth's [12] definition has proved to be a practical definition and has been used as a guide in the relevant studies. Kalseth [12] defined knowledge management as the endeavor of the organizations to take part in the continuous and uninterrupted process of gaining/creating, managing, sharing, and using collective knowledge in order to ameliorate the process of their decision making and to ensure their success in the competitive market.

Badriazarin et al. [18] pointed out that knowledge management has become one of the most essential aspects of strategic management in various organizations across the word due mainly to the fact that it enables them to maintain their long-term supremacy over their competitors in the market. As they explained, the organizations have changed their attitudes toward their main assets and have realized that state-of-the-art organizational knowledge and its efficient management constitute their invaluable assets. Likewise, Roos et al. [19] underscored the significant role of knowledge management as a type of intangible asset. As they explained, tangible assets constitute the physical and financial possessions of the organizations. On the other hand, intangible assets comprise the possessions that do not have a physical form. As a result, they may encompass the skills and knowledge of the staff members which are likely to increase the value of the organization in the future. Roos et al. [19] noted that knowledge management has proved to be one of the most important intangible assets of the organizations that have a noticeable impact on their ability to ensure their survival and to maintain their competitive advantage over the other organizations in the market.

Considering the above-mentioned discussions of knowledge management and its importance to the organizations in the era of information technology, the following section of this chapter expounds on the role of knowledge management in the employees' organizational culture, motivation, and success.

## 2. Knowledge management in organizations

### 2.1 The role of knowledge management in employees' organizational culture

An examination of the pertinent literature (e.g., [20]) highlights the fact that organizational culture has been defined in various ways. Schein [21] provided a practical definition of this concept. As he explained organizational culture encompasses a set of reasonable and valid assumptions that are made by the human resources of the organizations including their managers and employees based on their experiences and the challenges that are posed by the problems inside and outside the relevant organizations.

Likewise, Ravasi and Schultz [22] pointed out that, organizational culture encompasses the organization-related assumptions, which have a major influence on the behavior of the staff members in the organizations. According to them, these assumptions are considered to be the underlying principles of behavior in the organization. Consequently, the new members of the organization are provided with organizational-culture-based education in order to be able to adhere to the above-mentioned principles in a satisfactory way. As they concluded, the organizational culture of an organization determines the interaction patterns between its stakeholders and the degree to which the employees identify with it over the course of time.

Riches [23] argued that knowledge management has a profound impact on the employees' organizational culture. As he explained, providing the employees with adequate information on knowledge management is likely to make them cognizant of the significant role of group cohesiveness and may promote interaction among the diverse departments of the organizations. Moreover, this kind of information can remind the employees of the necessity of *consistency* in the performance of their tasks and can result in the enforcement of strong discipline in the organizations. Likewise, Bhatt [24] pointed out that the employees' understanding of knowledge management procedures has a beneficial impact on the establishment of their high standards of behavior and is likely to improve the efficiency of their pertinent organizations. Lastly, Herder et al. [25] noted that the employees' thorough understanding of the dynamics of knowledge management in their organization encourages their innovation and prompts them to formulate and implement innovative plans that are closely aligned with the underlying principles of professional behavior in their relevant organization. As they concluded, apprising the employees of the central tenets of knowledge management is likely to have a profound impact on their motivation in their pertinent settings.

### 2.2 The role of knowledge management in employees' motivation

In humanities, researchers have always been concerned with the motivation of individuals in various contexts including the occupational contexts. Radel et al. [26] defined motivation as the reason behind the individuals' initiation, continuation, and termination of various behaviors at specific points in time. As they explained, motivation can be explained in terms of specific states that range from the strongest to the weakest states. As they concluded, the stronger states are likely to affect the individuals' behaviors in a more noticeable way.

Likewise, Ryan and Deci [27] pointed out that motivation constitutes the reason for the individuals' engagement in objective-oriented behaviors in the course of their life. They distinguished *intrinsic motivation* from *extrinsic motivation* on the basis of their nature. More specifically, as they pointed out, intrinsic motivation depends on the individuals' internal factors and determines the degree to which a certain individual enjoys the performance of his/her relevant tasks and derives personal satisfaction from them. On the other hand, extrinsic motivation depends on the external factors and specifies the extent to which the individuals engage in various types of activities for gaining external advantages including rewards among others. According to them, extrinsic motivation may have a positive impact on the individuals' task performance in occupational contexts. Nonetheless, it may result in their burnout over the course of time. As they concluded, the individuals' intrinsic motivation is likely to have long-lasting beneficial impacts on their occupational performance in their pertinent settings.

Lastly, Wasserman and Wasserman [28] pointed out that the individuals' motivation may have *instrumental* or *integrative* orientations. As they explained, instrumental motivation encompasses the motivational orientation that prompts the individuals to perform their tasks in order to achieve their objectives. On the other hand, they noted that integrative motivation refers to the motivational orientation that encourages individuals to perform their tasks in order to be able to identify with their relevant organization. They concluded that integrative orientation has proved to be more beneficial for improving the employees' performance in their settings in comparison with the instrumental orientation.

Regarding the impact of knowledge management on employees' motivation, Rizwan et al. [20] pointed out that the employees' ability to strategically manage their organizational knowledge is likely to increase their intrinsic motivation in their relevant organization. As they noted, this issue stems from the fact that knowledge management gives the employees a deep sense of fulfillment and enhances their task-performance enjoyment. Likewise, Ekmekçi [29] noted that providing the employees with information on the knowledge management process makes them cognizant of the fact that their behavior and decisions are considered to be determining factors in the success of their organization. As he pointed out, this type of understanding enables the employees to take satisfaction from the performance of their tasks and improves their intrinsic motivation.

In addition, the employees' knowledge management capabilities are likely to exert a profound impact on their motivational orientation in their relevant organization [30]. Rotenberry and Moberg [31] pointed out that involving the employees in the knowledge management procedure makes them aware of their consequential role in the survival and success of their organization and empowers them to realize the significant role of their organization in the society. As they explained, this issue prompts the employees to identify with their organization in a stronger way and to support its principles and policies. They concluded that, the employees' integration into the process of knowledge management is likely to influence their success in their settings in a noticeable way.

### 2.3 The role of knowledge management in employees' success

The concept of knowledge management has been introduced to the field of management in order to positively influence the performance of the staff members in different organizations [4, 32, 33]. Considering this objective, a number of researchers (e.g., [34]) have focused on the role of knowledge management in the employees' success in the context of their organization. DeVitis and Rich [35] defined success as the condition in which an individual is able to satisfy his/her own or the other individuals' expectations in an acceptable way. As they explained, the individuals' success is assessed based on contextual criteria. Consequently, success is likely to be defined in various ways on the basis of the pertinent requirements in different contexts including the occupational contexts.

Mostafapour et al. [36] argued that knowledge management is one of the factors that may exert influence on the employees' use of technological advancements in their organizations. As they explained, the employees' knowledge about these advancements and their ability to use them in the process of task performance are likely to have a beneficial impact on their success in their occupational settings. Likewise, Rizwan et al. [20] noted that the engagement of the employees in the process of knowledge management encourages them to take advantage of various sources of information in order to gain knowledge about the dynamics of their organization and prompts them to use different types of technological advancements including various software in order to participate in the above-mentioned process in an effective way. As they concluded, these measures are likely to enable the employees to develop practical and technical skills which may have an advantageous impact on their success in the context of their organizations.

## 3. Conclusion

This chapter made an effort to expound on the role of knowledge management in the employees' organizational culture, motivation, and success. It was noted that, at the present time, strategic thinking and strategic management constitute invaluable organizational assets and are likely to increase the value of organizations over the course of time. Moreover, it was pointed out that knowledge management is the most central aspect of strategic management and involves the process of gaining/creating, managing, sharing, and using collective knowledge in order to ameliorate the process of decision-making in an organization and to ensure its success. It was concluded that, involving the employees in the process of knowledge management is likely to have a beneficial impact on their organizational culture, motivation, and success in their relevant organizations.

## Nomenclature list

information technology
instrumental orientation
integrative orientation
knowledge management
motivation
strategic management
strategic thinking
success
organization
organizational culture

## Author details

Seyyed Mohammad Kashef
Faculty of Sport Sciences, Department of Motor Behavior and Sport Management, Urmia University, Urmia, Iran

*Address all correspondence to: mm.kashef@yahoo.com

## References

[1] Rigby D, Bilodeau B. Bain's global 2007 management tools and trends survey. Strategy &Leadership. 2007;**35**(5):9-16

[2] Mintzberg H. The Rise and Fall of Strategic Planning. London: Prentice Hall International; 1994

[3] Mirakhoori A. Developing a Strategic Thinking Model Based on the Islamic-Iranian Pattern: Case Study of the Education Directorate of Tehran Province (Master's Thesis). Tehran, Iran: Payame Noor University; 2013

[4] Kashef SM, Ahmadi M, Kashkuli FE. The relationships between strategic thinking, knowledge management and intellectual capital in the Office of Youth and Sports of the selected provinces of Iran. Sport Science. 2018;**11**:78-84

[5] Adam S, Fuzi NM, Ramdan MR, Mat Isa R, Ismail AF, Hashim MY. Entrepreneurial orientation and organizational performance of online business in Malaysia: The mediating role of the knowledge management process. Sustainability. 2022;**14**(9):508-521

[6] Ahbabi A, Ali S, Singh SK, Balasubramanian S, Gaur SS. Employee perception of impact of knowledge management processes on public sector performance. Journal of Knowledge Management. 2019;**23**(2):351-373

[7] Ammirato S, Linzalone R, Felicetti AM. Knowledge management in pandemics: A critical literature review. Knowledge Management Research & Practice. 2021;**19**(4):415-426

[8] Granados ML, Mohamed S, Hlupic V. Knowledge management activities in social enterprises: Lessons for small and non-profit firms. Journal of Knowledge Management. 2017;**21**(2):376-396

[9] Tomé E, Figueiredo P. Knowledge management and politics at the highest level: An exploratory analysis. Management Dynamics in the Knowledge Economy. 2015;**3**(2):193-212

[10] Tomé E, Gromova E. Development of emergent knowledge strategies and new dynamic capabilities for business education in a time of crisis. Sustainability. 2020;**13**:45-68

[11] Zargar. The Impact of Intellectual and Social Capital and its Role on Organizational Effectiveness in Iranian Sports Organizations (Doctoral dissertation. Tehran, Iran: Islamic Azad University; 2012

[12] Kalseth K. Knowledge management from a business strategy perspective. Journal of FID Review. 1999;**1**:37-41

[13] Adali F. Knowledge Management: Movement beyond Knowledge. Tehran: Andisheh Metacognition Publication; 2005

[14] Ayatollahi H, Zeraatkar K. Factors influencing the success of knowledge management process in health care organizations: A literature review. Health Information & Libraries Journal. 2020;**37**(2):98-117

[15] Benabdellah AC, Zekhnini K, Cherrafi A, Garza-Reyes JA, Kumar A. Design for the environment: An ontology-based knowledge management model for green product development. Business Strategy and the Environment. 2021;**30**(8):4037-4053

[16] Chen Y, Luo H, Chen J, Guo Y. Building data-driven dynamic capabilities to arrest knowledge hiding: A knowledge management perspective.

Journal of Business Research. 2022;**139**:1138-1154

[17] Haider SA, Zubair M, Tehseen S, Iqbal S, Sohail M. How does ambidextrous leadership promote innovation in project-based construction companies? Through mediating role of knowledge-sharing and moderating role of innovativeness. European Journal of Innovation Management. 2023;**26**(1):99-118

[18] Badriazarin Y, Seyedameri M, Imanpoor A. Regression analysis of the relationship between knowledge management components and human resource performance. Sport Management Journal. 2013;**4**(15):35-50

[19] Roos J, Roos G, Dragonetti NC, Edvinsson L. Intellectual Capital: Navigating in the New Business Landscape. London: Macmillan Business; 1997

[20] Rizwan M, Khan DJ, Saboor F. Relationship of job involvement with employee performance: Moderating role of attitude. European Journal of Business and Management. 2011;**3**(8):77-86

[21] Schein EH. Organizational culture. American Psychologist. 1990;**45**(2):109-119

[22] Ravasi D, Schultz M. Responding to organizational identity threats: Exploring the role of organizational culture. Academy of Management Journal. 2006;**49**(3):433-458

[23] Riches P. Organizational coherence and knowledge management. KM Review Briefing. 2004;**7**(4):10-22

[24] Bhatt GD. Knowledge management in organizations: Examining the interaction between technologies, techniques and people. Journal of Knowledge Management. 2001;**5**(1):68-75

[25] Herder PM, Veeneman WW, Buitenhuis MDJ, Schaller A. Follow the rainbow: A knowledge management framework for new product introduction. Journal of Knowledge Management. 2003;**7**(3):105-115

[26] Radel R, Pjevac D, Davranche K, d'Arripe-Longueville F, Colson SS, Lapole T, et al. Does intrinsic motivation enhance motor cortex excitability? Psychophysiology. 2016;**53**(11):1732-1738

[27] Ryan RM, Deci EL. Self-determination theory and the facilitation of intrinsic motivation, social development, and well-being. The American Psychologist. 2000;**55**(1):68-78

[28] Wasserman T, Wasserman L. Motivation, Effort, and the Neural Network Model. Berlin: Springer; 2020

[29] Ekmekçi AK. A study on involvement and commitment of employees in Turkey. Journal of Public Administration and Policy Research. 2011;**3**(3):68-73

[30] Brown SP, Leigh TW. A new look at psychological climate and its relationship to job involvement, effort, and performance. Journal of Applied Psychology. 1996;**81**(4):358

[31] Rotenberry PF, Moberg PJ. Assessing the impact of job involvement on performance. Management Research News. 2007;**30**(3):203-215

[32] Dehghanpouri R, Kashef SM, Khodadadi MR. Designing the maturity model of knowledge management based on business strategies in Iran's sport. Applied Research in Sport Management. 2020;**9**(1):25-48

[33] Shafiepour F, Yarmohammadian MH. The organizational climate, job involvement and organizational trust with knowledge management culture: Educational systems of Esfahan

City (Iran). International Journal of Knowledge, Culture and Change Management. 2008;**11**(5):63-76

[34] Hansen MT, Nohria N, Tierney T. What's your strategy for managing knowledge? Harvard Business Review. 1999;**77**(2):106-116

[35] DeVitis JL, Rich JM. The Success Ethic, Education, and the American Dream. New York: State University of New York Press; 1996

[36] Mostafapour M, Kashef SM, Esmaeilpour HM, Akbarzadeh V. The relationship between knowledge management and the application of information technology in the departments of youth and sport organization of West Azarbaijan Province. Journal of Physical Education. 2014;**2**(1):29-34

Chapter 5

# Reason and Interdisciplinarity in Knowledge Management

*Steven T. Buccola*


## Abstract

We take a tour of what a valid and useful knowledge management would look like. To do so we distinguish between the two major types of organizational knowledge – human and technological – and show how rationality is to be differently understood in these two types. Human or personal reason is distinguished by a nonseparability of its concepts owing to the intuitive manner in which they are unified in the act of understanding, so that knowledge is a risky matter of interpretation and judgment. Technology instead requires a separability of concepts essential for reducing them to measurement, where they must stand visibly apart. We go on to show the paradoxical but essential need of these two knowledge types for one another, shown in the duality between unobservable and observable concepts necessary for judging an organization's value. We find that fact and counterfact, actual and possible, observable and unobservable are brought together in organizational knowledge.


**Keywords:** analytical, counterfactual, ends and means, interdisciplinary, intuition, organization, judgment, risk and uncertainty, technology, separability and nonseparability, synthetical, value

## 1. Introduction

By one account, knowledge management is the assessment and control of the data and know-how of an organization. Especially though, it is a matter of forming and using the data and knowledge, as only then can they inform both strategy and the processes of carrying it out.

Abstract definitions like this unfortunately only get us started. Few if any organizational improvements will be forthcoming from stated principles and purposes, explaining why our emphasis is usually on case studies, which cut through the generalities and offer a sense or feeling of what might work

Some insight however is to be had from asking what business knowledge is itself. What *is* that we call knowledge? How does knowledge lead to understanding, which must be knowledge's final goal? How will we know the best way to build the organization we are engaged with and how can these 'best-ways' be made accessible? To address these questions I step behind the important administrative and logistical questions to look in the opposite direction: at the sources of the ideas and concepts by which knowledge brings the understanding that effective management requires.

 IntechOpen

I begin with rationality itself, since in the absence of reason there would be no determinate solution to any organizational problem whatever, only a procession of *ad hoc* rules justifying any idea we came up with. We can envisage three cognitive steps in knowledge management, a reflection on: (i) rationality and optimality themselves, (ii) the appropriate optimization and performance procedures, and (iii) their logistics and administration. Of these I'll concentrate on the first while keeping the second and third in mind.

## 2. Reason: fact and counterfact

Our interest is in knowledge management itself. But what is knowledge? This is a metaphysical as well as epistemological question, bearing on the structure *of* reality as well as the structure of how we *know* reality. So it's worthwhile reflecting on both these questions. Something hangs paradoxical over the topic of knowledge management, at least when the knowledge is technical. For the question of managing something is simultaneous with, co-determined by, the question of how we value it. And technical knowledge is at a disadvantage when raising or answering questions of value.

### 2.1 Technology does not assess value, even its own

The difficulty is that value judgments can never be a matter of measurement; and it is with measurement that technology principally occupies itself. Reflections on measures and so on value are a matter of judgment. And judgment is a form of reason that transcends – though at the same time includes – any observability or measurability. Some aspects of the task before us therefore, insofar as we are forming judgments about technology management, will not themselves be technological. We must be economists, legal scholars, psychologists, or sociologists as well, and in some respect philosophers. Each in its way is a concern for the possibility of knowledge. As Martin Heidegger [1] put it, philosophy has for the past several centuries consisted mostly of "reflection on knowledge itself and its possibility." (297) And because, one way or another, the work of the philosopher is to reflect on essences, Heidegger paradoxically cautions us that "the essence of technology is by no means anything technological." [2].

A prime question in modern knowledge management, both in theory and practice, is the issue of the boundaries between knowledge fields. It is not just a matter of *where* a boundary lies but more fundamentally in *what* any boundary would consist. Can, should, and if so how and when might two knowledge disciplines be drawn together, or at least brought into conversation? These are relatively easy questions to answer in fields sharing a common epistemological attitude, where the standards for 'how can I claim that such-and-such is true' are the same. It is more problematic when their epistemologies or meanings differ, and even more so when their metaphysics do.

A crucial issue and theme of this essay will be the significance to knowledge management of *cognitive nonseparability*, which arises when one concept, assumption, or finding cannot be made sense of without considering others. Nonseparability is often indicated in multivariate equations when some interaction terms cannot be factored out of the remaining ones. As we will see, separability is a signal property of technological inquiry, and nonseparability a property found in the specifically human disciplines like economics. Indeed, separability virtually defines technical know-how, as nonseparability does human know-how. Yet the two fields cannot do without each other.

### 2.2 Technology is judgment-challenged, economics is observation-challenged

To the extent human understanding involves nonseparable concepts, rationality is something we can only dwell on rather than measure, since to measure is to stand outside of, be separate from, the object measured. And as psychologist J. H. Van den Berg [3] asked, "who could draw the line between the 'objective' and the 'human' world?" (99).

> *The object is; this means that the object in its abstraction is immediately and continually transcended into a whole of (human) interpretations, a whole which, eventually, always encompasses the entire world." (98).*

Those entire worlds are what confront us, or invite us, in every choice we make. It is what Van Dusen [4] calls being-in-the-world, (37) or as Medard Boss [5] puts it, "a world-unfolding and world-opening being." (85) A person is not then an 'individual' at all if by that is meant dissociable for inspection, which, Boss says, could "only be maintained on the basis of abstract intellectual constructions." (88).

For economics too, it is this same inner intuition, your sense of yourself-in-a-world, that is the basis of your empirical judgments. This is so not only in economics. An intuition or sense, originating in an inner subjectivity and awareness of one's self in a given situation, is the center of any rationality. This claim can neither be analytically proved nor empirically depicted. The reverse is so: it is the awareness of yourself and situation, projected onto your possible future, that offers the understandability of what you are reasoning and observing. That is nonseparability in a nutshell.

There is however a literal, empirical, and so entirely separable side to organizational thought – technology. As such, technology brings an important qualifier and co-interpreter of economic reason. Every human thought and decision is accompanied with and influenced by, for instance, emotive affects. Empirical, technical psychology is the study of these affects, as chemistry is of the environment and bioengineering is of gene splicing. Together they constitute part of the setting in which organizational analysis is conducted, the foundations of the supplementary theories necessary for business inference.

Economic models – directed to persons in the immediacy of their sense of a situation – therefore must buttress themselves with controlling factors from these technical disciplines. Immanuel Kant [6], who first clarified this problem in terms a modern ear can appreciate, wrote: "The sensible faculty of intuition is really only a receptivity for being affected in a certain way with representations." (A494, B522) One can go on and form judgments from these representations. But judgments are so closely connected to the initiating intuition that the reverse is also true: Kant says, "the same function that gives unity to the different representations in a judgment also gives unity to the mere synthesis of different representations in an intuition … [and its corresponding] analytical unity." (153) The prime implication of these words, and of the individuality or singularity of the person who forms the judgment, is that vague abstractions are finally to be ruled out.

It is *you* who judge. The 'I think', says Kant, "and which is the foundation of one's conceptualizing, must be able to accompany all my representations." Thus, "intuition has a necessary relation to the 'I think' in the same subject in which this manifold is to be encountered." (B131–132) (163) Sense and concept go hand in hand and it is in a person that they do. These are nonseparable and why technology alone is never finally adequate to knowledge management, just as abstract ideas and groupings aren't either. This is not to say that empirics and generalizations cannot be stressed in particular studies. They will be and must be.

## 2.3 Economic reason unites observables with unobservables

All this was well understood by the late 19th century expositors of modern economics. Leon Walras [7] for instance expressed nonseparability in the economic notion of *rarete*, a sense of a thing's scarcity, which remains the center of microeconomic theory. Scarcity combines, nonseparably, what we might otherwise think to be the most separable of all: the *desirability* of a good versus its *availability*. These two are never separable in a human decision, influencing one another instead. Each therefore has immediate implications for the other, so you can observe neither desirability nor availability on its own. There are no data on them as such because neither is an 'it' that can be isolated. Yet the greater your sense of scarcity the more you are willing to pay for it:

$$Scarcity \Rightarrow Price \tag{1}$$

By way of the marketplace on the other hand, prices *are* observable and measurable. Consequently the quantities of this good are observable and measurable too, for how could a per-unit price be observed if the quantities received for it were not? We also then have the relation:

$$Quantity \Rightarrow Scarcity \tag{2}$$

insofar as the greater the quantity on the market, the less its scarcity. Finally we combine the two to form:

$$Quantity \quad \Rightarrow \quad Scarcity \Rightarrow Price \tag{3}$$

and simultaneously

$$Price \Rightarrow Scarcity \Rightarrow Quantity. \tag{4}$$

Now note something fundamental in Walras' reasoning: what is unobservable here, the scarcity, is what is giving meaning to what is observable – the prices and quantities. In return it is these two observables that point to, and so help outline and reinforce, the sense of the unobservable: the scarcity. They are essential to each other. At the heart of both is what we would call an openness or receptivity to the decision maker's situation or 'world', the future into which she is always stepping.

The *synthetic a priori* reasoning Kant helped us recognize in ourselves *is* the form of reasoning we have outlined here and that Kant calls judgment. In it, our immediate sensible intuition of a manifold is formally (pre-empirically) combined into a single representation so as to render it conceptual and therefore articulable and interpretable. Such judgments are never dogmatic. They are *a priori* only, so must now be synthesized or tested in the presence of observable, empirical data. Scarcity – part of Kant's category of Limitation or finitude and in turn an element of what he calls Quality – is one such purely formal concept that provides the foundation of empirical work (B106). Because entirely formal, it is unobservable. But as representing a manifold of possibility, it is that by which we grasp and understand the prices and quantities that we observe and measure.

It is in this spirit that James Buchanan [8] shows in the theory of cost a tentative distinction between 'subjectivity', which is a matter of sense, and 'objectivity' a matter of concept. In the former, and what Buchanan calls the logic of choice, (45) "cost cannot be measured by someone other than the decision maker because there is no way that subjective experience can be directly observed." "Cost [therefore] must be reckoned in a utility dimension." (41) In what Buchanan calls the logic of prediction on the other hand, (40) where objectivity and so measurability are essential, we have "the familiar textbook diagrams, the objectively identifiable magnitude that is minimized." And as we saw in Walras, "this market value is reflected in the market prices for resource units."(40) [1] The unobservable then is being joined to the observable.

The highly specific nature of this conjunction of heterogeneous elements calls for metaphorical language. Buchanan says, "properly interpreted, [cost] theory's claim is limited to making predictions on the 'as if' assumption that men do so behave in some average or representative sense." (38) Metaphor is the only way, he concludes, that the objective and subjective elements of a theory can be integrated. In cost theory, the objective is only 'standing in for' the subjective. The business analyst is only 'standing in for' the customer, the stockholder, the banker, the CEO, or the Board who make the final decisions.[2]

Buchanan and I are employing *synthetic a priori* reasoning here ourselves, as opposed to the merely analytical or merely synthetical (empirical) one. As Lanier Anderson [10] writes in regard to Kantian epistemology in general, an implication is that,

> *the distinction between analytic and synthetic judgments is fixed independently from our strategies for forming concepts.... (32).*

The distinction between the analytic and synthetic, in how each stands toward or interrelates with the other, is already there in the structure of human reason so cannot be rearranged to suit the reasonings of an arbitrarily identified discipline or school. As Patricia Kitcher [11] discusses also from a Kantian standpoint, we cannot choose to take the analytical side over the empirical side, say, of some question simply by a nudge from the other. We cannot derive an analytical theory from a synthetical finding, or a synthetic theory from an analytical finding. They come together instead in every personal judgment.

### 2.4 The nature of counterfactual (interpretive) reason

Frank Knight [12] had, in more an economist's or statistician's than a philosopher's language, said as much in connection with the phenomenon of risk. "We have insisted

---

[1] Buchanan takes the word 'objective' to be synonymous with observable or 'real'.

[2] A valuable discussion of the use of metaphor appropriate to organization environments is in Richard Moran [9].

that there is a fundamental difference between '*a priori*' probability on the one hand and statistical" probability on the other. In the former the chances of something happening "can be computed on general principles, while in the latter they can be determined only empirically [synthetically]." (130) [3] This distinction of course bears on the ability to construct, and on the purpose for constructing, a counterfactual and so of the model that generates it.

Knight writes, "we must infer" by way of a model "what the future situation would have been without our interference, and what change will be wrought in it by our action." (118) Keep in mind we aren't speaking of just formal modeling here. Every time you stop and think about a specific organizational situation, you are constructing a model of it, where possibilities predominate over actualities. In sum:

*To model something is to generate counterfactuals (possibilities).*

*To be a counterfactual is to be estimated in a model.*

J-C Spender [16] adopts this same view in his assessment of what he calls organizational capital. In an extensive and careful critique of proposals to depict and measure the features of an organization – of say a capital asset – Spender concludes that none stand up to inspection. Indeed he remains a skeptic of any claim to capture these phenomena in mere concepts. Our references to reality must then be indirect, by way of pointing. There is no 'thing' out there that is 'an' asset, as it is too entwined with neighboring ones. Spender says, of human assets in particular: "From the theory side, one difficulty is the idea that either human or social capital can be conceived, measured or theorized independently of the other." (8–9) For, "employees are constantly educating each other and increasing each other's human capital in ways that make it difficult to distinguish the consumption" side of knowledge from the production side of it (6).

The underlying message is that, as in other human fields, business and economic concepts are for the most part nonseparable from one another. Pervasive nonseparability is acknowledged in ordinary qualifiers like 'sort of', 'semi', and 'partly'. "Elements of the organization's knowledge and skills are," Spender writes, "semi-public goods as far as that particular community is concerned." (9) Insofar as public, they cannot be reduced to any single 'I think', but achieve their public character when one person's 'I think' appeals to another person's 'I think'.

Efforts to escape or obscure such cognitive inseparability are frequent in the knowledge management literature. But finance, marketing, and employee relations are never really separate in the way that an assessment of one could simply be added to the assessments of the others. Considerations of each will require re-referencing every other in a step-by-step construction, as Westphal [17] demonstrates. Plans to reorganize a product assembly line, say, will have consequences for a recent bank loan agreement, in turn affecting a proposed new customer product, and around again to

[3] Bruce Caldwell [13] has discussed in this vein the relative merits of an apriorist (analytical) versus an empiricist critique of economics. He settles on Fritz Machlup's [14] view that characterizations of 'ideal types' of decision makers, as in Weber [15] and others, "emphasizes that 'rational economic man' is a theoretical construct; that is, it does not refer directly to 'the real world'... that no consumers or firms 'really' act that way...that empirical studies can never establish nor falsify a theory," but only to assist with our judgments. (167)

the assembly line problem. Joint, nonseparable phenomena of such sort are finally what matter in business, government, and economic life.[4]

We will put this even more succinctly. *Synthetic a priori* reason, in which a person's intuitions of a certain setting organize themselves under articulable categories, is nonseparable from intuitions of still other settings – unified as they are by the very nature of intuition. And because all such cognition is a matter of possibility, of a 'would be', it is a matter of a counterfactual, a 'might be'. In short, *counterfactual, unobservable-but-estimable, and nonseparable imply one another.*

## 3. Interdisciplinarity: economics and technology

In the above light therefore we ask more generally into the possibility of a valid interdisciplinarity, in which the necessarily mechanical modality of technology might, together with the a-mechanical reasoning of human personhood, help understand human ends and choices.

### 3.1 Measurement can be unified with concept

Max Weber [15] draws an incisive distinction here:

> *The term 'technology' applied to an action refers to the totality of means employed as opposed to the meaning or end at which the action is, in the last analysis, oriented. (160) The presence of a 'technical question' always means that there is some doubt over the choice of the most efficient means to an end. The only considerations relevant are those bearing on the achievement of a particular end .... (161).*

Technology for Weber is pure measurable efficiency, the least costly way, in measurable empirical terms, of attaining an end. Not so in economics:

> *There is, of course, an analogous principle governing economic action. But...it has a different meaning (161). Account must be taken of the quality, the certainty, and the permanence of the result....The definition of economic action must be as general as possible and must bring out the fact that all 'economic' processes and objects are characterized as such entirely by the meaning they have for human action in such roles as ends, means, obstacles, and by-products. (158–159).*

Economics' distinctive role is to choose the ends, though the means and their obstacles and byproducts are drawn into them. Ends are chosen for their quality and reliability, characterized Weber says "entirely by the meaning they have" and where prudence or judgment play a role.

What however will comprise quality and reliability? We have no sense in Weber that technology itself will answer this question in any way but an "efficient means"

[4] Patricia Kitcher [18] emphasizes that the source of these insights is Kant. She writes, "empirical cognition requires the simultaneous solution of two problems: (i) using the available sensible materials to represent an object in objective space and time,"; and (ii) "using the apprehension of those sensible materials to represent the empirical unity of a subject's consciousness." (9) Or as Kant says, "the understanding's pure synthesis ... lies *a priori* at the basis of the empirical synthesis." [6] (B140) Even empirical knowledge then is largely the internal act of the observer that we term judgment.

to do something we want done. Furthermore, 'want done' is never fully specifiable, extending itself in an indeterminate variety of directions, depending as it does on future contingencies. Technology then demands strict observability, declining to assert ultimate judgment but an element of the judgment's empirical foundation. For since it is not in a position to know a specific end for a specific person, technology is not in a position to project her future either. Only the organization or business is in the position necessary to appreciate a decision's 'by-products' (opportunity costs) and in that way its meaning. Only with a human view therefore – together with the accompanying data – can one point to the future, to the locus of judgment and purpose.[5]

Let us look more then at what this agency is that offers itself as a valuable auxiliary, that promises to supply us with the most efficient way of achieving whatever ends we have. Importantly, technology is not anything in-itself that you can hold up and literally look at. It is not your cellphone itself. It is a particular interpretation of it: what will help you achieve what you wish. Viewed this way, a phone is thoroughly observable in the literal way that 'observable' implies – empirical and measurable.

But it could be interpreted differently too. It could be among the organization's ends. There it is subject to, combined with, a whole manifold of other ends whose possibilities concatenate without clear limit, one building on another and so necessarily introducing uncertainty. Consider for instance the case of sourcing a newly redesigned cellphone part. It could easily be, compared to others: (a) more expensive, (b) more attractive, (c) more suited to a current advertising scheme, (d) easier to install, (e) more breakable, and (f) not yet fully tested. The data science staff, the engineers, the buyers, the stockers and inventory personnel, the accountants, are now, *as* technologists, over their heads. You've just entered the domain of economic reason if not the legal and sociological. The distinction between ends and means, and so between economics and technology, is itself then a matter of interpretation. And in the dimension of interpretation you are in the dimension of economics and other human, transcendental thought – namely transcending, and therefore judging, what *can* be literally observed. So if you regard yourself a technologist, keep in mind you spend much of your day a law theorist, economist, and psychologist as well – even if merely in crossing the street – where you are judging the net value of yourself and your organization as an end as well as a means.

As we have made clear and as Kant [6], Heidegger [20], and others show, the distinction between ends and means is co-relative to the distinction between a person and a thing. This distinction in turn is metaphysical because it presumes person and thing to be irremediably disjoint, that a person can never be a thing and vice versa. What it is to be a person then will always be correlative to the question of what it is to be rational, and because rational, conscious of uncertainty. To this uncertainty, technology has of itself no access. Technology is useful for addressing uncertainty but not in itself and as such. That only a person can do, *as* a person.

### 3.2 Fact and counterfact are synthetic a priori too: Buyer demand

We can then see why, in declining to put themselves 'above' their subjects, the human disciplines must somehow bring together what is observable (e.g. prices, quantities, technology) with what ultimately is unobservable (preferences). Only

[5] We should remember that Weber, an early sociologist as well, may be including sociology here, which he pursued under an epistemology much like Georg Simmel's [19], namely focusing on how individuals comport with each other in particular kinds of settings.

then can what is specifically human reveal itself. A central way economics does so is in the Marshallian [21] and Hicksian [22] demand functions, the former relating the quantity of a good desired to the money income $m$ of the person desiring it, and the latter to her preferences or utility $u$ instead. Both demands respond also to observable prices $p$. But while the income in the Marshallian is empirical to both buyer and analyst, the utility in the Hicksian is empirical to neither of them. $u$ is not observable, even to the buyer.

Let us represent these two explicitly, the Marshallian quantity demanded as $y\ (p,\ m)$ and the Hicksian as $h\ (p,\ u)$.[6] Now note, in addition to these demanded *quantities*, that the buyer in the Hicksian case is equivalently wishing, at the given prices $p$, to be minimizing the *expenditures* needed to achieve that given $u$. We will call this minimized expenditure $e(p, u)$. Substituting it for the money expenditure $m$ in the Marshallian demand $y(p, m)$ gives us $y[p, e(p, u)] = h(p, u)$, namely the Hicksian again. That is, *because* people want to minimize the cost of realizing their yet-unachieved dreams and preferences, we should depict their demand both in the *empirical* Marshallian dimension and in the *nonempirical* Hicksian dimension transcending the empirical. Each of these two demands is a check on the other.

Indeed they co-determine each other, since substituting $e(p, u)$ for $m$ – and vice versa – will allow us to move back and forth between the empirical $y(p, m)$ on the one side and the nonempirical $h(p, u)$ on the other. The unobservable is being 'revealed' in the empirical, while the empirical is being critiqued and judged by the yet unobservable cost $e(p, u)$ of realizing one's preferences. Because however we cannot observe $u$ or therefore $e(p, u)$ or $h\ (p, u)$, the Hicksian 'pushes' us to include in the Marshallian the observable factors $z$ that may be correlated with the unobservable but judgeable $u$. That is, the $h\ (p, u)$ *judgment* is what lets us *reflect* on and *specify* the $y(p, m)$ more fully, which then, upon estimation, provides the empirical results. Let us refer to this fuller Marshallian demand specification as $y(p, m, z)$.

Despite that such duality or mutual correspondence wasn't fully clarified until the mid-20th century (by John Hicks [22], in fact), it was implicitly being assumed by the late 19th. For the unobservable as well as observable dimensions of a decision are part of our daily experience. A price for instance is a weight one bears, and so, as a literal heaviness, is fully empirical. And income is countable money multiplied by its countable purchasing power, so equally empirical. Utility in contrast is a judgment of product usefulness or value and hence subject to the conditions of judgment – one's grasp of a situation and its possible conceptualizations. As possibility only, it is nonempirical and nonobservable while at the same time offering the insight needed to specify the fuller Marshallian demand $y(p, m, z)$.[7] Here then, in the specification of $z$ and thus of the final demand $y(p, m, z)$ is the opening for psychology, sociology, and political science, along with the technology and engineering needed – by reflecting on $e(p, u)$ – to understand $y(p, m, z)$.

Note that business, law, and economics in particular must now judge the stability and veracity of these other disciplines it is calling in to buttress themselves.

---

[6] See for example Varian [23] and Mas-Colell, Whinston, and Green [24].

[7] Frank Knight, quoted by James Buchanan [8], refers to the same literal heaviness Anderson does when he writes: "the cost of any value is simply the value that is given up when it is chosen; it is just the *reaction or resistance* to choice that makes it a choice." (Buchanan's italics). Every decision, by way of utility and its corresponding judgment, therefore endures a counterweight, namely the decision's antithesis. So it can be initiated only from an empirical 'spark' like a price. This is the 'matter' Anderson [10] says that, for Kant, is a decision maker's access to a 'thing itself' – the reality we encounter but never know as such.

Historically the first to be called in was physics, in the form of equation structures flexible enough to distinguish between an identity on the one hand and an equilibration (an insight, an effort, a risk) on the other. The second were the engineers and biologists to detail the technical connections between inputs and outputs, in particular the input combinations $x$ able to produce given outputs $q^o$ under a given technology and from which the cost-minimizing ones are to be selected.

### 3.3 The hybrid (dual) character of supply

Now that we have settled on consumer demand, consider the hybrid, techno-economic task of the supply side: isolating the input volumes – we'll call them $x$ – that not only can produce the given $q^o$ but in the least costly way. This is achieved by solving the producer's cost minimization problem $\min_x rx(q^o) = \min_x [r_1x_1(q^o) + r_2x_2(q^o) + ....,]$ yielding cost function $C(q^o, r)$, namely the least-cost way of producing quantity $q^o$ at given input prices $r$.[8] As you can see, this specifies the desired input volumes (conditional input demands) $x(q^o, r)$ – being the input purchases at alternative prices that minimize the total cost of producing the given output $q^o$.

Note what we have done here on the producer side, as in the Marshallian and Hicksian on the consumer, is to estimate counterfactuals, consumption and production *possibilities* under various possible price and other conditions. *Economics is more concerned and involved with counterfacts than with 'facts'.*

For all this, technical knowledge has been, though not sufficient, a necessary element. Technical contributions to economic thought and modeling include:

- By Discipline Area: science, engineering, statistics, depth psychology, empirical psychology, and empirical sociology.

- By Application Area: environmental, medical, manufacturing, construction, managerial, and financial.

Importantly, the technical possibilities these fields identify and generate can in turn, if bounded and finite, be recovered from the costs the economic decision maker incurs in their presence. That is to say, we have another duality. Technologies can be reverse-engineered: re-discovered from economic cost data alone, though only if the decision maker had been *trying* to minimize cost, as only then will the techno-economist's estimate of the minimum cost, and thus of the technology, be unbiased. It seems no other joint discipline (econ and tech) can accomplish this task – of returning, *as* digested and absorbed, the very information it had borrowed from another field. And because technology is what is being borrowed-from and interpreted here, and because cost minimization is economics' mode of borrowing and interpreting, we can say that *interpretation is being integrated with the interpreted*.

This integration or conjoining of the impersonal and technical with the personal and economic is yet another instance of synthetic a priori reason, a formal schema uniting the decision maker's inner sense of a situation with his conceptualizations and articulations of it, that Hume [25] first glimpsed and Kant [6] later confirmed. Here then is the nonseparability of what is subjective and what is objective, the nonseparability where real persons are making real decisions.

---

[8] For instance, Varian [23] (53).

### 3.4 Concluding comment: The plight of the counterfactuals

The initial or primal problem we have described here – in which technology is drawn upon to help minimize cost – is, as we have said, a matter of an observable pointing to a nonobservable: technology being the observable and empirical, and economic preferences being the nonobservable and nonempirical. Can you see that the dual problem then – reversing this direction by using the cost-minimizing input combinations to rediscover the technology that had been used – is by this token a matter of the unobservable judging the observable? As we have said, economics and technology are in deep need of one another.

If so, it is an interesting thought experiment to reverse these two poles. It would be to cast economics as the auxiliary, the external information-provider, and technology the interpreter of the information. It would be, that is, for economics (or psychology or sociology) to provide their services to technology. Economic findings then would have to be of the same order as the technical, namely technological themselves. The first thing to see about such a reversal is that the possibility of contextual, personal readings of economic language would be given up. Broad generalizations, emptied of the discrete, intuitive meanings that particular situations provide and that micro-economics is engaged in modeling, then replace them. Persons, the dimension of interpretation, judgment, and decision, are reduced to things.

What might, in an historical sense, explain such depersonalization? Two possibilities its seems to me. First, science and technology afford the unending stream of new curiosities that the human disciplines lack. The plethora of data becoming available in our era is, however, the second reason. Econometric structure, the distinction for instance between endogenous and exogenous variables, initially gives way to single-equation and other reduced-forms, where more abstract visions are allowed. Statistical structure then stands in for theoretical structure. Distinctions between cause and effect devolve into correlations. Generalizations, cut loose from a sense of particular circumstances, get freer rein but at the cost of credibility and meaning.

Yet the management of knowledge, especially of technical knowledge can never finally be technological. If it were, no one would finally be interested as it would have no human implications or meaning. Knowledge management therefore calls for symbolic, 'as-if' expression just as economics does. The way technical knowledge is interpreted is finally, as Heidegger [2] was saying, a human question. And to be human is to have a zone of privacy even from oneself. Not even the decision maker can ultimately peer inside and see how her decisions are made, so knowledge managers' depictions of decision processes are metaphorical and symbolical only. This is not to say metaphor is not effective. Quite the contrary, it is finally the most effective of all. Efforts nevertheless are underway – in artificial intelligence – to eliminate metaphorical, 'as-if' expression. That, I surmise, will be AI's chief problem.

## Nomenclature

| | |
|---|---|
| Epistemology (Methodology) | The study of the methods we use to know something and how the methods can be justified |
| Counterfactual | A model estimate of what would have happened had conditions been otherwise. In other words, the level |

| | |
|---|---|
| | an endogenous variable would have taken had the exogenous been at levels different from those at that same time and place |
| Empirical | Observable with the five senses |
| Endogenous Variable | A model variable whose value depends on others in the model |
| Exogenous Variable | A model variable whose value depends on no others in the model but affect others instead |
| Reduced Form | A single-equation simplification of what is presumed, in fuller reality, to be a multi-equation and more complex one |
| Separability | An independence or dissociability among variables implying each can be understood without reference to the others |
| Synthetic *a Priori* | A modeling procedure that involves both, and forms the unity of, conceptualization and empirical observation |

## Author details

Steven T. Buccola
Department of Applied Economics, Oregon State University, Corvallis, OR, USA

*Address all correspondence to: sbuccola@oregonstate.edu

## References

[1] Heidegger M. What Is a Thing? Transl. W. B. Barton, Jr. and Vera Deutsch. Chicago: Henry Regnery; 1967. Reprinted in "Modern Science, Metaphysics, and Mathematics," Martin Heidegger: Basic Writings, HarperPerennial, 1977, 1993

[2] Heidegger M. The Question Concerning Technology. HarperCollins; 1977. Transl. by William Lovitt; First published in 1954

[3] Van den Berg JH. The human body and the significance of human movement. In: Ruitenbeek H, editor. Psychoanalysis and Existential Philosophy. New York: E.P Dutton and Co.; 1962

[4] Van Dusen W. The theory and practice of existential Analysis. In: Ruitenbeek H, editor. Psychoanalysis and Existential Philosophy. New York: E.P Dutton and Co.; 1962

[5] Boss M. 'Daseinanalysis' and psychotherapy. In: Ruitenbeek H, editor. Psychoanalysis and Existential Philosophy. New York: E.P Dutton; 1962

[6] Kant I. Critique of Pure Reason. 1st and 2nd ed. New York: Random House (Modern Library); 1958. Trans. by Norman Kemp Smith. First published in 1781 (1st ed.) and 1787 (2nd ed.)

[7] Walras L. Elements of Pure Economics. 4th ed. Richard D. Irwin, Inc; 1954. Trans. William Jaffe; 1st edition 1874, 4th edition. Washington, DC; 1900

[8] Buchanan JM. Cost and Choice: An Inquiry in Economic Theory. Indianapolis: Liberty Fund, Inc; 1999

[9] Moran R. Metaphor. In: Hale B, Wright C, editors. A Companion to the Philosophy of Language. Oxford: Blackwell Publishers; 1997

[10] Anderson RL. The Poverty of Conceptual Truth: Kant's Analytic/ Synthetic Distinction and the Limits of Metaphysics. Oxford: Oxford University Press; 2015

[11] Kitcher P. Kant's Spontaneous Thinker and (More) Spontaneous Agent. In: Palmquist S, editor. Cultivating Personhood. Berlin: Walter De Gruyter; 2010

[12] Knight, Frank H. Risk, Uncertainty, and Profit. Boston: Houghton Mifflin, 1921. Reprinted in Adansonia Press, 2018

[13] Caldwell B. Beyond Positivism. Economic Methodology in the Twentieth Century. London: Allen and Unwin; 1982

[14] Machlup F. Methodology of Economics and Other Social Sciences. New York: Academic Press; 1978

[15] Weber M. The Theory of Social and Economic Organization. New York: Oxford University Press; 1947. Trans. A.M. Henderson and T. Parsonsl First published in 1922

[16] Spender J-C. Organizational capital: Concept, measure, or heuristic? In: Organizational Capital: Modeling, Measuring, and Contextualizing, Ahmed Bounfour. London: Routledge; 2009

[17] Westphal KR. How Kant justifies freedom of agency (without transcendental idealism). European Journal of Philosophy. John Wiley and Sons. 2017;**25**(4):1695-1717

[18] Kitcher P. Practical and empirical cognition of the cognitive self. In: Presented at the 97th Annual Meeting of the American Philosophical Association, Pacific Division, April 8, 2023. 2023

[19] Simmel G. The categories of human experience. In: On Individuality and Social Forms. University of Chicago Press; 1971. First published in 1908

[20] Heidegger M. Being and Time. New York: Harper-Collins; 1962. Trans. by John Macquarrie and Edward Robinson; First published in 1927

[21] Marshall A. Principles of Economics. New York: Macmillan and Co; 1890

[22] Hicks JR. Value and Capital. Oxford: Clarendon Press; 1946

[23] Varian HR. Microeconomic Analysis. 3rd ed. W.W. Norton and Co.; 1992

[24] Mas-Colell A, Whinston MD, Green JR. Microeconomic Theory. New York: Oxford University Press; 1995

[25] Hume D. In: Selby-Bigge LA, editor. A Treatise of Human Nature. Book I, of the Understanding. Oxford: Clarendon Press; 1893 First published in 1739

Chapter 6

# On Structuring of Media Information on Sensitive Issues

*Dora Gelo Čolić*


## Abstract

Structuring media information on sensitive issues is the optimizing process of information content to integrate the essential tension between two contradictory demands. In this case, it is a demand for openness, in other words, information of public interest. On the other side is the demand for secrecy with regard to the sensitivity of information with possible links to the specific parts of the national security concept. The content of the term public interest is determined by what is widely accepted as essential in terms of the long-term well-being of society and its members. The topic is approached within the framework of semantic information theory in such a way that the information published in the public media is analyzed in accordance with theoretical guidelines in a concrete environment, and the analysis isolates the elements of information that correspond to the given goal and those that do not.


**Keywords:** information, relevance, media, data quality, usefulness

## 1. Introduction

Structuring media information on sensitive issues is the optimizing process of information content to integrate the essential tension between two contradictory demands. One of them is demand for openness, demand to give access to information that is critical for citizens, in other words, information of public interest. The other one is the demand for secrecy with regard to national security.

The concept of public interest and its content could be debatable. However, it is unlikely that subtle differences in the perception would significantly erase the importance of factors such as the relevance of information, its truthfulness, clarity, and coherence of reporting.

"… there is the idea of 'public interest' as in the chapter title, used widely and diversely, sometimes misused and escaping an agreed definition except in very general terms (as a notion of the welfare of the public or society as a whole). However, Jay Blumler did suggest (1998) a fairly clear view of what it would mean, in terms of three key features: it refers to a vision of what is good for the many as instituted by some form of legitimate democratic authority (as are certain other functions in society, such as government or the justice system) and having an element of public responsibility as a consequence. It is an idea that requires a long time span, which takes into account the long-term needs and effects, thus of future as well as present generations.

In addition, the notion of a public interest has to recognize conflicts of interest and of perspective in implementation; it must permit compromise and adaptation to the realities of the time and place" [1].

Is that a problem worth solving? By simply observing, we can notice lots of lines of force in the public space. However, more often than not, we do not recognize their source or even their mutual interference, goals, or source's motivation. We might find that all of these are the factors producing or empowering the media noise we witness nowadays. It is not unfeasible to conclude that such media noise could be the reason for the fear that humans feel while deciding whether to believe something they have heard or not. Furthermore, that fear could be reflected in the opposite direction and make people not believe something that they actually should. Nevertheless, to analyze "what is what and who is who is the zoo" is not an easy task.

According to McQuail [2], media theory is a complex structure of socio-political and philosophical principles. He sees it as the knowledge that organizes ideas on the relationship between the media and society. In his classification, among a few other theories, there is normative media theory that deals with the issue of what the media should do rather than what they are really doing. Although the fact that McQuail categorizes theory in a few basic varieties, he adds that, in reality, there are no clean models; rather, what exists in a concrete society is a model combining theoretical elements and media types. He also believes that basic principles of media activity can be isolated as independence, diversity or pluralism, information quality, and the preservation of social and cultural order. He warns that some of these principles are conflicting but that one of the aims of regulation is managing tensions and settling conflicts. The conflict in focus in this research is between secrecy and openness, which we see as something that the national security system is entitled to do vs. the demand of the public as part of the norm of a democratic society. But it is just one of the many characteristics of this specific relationship between the system and the media. As stated by authors Peter Gill and Mark Phythian [3], a part of their relationship can also be marked by a combination of dependence, manipulation, support, and praise. Besides that, the similarity between these two is something that is worth mentioning as well. We can notice while looking at the relationship that both have specific connections with the source, which opens up the possibility of fraudulent and illegal behavior to obtain information that is not accessible to the public by regular means. These appearances [4] are also directly connected to the possible negation of basic principles like independence and information quality.

Can we solve it in the framework of science? We can exaggerate by saying that we will find the one and only solution in the framework of science and that we will resolve all of our problems with regard to media reporting. It is also possible to exaggerate in another direction and argue that the solution is not possible, not by any chance and not under any condition, but both perspectives cannot find a firm foundation if we look at science as something in the middle of those two, something that asks questions, seeks answers, gets partial answers, and tries again.

Is it applicable? It could be, and it will be presented in this paper. Firstly, a theoretical analysis of fundamental terms of information sciences was conducted. The results of the analysis were applied to a certain amount of units. By units, it is meant sentences from the chosen media article. An empirical analysis after the theoretical analysis filtered the applied results in a way that gave them space to live and be accommodated within a certain environment. That resulted in a concretization of the fundamental theoretical terms. The overall result will be shown in this paper, together with the process.

Is it real? In most of the discipline and not rarely in research, we do have that practice-theory relationship problem. We can find the same in this particular research and the discipline we lean on in this research. Information sciences, as in any other discipline, could have a theory that seems not to work in reality and a practical working solution that cannot be confirmed outside of the silent knowledge. According to many sources, gathering information is no longer a problem in today's world. As per some estimates, open sources contain a high percentage of required information, indicating an increased need to improve the decision-making process, mainly the analysis process [5]. That would be place where practice and theory should constantly meet, making each other real.

As a wide variety of problems in science, engineering, etc., can be posed as optimization problems [6], the goal of a former model, and hopefully an optimization algorithm in the future, is to calculate that right measure or the right language structure of the sentence and to optimize information, naturally following the results from the research process. Secondly, an alternative to optimizing every piece of information (in this research, information equals sentence) is to optimize the whole media article by picking only sentences that fall in the range of calculated values that are determined as those that legitimize publishing based on the scope and goal of the research.

Taking into account the need to have the possibility to change this model, as this particular optimization process must be understood as "learning by doing," we are thinking of using, for "very" further research, a learning process in the Artificial Neural Network's (ANN) context, that is, ANNs ability to learn automatically from examples. This can be considered as updating network architecture [6]. With this mode of applying the results, it is especially interesting that the ANN learns underlying rules from the given representative examples.

## 2. Methodology

The methodology used in this research is mostly inspired by Florian Kohlbacher's design, which implies applying qualitative content analysis as an interpretation method in a case study. Given the fact that the research in question is initial in nature and its main purpose is the processing of semantic theory of information in the context of its suitability for solving the given research problem as well as related problems, refining terminology, operationalizing concepts, and creating an analytical matrix of relationships between concepts, it is used a case study of the research principle with admixtures of the description principle. The latter is used for the purpose of transparency of empirical analysis, which should contribute to critical observation of the research process and its results.

In accordance with the need to resolve the essential tension that this problem contains and its multi-perspective, the needed methodological framework is the one that will result in the resolution of the problem and all its dimensions so that in future research, these dimensions can be specified more narrowly, and thus more precise in research questions/hypotheses which will potentially result in more precise answers.

The formulation of research questions is the first component of the research design, and in this study, a total of four research questions were asked. The choice of methodological strategy, including the type of methodology and methods, was previously explained, and here it should be emphasized once again that it was decided that, at this moment, it would be counterproductive and contrary to the basic goal of the research to set hypotheses and use any type of standard statistical or other quantitative methodology. For this reason, one cannot talk about a completed model of objective quantification of information but only about testing possible variables. In other words, at this stage, this would be a representation of the model that is aimed for, the model when all variables would be included in the calculation and more strongly modulated.

Consequently, an iterative analysis method is used, and due to that, at this stage is possible to talk only about an approximate solution and not the exact one as well as a gradual reduction of the error after each step. Considering the complexity of the system being processed, it is to be expected that a method of this character and scope will be used in the following research, possibly in a more complex form by narrowing down and determining the number of steps of information analysis and/or by introducing allowed limits of error reduction in the results in the sense of limiting the legitimacy of the results.

Firstly, a theoretical analysis was conducted. The fundamental concepts of information science were analyzed: relevance, usefulness, informativeness, data, and information. The paper presents brief considerations and the results of the theoretical analysis as initial settings for testing in the empirical analysis. Despite the large number of definitions of the fundamental concepts and concepts related to them and the many perspectives of their contents and relations, it was decided to use those that, in terms of their formation, best fit the framework of the specific research. As the goal of the research is to isolate an analytical framework for structuring information of public interest subject to the requirement of secrecy and to examine the adequacy of semantic information theory as a framework for establishing a balance between the requirements of secrecy and openness, the first starting point was to check whether semantic information theory is an appropriate framework for the research problem.

To achieve the subsidiary goal, that is, isolation of a specific preliminary model for testing the described publications in the media, it is examined:

a. whether truthfulness or informativeness is more important for the relevance of information,

b. which elements/categories are sufficient for building this model, and

c. what are the relations between them.

In the second phase, the results of the theoretical analysis were applied to a certain number of research units. They were analyzed by using structure analysis, syntax analysis, grammatical analysis, and narrative analysis. The number of research units for the empirical analysis was not determined in advance, but the analysis lasted until a conclusion was reached on all examined categories and elements, that is, until it was determined by the findings that the final conclusion could not be reached unambiguously.

In this particular research, a total of 34 research units were analyzed. The sentences were selected from the chosen media article, per the defined theme framework and based on the evaluation of the content in terms of participants, activities, events, and venues by convenient sampling from the daily or weekly national newspaper. In the selected article, research units (sentences) were selected as a representative part of the material (article) or a part of the material that was judged suitable for examining a certain category or relation.

With the results of the empirical analysis that filtered the applied theoretical terms, we created a matrix as the meeting point of theoretical terms and their empirical usage. By picking patterns during the matrix analysis, we produced a table containing formulas expressing connections between both empirical and theoretical examined elements.

In the third phase of research, the analysis was done based on the produced table, and the results were recorded. Considering the overall goal of the research, many more units have to be included in order to achieve a bigger number of representative examples.

Matrix results for relevance, usefulness, and average data quality are variables for the publication test. Given that 34 research units were analyzed and that the obtained values ranged from:

$$R = 0 - 7.65 \tag{1}$$

$$Kor = 0 - 105.65 \tag{2}$$

$$KV(g) = 0 - 66 \tag{3}$$

The sentence would pass the publication test if cumulative results for $R > 3.8$ and $Kor > 35.21$ or cumulative results for $R > 3.8$ and $KV(g) > 22$.

The choice is based on the evidence registered in the research. Relevance as one of the underlying variables must be above 0.5 of the range. Usefulness as the second fundamental variable is treated partially differently for the reason that we do not see the information we are processing here as a product that should stimulate the reader's action or articulated activity, but rather as media reporting with an unspecified goal in the context of the reader's activity. For media reporting, it is primary that the information is relevant to the highest degree possible, which means that it has a certain amount of correct and precise data and that the ratio of verifiable data in the total number of data it consists of is satisfactory. Usefulness is a category that is no less important in this relationship but has less impact on the publication test for the reasons stated above. Therefore, it was decided that any value above a third of the range makes the information publishable. Data quality as an empirical category that expresses the product of the sum of preciseness and correctness of data with the nominal number of verifiable data in the information is set in the alternative test variables, and its value must be higher than a third of the range for the information to be published.

The decision to introduce an alternative test model in which information, regardless of whether the usefulness is too low, if it has sufficient data quality, will be published, was made in order to develop the trend of openness of the system toward the public, and within the purpose of this research, to find the optimal measure of reporting on specific issues given by this framework in the context of public interest.

It is important to note that the publication test ranges of this preliminary model are determined within the data processed here. In the case of expanding the data set, each new result would potentially change the range and assessment of the information.

In the event that it turns out that standardized quantification is possible to some extent, it is assumed that a very large number of data that could be processed in an automated way would need to be included in that set. However, given the significant number of problems that exist in examining and evaluating information in this way, it is currently more appropriate to test the model on several small sets and analyze the possibilities of solving the underlying problems. Considering the fact that the analysis procedure, which begins with the extraction of data and continues with its characterization is more important than these simple hypotheses of calculations, which are only a reflection of the behavior of the categories in the evaluated information, even without presented preliminary result, expressed numerically, the average reader doing this process could be more acquainted with the value of the given information.

## 3. Theme framework

Considering the term "information" is often used to represent a variety of things, events, or expressions, it cannot be interpreted as things, events, or expressions themselves unless it is within a context and is understood meaningfully [7], so we put the research in a specific context to examine theory. Theme framework accordingly needs to be defined in order to create a scope for the research of fundamental theoretical terms in information sciences such as relevance, informativeness, and usefulness, and on the other hand, data and information.

The theme framework is related to the national security concept but in its specific nonmilitary aspects, like the inner structural weakness of the system, the vulnerability of the institution, and the vulnerability of the value system related to political stability and social cohesion.

Layeredness as a characteristic of the state's nature, and especially the specific structures and circumstances of a given state, makes it open to multiple threats. The idea of the state and its ideology are common targets of political threats. This especially comes to the fore when it comes to states where ideas and institutions are divided or opposed because such entities are highly vulnerable in the context of political penetration. However, internal division is an element that is not necessary but only contributes to vulnerability because even entities that are strong and influential can be objects of political threats. They can sometimes descend to a level where it is extremely difficult to distinguish whether it is an exchange of ideas and information or a threat to national security. Here we are talking about the issue of language, religion, and local cultural traditions that can also play a role in the creation of national identity, and in that sense, they can be objects of attack and necessary protection. Since political threats have become increasingly complex in terms of performance, they often do not occur directly and visibly but in such a way that external factors are involved in internal issues and discussions, taking sides that represent goals that are closer to the goal of a particular political intervention. In this sense, there are numerous variants of the process of influence and their goals, from which we can often single out the use of weak states to balance the forces, that is, to determine the patterns of the international order, at a given moment, by more influential or stronger political subjects. It is possible to conclude that the intertwining of types of threats and the scale of the vulnerability of a given society and state is difficult to definitively define unambiguously and in the long term, but it is possible and necessary to develop systems that would minimize the harmful consequences of various attacks, i.e., detect the sources and processes of threats as much as possible [8].

*DOI: http://dx.doi.org/10.5772/intechopen.1002541*

Following the aforementioned points, situations when hybrid threat activity, by applying combinations of tools, targets a state in the legal, diplomatic, information, and political domains are included. Each tool and its combination can target one or multiple domains, or the interface between them, by creating or exploiting a vulnerability or taking advantage of an opportunity [9].

Underlying idea of the theme framework is under the umbrella of finding a balance between democratic standards and registering hybrid threats in a timely manner, as the goal that is in this research considered as the goal of public interest.

## 4. Theoretical analysis

### 4.1 General definition of information

The general definition of information (GDI) is an operational standard that defines information as an item that:

1. is composed of one piece of data or more data that,
2. is well-composed, and
3. has meaning.

By well-composed data, we mean data that are composed in accordance with the syntax of a certain system, whereby syntax is seen as a term in a broader sense than linguistics, which includes the determination of form, construction, composition, and structure [10].

A primary characteristic of Floridi's semantic information, though not self-sufficient, is the meaning in a particular code, system, or language implying compliance with the chosen code, system, or language.

The fundamental nature of the data is where we see x different to y, where x and y are two uninterpreted variables, or in other words, the fundamental nature of data is exhibiting the anomaly.

The GDI endorses the thesis: a datum is a relational entity. It implies taxonomic neutrality due to the fact that nothing seems to be a *datum per se*, classifying it as a relation. Although we have the slogan "data are relata," the GDI is neutral with respect to the classification of data with specific relata.

The second implication of the GDI analyzed in this research is typological neutrality, meaning that information can consist of different data types as relata. Although the typology is not yet fixed and standard, it is quite common to have five classifications. Depending on the analysis conducted and the adopted level of abstraction, the same data can be understood as more than one type [11].

Considering the term "information" is often used to represent a variety of things, events, or expressions, it cannot be interpreted as things, events, or expressions themselves unless it is within a context and is understood meaningfully [7], so we put the research in a specific context to examine theory. Therefore, my research results are to be interpreted only as such. There is a strong possibility that the model would work in other conditions, but that would have to be proven in other contexts. Even this model will have to prove itself sustainable, and it is expected that it will grow and change as it is alive. This is also expected because we can anticipate changeable circumstances in which relations exist.

### 4.2 Data characteristics

To calculate the categories that characterize the information, it is necessary to evaluate the preciseness and correctness of the data that the information consists of.

The issue of assessing correctness and preciseness was solved during the empirical analysis by applying the initial settings for data correctness and preciseness. According to initial theoretical settings, incorrect data are considered those that are destroyed by errors or inconsistencies. In regards to data preciseness theoretically, precis is understood as a measure of the possibility of repeating the collected data.

When one of the implications of the GDI as an operational standard is taken into account, namely the taxonomic neutrality according to which the data are related, it was concluded that the correctness of the data is established when, at the sentence level, there is no contradiction between the data that the information consists of. The contradiction is examined at all levels – syntactic, semantic, and grammatical. In addition to the context, the data can also be examined in relation to external entities.

Due to analyzing data preciseness, the measure of data repeatability was also examined at all previously mentioned levels. It was concluded that precise data in this framework is data whose repetition brings meaningful value, and imprecise data is considered to be one whose repetition, although possible, neither in the first, nor in the second, nor in the tenth attempt does not bring meaningful value. As well as when testing correctness, data preciseness can also be tested in relation to external entities.

In the example:

"The fact that after some time SOKO ZI decided on its own initiative to pay penalties due to the delay of part of the delivery is also surprising."

Defined context of the media article as whole:

"the state was damaged by the payments under disputed contracts".

isolated data:

1. After some time, SOKO ZI decided on his own initiative

2. SOKO ZI paid the penalties after some time

3. The delivery was partially delayed

All data were assessed as correct because there is no contradiction between them at any examined level. All the data were assessed as precise because, in relation to the context, it is sufficiently precise that the decision was self-initiated, that the penalties were paid, and why they were paid. However, all the data could be characterized as imprecise in relation to external entities because in the first one, the duration of SOKO ZI deciding on its own initiative was not specified, so accordingly, it was not specified when it paid its penalties. The third data is also not precise because it does not bring content to the delay, i.e., it is not specified whether "partially" refers to the delivery time or the quantity or the quality of the delivery. It was concluded that, in accordance with the criterion of pragmatism, i.e., taking into account the constructive contribution in the practical aspect of the research, they are defined as precise in relation to the context. That is due to greater usefulness in knowing about activities and the reasons for these activities in a defined context than the harm that exists in connection with the inaccuracy of this data.

Defining criteria for the verification of data is very important. It is strongly advised not to keep a fixed number but to constantly update this list. Criteria naturally depend on the data we want to verify, so we started with kinds of self-evident criteria, such as the possibility of confirmation in transparent records, minutes, public reports, publicly verified documents, public registers, and transparent actions of the involved actors, such as direct tv interviews or any other similar direct source, five open sources that confirm information (today is not applicable due to substantial amount of web copying).

During the analysis, we observed a few more. In the examples below.

Data 5 Croatian citizens have started thinking about banks and the banking system that can hide many secrets – verifiable.

Data 6 Croatian citizens have started thinking that the president could lie and be connected to crime if he has an advisor who can lie and be connected to crime – verifiable.

Data 7 Croatian citizens began to think of other things as well – verifiable.

We see that the author used a very general syntagm, "Croatian citizens." We do not know their age, region in Croatia, education, or even the number of people, so we could apply very simple sociological research, take an undefined sample of Croatian citizens (as here), and try to include 1000 people so the research could be considered legitimate and verify/not verify this data. We can see that different data can be an inspiration for an indefinite number of criteria.

Specific environment characteristics of the data publishing also turned out to be crucial in defining the criteria for the verification. The examples shown here are from the time when the Croatian Act on the right of access to information [12] did not exist in the legal system. As Article 3 of the Act states, "The objective of this Act is to enable and ensure the exercise of the right of access to information and the reuse of information, as granted by the Constitution of the Republic of Croatia, to natural persons and legal entities, through openness and the publicity of the activity of public authority bodies." Therefore, from the moment the Act is valid in the country, we have many more verifiable data.

The criteria for data verification indirectly, through the category of truthlikeness, strongly influence the calculation of relevance, so they have to be considered carefully. However, it is expected to have changes in the research results, even changes in the model itself, due to environmental changes.

### 4.3 Relevance

Over time, relevance was explored in different directions, but it is possible to summarize it into four approaches to the nature of relevance. We found that the following emerged: systemic, communicative, situational, and psychological, and we can add to these a fifth or interactive framework based on a layered interaction model of information searching, where interactions include levels or layers. It is considered that there is not only one relevance but an interdependent system of relevances, which dynamically interact with each other within and between different layers or levels and adapt when necessary. A categorization of the manifestation of relevance was proposed, and it was cross-referenced with the system of relevance. It is considered that relevance has a set of general features that characterize its nature, which include:

a. relation

b. intention

c. context

d. inference by involving an assessment of a relation, often an advanced assessment of the success or degree of enhancement of a particular relation, such as an assessment of some information sought in relation to a context-directed intention

e. interaction meaning an inference is achieved as a dynamic, interactive process in which interpretations of other features can change depending on understanding [13].

Following this, in this research, we consider relevance between the author of the media article/its content and the reader as the element of efficiency strongly related to the characteristic of data, of which the particular information consists in the specific context. We find it is an unchangeable characteristic from the perspective of the time index. Counting on the fact that average preciseness and average correctness are not changeable, the only change we could expect in this is that of truthlikeness.

### 4.4 Truthlikeness as the best possible truthfulness

We had not included the concept of truth because we strongly believe that, because of its complexity, generally speaking, and especially in regard to this subject, it would limit the scope of the research and its usefulness. Therefore we are content with the term truthlikeness as the best possible concept one can work with.

As there might be a betweenness relationship among worlds [14] or even a fully-fledged distance metric, we can examine what is closer to the truth. The essence of the likeness approach is that the truthlikeness of a proposition is somehow dependent on the likeness between worlds. Graham discusses three main problems for any concrete proposal within the likeness approach:

a. an account of likeness between states of affairs – what does this consist of, and how can it be analyzed or defined?

b. the dependence of the truthlikeness of a proposition on the likeness of worlds in its range to the actual world: what is the correct function?

c. "translation variance" or "framework dependence" of judgments of likeness and of truthlikeness.

The truthfulness [10] that is a changing measure on this scale is actually the degree of realism of a particular claim or information, its proximity to the real state of affairs. The problem is determining the proximity to truth/reality/information. Considering what was mentioned earlier, it is concluded that the proximity to truth/reality/information could be expressed as truthlikeness that is the proportion of verifiable data from the total number of data.

$$ST = PP : UBP \tag{4}$$

PP – number of verifiable data.
UBP – total number of data.
and the relevance

$$R = (is + pr)xST \tag{5}$$

ST – truthlikeness.
is – correctness of data (total points for all data in the information).
pr – preciseness of data (total points for all data in the information).

### 4.5 Usefulness

In defining logical relevance, Cooper distinguished relevance and usefulness (utility). Relevance must deal with "what it is about," and it is finally defined by way of logical implication, while usefulness is a universal term that includes not only thematic connection but also quality, novelty, probability, and many other things. Building on this distinction, Cooper was the first to give an in-depth treatment of utilitarianism instead of relevance as a measure of search efficiency. He built his argument on the assumption that "the purpose of a search system is (or at least should be) to search for documents that are useful, not just relevant. Elaborating further: The success of a retrieval system must ultimately be judged on the basis of comparison of some kind involving costs and benefits" [15]. As in the pertinence point of view, in the pragmatic point of view, the approach was to divide the notion of relevance to differentiate and show that relevance is one thing and pertinence or utilitarianism another, although they are related.

Starting mainly from the distinctions established in Cooper's work, by examining the sentence as the information carrier, in these specific conditions we look at the usefulness of the information as something that is considered to be in the public interest as it is defined earlier. That means that even when calculation is not very high, the information could be in public interest and, therefore, useful for publication, especially when it comes to exposing corruption that is not easy to verify in the sense of data verifiability.

$$Kor = (KV(g) : IGP)x\ DxI \tag{6}$$

KV(g) – average quality of data

$$KV(g) = PP(is + pr) \tag{7}$$

is – correctness of data (total points for all data in the information).
pr – preciseness of data (total points for all data in the information).
D – time index (D - > 0 day-2 days = 10 points, 3–5 = 9, 6–8 = 8, 9–11 = 7, 12–14 = 6, 15–17 = 5, 18–20 = 4, 21–23 = 3, 24–26 = 2, 27–29 = 1, 30.. = 0) number of days from the zero event day, or connected (thematically related to the zero event) event day to the day of publishing the article.
IGP – total number of nouns, verbs, and adjectives in the information.
I – informativeness

$$I = 10 - X \tag{8}$$

$$X = 1 + (SP/PRP) \tag{9}$$

SP – secondary data.

PRP- primary data.

Here, a few things could and should be discussed. Why is it that calculating relevance includes truthlikeness, which stands for the proportion of verifiable data from the total number of data, and while calculating usefulness, we use an exact, nominal number of verifiable data? The decision was made due to a discussion on relevance and the possibility of partial relevance, which can be viewed as a range of nuances. By including the principle of relativity in the assessment of relevance [16], it is possible to find a measure that is not determinable in two extremes – yes or no – but also as a sequential value. In this framework, relevance is measured, having as a possible outcome a range within which the calculated values are observed in relation to the highest and lowest values obtained in the analysis. The situational approach of the Syracuse School, which considers the situation, social context, multidimensionality, time dependence, and dynamics as the key elements and properties that characterize the nature of relevance and the processes by which relevance relations are established, also influences our choices. Relevance is "a dynamic concept that depends on the user's judgments on the quality of the relationship between information and information needs at a certain moment" [18]. By this analogy, the user's judgments in this research correlate with the defined theme framework as explained earlier. Finally, we concluded that it is important to include the relationship between verifiable data and unverifiable data because it shows the situation in that the information was published in, and in a way, it shows intention, relation, and connection to that social context as well. The time dependence the group is working with while exploring situational relevance was connected to usefulness, and the usefulness is actually situational relevance for some authors.

Clearly, our choice is to divide usefulness and relevance based on previous discussions, using more content of discussed terms rather than the terms themselves trying to make them vivid in the given research framework.

Several things could and should be discussed here.

Why does the calculation of relevance include truthfulness, which indicates the proportion of verifiable data in the total number of data, and the calculation of usefulness dependent on average data quality includes the exact, nominal number of verifiable data? The answer depends on two things. One of them is stated when distinguishing the structure of the average data quality and relevance in the context of decomposition using different coefficients in the formula proposals. Another reason is in the discussion of relevance and the possibility of partial relevance, which can be seen as a series of nuances [16].

Greisdorf also states that relevance is defined very differently, so he singles out Goffman [17], who defines relevance as a measure of information delivered by a document in relation to a query and determines that the connection the document has with the query is not sufficient to determine relevance. Furthermore, since relevance can be defined as a measure of information, it must depend on what is already known, which is a fact that must be recognized in any assessment of the relevance of the document in relation to the query. He concludes that for the assessment of relevance, the connection of the document with the query is not sufficient, but the measure of relevance is also evaluated in relation to the set of documents that contains the document whose relevance is assessed. Therefore, if we include the moment of relativity in the assessment of relevance, there is a possibility to obtain results of measuring in a graduated sense and not in two extremes – yes or no. Consequently, there is a way to find a gradation of relevance. There are many authors who analyze the concept of graded relevance, but also a few who strongly advocate the position that relevance exists or not, and that what supporters of graded relevance call degrees should be categorized in a different way.

The situational approach of the Syracuse School, which considers situation, social context, multidimensionality, temporal dependence, and dynamics as key elements and properties that characterize the nature of relevance and the processes by which relevance relations are established, also influenced the said choice. Relevance is "a dynamic concept that depends on the user's judgment of the quality of the relationship between information and information needs at a given moment" [18]. Analogously, user judgments in this research correlate with the determinants defined by the topic framework. During the research, it was concluded that it is important to include the relationship between verifiable and unverifiable data as an indicator of the situation in which the information was published and indirectly as an indicator of intention, relationship, and connection with the social context. On the other hand, usefulness as an indicator of the characteristic "being in the public interest" increases with the largest number of verifiable data, regardless of the total number of data.

A significant difference can also be observed in the dependence on the time of publication on which the calculation of usefulness depends, while information, once marked as relevant, if the circumstances that affect the assessment of data verifiability do not change, is a time-resistant, that is, unchanging category in the context of the time index. Consequently, in this research, relevance is considered a category that is strongly related to the features of the data that a particular piece of information consists of in a specific context. It is not viewed as a measure of concordance with the thematic framework but as a measure of the amount of information found in relation to the given thematic framework of the research in which, as previously stated, media articles are selected in relation to activities, persons, and events, that is, as a "measure of the effectiveness of contact between source and destination in the communication process" [13].

### 4.6 Average quality of data

To calculate the average quality of data, first we must identify the type of data. As we mentioned earlier, the second implication of the GDI that interests us is typological neutrality. It means that information [11] can consist of different types of data as relata, and although the typology is not yet fixed and standard, it is quite common to have five classifications. Depending on the analysis conducted and the adopted level of abstraction, the same data can be understood as more than one type.

1. primary data – basic data stored in a database

2. secondary data – they are the opposite of primary data and represent their absence (anti-data) – silence can be very informative

3. metadata – indicators of the nature of some other data, usually primary data

4. operational data – data on the operation of a data system as a whole

5. derived data – data that can be derived from some other data and then we consider these other data as an indirect source

Classifying data, that is, determining the type of data, is done in accordance with the classification in connection with the second implication of GDI, that is, typological neutrality, which means that information can consist of different types of data that are relationships. Data within the framework of typological neutrality are classified in relation to the context of an operating system. The context of the sentence is determined by the content analysis of the article in which it is found, and in this sense it is the operating system in which it functions.

Following the aforementioned parallel, the primary data that is originally the basic data stored in the database in this frame is the data as a set of words that are the core of the context. Secondary data are the opposite of primary data and represent their absence (anti-data), which in this framework means that the data tends to be primary, but the given set of words nevertheless does not provide information, that is, the set of words is an anomaly in relation to the previous state and tends to be the core of the context, but does not provide recognizable content. Derived data is data that can be derived from some other data, and then this other data is considered an indirect source. In this framework, derived data are those that are not an integral part of the context. During the analysis, a problem arose with the adjustment of the term derived data, given that the type of data is determined in relation to the context. However, the solutions during the analysis showed that they were extracted from the information and classified in relation to the context. It was done in that way because it is only in relation to the context that it is possible to determine that they are not part of it. The fact that they exist in information makes them an integral part of the system in a specific way. Accordingly, they, as such, derive from some other source but have a specific function in the system. One of the results showed that they are in the function of supporting the context but that they can also have the opposite effect.

In the sentence example.

"Radoš assumes that the money that Croatia sent to Mostar during the war in 1993 and 1994 was nothing less, in fact, it could only have been greater because war costs money."

the context is determined:

proving the international character of the conflict in BiH through Croatia's involvement in that conflict.

and the data are isolated:

1. Radoš assumes

2. 1993 and 1994 were war years

3. Radoš assumes that the money that Croatia sent to Mostar during the war in 1993 and 1994 was no less (information in the previous sentence)

4. the money could only be bigger (information in the previous sentence)

5. Radoš assumes that war costs money

and classify

1. derived – the conclusion that Radoš assumes is derived from another source

2. primary – temporally determines the conflict in question, the international character of which is proven

As already mentioned above, given that data classifying is still not standardized, sometimes some data can be classified as multiple types. Given that this data could be metadata if the core of the context was strictly interpreted. The conclusion regarding the specific classification was made as a consequence of the interpretation of the core of the context in terms of temporal and spatial determinants without which the context would be seriously damaged, i.e., as a consequence of the interpretation that proving the international character of the conflict would be incomplete if there were no data on the years of the conflict.

3. secondary – the data tends to be primary, but the verb "assume" introduces weakness into the set of words, that is, into the data;

   The fact that we learn that the amount "was no less" than other specific amount makes that amount determinable, but at the same time, introduces weakness in the information that tends to be primary. A possible objection to this classification could be due to the fact that the determination of the amount does not necessarily have to be part of the core that proves or does not prove the international character of the conflict through Croatia's involvement in that conflict, but could be characterized by supporting context. However, the fact that derived data is considered to support the context does not lead to the fact that every set of words whose composition and consequently content can mean supporting the context should be considered derived data. The essential determinant of the derived data is that the data is from another source, and here it is unlikely that data 3 and 4 have a different source than data 2.

4. secondary-"only bigger" has the same status as "was no less"

5. derived – if you look at the set of words "war costs" within the sentence to which it belongs, it can be concluded that it is generalized view that any war costs money, so in that sense it is derived from another source. It is not clear from the sentence whether this is Radoš's data, and further to data 3 and 4, when classification could be done in such a way that this data is classified as secondary. Another possibility is that it is a comment by the author. In the case that it was Radoš's data, the classification would go in the direction of secondary data because the set of words, apart from representing an anomaly in the fundamental sense, does not bring specific content in this context, so it cannot be primary data in a sense – The war in Bosnia and Herzegovina costs X. Decision on type was eventually done for all the above reasons, especially because of the greater probability that is the general attitude of Radoš or the author, which has its source somewhere outside the core of the context. The functionality of this derived data in terms of context support is questionable.

Following the parallel between the operating system and the context, metadata as indicators of the nature of some other data, usually primary data, require the least adjustments because the definition is directly applied to the scope of this research.

Operational data, which are originally data about the operation of the data system as a whole, in this framework are data that speak about the consequences of the context content, the implementation of the context content and its internal functioning.

In the example sentence.

"The fact is that the contracts for the procurement of various spare parts for Hrvatsko ratno zrakoplovstvo (HRZ) (Croatian Air Force), and the affairs behind them, have led to the fact that today only one combat aircraft and one transport helicopter are flying."

the context is determined:

the state was damaged by the payments under disputed contracts.

**data are isolated:**

1. contracts were concluded on the procurement of various spare parts for HRZ

2. are having affairs

3. contracts produced consequences

4. affairs produced consequences

5. consequence is that only one fighter plane flies

6. consequence is that only one transport helicopter flies

1 – primary data.

2,3,4 – metadata – data about the nature of the primary data, which is such that affairs are dragged on, that consequences are produced.

For data 4, the classification is questionable. In the case of narrow interpretation of metadata, and if data 2 is correctly typed as metadata, data 4 would be metadata of metadata. The conclusion is that data 4 is typified as metadata because in the very definition of metadata, it is indicated that metadata is an indicator of the nature of other data, and that it is most often primary data. Therefore, such a definition also allows metadata as the type of data metadata could be an indicator of their nature. In this framework, given that the data is isolated and classified in relation to the context, that metadata 2 is an indicator of the nature of data 1 and that, in terms of content, the affairs are directly tied to the conclusion of the contract, metadata 4 is metadata of metadata 2, and in compared to primary data, it is metadata in the second degree.

5 and 6 – operational data – brings content to the consequences or causes of the content of the context and shows the internal functioning of the context.

After classifying all data in the information, we give points to every data for correctness and preciseness and then add up all the points for correctness and all the points for preciseness so we get the overall result for is and pr. We multiply that sum with the number of verifiable data (PP).

$$KV(g) = PP(is + pr) \tag{10}$$

is – correctness of data (total points for all data in the information).

pr – preciseness of data (total points for all data in information).

### 4.7 Informativeness

The type of data is important for calculating informativeness. Although terminology [11] is not yet standard and fixed, typological neutrality as another implication of the general definition of the information consequently gives us five types of data classification. They are not to be understood exclusively or rigidly because, depending on the sort of analysis and the level of abstraction adopted, the same data may fit different classifications.

$$I = 10 - X \quad (11)$$

$$X = 1 + (SP/PRP) \quad (12)$$

SP – secondary data.

PRP – primary data.

Taking 10 as the maximum for informativeness as regards the interpretations following the perspective stating that the more the probability of the message decreases, the more its informativeness increases, but when the endpoint is reached, the statement implodes – Bar-Hillel – Carnap paradox (BCP) – this is too informative to be true [10]. Despite the fact we did not include in this research the truth concept but the concept of truthlikeness as the instrument we can work with, we cannot deny that the truth is one of the essential goals of the relevant information. Accordingly, we expect that 1 (or in our case 10) is too informative to be true, so we calculate everything under 10 using x as the changeable element while defining change as the changeable proportion of the secondary data in the number of primary data in the particular information.

By using the number of primary data as the basic data stored in a database and the number of secondary data as the opposite of primary data that represents their absence (anti–data), we tend to confirm secondary data also as a carrier of informativeness. In this research, as Beard [19] writes, "(it) might be said that a system is any entity, conceptual, or physical, which consists of interdependent parts and that a systemic approach consists in trying to look upon things as a whole. We need to be able to appreciate the importance of both 'detail complexity' and 'dynamic complexity' at the same time." We were obliged to translate the definitions of particular types of data. At the beginning of the research, we defined types of data with regard to the event (zero events or any following event). Going further, it showed that the more logical choice would be to define them in relation to the context. Sometimes, we noticed overlaps by getting the same or similar results. Nevertheless, the conclusion is that the right analogy would be system-context and not system-event. If we look at the sentence in context and if it is written after the event, known or unknown, it happened in the system, that is, syntax or context. The share of secondary data in the number of primary data should show a relationship between data omissions and data presentations.

A problem we could and should discuss here is how data is actually defined, but for now, we are satisfied with the fact that it was done consistently throughout the whole research. Also, as mentioned before, there are general uncertainties about this neutrality, so we can consider this procedure as one of the ways to test it.

Furthermore, informativeness was shown as a characteristic that does not have much impact on deciding whether a sentence should be published or not. As theories already show, it is an interesting concept for research and can be the source of deeper insight, generally speaking, but we did not attach any major importance to it in the practical aspect of this framework.

## 5. Example

Within the theme framework, a media article is chosen. One example of matrix analysis (third research phase) will be presented in this paper.

It is important to emphasize that this research has been done in Croatian, so slightly different results are expected regarding the parts inherent to the specific language. It is doubtful, nevertheless, that the coefficient of the variations would be significant. Example presented here have been done in Croatian and here we see only translations of them and not the adaptation to possibly different rules for the analysis in English.

Nacional 518/2005.

"Two investigations against Nobilo"

1. From the article, one to two sentences will be picked based on the narrative analysis as one or two of them are representative of the article as a whole. Sentences in this research are considered as information. The context of the sentence will be defined simultaneously.

   "The 'Dubrovačka banka' affair heralded the beginning of the end of Tudjman's ten-year rule, but in a way, it was an indication for revealing the affair that followed: 'Banks and the banking system can hide many secrets', 'If the adviser to the president can lie and be related to crime, why could not it be the president himself?' These are just some of the things that Croatian citizens have started to think about."

   Context: The Dubrovačka banka affair overthrew the all-powerful HDZ

2. The next step is defining the zero event as the event that is the motive of the published article. If we talk about serial reporting, it is necessary to register connected events which happen after the zero event and which are the motive for the published article.

   0event: 26.02.1997. A stored secret partnership agreement by which partners were to become majority owners of Dubrovačka Banka without investing a single kuna in shares

3. Using structural analysis, syntax analysis, and grammatical analysis, we extract data from the information

   Data 1 The Dubrovačka banka scandal signaled the beginning of the end of Tudjman's ten-year rule.

   Data 2 The scandal was, in a way, a starting point for revealing the scandals that followed.

   Data 3 Banks and the banking system can hide many secrets.

   Data 4 If the president's adviser can lie and be involved in crime, there are suspicions that the president could be doing the same.

   Data 5 Croatian citizens have started thinking about banks and a banking system that can hide many secrets.

   Data 6 Croatian citizens have started thinking that the president could lie and be connected to crime if he has an adviser who can lie and be connected to crime.

   Data 7 Croatian citizens began to think of other things as well

4. Counting the total number of verbs, nouns, and adjectives in the information

   IGP = 34

5. Checking the verifiability of data

   Nowadays the right to access information does exist, which makes more data verifiable. The chosen article is from the beginning of the 2000s when other criteria were applicable and we had to adhere to that. Here we found two unverifiable and five verifiable data.

   Data 1 The Dubrovačka banka scandal signaled the beginning of the end of Tudjman's ten-year rule – unverifiable.

   Data 2 The scandal was, in a way, a starting point for revealing the scandals that followed – unverifiable.

   Data 3 Banks and the banking system can hide many secrets – verifiable.

   Data 4 If the president's adviser can lie and be involved in crime, there are suspicions that the president could do the same – verifiable.

   Data 5 Croatian citizens have started thinking about banks and a banking system that can hide many secrets – verifiable.

   Data 6 Croatian citizens have started thinking that the president could lie and be connected to crime if he has an adviser who can lie and be connected to crime – verifiable.

   Data 7 Croatian citizens began to think of other things as well – verifiable

6. Classifying data

   Data 1 The Dubrovačka banka scandal signaled the beginning of the end of Tudjman's ten-year rule – primary.

   Data 2 The scandal was in a way a starting point for revealing the scandals that followed – secondary.

   Data 3 Banks and the banking system can hide many secrets – derivative.

   Data 4 If the president's adviser can lie and be involved in crime, there are suspicions that the president could be doing the sane – metadata.

   Data 5 Croatian citizens have started thinking about banks and a banking system that can hide many secrets – operational.

   Data 6 Croatian citizens have started thinking that the president could lie and be connected to crime if he has an adviser who can lie and be connected to crime – operational.

   Data 7 Croatian citizens began to think of other things as well – operational

7. Quality of data

   Data 1 The Dubrovačka banka scandal signaled the beginning of the end of Tudjman's 10-year rule – is.

Data 2 The scandal was in a way a starting point for revealing the scandals that followed – is.

Data 3 Banks and the banking system can hide many secrets – is.

Data 4 If the president's adviser can lie and be involved in crime, there are suspicions that the president could be doing the same – is, pr.

Data 5 Croatian citizens have started thinking about banks and a banking system that can hide many secrets – is.

Data 6 Croatian citizens have started thinking that the president could lie and be connected to crime if he has an adviser who can lie and be connected to crime – is, pr.

Data 7 Croatian citizens began to think of other things as well – is

8. Informativeness

$$I = 10 - x \tag{13}$$

$$x = 1 + 1 : 1 = 2 \tag{14}$$

$$I = 10 - 2 = 8 \tag{15}$$

## 6. Results

$$ST = 5 : 7 = 0,71 \tag{16}$$

$$R = (7 + 2) \times 0,71 = 6,39 \tag{17}$$

$$KV(g) = (7 + 2) \times 5 = 45 \tag{18}$$

$$Kor = (45 : 34) \times 0 \times 8 = 0 \tag{19}$$

## 7. Conclusion

The optimal structure of media reporting on sensitive issues related to national security would be the optimal amount of information to integrate the essential tension between two contradictory demands. Although these are preliminary formulas, this research showed that it is possible to think about a certain kind of quantifying information in order to decide on its value. We aimed to do it by using the tools from the information sciences mostly, but also by including basics from other disciplines, such as related philosophy, logics, and language. There are still open questions and a need to go further to the possible extent in order to resolve uncertainties.

Basic conclusions are formed as answers to research questions. 1) Semantic information theory, understood in a broader sense where the segmented parts of the theoretical framework were applied, is the appropriate framework in the described scope for the analysis of the research problem. After the selection of units for future analysis, segmented parts of the theoretical framework were applied. The aforementioned selection was done in accordance with the assessment of purposefulness, i.e., in accordance with the estimated anticipation of the result's usefulness in the context of the research goal. The value of this framework is most evident in its comprehensiveness, which opens up space for in-depth analysis of the information. The general definition of information is certainly not a precise definition that excludes a lot of items and reduces the definition of the term information to make it precise, but this is a consequence of the nature of the object of definition. It would be unnatural, unscientific, and unnecessary to define any term arbitrarily without one being able to defend it, not only theoretically but also empirically. In this sense, a large number of authors try to encompass the content in different ways described in the theoretical analysis. Each of the definitions considered here has left its mark on the results of analyses. Besides using the general definition of information in this framework, with some adaptation, information can be defined as a subset of data or a subset of data extended by an additional part deduced or calculated or refined from that subset. In the original definition, Fricke [20] defines information as a subset of relevant data together with the results of conclusions derived from that data, so it clearly follows that the subset can be enlarged by additional parts that have been derived or calculated from the subset. In this research, the category of relevance is linked to information, not data, but in its calculation relevance depends on the characteristics of the data it consists of. The definition is therefore adapted to this default, and thus does not lose its value and essence, contained in the word subset. That conclusion emphasizes the cohesive-reductionist property of information.

The compatibility of the theoretical framework and empirically established relationships are manifested in the empirical finding that a sentence does not have to be useful to be relevant. In other words, results were found for the sentence where the usefulness was calculated to be zero, and the relevance to some value above zero, but there is no opposite result. Usefulness directly depends on the time index, and in this sense, the value of information is variable. However, if the time index is greater than zero, its growth is more influenced by the average data quality. Relevance does not depend on the time index; therefore, it is a conditionally unchangeable value of information. A change in its calculation may occur due to an external agent that would have an effect on the verifiability of the data that the information consists of. Informativeness does not depend on the verifiability coefficient and has no significant effect on the test of publication of information. If there is no primary data in the information, its informativeness is not affected by the existence of secondary data. The level of informativeness is positively influenced by a larger number of primary data compared to the number of secondary data in the information.

Foundations for further research have been established, and depending on one's interest, investigations could go in different directions. Some of them have already been outlined in the text, and some are yet to be identified, but nevertheless, we have results we can work with in the future by confirming them, improving them, or even negating them.

## Abbreviations

| | |
|---|---|
| R | Relevance of the information |
| Kor | Usefulness of the information |
| KV(g) | Average quality of data |
| GDI | General definition of information |
| ST | Truthlikeness of the information |
| PP | Number of verifiable data in the information |

| | |
|---|---|
| UBP | Total number of data in the information |
| is | Correctness of data in the information |
| pr | Preciseness of data in the information |
| D | Time index |
| I | Informativeness of the information |
| SP | Secondary data |
| PRP | Primary data |

## Author details

Dora Gelo Čolić
University of Zagreb, Zagreb, Croatia

*Address all correspondence to: doragelo@gmail.com

## References

[1] McQuail D. Political communication research in the public interest. In: Coleman S, Moss G, Parry K, editors. Can the Media Serve Democracy? London: Palgrave Macmillan; 2015. pp. 76-86. DOI: 10.1057/9781137467928_7

[2] McQuail D. Mass Communication Theory. 6th ed. Los Angeles, London, New Delhi, Singapore, Washington D.C.: SAGE Publications Ltd., SAGE Publications Inc., SAGE Publications India Pvt Ltd., SAGE Publications Asio-Pacific Pte Ltd; 2005. 632 p

[3] Gill P, Mark P. Intelligence in Insecure World. Oxford: Polity Press; 2018. p. 288

[4] Gelo D. Media freedom and regulation in the context of reporting on national security issues. In: 7th International Conference the Future of Information Sciences INFuture 2019: Knowledge in the Digital Age Zagreb; 21-22 November 2019. Zagreb: Faculty of Humanities and Social Sciences, University of Zagreb, Department of Information and Communication Sciences, FF Open Press; pp. 183-189

[5] Omand D. Reflections in intelligence AnaInlysts and policymakers. International Journal of Inteligence and Counterinteligence. 2020;**33**:471-482. DOI: 10.1080/08850607.2020.1754679

[6] Jain AK, Mao J, Mohiuddin KM. Artificial neural networks: A tutorial. Computer. 1996;**29**:31-44. DOI: 10.1109/2.485891

[7] Ma L. Meanings of information. The assumptions and research consequences of three foundational LIS theories. Journal of the American Society for Information Science and Technology. 2012;**63**:716-723. DOI: doi.org/10.1002/asi.21711

[8] Buzan B. People, States, and Fear: The National Security Problem in International Relations. Brighton, Sussex: Wheatsheaf Books; 1983. p. 262

[9] Giannopoulos G, Smith H, Theocharidou M. The Landscape of Hybrid Threats, a Conceptual Model, EUR 30585 EN. Luxembourg: Publications Office of the European Union; 2021. DOI: 10.2760/44985

[10] Floridi L. The Philosophy of Information. Oxford: Oxford University Press; 2011. p. 405

[11] Floridi L. Philosophical conceptions of information. In: Sommaruga G, editor. Formal Theories of Information: From Shannon to Semantic Information Theory and General Concepts of Information (Lecture Notes in Computer Science 5363). 2009th ed. New York: Springer; 2009. pp. 13-53. DOI: 10.1007/978-3-642-00659-3_2

[12] Act on the right of access to information, Official Gazette of the Republic of Croatia no. 25/13 and 85/15

[13] Saračević T. Prilozi Utemeljenju Informacijske Znanosti (Contributions to Foundation of Information Science). Osijek: Filozofski fakultet; 2006. 266 p

[14] Oddie G. Truthlikeness. The Stanford Encyclopedia of Philosophy. In: Edward NZ, editor. 2016 Edition. Stanford: Metaphysics Research Lab Stanford University; 2016. Available from: https://plato.stanford.edu/archives/win2016/entries/truthlikeness/

[15] Saračević T. Relevance: A review of the literature and a framework for

thinking on the notion in information science. Part II: Nature and manifestations of relevance. Journal of the American Society for Information Science and Technology. 2007;**58**: 1915-1933. DOI: 10.1002/asi.20682

[16] Greisdorf H. Relevance, an interdisciplinary and information science. Informing Science. 2000;**3**:67-72

[17] Goffman W. On relevance as a measure. Information Storage & Retrieval. 1964;**2**:201-203

[18] Schamber L, Eisenberg MB, Nilan M. S: A re-examination of relevance: Toward a dynamic, situational definition. Information Processing and Management. 1990;**26**:755-776. DOI: 10.1016/0306-4573(90)90050-C

[19] Beard AN. Some ideas on a systematic approach. Civil Engineering and Environmental Systems. 1999;**16**: 197-209. DOI: 10.1080/0263025990 8970262

[20] Fricke M. The knowledge pyramid: A critique of the DIKW hierarchy. Journal of Information Science. 2009;**35**:131-142. DOI: 10.1177/ 0165551508094050

Chapter 7

# Enhancing BIM through Mixed Reality for Facility Management

*Massimo Vaccarini, Alessandro Carbonari, Francesco Spegni and Alberto Giretti*


## Abstract

Implementation of processes in facility management asks for coordination and collaboration among several factors, each implementing its own sub-process. This goal must cope with several challenges caused by the fragmentation of the AEC (architectural, engineering, construction) industry. In the specific case of facility recommissioning, further constraints are determined by limitations posed by the current status of the existing facility whose knowledge is often limited to coarse preliminary surveys. In this chapter, the benefits determined by the integration between BIM and mixed reality will be presented, along with a prototypical platform that realizes an efficient, distributed collaborative workflow enabling asynchronous collaboration among members of the facility management office, the owner, the design team and technical specialists that may be appointed in recommissioning workflows. Technically, this approach provides an immersive mixed-reality environment capable of seamlessly displaying project information, through which specialists can evaluate and refine different recommissioning options. In addition, the platform supports on-site enrichment of BIM models for a facilitated, yet asynchronous, collaboration between remote and on-site users. This technology was validated by means of real-life experiments regarding a hypothetical recommissioning project of the Construction Division of the DICEA Department at Università Politecnica delle Marche (Ancona, Italy).


**Keywords:** facility management, asset recommissioning, BIM, AR/MR, mixed reality, efficiency

## 1. Introduction

### 1.1 Facility management

Facility Management is inherently a management discipline that is articulated within the context of a very broad and disparate set of technical-operational domains. Consider in primis the areas of maintenance, energy efficiency and sustainability, safety and resilience, organization and usability of spaces. In addition to these purely technical areas, there is the economic-financial management of both current activities and new construction projects. Finally, at the top of this challenging pyramid is


IntechOpen

perhaps the most important organizational aspect, the management of the quality of the day-to-day service offered by facilities in relation to their intended use and their ability to adapt to the sudden changes in the operational processes that take place there. Today, the holistic and managerial view of Facility Management, therefore, accompanies every phase of the building life cycle and represents a key competence of construction management engineering [1]. Although many studies have highlighted the importance of consistency and interoperability in FM, the processes used in facilities still lack an adequate conceptual framework to support informed and data-driven decision-making. Like any management activity, Facility Management is data intensive. A correct, complete, and timely information flow is of fundamental importance for supporting decision-making processes, extending from medium-term strategic level decisions to the real-time management of events [2].

### 1.2 The BIM promise for the FM revolution

Building Information Modelling (BIM) can play a key role as an operational framework for coordinating FM operations. BIM has the potential to enable the facility manager to manage the complexity of processes through a structured, referenced, and easily accessible data flow [3]. The BIM data interchange structure is based on the official Industry Foundation Classes (IFC) standard. An IFC model can map a complete facility model, topography, and technical systems, including 3D representations, structural design, and all technical features. In its possible extensions, IFC allows, through the CoBie MVD [4], handovers management and the inclusion of management data, such as maintenance plans, technical specifications, operating instructions, warranty and service contract information, and costs. From an ICT perspective, the use of a BIM-based operational framework in a cloud platform has the potential to integrate and make enriched data (e.g., from energy simulations or predictive maintenance assessments) accessible to all stakeholders [5]. Finally, from the pure operational standpoint, the virtualization of the facility model allows the evolution of the operational workflow through the use of new mixed reality techniques [6].

### 1.3 Integrating BIM into FM workflows

The multifaced influence of the BIM technology in the Facility Management operational framework requires therefore a careful analysis to meet operational requirements. FM mainly concerns assets and processes operating on assets. BIM integration in FM cannot be limited to information mapping, e.g. [7] because this narrow scope fails to capture the real FM perspective. Assuming a systemic view of FM processes, the requirements analysis must identify the operational context, as the set of processes, assets and services oriented to support one or more well-defined core processes, and on this basis characterize the entire information profile, according to the four fundamental qualities of an information profile:

- What information is to be processed,
- How it is to be stored and retrieved,
- Where it is to be stored,
- When it must be stored and used.

In other words, to meet the operational requirements of FM processes, not only the information content must be defined but also the way it is stored and retrieved as well as the storage location. Consider, for example, the asset management process, in the context of sustainable Facility Management. In a circular economy perspective, a building component, e.g. a window or doorframe, has a life cycle that goes beyond the simple usage phase. It is in fact produced through processes that tend to minimize the use of resources, used in such a way as to guarantee the best performance in terms of energy, and recovered as far as possible in its materials or sub-components after its disposal from the FM cycle.

Therefore, the asset's information life cycle, while intersecting to a large extent with the life cycle the asset management information profile has a much more extended scope, involving both the production and the recovery phases, themselves complex processes with highly articulated information structures. This scenario is not purely conceptual. In fact, it has a definite impact on the technology that manages the information. The transition of information from one phase to another involves the transition between different management systems. At the practical level of the construction production system, given the quantity of materials and the diversity and spread of manufacturers, this transition is difficult to manage through communication between different information systems for the usual reasons of standardization of protocols and accessibility. More effectively realized is the embedding of information in the component itself through inexpensive RFID tags [8–10]. Ultimately, the integration of BIM-based technologies into FM processes requires the extension of the simple mapping of information into the IFC interchange structures and the inclusion of the entire process workflow, making explicit the specific operations that emerge from the adoption of a particular technology in the operational process, especially for on-site processes.

In the next Section 2, the scientific background concerning the integration between BIM and advanced visualization techniques will be reported, with a specific focus on mixed reality and applications to facility management. Section 3 suggests an efficient cooperative workflow enabling asynchronous interactions between remote and onsite users in the Facility Management context. This is the premise for the development of a prototypical web platform for *Asynchronous Collaborative Onsite Survey* (ACOS), which is the subject of Section 4, where its architecture, GUIs, alignment, and onsite apps will be reported. Experimental results and remarks about the management of a recommissioning project in a hypothetical real-life test case are then presented in Section 5. Finally, Section 6 ends this chapter with conclusions.

## 2. Scientific background about mixed reality

The basic technology requirement for Mixed Reality (MR) systems is that they provide a sensory, visually coherent set of stimuli. This is fundamentally different from other competing or complementary technologies [11]. The conventionally held view of a Virtual Reality (VR) environment is one in which the participant-observer is totally immersed in, and is able to interact with, a completely synthetic world. Augmented Reality (AR) is characterized by digital content superimposed on the users' real surroundings; Augmented Virtuality (AV) involves real content overlapped on the user's virtual environment.

In Mixed Reality, users are placed in the real world and digital content is totally integrated into their surroundings so that they can interact with both digital and real content, and these elements too can interact [12]. The basic elements of a mixed reality environment are interaction, lighting, objects, and the real environment [11]. They involve both hardware and software issues, such as the technical performances of head-mounted displays and scene reconstruction combining both real and virtual content.

Building Information Modelling is being increasingly used in the construction industry not only to produce n-Dimensions data-rich models but also to promote the use of on-site models. This application can enhance communication among all stakeholders. For this reason, BIM and visualization technologies, such as VR, are integrated to create an immersive environment to be used for assessment tasks. Examples range from site layout and planning to the evaluation of construction scenarios, inspection, and maintenance. Indeed, VR broadens the vision of potential end-users about what output to expect after the completion of the project [13]. The potentials of improved visualization enabled by BIM have been discussed from several points of view:

- interactive MR visualization can connect virtual models and digital planning information based on BIM with the physical building or production site for self-inspection and self-instruction; this means, respectively, that workers on-site can check their own working processes and results in collaboration with others, and that actors on-site can be provided interactive guidance to prevent incorrect actions, even helping workers to rectify errors immediately, if any [14].

- BIM can provide technical information as integration of management functions supported by computerized maintenance management systems (CMMS) that can facilitate data collection and data entry, as well as visualization when and where needed; more specifically, the technical office can update the inspector with information from the database or can monitor and advice him/her by sharing the inspector view; in addition, data collected by an inspector operating on-site, such as defects and their attribution, can be saved in the database and immediately shared with the technical office [15].

- data from different sources can be linked within a BIM environment, provided that a platform for big data management has been put in place; then, several layers devoted to data extraction, integration, analysis, and man-machine interoperability can facilitate several tasks in the facility management where operators are usually involved, such as interacting with asset data in a 3D environment [16].

As an additional application, advanced visualization provided by AR in a BIM environment has been used as a tool to enable untrained individuals (ranging from professionals down to unskilled personnel) to complete construction tasks [17]. These tests found out that the use of such a technology can be of great advantage for all the considered categories of workers, with some limitations to the simplest tasks for the under-trained individuals.

Overall, mixed reality setups can allow the generation of distributed collaborative construction processes, where personnel located on remote sites and equipped with smart see-through glasses cooperate in the construction of a virtual 3D model combining tangible and virtual objects. Such a collaboration environment is characterized by multiple client instances, each of them defining the environment which will run at a remote site. Those instances must communicate via a middleware allowing data flow concerning three main types of data: real objects incorporated by means of the user's scene visualization; virtual objects and information that are retrieved from the construction model and relocated to the remote site; the gesture recognition component that informs about physical interactions with virtual objects [18, 19]. Another specific application involves a BIM system, coupled with AR and integrated with a location-based management system, to provide context-specific information on construction projects, as well as evaluation of performance indicators on the progress and execution of construction activities. Such information is displayed within head-mounted displays put on by managers while they are walking through the construction site [20]. The main challenges addressed by the authors are the integration between BIM and the development environment, and the interface of position systems in the BIM environment.

The target of the solution showcased in the present contribution is to improve the efficiency of planning renovation actions in asset management. This might concern both repairs of built assets and replacement or changes of building sub-systems and components [21]. More specifically, the data exchange processes described in the next paragraph can be made more efficient thanks to enhanced collaboration between the technical office and on-site personnel. In order to successfully apply MR technologies in the field of FM, the full integration between reality and virtuality is required. The users' perception of the real environment can be improved by showing information that users cannot directly acquire otherwise. One essential requirement to use MR technology for on-site FM purposes is the alignment of the virtual BIM model so that it perfectly matches its physical counterpart [22]. Some applications (e.g. Trimble Connect [23, 24]) support model alignment functions. In the following of this chapter, four methodological and technical challenges will be tackled. The first one concerns the development of a workflow supporting recommissioning in facility management. The second one reports the technical development of a web platform facilitating collaboration in facility management, which is an extension of some technology developed within the H2020 EU project Encore (Id:820434) [27]. The third challenge presents the details of a technique to align virtual models over virtual facilities during on-site surveys. Finally, the use of the platform is showcased in the case of a hypothetical recommissioning project.

## 3. Workflow and information model

In order to fully exploit the potential of novel technologies, it is of paramount importance to have a clear understanding of how they impact existing workflows, understand what tasks are eased or even automatized, and who will benefit from such innovation. In the following, the workflow of Facility Management is described as a collaboration among several actors, each implementing its own process. Next, the activities that are supported by the presented approach are exploded and analyzed in detail.

### 3.1 Workflow for facility management

Recommissioning can be described as the interaction among three main actors: the *client*, the *facility management office*, and the *design team*. The former is responsible for expressing the project needs, allocating the budget for the project, and has the final word about which design should be accepted among the several alternative ones.

The facility management office receives the needs of the client and through careful analysis, the process isolates the set of requirements that the recommissioning must or should meet in order to satisfy the client's needs. Such requirements express both technical constraints or desiderata (e.g. as in the case of seismic or energy retrofits) as well as non-technical ones (e.g. as in the case of budget constraints or safety regulations).

The facility management office is in charge of managing the overall recommissioning project and coordinating several technical specialists on behalf of the client. Most of the time, indeed, the latter is not able by itself to identify how the many possible technical solutions may impact the ability to meet the desired needs. In the recommissioning workflow, a tight interaction between facility management office and one or more design teams is needed. For the sake of simplicity, and without loss of generality, in this work, it is assumed that there is only one design team responsible for producing the desired design options. Finding the best design, that is able to satisfy the client's needs, is an iterative process. One attempt is never enough, and thus usually a sequence of design options is produced by the design team and then assessed by the facility management office. The main purpose of this loop is only the design team and the facility management office and its purpose is to set a great amount of technical and non-technical details, ruling out solutions that do not fit in the client's budget or that do not meet the client's needs. Usually, after some attempts, the design team and the facility management office agree that a small set of the produced design options meet all the relevant requirements, and the facility management office decides that they are ready to be presented to the client which in turn is in charge of selecting the final design (**Figure 1**).

Even the process of selecting the final appointed design can be iterative, since the client can ask the facility management office and the design team to provide different solutions, thus causing a new round of generating new design options and assessing them. If the presented design options, on the other side, satisfies the client's expectations, the client itself is able to select one of them as the appointed design, thus passing

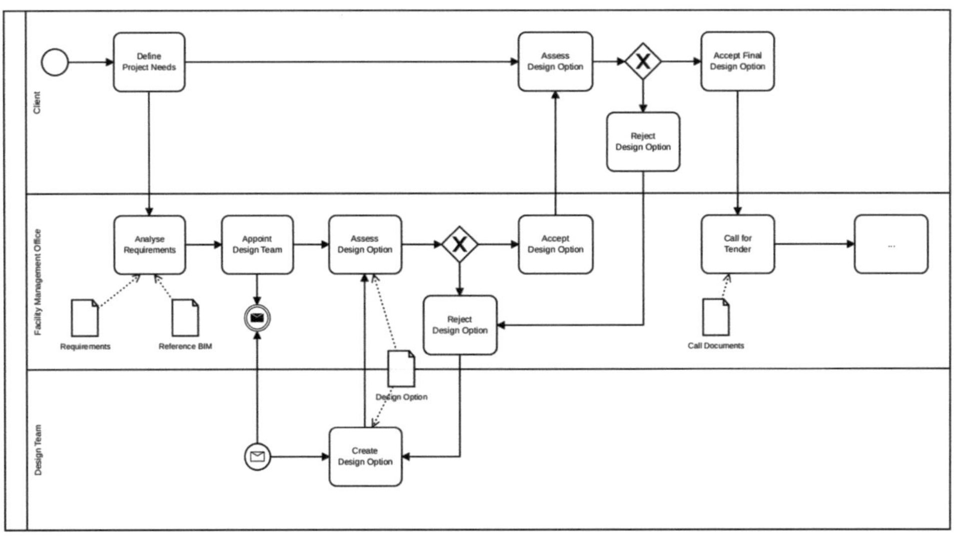


**Figure 1.**
*Recommissioning workflow.*

it over to the next steps (e.g. involving a call for tender, selecting the constructor company, executing the designed project, and so on).

The degree and quality of the interaction among the involved parties in the workflow strongly determine the realizability of the overall recommissioning project and the quality of the final renovated building or infrastructure: on one side, each new loop between the client, the facility management office, and the design team may introduce a delay in the project schedule; on the other side, a superficial assessment of the design options may speed up the project schedule in the first stages at the cost of overlooking significant design flaws that will be caught only at execution phase, causing increments of the project costs and even greater delays in the overall project schedule.

This motivated the definition of the aforementioned methodology called ACOS, assisting the parties during two critical steps of the overall recommissioning workflow, viz. the design assessment involving a tight interaction between the facility management office and the design team, and the final design selection, which involves a tight interaction between the client and the facility management.

### 3.2 Workflow about the usage of the information platform

The ACOS platform usage workflow depicted in **Figure 2** begins with the facility management office creating a recommissioning project in the platform itself, collecting the requirements elicited analyzing the project needs as expressed by the client. The recommissioning project is then shared with the design team, which in turn is required to produce and upload design options that should meet the given (technical as well as non-technical) requirements.

The design team usually works with a wide range of BIM authoring tools in order to produce design options. The ACOS platform is compatible with all the BIM authoring tools that can export the produced design options as IFC files. For every IFC file, a new design option can be created in the ACOS platform, within the given recommissioning project, and the IFC file is uploaded into the just produced design option. Once the IFC dataset is imported, the platform triggers an automatic conversion service extracting two different pieces of information from the IFC file: on one side, a 3D model representation is saved as a GLTF object, while on the other side a

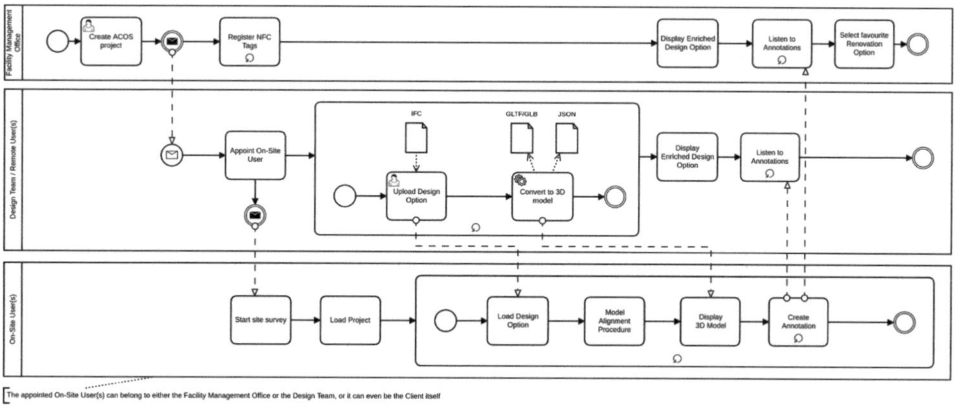


**Figure 2.**
*The ACOS platform usage workflow.*

JSON document represents the graph of objects contained in the IFC model (walls, windows, doors, furniture, ...) together with their properties and relevant IFC metadata (e.g. the GUID identifying each object). After this stage, the facility management office or any appointed technical specialist can go on-site, wear the MR headset and in turn exploit WiFi and Internet connectivity in order to select the design option that she wants to assess directly on site.

Once the onsite user assessing the project has some comments to do about one or several components, he/she can point at them exploiting the capability of the MR headset of interpreting the user gestures and start recording an audio comment as an MP3 file which is then uploaded onto the web server and linked to the pointed GUID of the assessed design option. The uploaded comment will be wrapped onto an annotation that in turn is linked to the specified GUID of the current design option. The assessment activity ends when the facility manager or technical specialist in charge has no more notes to leave.

Let us underline that while it is very likely that in medium or big organizations the client does not show up on the site of the building or infrastructure to be recommissioned, nothing prevents the clients from using the same technology in case they want to assess in first person the options that have been designed. In this case, the client can wear the same MR headset, add annotations and contribute to the BIM enrichment process that will link extra information to the objects present in each design option.

Remotely, both the remote users of the design team and the facility management office, as well as the client itself, are able to access the web interface of the platform, display the 3D representation of the enriched BIM, and listen to the recorded annotations. The enriched project information model obtained using the ACOS platform becomes a key enabling factor for increasing the quality of interaction among clients, facility management office, design team members, and appointed technical specialists. This in turn translates to a better recommissioning process and helps intercept design flaws during the early stages of the overall recommissioning project, reducing the cost of fixing them.

## 4. Technology implementation

### 4.1 Architecture

The ACOS methodology has been implemented on a platform whose architecture is depicted in the UML component diagram in **Figure 3**. One of the main purposes of the platform is to ease the collaboration between two types of users: Remote Users and On-Site Users. The former has at its disposal tools to be used on a desktop computer, while the latter can work on the field using wearable devices such as an MR headset and mobile devices such as a smartphone or a tablet. The synchronization among the tools is made possible using Internet and JSON web services implementing a RESTful API. The latter offers a unified view of the information in the system, allowing all the distributed tools to access the most updated information available.

The components in the server are deployed realizing a microservice-based architecture, where each offers a separate service and runs on a separate environment called *container*. This architectural pattern has several known advantages that pay back for the added complexity required in the configuration phase.

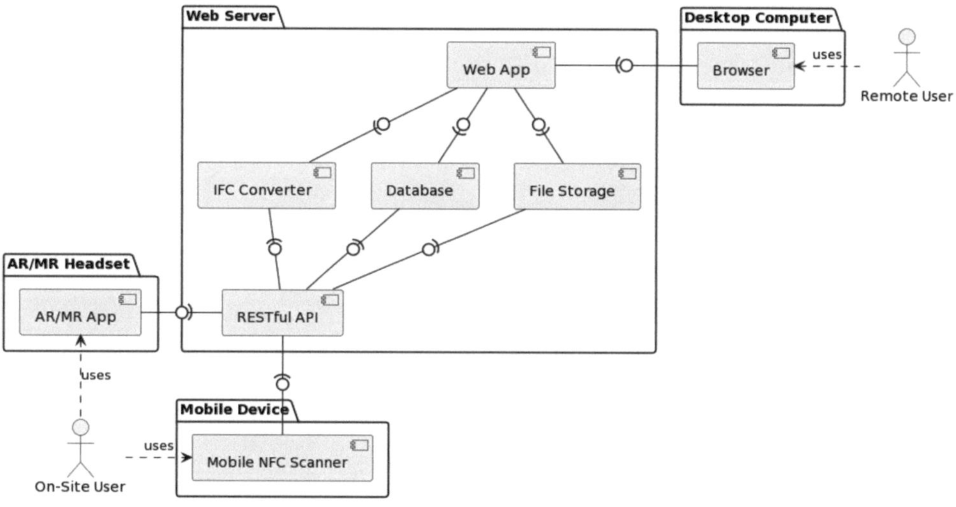


**Figure 3.**
*Architecture of the ACOS platform.*

First, running services on separate containers make each of them more secure and able to protect its own datasets from intruders or non-authorized users trying to steal sensitive information about the managed projects. Second, the architecture is more scalable and can rapidly migrate from deployment on a single server to deployment on a pool of servers where each component runs on a separate machine, globally achieving higher performance levels. Third, it eases the maintenance activities of the services themselves over a longer period of time, because each service can be replaced by any other better implementation of the same service, as long as the service interface is respected by the new implementation. Fourth, services running in containers generally ensure a higher availability to the service clients, because one of the main characteristics of containers is that they can be easily programmed to be restarted even when critical errors happen, thus limiting the disconnection time for each service and allowing to reach the so-called "five-nines" availability target, i.e. ensuring that a service is up and responding for 99.999% of the daytime.

All the aforementioned features are very desirable for cloud-based architectures that may transition from being a prototype in a test environment to being an actual business service in a production environment.

The platform organizes information in objects known as *entities* that are stored persistently on a database. Each entity has a type, called *entity type*, and entities are linked among themselves through *relations*. **Figure 4** is a UML Entity-Relationships diagram documenting the core entity types and relations used to implement the platform.

The core entity types are *Users*, *Projects*, *Design Options*, *Conversions*, *Annotations*, *NFC Tags*, and *NFC Readings*. An instance of User stores some basic metadata about the users allowed to access the platform, in order to implement standard authentication and authorization mechanisms (e.g. username, password, first and last names, contact information, ...). Projects store information concerning the overall facility management project (e.g. project name, owner, contact information, project begin and end dates, ...). Design Options are developed by the design team using their favorite authoring software tools, and can be updated in the form of IFC files on the platform. Conversions store the 3D object model in the form of a GLB/GLTF file together with a JSON representation of the product objects that are described in the

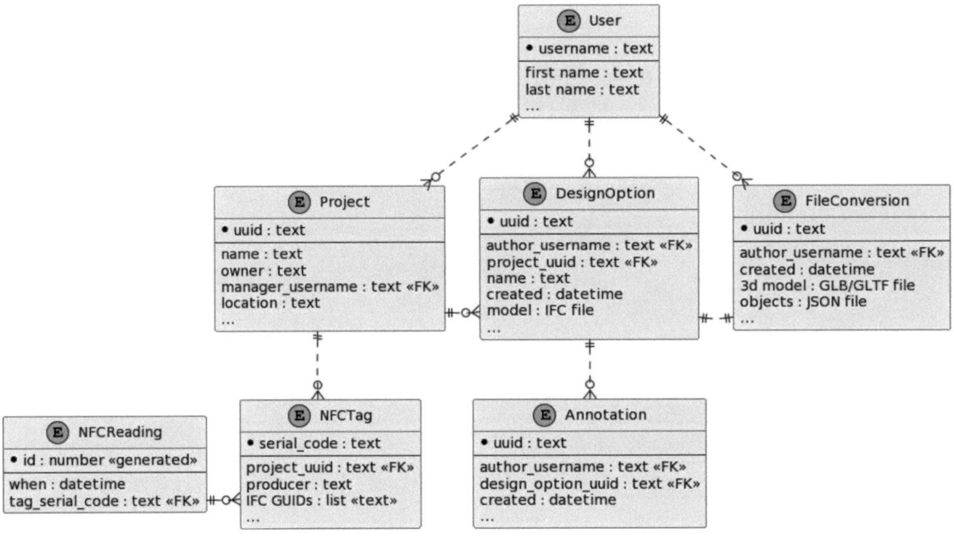


**Figure 4.**
*Entity-Relationship UML diagram of the data model implemented by the platform.*

original IFC file. Both the GLB/GLTF file, as well as the JSON file, are generated automatically using the IFC Converter component described in the architecture. Annotations wrap audio files recording the comments of On-Site Users expressing their opinions about specific objects of the IFC model they are assessing. The IFC object is referred to through its GUID, detected when the user points to a virtual object in the AR/MR Headset App. Finally, NFC Tags store information of each tag deployed on the facility that is used to complete the model alignment procedure, while the NFC Readings store the serial identifier of tags that are scanned using the Mobile NFC Scanner, as well as the timestamp of the scan operation. Later, in Section 4.3.1, it is explained in further detail why, for alignment purposes, it is more suitable to rely on NFC tags rather than other RFID technologies.

## 4.2 Desktop/remote tools

Through their desktops and browsers, Remote Users access the Web Application through a web GUI obtained by combining HTML and Javascript. The Web Application component is realized using the Python Django framework and is deployed on the server. The purpose of the Web Application component is to generate the web GUI that the Browser displays to the user.

The web GUI allows the Remote Users to access the Web Application entities (projects, design options, ...). Different users can have different privileges over the platform, and thus they can see or modify different entities, depending on the authorization they have been assigned to. For each entity type in the platform, the user has several operations available: list all the entities of the given type, search and filter the list of entities, create a new entity, change an existing entity, and delete an existing entity. In **Figure 5** the Remote Users can see the available entity types they can operate upon, while in **Figure 6** the same users can edit a single entity, in this case, an Annotation containing an audio comment uploaded from the On-Site User through the AR/MR Headset and linked to the IFC GUID the comment is referring to.

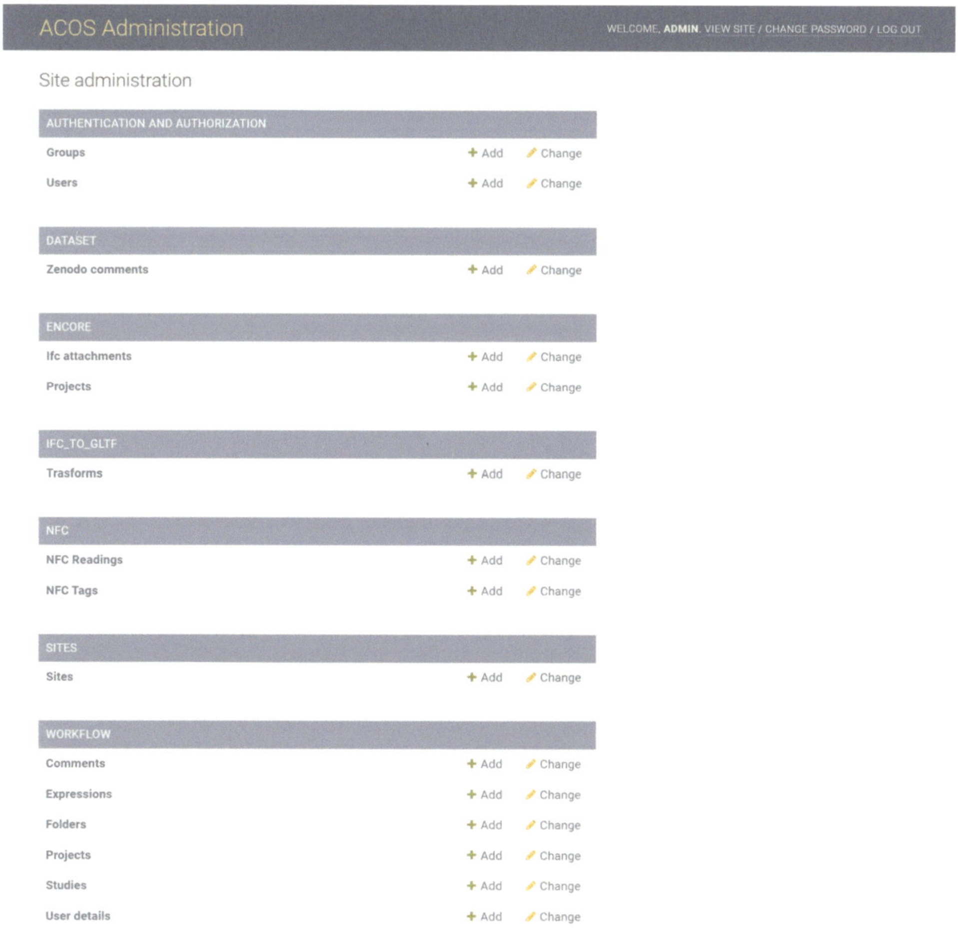


**Figure 5.**
*The web GUI shows the available entity types to the Remote User.*

## 4.3 On-site tools

### *4.3.1 The alignment tool*

For successfully applying mixed reality technologies on field, the full integration between reality and virtuality is required. In MR devices, this integration requires a set of enabling technologies [25, 26], namely: displays, calibration, tracking, registration, and interaction. Among these, the tracking and registration tasks are the most challenging and play a key role in Facility Management. Tracking task is strictly connected to the registration problem, which aims to achieve a precise real-time alignment between virtual and real elements. Especially indoors, due to the absence of an absolute tracking system, there is an unknown offset between the coordinate system of the virtual model and one of the 3D representations of the environment.

Feature recognition could be exploited for tracking and registration tasks when the visible features can be exactly matched with the virtual model, but this is not always the case, for instance during building construction. The currently adopted approaches

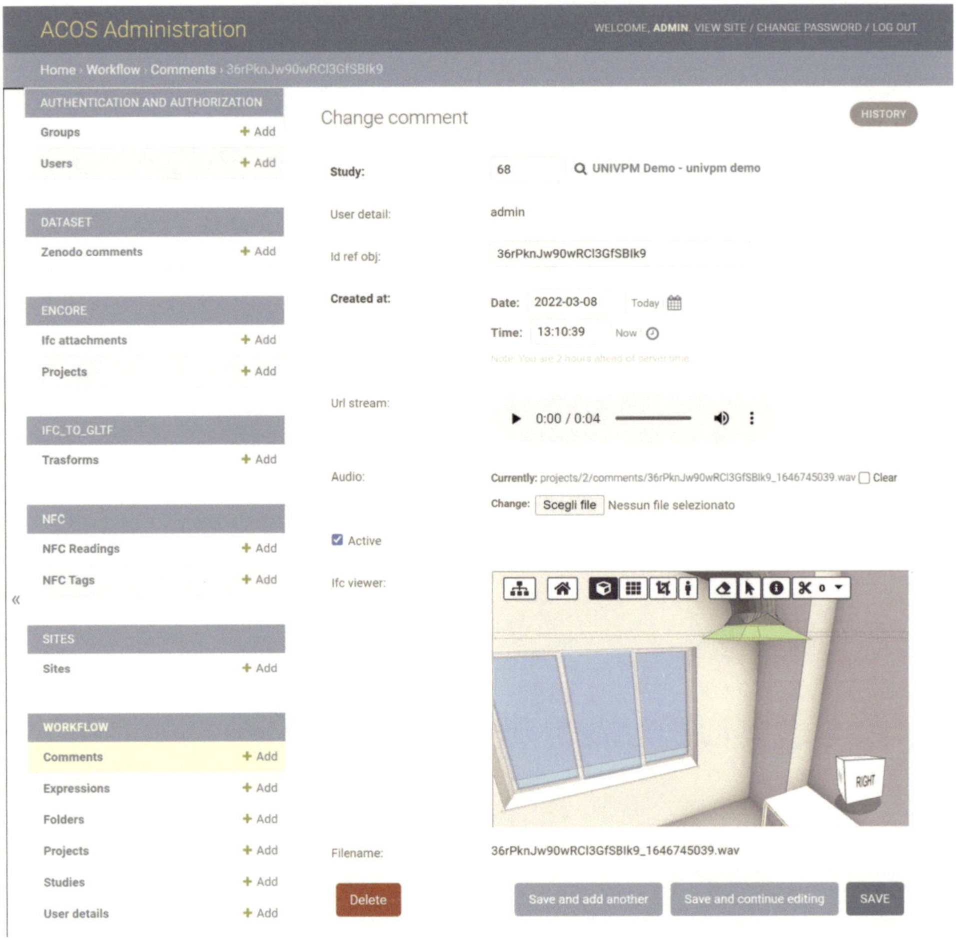


**Figure 6.**
*The web GUI allows to view and edit a single entity (in this example, of type Annotation).*

for addressing the registration issue by the commercially available devices, such as Trimble™ XR10 for Microsoft™ HoloLens, are the semi-manual alignment and the markers-based one. The first method consists in aligning any two surfaces in the model with the corresponding real ones. Then, a manual scaling and rotation of a cube for fine-tuning are required. This method produces a rough but acceptable alignment, provided that two conditions are fulfilled. First, the user must be aware of his/her position in the virtual space; secondly, he must be enabled to visually select any item, even those usually hidden by other holograms. Moreover, such an alignment method can be applied only with reference to virtual elements that have their physical and stable counterpart in the real world. Such requirements could be hard to meet in AEC scenarios that continuously evolve (e.g. during work progress) and may not offer stable references. The markers-based alignment method overcomes those issues by aligning the BIM model based on the user position, retrieved by scanning a real and visible marker, e.g. a QR code or a target image, having its virtual replica [23, 24]. Although the correctness of visual markers' positions must be verified before each scanning, this method ensures a pretty good model alignment.

In this chapter, the Microsoft™ HoloLens 2.0 device is adopted for addressing all the above MR requirements, except for the registration that is achieved by means of the tracking capability of the MR device, together with an offset elimination procedure (that we call model alignment) that must be implemented for each specific model. The developed approach uses RFID tags together with a handheld device (e.g. a smartphone) capable of reading them. We assume such tags have been previously and once for all embedded in the building (e.g. during the construction or during the first on-site survey). They can be also embedded in building components thus making them not visible and persistent through the whole building life-cycle. In addition, this approach overtakes the need for having the real counterpart of a virtual element, which is compulsory for the manual/semi-manual alignment methods. This improves and generalizes the alignment process both in terms of efficiency and quality of results.

Various RFID technologies can be exploited for model alignment, but MIFARE-type (ISO/IEC 14443A and ISO/IEC 14443) Near Field Communication (NFC) family tags have several advantages over others: they can be read only at short distances, thus allowing their location in space to be more accurate (within a few centimeters); they

**Figure 7.**
*First-person view of the expert while reading an NFC tag.*

do not require batteries since they are passive and powered by the reader; both the tag and the reader are very small and inexpensive compared to other technologies; furthermore, their packaging can be very strong and durable, thus allowing persistent incorporation within building components. The counterpart of the first advantage is the need to know almost exactly where they are located in order to read them, but this problem can be overcome by including them under small notable elements (e.g., near corners) or under nameplates usually attached to certain elements (e.g., doors, equipment, electrical panels, etc.).

Alignment of models with the physical world is made by means of a visual localization of the handheld device when reading a tag and calculating its relative position w.r.t. the model (**Figure** 7). The offset between its position in the model and its actual position is used for aligning models over the physical world. When the NFC scanner embedded in the mobile detects a NFC tag, it sends a request to the RESTful API to save a new NFC reading entity. The latter stores the tag serial code together with the timestamp of the reading event. If the communication with the RESTful API is successful, a target image is shown on the display of the mobile that is recognized by the MR application that precisely and rapidly localizes it in space by exploiting capabilities of an AR engine; in our application, we have embedded Vuforia™ engine for this purpose.

Since the detected distance from the observer is highly sensible to scale variations of the target image, only the observer direction is used for image detection and the actual distance is measured by exploiting the raytracing capability of the MR headset. The resulting position is then always snapped to the observed surface regardless of image scaling issues.

The alignment procedure based on NFC tags assumes that at least two NFC tags have been placed in known positions in the BIM model of the building with their GUID as identifier. The same tags must be registered in the web GUI under NFC tags in order to link the GUIDS with the serial codes of the corresponding tags.

For the sake of simplicity, but without loss of generality, the model is assumed horizontal since the inertial sensors of the MR headset are usually accurate enough to ensure this. Therefore, the remaining degrees of freedom to align the model with reality are just four: three for translation and one for rotation around the vertical axis. This implies that just two reference points are enough to perform alignment: the first point allows to translate the model and the second one is used for rotating it.

In the beginning, the loaded model is placed in position $P$ with respect to the right-handed reference system of the MR device. When the image target is visually detected for the first time, its position in space $i_1$ is returned by the MR headset and the handheld device sends the serial code of the NFC tag to the server for matching it with the model and retrieving its GUID and the position of the tag $t_1$ in the model. Since the two positions should overlap, the first alignment operation is a translation of the model by the detected offset $P' = P + (i_1 - t_1)$.

Then, the user looks at the second image target in position $i_2$ at which corresponds to the tag in position $t_2$ in the model. The distance vectors among a couple of image targets in reality $i_{21} \doteq i_2 - i_1$ and a couple of tags in the model $t_{21} \doteq t_2 - t_1$ are then used to determine the rotation that overlaps also the second tag. The horizontality assumption allows us to project them to the horizontal plane and to perform just a rotation around the vertical axis.

By denoting the projections of vectors $i_{21}$ and $t_{21}$ on the horizontal plane with $\bar{i}_{21}$ and $\bar{t}_{21}$, and by defining their unit vectors $\bar{i} \doteq \bar{i}_{21}/\|\bar{i}_{21}\|$ and $\bar{t} \doteq \bar{t}_{21}/\|\bar{t}_{21}\|$ respectively, the rotation matrix that rotates $\bar{i}$ onto $\bar{t}$ by a counter clockwise angle $\theta$ is given by

$R = \left[\begin{pmatrix} c & -s & 0 \\ s & c & 0 \\ 0 & 0 & 1 \end{pmatrix}\right]$, where $v \doteq \bar{i} \times \bar{t}$ is the cross product of the two unit vectors with module $s \doteq \|v\| = \sin\theta$, $c \doteq \bar{i} \cdot \bar{t} = \cos\theta$ is the dot product of the two unit vectors.

Since the two vectors are applied to a common point $i_1 = t_1$ generally not placed at the origin, this pivot point must be placed at the origin before rotation by applying translation $P'' = P' - t_1$, then the model must be rotated with rotation matrix $R$ (eventually regularized by the use of the corresponding quaternions), and at the end, it must be translated back to the original position by $P' = P'' + t_1$. Due to unavoidable uncertainties, the distance between the image targets will always be slightly different from that one between the tags in the model. Once the planes containing the tags and the one containing the image targets overlaps, the two remaining degrees of freedom are used to fine-tune the position of the model by moving it along this plane in order to minimize the distance among the two couples $P''' = P' + (i_2 - t_2)/2$.

In order to avoid unnecessary computational burden, for the implementation in the MR device, all the transformations are done on a not rendering dummy game object and, only at the end of the alignment, they are applied to the building model. In case more than two reference points are detected, the procedure can be repeated by considering the most significant couple of tags (e.g. the last two or the farthest). A regression approach can also be implemented for progressively refining the alignment when many tags are considered simultaneously.

#### *4.3.2 The MR app*

The MR application for Microsoft HoloLens has been developed under Unity3D 2019 environment with Microsoft Visual Studio 2019 and Mixed Reality Toolkit (MRTK) for Unity. The on-site app is a client for the ACOS server that hosts all the information used and produced by it. As reported in Section 4.2, at least one project and one design option must be loaded via the remote tools into the server and the corresponding "Conversion" entity must be generated.

The assessment task starts as soon as an expert gets on site and establishes Internet connectivity. Then, he/she wears the MR headset, logs in into the device and runs the app. At this time a virtual menu appears in front of the user that is enabled to switch across different alternative options by selecting the desired project (**Figure 8a**) and, within it, the desired design option (**Figure 8b**). After the selection of the design option, the MR app queries the RESTful API for the related "Conversion" entity (GLTF object and JSON document). Once the download has been completed, the "Assessment menu" pops up (**Figure 8c**) for managing the loaded model that is not displayed on the MR app, yet. This menu is made of several virtual buttons that allow the user to manage the model, align it via RFID tags, adjust it manually, or to hide/show specific IFC categories of objects. As shown in **Figure 8c**, by using the buttons in the last two columns of the menu, any components corresponding to pre-defined IFC types can be hidden/shown in order to keep visible only those parts of the renovation options that are useful to perform the assessment task and to hide objects that may obstruct the observer's view with respect to model parts to be assessed.

Moreover, every component of the virtual model can be selected by gazing it and performing an "air tap" gesture. The selected object is highlighted, and a new virtual menu is shown (the "Recording menu" of **Figure 8d**) that enables the user to record a

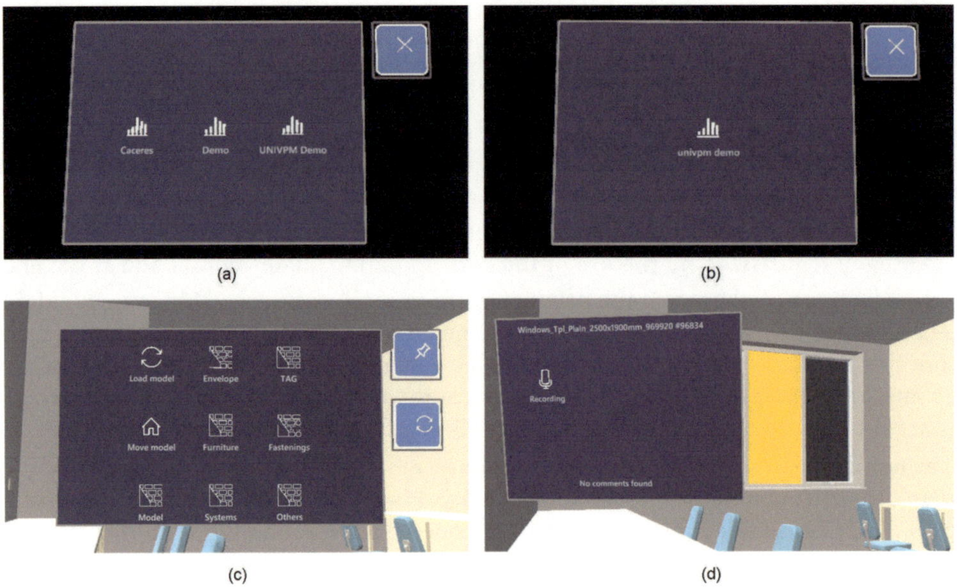


**Figure 8.**
*Main menu to select the project options (a) and design options (b); the virtual menu to navigate on-site (c) and to attach an audio comment to an IFC object (d).*

voice comment as an audio file. Once the recording phase is over, the file is sent to the ACOS server together with the GUID of the object at which it should be attached, and it is shown as an available file on the right side of the "Recording menu" (**Figure 8d**). As a result, the final assessment of a design option will be made of a set of Annotation entities attached to IFC elements of the available design options. Each such entity wraps an audio file that can be played back both on-site by technical specialists, using the MR application, as well as remotely and asynchronously by the facility manager, using the web GUI.

## 5. Experimental results

### 5.1 Case studies

This ACOS web platform can support various types of case studies that have been tested by the authors. Among them, it is worth mentioning:

1. productivity improvement in maintenance processes, thanks to on-site localization and visualization of components, retrieval and display of information relevant for repairing; previous tests regarding a scenario of potential failure of a communication plug in an office room showed that, once the virtual model of the communication system has been aligned over the real asset, an operator using the MR app and aiming at the switch-board, can query the model to single out which switch in the board is connected to the failed plug [27];

2. enabling the asynchronous cooperation between designers and specialists involved in the assessment of a set of alternative renovation projects of

residential buildings, which asks for the evaluation of some factors that can be assessed only through on-site surveys; in particular, a group of volunteers was committed to test how efficient an MR application is in the on-site display of renovation design options regarding a residential building located in Caceres (Extermadura, Spain); those renovation options were assessed and some constructability issues were found and fixed in order not to hamper the execution of renovation works [28];

3. this paper section reports real-life tests regarding a facility management scenario, carried out in the construction division laboratory of the DICEA Department at the Engineering Faculty of Università Politecnica delle Marche (Ancona, Italy); these tests highlighted the validity of the automatic alignment approach carried out by means of the alignment tool; in addition, appointed technical specialists were shown to be able to check and enrich models of recommissioning projects of the asset, and gradually enrich and refine such models by wondering throughout the asset and generating annotations.

More specifically, the last scenario mentioned in the above list concerns the recommissioning of two laboratory rooms of the Construction Division at the DICEA Department (**Figure 9a**). Such a recommissioning involves three categories of actions:

- installation of a new air supply system in both rooms and modifications of the ceiling;
- construction of a new partition that creates a new shared entrance room leading into the two laboratory rooms;
- installation of two doors as the new entrances into the laboratory rooms.

The changes listed above are also depicted in **Figure 9b**, where the addition of a new shared entrance with two doors and the new air supply system are visible in the model. Both models have been uploaded on the web platform as shown in **Figure 10a**.

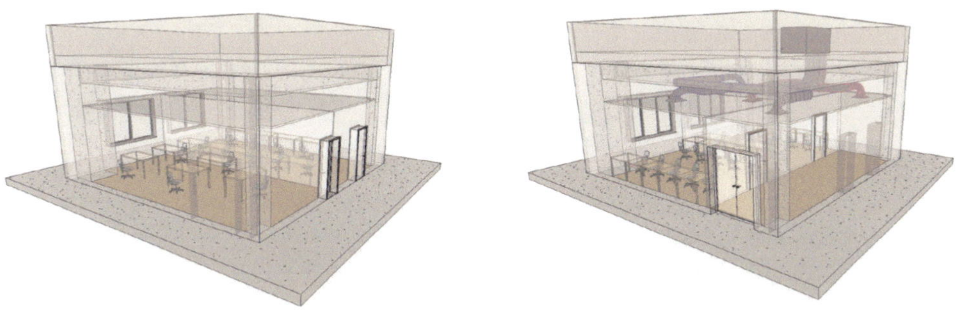

(a) (b)

**Figure 9.**
*Current layout of the two laboratory rooms (a) and renovation model (b), both developed in a BIM authoring software tool.*

Comparing the two sides of **Figure 9**, possible critical issues that might emerge after an on-site assessment may relate to conflicts between the new partition and secondary elements of existing electrical and communication systems (e.g., switches and plugs). Also, the installation of the new modular partition requires that connections with existing prefabricated modular wall panels have been put in place, that must be constrained at specific locations and that may intersect other non-compatible elements. In addition, unacceptable clashes between the new partition, the air supply system and other systems accommodated in the ceiling panels may be detected. From a functional point of view, the size and relative positions of doors must be assessed in relation to the actual use of the shared room. In this regard, an immersive view, as the ones shown in **Figures 10b** and **11a**, is required. In particular, the view in the second picture is able to show a clash between the virtual air inlet included in the recommissioning and the existing light appliance embedded in the ceiling. Finally, **Figure 11b** shows how the operator usually relates with the environment where he/she is immersed, thanks to the capability of selecting components and enriching them with annotations. In other words, this case study allowed developers to test the reliability of a step-by-step enrichment of the initial recommissioning model with specialists' opinions and other information helpful to refine it and converge towards a correct and approved version of the model.

(b)

(a)

**Figure 10.**
*Alternative design options uploaded on the web service for each project (a), and first-person view of the operator while wandering in the room and looking at the "Renovation Demo" design option for "UnivPM" project (b).*

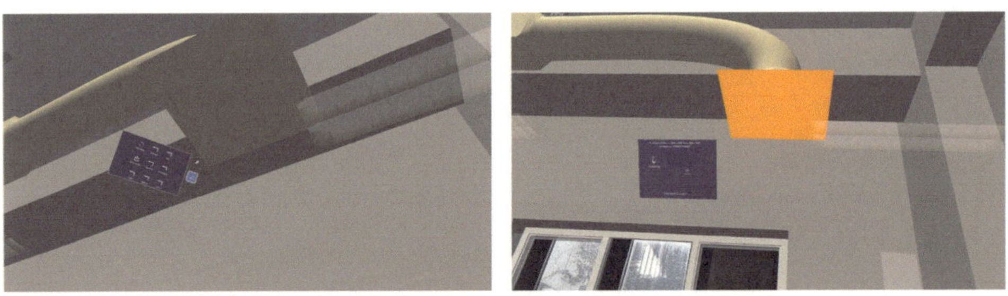

(a) (b)

**Figure 11.**
*First-person view of the on-site operator while checking a clash (a) and while recording an annotation with audio comments about the observed clash (b).*

### 5.2 Assessment of results

As described in the previous section, the case study concerns two laboratory rooms of the DICEA Department at the Engineering Faculty of Università Politecnica delle Marche (Ancona, Italy) (see **Figure 9a**). For some reason, the dean of the faculty (the client) presents to the facility manager office the need to renovate the two rooms by creating a new shared room before the entrances of the two rooms, by installing two new doors in the new partition and a new air supply system.

The FM office, using the Desktop/Remote tools (see Section 4.2), creates a new project and registers the two NFC tags already placed inside the building by means of the web GUI in **Figure 5**. After an appropriate selection procedure for the design team, it hands them the requirements and a reference BIM (**Figure 9a**). This model also includes the NFC tags embedded in building components; in this, a couple of tags have been embedded in each partition wall.

After some time, the design team produces a design option (**Figure 9b**) that is submitted to the facility manager for approval. The latter uploads this option into the previously created project (**Figure 5**), and this event triggers IFC conversion into 3D holograms. The facility manager tells a technical specialist to evaluate the corresponding solution directly on site and provides her/him with a summary of the evaluation task (e.g. drawings with annotations in PDF format) in which tag locations and major renovations are highlighted.

The technical specialist, as soon as possible, goes onsite with the MR headset and the smartphone, selects a project among the available ones and then loads the renovation option through virtual menus depicted in **Figure 8a** and **b**. With the support of the drawings, It looks for the first NFC tag by sliding the smartphone over the wall and, when this displays a target image, the MR app surrounds it with a transparent blue square (**Figure 7**) and the user makes a tap gesture on it in order to lock the tag and store its position. Then, the same procedure is repeated for the second one (see Section 4.3.1).

After the second tag is locked, the holograms of the design option are automatically displayed superimposed on reality and the technical specialist is in an immersive view (**Figure 10b**). Wandering inside the building, the user checks the location and appearance of the new partition wall and door inside each room. He also checks that the new furniture does not interfere with the door opening space and wall plugs, which are not modeled in the IFC file. Then, he hides the countertop holograms (by air tapping the corresponding button of the virtual menu in **Figure 8c**) to uncover and check the new ventilation system above it. He notices that a ventilation outlet partially overlaps an existing light fixture (**Figure 11a**) and decides to leave an annotation for the facility manager. By making an air-tapping gesture on the socket, this object is highlighted and the recording menu is displayed (**Figure 11b**); then the operator selects the microphone button and starts talking.

After some time, the technical specialist decides to close the assessment as no problems with the other elements are detected. The facility manager, notified by the specialist of the conclusion of the assessment, opens up the Desktop/Remote tool (**Figure 5**), selects the "Annotation" entities, and checks the results of the assessment. By exploiting the embedded viewer, the user can browse the construction elements with annotations and listen to the audio comments by using the multimedia controls and the model viewer in **Figure 6**. The facility manager then asks the design team to fix the problem and to provide a new solution that could be eventually object for new assessment.

When the design options are finalized, the client itself can ask for an on-site survey in order to better evaluate the proposed solutions and to better make the final decision.

It is noteworthy that, as is often the case, due to lack of information at the design stage, the problem was only discovered on site. In fact, many elements of the building, such as lighting fixtures, plugs, etc., are fully defined only as built and are subject to many changes during the building's life cycle. Since time and resources are always limited, it is not possible to capture all the details of the existing building during any preliminary surveys. This case study demonstrates that this situation is successfully solved by the ACOS platform, avoiding future constructability problems of the planned renovation and improving the final result in terms of execution time and quality.

## 6. Conclusions

One of the tasks of facility managers is the adaptation of facilities to the sudden changes they may undergo over their everyday operational process. This may trigger a recommissioning process that involves several parties, each implementing its own process, all steered by the facility management office. In order for this process to be successful, the ACOS platform implements mixed reality technology in a BIM environment to generate distributed collaborative construction processes and to ensure a timely information flow and enhanced collaboration among the parties. Technically, an information platform and an MR application supporting the most critical steps of the workflow were developed. The platform enables asynchronous collaboration between remote users (e.g. facility manager and owner) and on-site users (e.g. technical specialists). Thanks to the mixed reality app, appointed technical specialists can work in an immersive environment to enrich and refine BIM recommissioning projects directly on-site. Then, the outcomes of this task constitute the basis for the decision-making process charge of the manager and owner. Validation tests showed that the ACOS platform allows a better assessment process for the recommissioning workflow; it helps intercept design flaws at the early stages of the workflow and, as a consequence to that, it reduces efforts and costs involved in the recommissioning process.

### Funding

This work was partially supported by the EU H2020 ENCORE Project (Grant Agreement No. 820434).

### Thanks

The authors wish to thank the master's students Eng. Eleonora Monaldi and Eng. Filipe Mate, who contributed to the technical setup of validation tests.

## Author details

Massimo Vaccarini*, Alessandro Carbonari, Francesco Spegni and Alberto Giretti
Department of Civil and Building Engineering and Architecture (DICEA), Università Politecnica delle Marche, Ancona, Italy

*Address all correspondence to: m.vaccarini@univpm.it

## References


[1] Brunet M, Motamedi A, Guenette LM, Forgues D. Analysis of BIM use for asset management in three public organizations in Québec, Canada. In: Built Environment Project and Asset Management. 2019;**9**(1):153-167

[2] Patacas J, Dawood N, Kassem M. BIM for facilities management: A framework and a common data environment using open standards. Automation in Construction. 2020;**120**:103366

[3] Pishdad-Bozorgi P, Gao X, Eastman C, Self AP. Planning and developing facility management-enabled building information model (FM-enabled BIM). Automation in Construction. 2018;**87**:22-38

[4] 2013. Available from: http://docs.buildingsmartalliance.org/MVD_COBIE/

[5] Matarneh ST, Danso-Amoako M, Al-Bizri S, Gaterell M, Matarneh R. Building information modeling for facilities management: A literature review and future research directions. Journal of Building Engineering. 2019; **24**:100755

[6] Jurado D, Jurado JM, Ortega L, Feito FR. GEUINF: Real-time visualization of indoor facilities using mixed reality. Sensors. 2021;**21**:4

[7] Marmo R, Polverino F, Nicolella M, Tibaut A. Building performance and maintenance information model based on IFC schema. Automation in Construction. 2020;**118**:103275

[8] Jaselskis EJ, El-Misalami T. Implementing radio frequency identification in the construction process. Journal of Construction Engineering and Management. 2003; **129**(6):680-688

[9] Tzeng CT, Chiang Yc, Chiang Cm, Lai Cm. Combination of radio frequency identification (RFID) and field verification tests of interior decorating materials. Automation in Construction. 2008;**18**(1):16-23

[10] Naranje V, Swarnalatha R. Design of tracking system for prefabricated building components using RFID technology and CAD model. Procedia Manufacturing. 2019;**32**:928-935

[11] Collins J, Regenbrecht H, Langlotz T. Visual coherence in mixed reality: A systematic enquiry. Presence: Teleoperators and Virtual Environments. 2017;**26**(1):16-41

[12] Milgram P, Kishino F. A taxonomy of mixed reality visual displays. IEICE Transactions on Information and Systems. 1994;**77**(12):1321-1329

[13] Muhammad AA, Yitmen I, Alizadehsalehi S, Celik T. Adoption of Virtual Reality (VR) for site layout optimization of construction projects. Teknik Dergi. 2020;**31**(2):9833-9850

[14] Riexinger G, Kluth A, Olbrich M, Braun JD, Bauernhansl T. Mixed reality for on-site self-instruction and self-inspection with building information models. In: Procedia CIRP 51st CIRP Conference on Manufacturing Systems. 2018

[15] Ammari KE, Hammad A. Collaborative BIM-Based Markerless Mixed Reality Framework for Facilities Maintenance. Computing in Civil and Building Engineering. Edited by Raymond Issa Issa and Ian Flood. Orlando, Florida: ASCE; 2014. pp. 657-664

[16] Farghaly K, Abanda H, Vidalakis C, Wood G. BIM big data system

architecture for asset management: a conceptual framework. In: Proceedings of the Joint Conference on Computing in Construction Congress (JC3). Heraklion, Greece; 2017. pp. 289-296

[17] Chalhoub J, Ayer SK, Ariaratnam ST. Augmented reality for enabling un-and under-trained individuals to complete specialty construction tasks. Journal of Information Technology in Construction. 2021;**26**:128-143

[18] Blank C, Eckhoff M, Petersen I, Wege R, Wendholt B. Distributed Collaborative Construction in Mixed Reality. In: Proceeding of ACHI. Lisbon, Portugal; 2015

[19] El Ammari K, Hammad A. Remote interactive collaboration in facilities management using BIM-based mixed reality. Automation in Construction. 2019;**107**:102940

[20] Ratajczak J, Riedl M, Matt DT. BIM-based and AR Application Combined with Location-Based Management System for the Improvement of the Construction Performance. Buildings. 2019;**9**(5):118

[21] Cotts D, Roper K, Payant R. The Facility Management Handbook. New York, NY: AMACOM; 2010

[22] Huang Y. Evaluating mixed reality technology for architectural design and construction layout. Journal of Civil Engineering and Construction Technology. 2020;**11**(1):1-12

[23] Trimble Inc. Aligning a Model to Site in Trimble Connect for HoloLens. 2020. Available from: https://www.youtube.com/watch?v=AUfv2dRGcNc [Accessed: May 27, 2022]

[24] Trimble Inc. Aligning Models Using Markers in Trimble Connect for HoloLens. 2020. Available from: https://www.youtube.com/watch?v=n5TKyeQ8QOU [Accessed: May 27, 2022]

[25] Azuma R, Baillot Y, Behringer R, Feiner S, Julier S, MacIntyre B. Recent advances in augmented reality. IEEE Computer Graphics and Applications. 2001;**21**(6):34-47

[26] Costanza E, Kunz A, Fjeld M. Mixed reality: A survey. In: Lalanne D, Kohlas J. (eds). Human Machine Interaction. Lecture Notes in Computer Science, vol 5440. Berlin, Heidelberg: Springer; 2009. pp. 47-68

[27] Naticchia B, Vaccarini M, Corneli A, Messi L, Carbonari A. Leveraging Extended Reality technologies with RFID to enhance on field maintenance of buildings. In: Proc. of the 38th International Conference of CIB W78, Luxembourg; 2021. pp 378-387

[28] Carbonari A, Vaccarini M. Pictures and Videos Collected during ODAVS Activity. Zenodo; 2022; Available from: https://doi.org/10.5281/zenodo.6531860 [Accessed: May 27, 2022]

Chapter 8

# Knowledge Dynamics: Educational Pathways from Theories to Tangible Outcomes

*Saba Qadhi*

## Abstract

In the intricate dance between theory and application, "Knowledge Dynamics: Educational Pathways from Theories to Tangible Outcomes" delves into the transformative journey of knowledge from conceptual understanding to actionable execution within educational settings. This investigation highlights modern education's progressive pedagogical approaches and methodologies to address the disparity between theoretical knowledge and its practical implementation. This story emphasizes the need to cultivate flexible learning environments by thoroughly examining case studies and analyzing current trends. These educational settings provide students with fundamental theories and enable them to develop the necessary abilities and self-assurance to use this information effectively in their specific areas of study. This chapter is a crucial resource for educators, policymakers, and scholars who seek to effectively manage and enhance the dynamic relationship between theory and practice within the ever-changing educational environment of today.

**Keywords:** education administration, knowledge era, education systems, educational policies, adaptive learning

## 1. Introduction

The educational environment is experiencing a significant shift, driven by technological developments and the growing need for practical skills that align with the constantly changing job market. Consequently, there is an increasing trend toward reassessing the longstanding conflict between theory and practice to achieve a harmonious equilibrium that equips students with a comprehensive grasp of concepts and the ability to apply them in practical scenarios [1]. The idea of "knowledge dynamics" involves the dynamic and fluid transition between different forms of knowledge, emphasizing the importance of educational pathways that balance a solid theoretical foundation with the ability to generate practical and significant results [2].

Theories serve as a fundamental basis for comprehension and a structure for analytical reasoning. However, it is via practical implementations that these ideas are examined, questioned, and frequently enhanced. According to Fullan and Scott, the task involves establishing an educational setting where students can seamlessly transition between theoretical concepts and practical applications. This approach aims to cultivate a more comprehensive and well-rounded comprehension of the studied subjects [3]. Furthermore, considering the increasing complexity of global challenges such as climate change, public health crises, and socioeconomic inequality, educational institutions need to modify their curricula to incorporate the skills and knowledge required to tackle these issues [4].

This chapter aims to investigate the developing methods, approaches, and technologies that enable a smooth transition, utilizing illustrative examples and case studies from diverse educational sectors across the globe. By doing so, the study aims to offer educators, scholars, and policymakers' valuable insights and recommendations to improve the effectiveness and pertinence of current educational practices.

## 2. Theoretical background

Knowledge dynamics is grounded on recognizing that knowledge is not fixed but undergoes constant evolution through its interactions with many elements such as technology, culture, and societal demands. According to Drucker [2], knowledge has been highlighted as the paramount economic resource in the post-capitalist society. This perspective underscores the shift from conventional capital and labor to learning as the principal catalyst for productivity and expansion.

The phrase 'knowledge dynamics' inherently implies the presence of motion, development, and transformation within the knowledge domain. According to Robinson & Lee [1], within the realm of education, there exists a notable change in the paradigms governing instructional methods and knowledge acquisition. This underscores the necessity for an educational strategy characterized by flexibility and adaptability. This method encompasses the transmission of academic knowledge and the cultivation of creativity and invention in learners, equipping them with the necessary abilities to traverse a dynamic and constantly evolving world.

Tapscott & William's study [5] argued that a more nuanced exploration of their interplay can challenge the conventional perception of a strict dichotomy between theory and practice. However, it is essential to note that a continuum exists in which approach influences practice and vice versa. The interaction between theory and practice is particularly significant in contemporary educational environments, as they require individuals to possess a solid theoretical basis and the ability to apply and modify that knowledge to address real-world difficulties successfully [4].

Theoretical foundations of knowledge dynamics highlight the interconnectedness between theory and practice within educational environments. As individuals in the field of education, it is crucial to acknowledge and encourage this dynamic process, guaranteeing that students are adequately equipped to use their knowledge and abilities effectively and meaningfully in practical contexts.

### 2.1 Evolution of knowledge dynamics in the digital age

The advent of the Digital Age has played a crucial role in facilitating the transition toward knowledge dynamics. The notion of the "wikinomics" model was presented by Tapscott & Williams [5], who argued that the Internet and collaborative technologies have facilitated the democratization of knowledge, hence dismantling conventional boundaries and hierarchies in the realms of education and business.

In the contemporary context, the distribution of knowledge is not solely reliant on hierarchical structures but rather involves a collaborative process of co-creation, refinement, and widespread dissemination.

One of the primary consequences of the digital revolution on the dynamics of knowledge is the increased accessibility and facilitation of knowledge retrieval and dissemination. The theory of connectivism was developed by George [6], which suggests that in a digitally networked world, learning takes place in complex and dynamic contexts characterized by the formation of networks rather than traditional hierarchical structures. In the context of George, the acquisition of the capacity to establish correlations among various sources of information and make prompt decisions assumes a pivotal role as a valuable cognitive aptitude.

In addition, Seely Brown and Adler [7] put out the notion that the advent of the Web has facilitated a transition from a focus on acquiring knowledge to a focus on developing one's identity, highlighting the significance of active engagement and deep involvement in the learning process rather than passive reception of information. The increasing popularity of Massive Open Online Courses (MOOCs) and other digital learning platforms has resulted in a convergence of formal and informal education, prompting educators to reconsider conventional pedagogical approaches to fully use the capabilities of digital tools [8].

To effectively navigate this ever-changing environment, educators must stay updated on technological innovations and the resulting changes in learning mechanics. The task at hand necessitates not only comprehending but also critically assessing the ramifications of these alterations on the dissemination and generation of knowledge.

### 2.2 The role of educators in facilitating the integration of theory and practice

Educators encounter a dual set of obstacles and prospects in an era marked by the swift dissemination of information and the erosion of conventional educational boundaries. One of the primary duties involves facilitating the extensive reservoir of information, equipping students with the necessary skills to assess and utilize knowledge in practical situations.

The concept of communities of practice was first presented by Wenger [9], who emphasized the significance of social learning in developing individuals' understanding and expertise. Within these communities, wisdom transcends individualism and becomes a collective endeavor wherein learners engage in navigation, negotiation, and collaborative knowledge construction. In this particular environment, the educator assumes the role of a facilitator, guiding students. At the same time, they engage in intricate problem-solving activities, promoting teamwork and prioritizing the application of knowledge rather than mere memorization.

Dewey [10] previously addressed the significance of experiential learning, asserting that authentic education emerges from the interplay between knowledge and experience. In modern education, educators are responsible for designing educational encounters that correspond with real-life situations, enabling students to apply theoretical knowledge to practical obstacles [11].

Moreover, following the progress of technology [12] posited that digital tools present a distinctive prospect for establishing dynamic and interactive learning environments. Nevertheless, the effectiveness of these tools lies not in their novelty but in their capacity to replicate real-world obstacles, enabling students to engage in experimentation, experience failure, acquire knowledge, and engage in iterative processes. In doing so, these tools serve to connect theoretical concepts with practical applications.

Educators, as custodians of knowledge dynamics, have a responsibility beyond the simple transmission of information. Educational institutions should cultivate conducive settings that facilitate the development of critical thinking, teamwork, and practical application skills, thereby equipping students with the necessary competencies to tackle the complex and diverse challenges prevalent in contemporary society.

## 3. Modern pedagogical approaches in knowledge dynamics

The evolution of educational thought, especially in the last few decades, has witnessed a remarkable shift toward innovative pedagogical strategies that align with modern knowledge dynamics and prepare students to navigate the multifaceted challenges of the real world.

### 3.1 Project-based learning: a nexus of theory and practice

Project-based learning (PBL) is an educational approach that promotes student learning via active participation in authentic and personally significant projects. According to Thomas [13], PBL is an all-encompassing pedagogical approach that actively includes students in exploring genuine problems during classroom instruction and learning activities. This educational approach enables students to acquire theoretical knowledge and comprehensively understand its practical implementation in real-world contexts, effectively bridging the gap between knowledge and practice [14]. As we transition into an information-driven era, applying theoretical knowledge practically has become paramount. PBL provides an ideal platform for this. Bell [15] notes that PBL helps students develop skills for living in a knowledge-based, highly technological society. The process enables students to think critically about and solve challenging, real-world problems [16]. Unlike traditional learning methods that rely on rote memorization, PBL emphasizes developing problem-solving skills, critical thinking, and collaborative team efforts. Helle et al. [17] also pointed out that PBL can significantly improve content retention and cultivate a genuine enthusiasm for lifelong learning.

### 3.2 The role of flipped classrooms in cultivating independent inquiry

The concept of ‘flipped classrooms’ was presented by Bergmann & Sams [18]. In this pedagogical approach, the usual teaching method is reversed, enabling students to engage with lectures and instructional materials outside of the physical classroom environment, often utilizing digital platforms. This educational framework facilitates classroom time for engaging in interactive exercises, facilitating group discussions, and cultivating a more profound comprehension of the subject matter. It promotes the development of self-directed learning and offers avenues for cooperative problem-solving. Bishop and Verleger [19] found that flipped classrooms can increase student satisfaction and improve learning outcomes. Moreover, Tucker [20] noted that flipped teaching provides a more significant opportunity for students to work at their own pace and engage with materials tailored to individual learning styles.

### 3.3 Interdisciplinary studies: fostering integration in the contemporary knowledge landscape

In the contemporary period, knowledge is not confined to isolated domains but is intricately interconnected throughout several fields of study. Interdisciplinary studies involve integrating knowledge and methodologies from several academic disciplines, synthesizing multiple approaches comprehensively. This educational approach provides pupils with an expanded viewpoint and promotes adaptable cognitive processes, essential competencies in the contemporary and ever-changing global landscape. According to Klein [21], the advantages of employing interdisciplinary methodologies in education have been underscored, particularly emphasizing its capacity to foster creativity and innovation. Mansilla & Duraising [22] argue that interdisciplinary instruction allows students to perceive and analyze complex systems more holistically. Such a broadened perspective prepares students to tackle real-world challenges by drawing insights from multiple disciplines, fostering a more rounded and holistic form of problem-solving. It also promotes flexibility in thought, a more valuable skill in a rapidly changing world.

### 3.4 Adaptive learning systems: individualized approaches to knowledge acquisition

The educational landscape has been transforming because of the emergence of adaptive learning systems, which may be attributed to technological advancements [23]. These systems employ algorithms to adapt content dynamically, customizing instruction to cater to the specific needs of each student. The content is dynamically changed to optimize learning by analyzing a student's interactions and performance [24]. This strategy guarantees that the pace of learning is tailored to suit the needs of individual students, thereby optimizing their understanding and ability to retain information. This indicates a shift toward an educational strategy that prioritizes personalization and student-centeredness.

## 4. Digital tool and platforms: amplifying real-world application

In the digital age, the realm of education has been fundamentally transformed by the advent of innovative tools and platforms. Digital solutions have significantly broadened the scope of educational opportunities, surpassing conventional teaching methods by establishing connections between theoretical concepts and practical, real-life scenarios. This analysis delves further into the impact of these tools and platforms on the educational environment.

### 4.1 The emergence of virtual reality (VR) and augmented reality (AR) in experiential learning

Virtual reality (VR) and augmented reality (AR) tools can bring about significant changes in the field of education. Using realistic simulations, these technologies can transport pupils to many locations, ranging from historical battles to molecular structures. The authors of the study conducted by Radianti et al. [25] highlight the advantages associated with the utilization of AR and VR technologies in the context of emergency preparedness training. They argue that using realistic simulations in these training programs can significantly improve learners' abilities in decision-making and analysis. In disciplines such as architecture and medicine, utilizing VR and AR technologies offers students the opportunity to get practical experience that circumvents the limitations imposed by physical logistics and the potential risks connected with hands-on practice. Moreover, these technologies have the potential to significantly empower students with disabilities by offering accessibility features and personalized interactive experiences that cater to their specific needs.

### 4.2 The utilization of gamification to foster engagement among learners in both theoretical and practical contexts

In addition to the initial appeal of badges and leaderboards, gamification can make learning interactive and captivating. According to Hamari et al. [26], gamified systems can augment motivation levels and foster more user involvement, hence crucial in facilitating the learning process.

An exemplary illustration may be found in educational games within the STEM (Science, Technology, Engineering, and Mathematics) fields, where evidence has demonstrated their capacity to cultivate critical thinking and problem-solving abilities. Games give a joyful avenue for engaging with intricate topics and offer learners the advantage of receiving prompt feedback, enabling them to adapt and enhance their techniques in real-time.

### 4.3 Artificial intelligence and adaptive learning platforms: customizing educational trajectories

Artificial Intelligence (AI) holds significant relevance in education, extending beyond a mere term. Contemporary artificial intelligence (AI)-based platforms can efficiently analyze extensive quantities of student data to discern discernible patterns, areas of deficiency, and areas of proficiency. Using data-driven methodologies guarantees learners a personalized educational experience specifically designed to cater to their requirements.

Muhie and Woldie [27] underscored the significance of AI in developing intelligent content, encompassing tailored reading materials, problem sets, and study aides. The adaptive material undergoes continuous development in response to a student's progress, ensuring that the difficulties presented appropriately match their existing expertise level. In addition, chatbots powered by artificial intelligence have the capability to promptly address students' uncertainties, hence diminishing obstacles to ongoing education.

## 5. Case studies: effective synthesis of theory and concrete results

### 5.1 The finnish model: striking a balance between theoretical knowledge and practical skills

The educational model of Finland has continually attracted attention due to its exceptional quality. A key factor contributing to its achievement lies in integrating academic comprehension with practically implementing this knowledge within real-life contexts. The Finnish educational system has a significant confidence level in its teachers, as most have completed extensive training and possess master's degrees [28].

The utilization of theoretical knowledge in practical contexts is a fundamental aspect. Students frequently participate in projects that simulate real-life situations, facilitating the integration of theoretical knowledge acquired in the classroom with its practical implementation. As an illustration, mathematical principles can be applied in functional scenarios, such as coordinating a community event or allocating funds for diverse activities.

### 5.2 Singapore places a significant emphasis on problem-based learning

Singapore's educational system is widely recognized internationally and is particularly notable for its PBL methodology. In this educational setting, students are exposed to intricate real-world challenges that necessitate collaborative problem-solving. According to Tan [29], this approach promotes active engagement among learners and fosters the development of critical abilities such as evaluation, questioning, and knowledge synthesis. The strategy guarantees that students are adequately prepared for contemporary work environments, where the ability to engage in critical thinking and problem-solving is highly valued [30].

### 5.3 Massive open online courses (MOOCs) and the democratization of global education

The emergence of Massive Open Online Courses (MOOCs) has facilitated the democratization of global, high-quality education. The advent of online learning platforms such as Coursera, edX, and Udacity has played a pivotal role in enabling the proliferation of this educational paradigm. These platforms have effectively amalgamated theoretical instruction with practical applications by including real-world case studies, simulations, and assessments [31]. According to Shah [32], the existence of these platforms highlights the worldwide need for adaptable and flexible learning, enabling individuals, both students and professionals, to consistently develop and adapt to the dynamic requirements of the global economy.

## 6. Future directions and conclusions

### 6.1 Anticipating the evolution of knowledge dynamics in the subsequent decade

The forthcoming decade holds the potential for significant changes in knowledge dynamics, particularly within educational settings. The convergence of AI, sophisticated analytics, and ongoing developments in pedagogical research will fundamentally transform the processes of knowledge generation, dissemination, and application.

It is anticipated that the rapid progression of technology will facilitate the development of increasingly immersive learning environments. According to Johnson et al. [33], the integration of AR, VR, and mixed reality can significantly transform educational settings by enhancing the accessibility and tangibility of remote historical events and intricate concepts for students.

Moreover, the conventional confines of traditional educational settings are expected to become less distinct because of the influence of e-learning platforms, collaborative online forums, and the emergence of digital nomadism. These factors are transforming the learning landscape, altering the location and way educational experiences take place. A foreseeable trend in education is the transition toward learner-centric paradigms, characterized by a growing emphasis on personalization, adaptability, and responsiveness to individual requirements [34].

### 6.2 Suggestions for educational institutions and policy makers

Educational institutions should pursue the active integration of developing technology into curricula. This entails more than simply obtaining the most recent technological devices but comprehending and implementing them pedagogically and appropriately.

Continuous professional development (CPD) is paramount in providing educators with the necessary skills and knowledge to navigate the ever-changing educational landscape effectively [35]. According to Darling-Hammond & Hyler [36], it is crucial to prioritize regular training sessions, seminars, and opportunities for exposure to novel educational methods.

Policy flexibility refers to the ability of a policy to adapt and respond to changing circumstances and needs. It involves the capacity in a constantly evolving environment; inflexible policies can impede innovation progress. Policymakers should prioritize cultivating adaptability, granting educational institutions the freedom to engage in experimentation and innovation while upholding fundamental academic norms and objectives.

The importance of collaboration in achieving success. It is imperative to foster collaborative alliances among educational institutions, technology corporations, research bodies, and governmental entities. Association of this nature has the potential to promote innovation, facilitate research endeavors, and facilitate the adoption of optimal methodologies across international boundaries [37].

### 6.3 Predating the evolution of knowledge dynamics in the next decade

The next decade promises profound transformations in knowledge dynamics, especially within educational contexts. The convergence of artificial intelligence, sophisticated analytics, and ongoing developments in pedagogical research will fundamentally transform the processes of knowledge generation, dissemination, and application.

It is anticipated that the rapid progression of technology will facilitate the development of increasingly immersive learning environments. According to Johnson et al. [33], integrating AR, VR, and mixed reality can significantly transform educational settings by enhancing the accessibility and tangibility of remote historical events and intricate concepts for students.

In addition, it is anticipated that the conventional confines of physical classrooms will become less distinct because of the influence of e-learning platforms, collaborative online forums, and the emergence of digital nomadism. These factors are expected to significantly alter the locations and methods through which educational experiences take place. A foreseeable trend is the emergence of learner-centric paradigms in education, characterized by a growing emphasis on personalization, adaptability, and responsiveness to individual requirements [34].

### 6.4 Final remarks on the ongoing progression of knowledge dynamics

At its essence, knowledge dynamics encompasses the dynamic and growing relationship between theory and practice and the interplay between tradition and

*DOI: http://dx.doi.org/10.5772/intechopen.1002979*

innovation. Considering imminent technological and pedagogical transformations, it is imperative to consider the ultimate objective: fostering individuals who can think critically, adapt effectively, and engage meaningfully with the evolving global landscape.

The process of knowledge dynamics is characterized by its perpetual nature, wherein successive generations actively contribute to, modify, and expand upon the accumulated wisdom of their predecessors. This statement calls upon educators, learners, and policymakers to maintain a perpetual state of curiosity, continuous growth, and unwavering commitment to achieve significant and influential education.

## Nomenclature

CPD continuous professional development

## Author details

Saba Qadhi
Qatar University, Qatar

*Address all correspondence to: sabaa@qu.edu.qa

## References

[1] Robinson K, Lee JR. Out of our Minds. Wiley Online Library; 2011

[2] Drucker P. Post Capitalist Society. New York: ButterWorth-Heinemann; 1993a

[3] Fullan M, Scott G. Turnaround Leadership for Higher Education. John Wiley & Sons; 2009

[4] Selingo JJ. College (un) Bound: The Future of Higher Education and What it Means for Students. Houghton Mifflin Harcourt; 2013a

[5] Tapscott D, Williams AD. Wikinomics: How Mass Collaboration. Changes Everything. 2006

[6] George S. Connectivism: A learning theory for the digital age. International Journal of Instructional Technology and Distance Learning. 2005;**2**(1):3-10

[7] Seely Brown J, Adler RP. Open education, the long tail, and learning 2.0. Educause Review. 2008;**43**(1):16-20

[8] Pappano L. The year of the MOOC. The New York Times. 2012;**2**(12):1-7

[9] Wenger E. Communities of Practice: Learning, Meaning, and Identity. Cambridge University Press; 1999

[10] Dewey J. Experience and Education. 1997 edition. New York: Touchstone; 1938

[11] Kolb DA. Experience as the Source of Learning and Development. Prentice-Hall: Englewood Cliffs; 1984. pp. 31-61

[12] Bower M. Teaching as a Design Science: Building Pedagogical Patterns for Learning and Technology. New York & London: Routledge; 2018. p. 258. Revista Fuentes, 20(1), 89

[13] Thomas JW. A Review of Research on Project-Based Learning. San Rafael, CA: Autodesk; 2000

[14] Nosair MR, Qadhi S, Hendawi M. Evaluating preparatory programs and novice teachers teaching performance and its influence on students' learning process in Qatar University. Educational Administration: Theory and Practice. 2021;**27**(3):1133-1149

[15] Bell S. Project-based learning for the 21st century: Skills for the future. The Clearing House. 2010;**83**(2):39-43

[16] Romanowski MH, Qadhi S. Teach for Qatar: Teachers' challenges and resources in Qatar's government schools. SAGE Open. 2022;**12**(2):1-13

[17] Helle L, Tynjälä P, Olkinuora E. Project-based learning in post-secondary education–theory, practice and rubber sling shots. Higher Education. 2006;**51**:287-314

[18] Bergmann J, Sams A. Flip Your Classroom: Reach Every Student in Every Class Every Day. International Society for Technology in Education; 2012

[19] Bishop J, Verleger MA. The flipped classroom: A survey of the research. In: 2013 ASEE Annual Conference & Exposition. 2013. pp. 23-1200

[20] Tucker B. The flipped classroom. Education Next. 2012;**12**(1):82-83

[21] Klein JT. Interdisciplinarity: History, Theory, and Practice. Wayne State University Press; 1990

[22] Mansilla VB, Duraising ED. Targeted assessment of students' interdisciplinary work: An empirically grounded

framework proposed. The Journal of Higher Education. 2007;**78**(2):215-237

[23] Qadhi S, Alkubaisi H. Teachers' education in Qatar: Devolution and decentralization. In: Khine MS, editor. Handbook of Research on Teacher Education: Pedagogical Innovations and Practices in the Middle East. Singapore: Springer Nature; 2022. pp. 13-28. DOI: 10.1007/978-981-19-2400-2_2

[24] Woolf BP. Building Intelligent Interactive Tutors: Student-Centered Strategies for Revolutionizing e-Learning. Morgan Kaufmann; 2010

[25] Radianti J, Majchrzak TA, Fromm J, Wohlgenannt I. A systematic review of immersive virtual reality applications for higher education: Design elements, lessons learned, and research agenda. Computers & Education. 2020;**147**:103778

[26] Hamari J, Koivisto J, Sarsa H. Does gamification work?--a literature review of empirical studies on gamification. In: 2014 47th Hawaii International Conference on System Sciences. 2014. pp. 3025-3034

[27] Muhie YA, Woldie AB. Integration of artificial intelligence technologies in teaching and learning in higher education. Science and Technology. 2020;**10**(1):1-7

[28] Sahlberg P. Finnish Lessons 3.0: What Can the World Learn from Educational Change in Finland? Teachers College Press; 2021

[29] Tan O-S. Problem-Based Learning Innovation: Using Problems to Power Learning in the 21st Century. Gale Cengage Learning; 2021

[30] Hung W, Jonassen DH, Liu R. Problem-based learning. Handbook of Research on Educational Communications and Technology. 2008;**3**(1):485-506

[31] Reich J, Ruipérez-Valiente JA. The MOOC pivot. Science. 2019;**363**(6423):130-131

[32] Shah D. By the Numbers: MOOCS in 2016. Class Central's MOOC Report. Class Central; 2018

[33] Johnson L, Becker SA, Cummins M, Estrada V, Freeman A, Hall C. NMC Horizon Report: 2016 Higher Education edition. The New Media Consortium; 2016

[34] Weller M. 25 Years of Tech. Athabasca University Press; 2020. DOI: 10.15215/aupress/9781771993050.01

[35] Qadhi S, Floyd A. Female English teachers perceptions and experience of continuing professional development in Qatar. Education Sciences. 2021;**11**(4):1-14. DOI: 10.3390/educsci11040160

[36] Darling-Hammond LH, Hyler M. Effective Teacher Professional Development. Learning Policy Institute; 2017

[37] Schleicher A. World Class: How to Build a 21st-Century School System, Strong Performers and Successful Reformers in Education. OECD Publishing; 2018

Chapter 9

# Optimising Project Stakeholder Value through Knowledge Management: A Social Capital Lens

*Hakem Sharari*


## Abstract

Knowledge is the essence of organisational performance; without knowledge nothing would be produced. Knowledge management can be simply seen as the processing of information to be introduced as business outcomes: projects, services and products. Having said this, organisations must be keen to put knowledge into practice. By adopting a social capital lens, this paper aims to shed light on the link between knowledge as a theoretical construct and its practical implications. The paper explores the role of social capital and networks in optimising project stakeholder value within three Jordanian telecommunication companies operating in a competitive, technology-based context. The structural, relational and cognitive dimensions of social capital are employed to understand how project stakeholders create, exchange and exploit knowledge to achieve their as well as their organisation's objectives. The paper offers findings that support knowledge management as a determinant of overall organisational performance and help project managers to capitalise on social networks to optimise project stakeholder value.


**Keywords:** stakeholder value, social capital, knowledge management, organisational performance, social networks, telecommunication

## 1. Introduction

Projects are increasingly considered as the means of creating stakeholder value [1]. This view is more in keeping with the challenges of modern society, in that project value cannot only be measured according to the traditional budget, time and scope constraints, but it also has to consider stakeholder satisfaction. The role of a project manager should thus exceed that of planning and controlling activities to effectively and efficiently managing stakeholders, who are seen as actors in a collaborative project network [2].

Value is mainly created at the front end of projects, making it a strategic phase in which stakeholder needs, requirements, expectations and goals are captured [1]. The front-end phase ensues with the very early point in the generation of a project idea, all the way to its final development to be either approved or shelved [3]. This phase is however known as fuzzy; it lacks definition and alignment due to the unsettled project network and the scarcity of knowledge about the novel, explorative project idea.

This paper employs a social capital lens to understand how project networks can be formed to create, share and exploit knowledge to optimise stakeholder value. The paper maps the best front-end interactions and relationships, leading to the development of a holistic model that demonstrates the preferred structural, relational and cognitive network attributes to enhance stakeholder alignment and facilitate decisions. Having such conceptualisation of projects as being embedded in complex networks of relationships lags behind [4], prompting the following questions:

1. How does social capital help in managing knowledge and optimising stakeholder value in the front end of projects?

2. What social network attributes should be maintained to facilitate decisions and optimise stakeholder value in the front end of projects?

Addressing these questions contributes to an enhanced understanding of how best project stakeholder value is optimised, which can only be done by considering social capital and networks in the highly turbulent and fast-changing environment of the fuzzy front-end phase. Next, the paper reviews the existing literature to explain the related concepts and views and develop the research propositions. The paper later explains the methods used and the context within which the research was pursued, ending with discussing the findings and conclusions.

## 2. Literature review

Organisations currently rely on fast transformation through developing project models that cope with ever-changing business needs and optimise stakeholder value. To understand this issue, the literature on project management and social capital is reviewed to shed light on the dependability of stakeholder value on the nature of knowledge channelled within project networks.

### 2.1 The modern view of projects

Projects can be viewed as social networks initiated with the aim of creating stakeholder value within collaborative settings [3]. Within this 'modern view', projects are much broader than conceived when positioned on the instrumental base of planning and monitoring [1]. This change in view has reshaped the context of project management to address the requirements of the political, economic and social forces, imposing new actions to be considered in the front end of projects: ensuring that the needs and requirements of stakeholders are clearly captured; managing the impact of those stakeholders on the project vision; and aligning the expected project value with their strategic intent. These actions are inevitable for project managers to link project value to the objectives of related forces [5].

### 2.2 The fuzzy front end

The front end is part of an expanded project life cycle with a strategic role as the initiation phase [6]. This view of the front end is more concerned with the activities related to managing stakeholders rather than managing processes. The focus of the front end is to align the goals of stakeholders in a holistic project definition, all the way to submitting a value-optimised proposal to decision-makers to approve its finance. The front end is therefore seen as a network of relationships and not a set of well-defined tasks [7].

Throughout the front end, three sub-phases take place: idea generation, idea development and evaluation and project definition [3]. These sub-phases occur when a formal review is undertaken to discuss progress and evaluate the various alternatives for underlying issues (e.g. human capabilities, technological solutions and market opportunities). The result of each sub-phase comes in the form of a decision on whether to proceed to the next (**Figure 1**). The final sub-phase usually involves the participation of the top management to agree on the documentation and sign the project proposal, triggering the planning and implementation activities [8].

Managing the front end for value creation requires considering the different needs and perspectives of stakeholders. It requires viewing the front end as a social network in which stakeholder relationships are treated as crucial resources of knowledge and alignment [6]. Cooperation and coordination between project stakeholders can lead to various benefits, including improved communication, timely conflict resolution, effective decision-making and creative problem-solving [9]. These benefits create an environment that supports learning and knowledge exchange and exploitation, enabling the alignment of divergent stakeholder goals around an agreed project definition to capture a higher value end-state [10].

### 2.3 Social capital and networks

Social capital is a concept that initially appeared in community studies, where social networks are used to study the basis for trust, cooperation and access to resources. Social capital is channelled within social networks to form the patterns of relationships among actors according to three dimensions: structural, relational and cognitive [11].

The structural dimension refers to the number of existing ties and the power of actors, affecting their centrality and connectivity [12, 13]. The relational dimension focuses on the strength of ties and trust among actors [14]. Both dimensions are critical for knowledge creation and exchange [15]. The cognitive dimension focuses on having shared goals (i.e. the degree to which actors have a similar understanding of

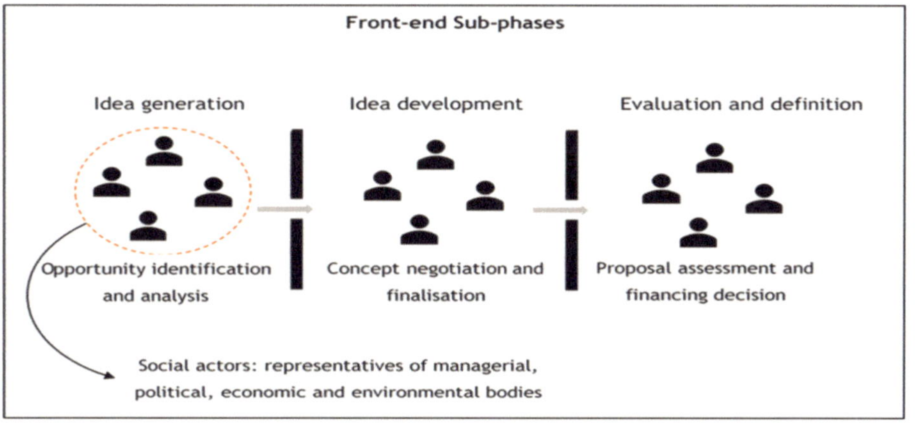


**Figure 1.**
*Front-end sub-phases.*

project value) and culture (i.e. the degree to which network relationships are governed by the same norms of behaviour). This dimension studies the network resources from which shared meaning and understanding of available knowledge is reached, enabling better exploitation [11].

Social capital can enhance project value through capitalising on the interactions and relationships of the involved actors [16, 17]. Since social capital is considered as a project resource, then more ties or trust should support more value [18]. This was the dominant thought until research found that 'sociability cuts both ways' ([19], p.18), meaning that social capital has a dark side. This dark side of social capital manifests itself in two main aspects: reinforcing inequality and supporting siloing and antisocial behaviours [20]. Knowing this opens the door for exploring the favourable network attributes to channel social capital and resources in a way that optimises stakeholder value in the front end of projects while avoiding its negative impact.

### 2.4 Research propositions

Engaging powerful actors in the early project network provides more knowledge for idea generators about the expected project outcomes [21]. In such a network, decision-makers are also provided with a sense of what can really be achieved, which affects stakeholder objective alignment and decision-making criteria. Regarding the structural network attributes, high interaction among desirable actors is seen to facilitate front-end value:

- *P1: High interaction among desirable network actors increases the likelihood of idea adoption and optimises front-end stakeholder value.*

The nature of actor relationships surrounding an idea would affect its maturity and selection. The various ties that span across a network determine the nature of knowledge creation and exchange [22]. Knowing that strong and weak ties have their merits and drawbacks [23], it is likely that both types of ties should be supported throughout the front end to enhance value creation:

- *P2: Networks of actors that evolve from weak to stronger ties increase the likelihood of idea adoption and optimise front-end stakeholder value.*

Front-end value creation requires actors to build interpretative frameworks that reflect their individual understanding of concepts [24]. Actors may have discrete goals and different purposes when they jointly discuss project contents [7]. Developing mutual understanding among network actors allows for the effective exploitation of knowledge, which increases the likelihood of idea adoption:

- *P3: Building mutual understanding among network actors increases the likelihood of idea adoption and optimises front-end stakeholder value.*

The three propositions represent the road map for exploring how social capital and network dimensions can optimise project stakeholder value in the fuzzy front-end phase through better channelling and exploitation of knowledge. The next section discusses the context selected, and the methods employed, to pursue the research enquiry, leading to discussing the findings and conclusions.

## 3. Methodology

### 3.1 Research context

The total Jordanian telecommunication sector was studied, one global and two regional companies. The three companies are anonymised as Company1, Company2 and Company3. Whereas Company1 employs 550 employee and holds 30% of the market share, the other 2 companies enjoy 35% of the market share each, but with 1000 employee working for Company2 and 1800 working for Company3. These companies compete aggressively, creating a huge pressure to optimise project stakeholder value. In such dynamic and competitive environment, projects require noticeable exploration in their early phases to be approved and adopted by decision-makers.

### 3.2 Method and design

A qualitative method was employed as the means of studying the network attributes within which social capital can optimise stakeholder value in the front end of projects [25]. This helps to answer the 'how' element of the research enquiry due to its explorative nature [26, 27]. This allows developing the propositions to build on existing theory. For the 'what' element of the research enquiry, a multiple case study design was adopted to compare the effects of social network dimensions on front-end value creation across organisations to gain a detailed insight [28].

### 3.3 Research approach

This research relies on the inductive approach to build on the theory related to social capital and networks and front-end project management [29]. Such an approach suits this qualitative research where limited literature is available and primary data is collected from a small sample, focusing on a specific context to make inferences about the enquiry domain [30].

### 3.4 Data collection

Thirty-one semi-structured interviews were conducted with project managers, product owners, project management office managers and top management personnel (**Table 1**). Using purposive sampling, the HR department in each company was contacted and provided with the interview guide. Based on the provided questions, nine experts were chosen as a core sample (three from Company1, two from Company2 and four from Company3). The sample then was snowballed by asking interviewees at the end of every interview to name potential experts who could provide further insight. Field notes were compiled during interviews to flag the main codes and topics and identify the gaps in the collected data [31]. After thirty-one interviews, both the interviews and supportive documents were unable to provide new insights; thus, data collection was ceased due to saturation [32].

### 3.5 Data analysis

The 31 interviews resulted in having 25 hours of voice recordings that were transcribed into 256 pages of text. These scripts were cleansed to enhance meaning and

| Managerial level | No. of interviewees | Gender | Average duration |
|---|---|---|---|
| Top management | 8 interviewees | 1 female–7 males | 60 minutes |
| Middle management | 13 interviewees | 3 females –10 males | 45 minutes |
| Lower management | 10 interviewees | 3 females–7 males | 50 minutes |

**Table 1.**
*Interviewing details.*

clarity since interviewees were second language English speakers. Summaries were produced for interviews to register any notes related to the content and context of the interviews to better interpret any variance in responses [33]. The personal and organisational names of interviewees were anonymised, keeping with the ethical obligations of the interviews.

Content analysis was conducted using NVivo software to explore the available scripts. Different types of codes were utilised for this purpose, including *in vivo* codes, descriptive codes and process codes, highlighting the main passages of the text and identifying key themes and categories [34, 35]. This process was supported by running word frequency, text search and other NVivo queries to further explore the text and dive into key topics. Higher-level inferences were drawn, which were then examined in line with the supportive documents [36]. During the content analysis, the iteration between the data-driven codes, categories and themes and theory was carefully maintained to ensure data validity and reliability.

## 4. Findings

Twenty-one out of 26 projects explored in this research were reported by interviewees to be satisfying; value was created for the stakeholders on both personal and organisational levels (**Table 2**). While organisational value is derived from meeting the sustainability and expansion objectives such as increasing sales and market share numbers, personal value is derived from aspects like incorporating stakeholders' needs in project definitions, achieving career-related promotions, appreciating their contributions and recognising learning opportunities. In some situations, especially with top management personnel, stakeholder value was intertwined so that achieving personal goals was linked to organisational objectives:

'This project was requested by [the group name] because of customer needs and complaints, and that we have objectives to meet: time to deliver and time to repair. These are strategic objectives to the company and to [the group name]. When we first presented the project to the top management, we tried to cover every single point that

| Projects done by | Satisfying | Dissatisfying | Description |
|---|---|---|---|
| Company1 | 5 projects | 2 projects | Some projects were chosen by several interviewees as the focus of interviews |
| Company2 | 5 projects | 1 project | |
| Company3 | 11 projects | 2 projects | |

**Table 2.**
*Perception of stakeholder value in the front end of projects.*

| Measure | Synonyms sample | Example quote |
|---|---|---|
| High | Usual, more, high, similar, always | 'When we first discussed the concept, we had more interaction' |
| Low | Alone, sometimes, low, different | 'Then we took some time alone to do our homework to prepare the business case' |
| Medium | Maintained, medium, less often, moderate | 'It is maintained, we cannot say that we were isolated, we always have interactions' |
| Strong | Frequent, strong, deep, increased | 'Due to that we built a strong relationship together, we started to share information' |
| Weak | Normal, weak, not yet, cautious | 'It started to increase in the middle phase, in the start, we were not afraid but cautious' |

**Table 3.**
*The process of identifying the network attributes.*

may help us achieve our objectives and meet all stakeholder requirements. The top management reviewed the project proposal, and the result was to go. We developed the project based on the proposal and once we completed the project and presented the results, all stakeholders were satisfied' [IT & Network Build Coordination and Support Manager, Company3].

Within these project networks, several attributes were considered as common to enhance stakeholder value accrual in the front end. These attributes were tracked according to the dimensions of social networks (i.e. structural, relational and cognitive) within each front-end sub-phase (i.e. idea generation, idea development, evaluation and project definition). A holistic model was therefore developed including the social network attributes that should take place throughout the front end of projects to optimise stakeholder value. It is worth noting however that the measures used to describe these network attributes were derived from the interviewees' own words, making them context sensitive (**Table 3**).

### 4.1 Structural network attributes

This dimension explores the social attributes related to the network size and frequency of interaction: both with whom they should take place and how they should change as the front end unfolds for optimised stakeholder value. The first finding explains that higher interactions among the right actors is critical to spark creative insights and encourage coordination in project networks (**Figure 2**). This helps transforming project ideas from the phase of being plain thoughts (i.e. idea generation) into more comprehensive and well-considered plans (i.e. idea development) where the organisational orientation and stakeholder ambitions are reflected in a holistic project documentation (i.e. evaluation and definition).

As shown in **Figure 2**, in the idea generation phase, network actors were found to build multiple ties and to have multilateral and interdepartmental interactions with less involvement of powerful actors. In this early phase, the large network size and heterogeneity was helpful to increase the pool of available knowledge that was needed to allow more innovative thoughts and suggestions regarding the various aspects of the project idea. Heterogeneous ties were also helpful to decide on the number and type of actors needed to guarantee that the proposed form of the project idea

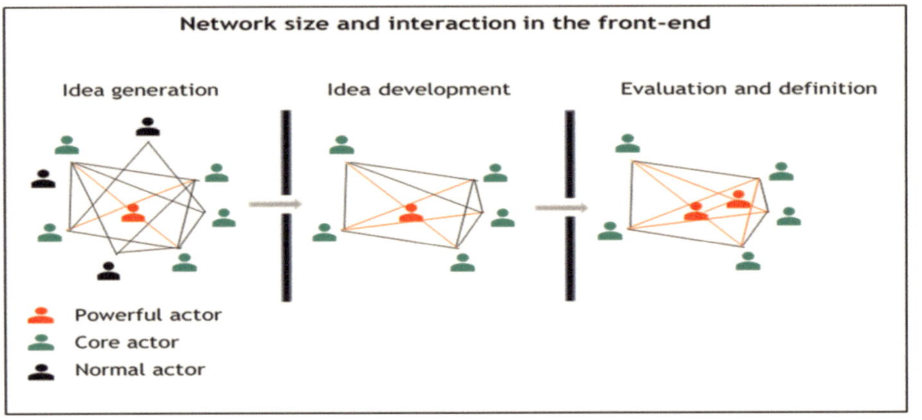


**Figure 2.**
*The recommended network size and interaction for optimised value.*

contained the needs and requirements of all stakeholders. This, as shown in **Table 2**, led to more stakeholders perceiving better value being created from project ideas.

Moving to idea development, interactions were higher and more concentrated in the core project network while keeping a lower level of contact with less related actors. Turning into a more cohesive project network was crucial in this phase, as twenty-one interviewees explained, to reduce distraction and validate the main aspects of the project idea that must be further developed. With such structural dynamics, network actors were able to abandon aspects of the project idea that had marginal benefits and focus on the long-term value:

> *'The structure dynamics varied according to the level of interaction. When we first discussed the concept, we had more interaction. Then, we took some time separated to prepare the business case and the model itself. After that, we had more interaction to validate the concept and ensure that everything is going well. However, we cannot say that we were totally isolated at any point in time, we always have interaction' (Pricing & Business Planning Manager, Company1).*

As opposed to the idea generation phase, a high level of engagement from powerful actors in the evaluation phase was required to avoid any potential scope creep (**Table 4**). Although ideas in the generation phase were more vulnerable to be biased to the benefit of powerful actors, the existence of those actors in the evaluation phase was essential to keep the balance between actors' objectives. This balance ensured relevant decisions were made, which raised the probability of top management adopting and financing project ideas. Such observation explains what was earlier

| Front-end sub-phase | Level of interaction | Network cohesion | Powerful actor involvement |
|---|---|---|---|
| Idea generation | High | Low | Low |
| Idea development | High | High | Medium |
| Evaluation and definition | High | High | High |

**Table 4.**
*Social network attributes related to the structural dimension.*

proposed about the critical need to direct the interaction in each phase to the right network actors to arrive at comprehensive project definitions:

> *'The top management nominated X as the Business Owner for this product. But down the road, I started to understand who the real decision-maker is, and I knew that X is just a messenger from that person who is not free working on another project. I used to talk to the Business Owner, then I jumped to his manager who had all details. This was very important to accelerate decisions by ensuring that I had the full details of the business rules and that they would not change later on' [Project Management Office Manager, Company1].*

The higher the interaction among desirable project actors during the front end, the more benefits attained by stakeholders. These benefits ranged between providing enough room for learning through answering several inter-functional questions, easing control over work and facilitating relevant decisions. In contrast, networks that had poor frequency of interaction and haphazard involvement of actors leaned towards arriving at defective value, since project definitions were only reflecting the needs and goals of specific stakeholders without a clear link to the organisational strategy:

> *'We had high interaction with all parties to be able to answer their concerns and questions from one aspect and to speed up the approval cycle from another. This is because the project itself took a month from the idea to the approval of the implementation, and we had many concepts and parameters to include as part of the business case of this new project. Thus, we had high interaction to ensure that we are covering all these KPIs or parameters' [Pricing & Business Planning Manager, Company1].*

> *'Because I dealt with many stakeholders in this project: Finance, Supply Chain, Technical and IT, I gained a very good knowledge and experience from them. I gained information that I did not recognise before; I started to understand the meaning of server storage users and the beverage of the users' [IT & Network Build Coordination and Support Manager, Company3].*

> *'During that analytical phase, one of the major stakeholders, who was a manager from IT, managed to convince the Business Owner to develop the product in an inefficient way only because it was easier for him to implement. For the Business Owner, he managed to have the product on the portal, and for me, it was okay, but the pain for the company was to lose the full integration between all systems' [Project Management Office Manager, Company1].*

Developing ideas and solutions without proper representation of the opinions of actors can lead to catastrophic outcomes if they manage to pass the different front-end check windows to implementation. Such ideas and solutions might allow for temporary and marginal benefits, but they have multiple negative impacts on the overall project journey. These impacts can cause major resource losses and poor customer satisfaction and exhaust other project stakeholders who may have less negotiation power when trying to reconcile these impacts:

> *'The Commercial Owner attempted to launch the solution in less than thirty days to claim establishing a new enterprise e-commerce platform in a short time. But after a*

> *while, many complaints will be received about bad customer experiences. He will then be punished by the top management, and he will start asking for a change request from the vendor. This will put us in a weak negotiation state because the vendor is the developer of the solution, and it is the only entity that can do the change request. Thus, he will put a huge cost on us, and we will accept it as we will not have any bargaining power, and the Commercial Owner will lose his position' [Product Development Manager, Company1].*

In such situations, the involvement of powerful actors in the evaluation phase is important to interrupt this unsophisticated development of the idea to correct the project direction towards better stakeholder value:

> *'I interrupted the project, and I convinced the Commercial Owner that he needs to consider this e-commerce platform as an additional communication channel for the customer to subscribe, manage her/his profile and submit payments, but not as an isolated channel. Then, the whole project was reviewed, and the scope of the documentation was changed, and we started the project from the scratch, or from my point of view, we corrected the whole project to get more value for the end user' [Product Development Manager, Company1].*

To compare the three cases, in Company1, the processes lacked stickiness as a result of higher personal relationships, which required continuous scrutiny of actor engagement to reduce the probability of individuals opportunistically attempting to reap benefits for themselves. In Company3 and Company2 (but especially the latter), such structural dynamics were easier to maintain due to well-defined business procedures. However, in all cases, involving the right actors with the advisable interaction level occurred in all satisfying projects. This confirms and develops the first research proposition:

- *P1: High interaction among desirable network actors optimises stakeholder value through encouraging coordination that sparks creative insights and increases the likelihood of project idea adoption.*

### 4.2 Relational network attributes

This dimension discusses the strength of ties among network actors; when, how and with whom they evolve throughout the front end for optimised stakeholder value. The second finding explains networks that evolve from weak to stronger ties to optimise front-end stakeholder value. Building strong ties was difficult in the early phases when the number of actors was high but manageable afterwards when fewer actors were involved (**Figure 3**). With such network dynamics, actors used to take enough time to decide on knowledgeable and experienced candidates with whom to discuss their shared interests and build trusting partnerships (i.e. idea generation) that assist in collectively improving project concepts (i.e. idea development) and to make decisions that increase the probability of ideas adoption (i.e. evaluation and definition).

Networks of actors, as shown in **Figure 3**, were found to coalesce around weak ties with lower emotional intensity and intimacy in the idea generation phase. This phase included actors who sometimes had to adopt conflicting positions in their pursuit of proving the superiority of their needs. Actors were also exploring knowledgeable and

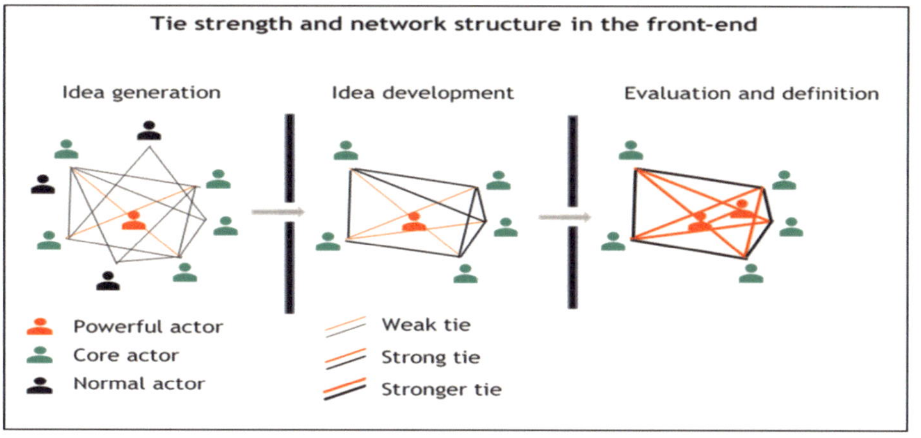


**Figure 3.**
*Combining the recommended structural and relational attributes.*

experienced candidates with whom to develop strong ties. With several multilateral departments involved in this phase, such cautious behaviour helped actors to review their choices of viable future partnerships:

> *'At the beginning, we only had the product concept, and we did not have much knowledge about the project itself. We were still exploring the different vendor approaches and what is the model that each one of them is adopting accordingly. For example, if we wanted to discuss anything with the Technical team, we used to only ask them if they have this or that thing and, in a nutshell, they just tell us, yes, this is something that we already do, and we can provide. Once we selected the vendor with the most suitable business model and reviews, we started working with them and we went more into details about the technical and commercial aspects, and the involvement of the related teams started to get deeper then' [Digital & VAS Products Management Expert, Company2].*

> *'At the beginning, the relationships were normal since it was a team formation process until we reached the storming stage where everybody was trying to prove her/himself right. Then, we moved to team norming, and everybody was working aligned together. But it was difficult at the beginning to set the rules and to clarify who is responsible for what' [Customer Experience & Quality Director, Company3].*

In the idea development phase, where the network size tends to be smaller and ties shift from being heterogeneous to more cohesive ones, interactions were denser and could support building strong ties and dyadic collaborations. This resulted in actors starting to exchange extensive information, which increased their knowledge and awareness about project concepts and visions and pushed them for better development:

> *'I got in touch with a guy from IT who I never met before this project. We started to get in touch more often to talk and share ideas and thoughts. Due to this strong relationship that we built in this project, we shared knowledge and experiences, and I started to understand things technically about the network that I did not use to know, which*

*helped me to make efficient decisions' [IT & Network Build Coordination and Support Manager, Company3].*

The impact of building strong ties in the development phase was not only about increasing the density and depth of communication but also about reducing the time needed to complete explorative tasks of the front end. Actors who built strong ties in the development phase reported easier communication processes and patterns, which, according to seventeen interviewees, resulted in shorter development periods when compared to the long period of time consumed in the generation phase when ties were weak and scattered. This was critical in the dynamic and fast-changing telecommunication sector to avoid outdated launches:

*'The early project preparations took long time as the relationships were not yet built. But the development took only one month because our communications started to be more friendly. For example, when I used to call a person, her/his reply was like okay, I am busy today, you can call me tomorrow, which made the process faster, and the development was faster' [Senior Business Demand Analyst & Technical Project Manager, Company3].*

Network ties in the evaluation phase were mostly stronger and triggered extra cooperation efforts to create a fit between the various needs and requirements of project actors (**Table 5**). The cooperation efforts also eliminated individual obstacles to help identify holistic objectives. In so doing, the probability of ideas adoption was higher as actors collectively worked towards convincing the decision-makers (i.e. top management) of the feasibility of their suggestions:

*'When we started the Fibre project, we used to sell the Fibre services without providing Wi-Fi solutions to our customers. These solutions are expensive and need a large budget, which made some project stakeholders think that they are not necessary. They justified their decision by the fact that we already had Internet services and that we did not provide such service before. Me and my Technical partner were not convinced, and insisted that the Wi-Fi solutions are needed by customers. We provided full presentations to the top management, and we repeated them several times. Eventually, we managed to get through and convince them that this is a point of improvement that we should do' [Customer Experience & Quality Director, Company3].*

*'We were cautious in the start and middle of the project preparation. When we approached the last phase of the preparation, trust between us was higher, and we could rely on each other, so we could share information and ideas with each other. This is because we were together in the ups and downs in each single step. The time was an*

| Front-end sub-phase | Strength of ties | Cooperation and coordination | Scarcity of knowledge |
|---|---|---|---|
| Idea generation | Weak | Low | High |
| Idea development | Strong | Medium | Medium |
| Evaluation and definition | Strong | High | Low |

**Table 5.**
*Social network attributes related to the relational dimension.*

*important factor to build trust and it increased after the middle phase of the preparation till the end' (Channel Events & Brand Activation Team Leader, Company2).*

The relationship between tie strength and decisions and stakeholder value creation in the front end of projects was evident. The 31 interviewees explained in more than 66 occasions that strong ties and trusting relationships had led them to achieve multiple advantages, including promoting knowledge exchange, bridging interest gaps, encouraging extra cooperation and supporting easier and faster delivery. However, strong ties were not without disadvantages as they required extra effort and emotional intensity to keep and limited distant network actor suggestions in a way that confined the understanding of network actors to the views of their close ties.

Although the identified relational network attributes were common in most projects, they can vary based on the structure and business dynamics of companies. Since the three companies employ non-dedicated teams (i.e. employees reported to both functional and project managers), some projects involved actors who already had existing ties due to previous experience working together. These projects, as found with nine interviewees, showed slightly different social network dynamics throughout the front end. Actors within these networks exhibited more readiness to have high interaction frequency from the idea generation phase onward because they did not need to spend time deciding on their partnerships:

*'Because I have been in Company3 for seven years, and in the Marketing team for almost three years, relationships were already built. I already knew other people and there was no big gap between us because we worked together on several projects. So, the relationships were not only from this project, but also built from other projects and still developing' (Marketing Team Leader, Company3).*

*'I think our relationships do not come in one project and disappear in another; they are built over the years. I have had almost fourteen years in Company1, which is a long time during which I established trust. Healthy relationships come from good experiences and trust, and feeling that each party is careful about the success of the other and the project we are working on. Once all parties feel that you are responsible and trustable, and that you are not faking communication just to avoid blaming, they will be interested in building a good relationship with you' [Business Development Manager, Company1].*

Actors within networks were compromising the risk and cost of committing to a strong tie with the reciprocal benefits that can be obtained. This explains why in Company2, as an early mover in the market, building strong ties and trusting relationships used to require extra time and scrutiny to decide on the credibility of other actors and to guarantee confidentiality when introducing new solutions. Company1 and Company3 (but especially the former) had different dynamics, since actors exhibited easier development of strong ties as these companies are usually late movers in following the technological trends set by Company2, which further supports and develops the second research proposition:

- *P2: Project networks that evolve from weak into stronger ties optimise stakeholder value through promoting trusting partnerships and cooperation that assist in making relevant decisions and increase the likelihood of idea adoption.*

### 4.3 Cognitive network attributes

This dimension explores actors' understanding of project ideas, needs and goals; both the level of similarity and how it changes throughout the front-end for better alignment. The last finding insists on building mutual understanding and a similar background within project networks to optimise stakeholder value in the front end. Bridging mental and business gaps among actors was necessary to avoid divergence in understanding project underpinnings (**Figure 4**). Mutual understanding helps blend the needs and requirements of network actors (i.e. idea generation) into commonly shared objectives (i.e. idea development) that are later finalised in a convincing project proposal submitted to decision-makers to be agreed on (i.e. evaluation and definition).

As shown in **Figure 4**, in the idea generation phase in which the kick-off meeting takes place as the first formal point of discussion, divergent understandings of the project vision were found to surface due to the diverse backgrounds of the actors involved. Network actors, in this early phase, were cognitively biased to perceive ideas and concepts in a way that better serves their own interests and priorities. Such behaviour was reinforced by the existence of many weak ties and the poor cooperation and coordination among network actors:

> *'One of the reasons why this project was delayed is that each party had different interests. We had two major stakeholders and each one needed something from the project that the other did not care about. The first one is from the Business side, and only wanted to launch to claim digitalising a product. While the main interest of the other Technical guy was to deliver the new product rather than the old product; the Technical team only wants to deliver' [Project Management Office Manager, Company1].*

In the idea development phase, having closer ties and dense communications facilitated similar understanding among network actors. This was more noticeable in projects where networks were early finalised, which allowed for a longer period of adaptation needed for actors to be aligned through framing mutual interpretations of ideas and concepts:

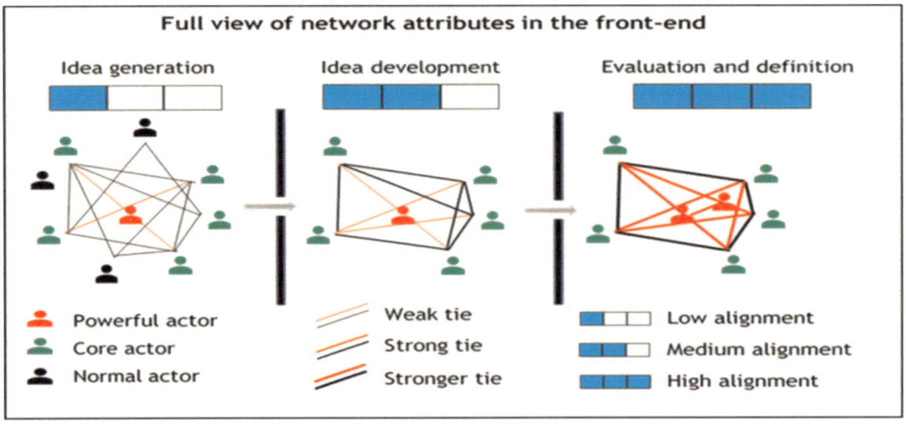


**Figure 4.**
*The full network attributes preferred for optimised stakeholder value.*

*'Close the whole cycle from day one, and if it is not closed from early stages, you can keep closing it. You have to list all areas down to know that this is a pending area that is still open. But never ever complete the development without closing all areas. You also need to clarify related stakeholders at early stages to know the remaining areas or the pending tasks in this project, so not to miss them later on' [Product Development Manager, Company1].*

With more engagement of powerful actors in the evaluation phase, network actors were able to reach some sort of final compromise about their needs and goals. Powerful actors, because of their holistic views gained from their central positions, managed to trigger collaboration efforts to inform project actors about the reasons for their recruitment and the top management expectations from their streams. These efforts also allowed the top management to envisage the potential outcomes, which helped them amending their decision-making criteria to meet network capabilities and ease actors' agreement on project objectives (**Table 6**):

*'Everything went well in this project because, as the assigned Project Manager, I used to describe everything to everyone. I started at the very beginning to clarify the goal of the project to them and what we need from each one of them, and why they were invited. It is very important to prepare this ahead because it is the responsibility of the Project Manager to clarify to the team why they are joining the project, and then to point roles or tasks to each one of them' [Marketing Manager, Company3].*

*'In the start of the preparation, the project vision was not the same for us all. In the middle of the preparation, I think we shared eighty percent of the project vision and with time, it started to increase. In the end of the preparation, the project vision became clearer for all of us as we had more opportunity to meet and discuss the project idea and its ultimate goal' [Agile Supervisor & Application Development Specialist, Company1].*

New project concepts that involve less extant knowledge usually accept various interpretations and trigger cognitive gaps. These concepts require long time and extra creativity from network actors to realise their mutual value. They also require having a common language to collectively understand and exploit the available tacit and explicit knowledge. This ensures the development of these concepts fits with overall organisational objectives. The following compares the difficulties faced by project actors when dealing with both completely new and well-established project concepts in the exact same context (i.e. Company2):

*'In the preparation phase, it was hard to be aligned together since the project was completely different with zero commercial goals. When we were trying to set the budget*

| Front-end sub-phase | Divergence of understanding | Alignment of actors | Disparity of objectives |
|---|---|---|---|
| Idea generation | High | Low | High |
| Idea development | Medium | Medium | Medium |
| Evaluation and definition | Low | High | Low |

**Table 6.**
*Social network attributes related to the cognitive dimension.*

*for this project, we started to negotiate and to brief about the outcome that we want to achieve. It was actually hard in the beginning of the preparation to be aligned with all stakeholders' [Channel, Events & Brand Activations Team Leader, Company2].*

*'With time moving forward, things were getting clearer, and everyone started to understand the vision of the project in the same way. The project idea was easily agreed because it bridges a gap that everyone could see. All participants in the preparation of the project were aware of its topic and were well prepared. It was noticed that everyone had enough knowledge about the purpose, the details and the goals of the project' [Sales Support & Development Analyst, Company2].*

In both situations, twenty-three interviewees explained that selecting the right communication channels to discuss project concepts was important to improve actor alignment. While formal patterns were insufficient to reduce divergence in sense-making, flexible patterns (i.e. formal and informal) were enough to encourage effective discussions to agree on project objectives:

*'Having misunderstandings or different opinions over a matter happens in all projects. We have different mindsets, and at the end of the day, I may understand something that my colleagues might not understand in the same way. But we usually discuss and get to a middle area either through a meeting or a phone call; it depends on how many people are involved and who are the people I am dealing with' (Value Adding Services Expert, Company3].*

*'It is important to select the right communication method; when to communicate verbally, via emails or by having a meeting. This is because meetings may waste stakeholders' time, so they stop responding to other meeting calls. Stakeholders must feel that they are spending their time on something that adds value, instead of reading emails to agree on vague points' [Product Development Manager, Company1].*

*'I learned that by setting the right communication at the right time using the right channel, I can reach people and make them work together to overcome obstacles; and by having a clear vision from the beginning that sticks in the minds of everybody, I can achieve better results' [Consumer Experience & Quality Director, Company3].*

It is worth mentioning that in a couple of projects, alleviating the distraction caused by the functional departments of network actors was critical to minimise the impact of their business backgrounds on the understanding of project concepts. In these situations, actors had to separate the locations in which they meet to discuss project concepts (e.g. designated meeting rooms, subsidiary locations) from their functional locations where they perform their day-to-day routine work (e.g. offices, company meeting rooms), which facilitated better alignment:

*'When we wanted the team members to be isolated to minimise the business interruption, we invited them to have brainstorming sessions in [the name of a subsidiary business incubator]. We used to reserve a room there to meet all and discuss the project. We used to make sure that all stakeholders are included to exchange ideas and be able to come up with a document that is agreed by all of us in the end of this session' (Product Development Manager, Company1).*

*'In the beginning of the project, I tried to create a family-like environment, which triggered the idea of the Fibre Wareroom. The Fibre Wareroom is a room where we brought all team leaders who were working on the Fibre project to have open discussion meetings. These meetings had no dedicated time because in the beginning of the project, we needed to have communication between people who were not communicating very well before. So, we had to make them feel important and have what is needed to deliver and achieve our global target' [Fibre Project Manager, Company3].*

The choice of suitable communication channels for an organisation is understood in terms of its workplace and market environments. Company1 and Company3 (but especially the former) place more value on personal relationships and tend to use flexible discussions and dialogues. Company2, on the other hand, is more process-oriented, and for that reason, it has less flexibility. Although flexible communications may be recommended, the choice of Company2 is justifiable since it is the market leader, which forces communicating behind closed doors and with highly conservative networks of actors to avoid any leakage of information.

Developing a mutual understanding of project ideas, needs and goals is necessary not only for better network alignment but also to motivate actors by increasing their knowledge about the value of their engagement. Actors who are not properly involved in project visions show fewer links to strategic objectives, thus providing shallow contributions. This explains why in the satisfying projects, effective discussions were frequently taking place to reflect on project ideas and concepts and to enhance actors' exploitation of knowledge, leading to acceptable project definitions. This confirms and develops the third research proposition:

- *P3: Building a mutual understanding among network actors triggers collaboration efforts that stimulate alignment around objectives to amend decision-making criteria and increases the likelihood of project idea adoption.*

## 5. Discussion

### 5.1 Answering the research questions

The research findings suggested a correlation between carefully facilitated social capital and optimised project stakeholder value. They identified a comprehensive set of network attributes that commonly occur in the front end of most satisfying projects. Following is a reflection on how these findings answer the two research questions.

The first question is: how does social capital help in managing knowledge and optimising stakeholder value in the front end of projects? Social capital (e.g. actor power, tie strength) was found to promote knowledge creation and exchange and organisational learning. Proper social capital, which is defined based on the identified network attributes, enables creative ideas to come through, thus determining the likelihood of the developed solutions to meet stakeholders' objectives. In contrast, too much social capital such as excessive interactions and uncontrolled relationships leads to wasted resources and unwelcome behaviours (e.g. high information load, irrelevant conversations, procedural breaches and siloing and antisocial behaviours).

Social capital is not like any other project resource (e.g. time, money and technology) where always more is better; it should be wisely used to avoid scope creeps and catastrophic consequences. For example, while lower stakeholder alignment around project objectives in the idea generation phase promotes creative insights and diverse suggestions, it hinders arriving at an acceptable project definition if it continues to occur in the development and evaluation phases. Social capital hence should not be haphazardly channelled within project networks, but should be reviewed according to their unique nature and needs as well as the ultimate front-end goals to optimise stakeholder value.

The second research question is: what social network attributes should be maintained to facilitate decisions and optimise stakeholder value in the front end of projects? Networks should include a larger group of actors with multiple weak ties and high interaction in the idea generation phase (**Table** 7). Although these network attributes may spark issues of control and lower alignment, they allow for accessing a broader range of internal and external knowledge and facilitate novel concepts. In the idea development phase, networks are recommended to move into focused groups with more cohesive and strong ties and higher interaction among core actors. This allows extra focus on essential expansion aspects to better shape and validate project ideas to fit with the strategic orientation of organisations.

Moving to the evaluation and project definition phase, higher engagement of stream leaders and decision-makers should take place to facilitate effective discussions and encourage alignment around objectives. This higher interaction with desirable network actors assists in building stronger ties and mutual understanding towards the evaluation phase, which raises the likelihood of project definition consensus and idea adoption.

## 5.2 Theoretical implications

Building on prior research exploring projects as networks of interorganisatioal relationships [4], this paper identified a list of social network attributes that should be sought throughout the front end to ensure a higher probability of project ideas adoption. The list extends the one from Kijkuit and Van Den Ende [21] through covering detailed attributes within the structural, relational and cognitive dimensions of social networks and discussing the dynamisms in which these attributes interact to optimise stakeholder value. It also contains some discrepancies to previously identified network

| Front-end sub-phase<br>Dimensional attributes | | Idea generation | Idea development | Evaluation and definition |
|---|---|---|---|---|
| Structural | Level of interaction | High | High | High |
| | Network cohesion | Low | High | High |
| | Powerful actors' involvement | Low | Medium | High |
| Relational | Strength of ties | Weak | Strong | Strong |
| | Cooperation and coordination | Low | Medium | High |
| | Scarcity of knowledge | High | Medium | Low |
| Cognitive | Divergence of understanding | High | Medium | Low |
| | Alignment of actors | Low | Medium | High |
| | Disparity of objectives | High | Medium | Low |

**Table 7.**
*The full list of attributes within network dimensions.*

attributes, particularly the ones unique to the explorative, highly dynamic and fast-changing telecommunication sector.

When looking at key works from Kijkuit and Van Den Ende [21], Morris [1], Stevens [24], Matinheikki et al. [7] and Sydow and Braun [4], this paper offered a holistic view of how stakeholder value is optimised in the front end of projects. A view focusing on the dimensional elements of social capital and networks to promote innovation capabilities and induce value creation. It is a view that fits with the 'age of relevancy' issued by Morris [1] to ensure that stakeholders' needs and goals are driving project initiatives. This revolutionises project management through providing relevant social indicators of project performance outcomes.

### 5.3 Practical implications

Social interactions and relationships within projects are usually dealt with as a secondary resource managed on a situational basis. To explain, project managers only take actions to address social issues when they occur, without having a prepared framework to govern them. These situational responses are insufficient to capture the benefits of social capital. Changing the managerial perception about social capital to be perceived as an essential determinant of stakeholder value is necessary in modern project management. Project managers should focus on developing strategic planning and communication competencies to be able to facilitate proper stakeholder engagement and relevant project outcomes.

Project managers and decision- and strategy-makers can use the proposed list of network attributes to decide on social dynamisms preferred to navigate the project to its objectives. These include actor interaction, tie strength, trust and alignment, as well as when it is best for these elements to take place and their respective weights, which cannot be allowed to be random. It is of high significance for decision-makers to decide on these elements to avoid their dark side. This paper explained several occasions where social capital was administered to reduce the dominance of specific actors and control their engagement in front-end decision-making. A lesson to emphasise is that social capital cannot be optimal at any end of the spectrum; it is optimal when wisely balanced in light of its distinct contextual conditions.

Top management must invest in both formal and informal project relationships. Such approach fits with recent PMI updates for its PMBOK™ Guide that included stakeholder management as one of the ten project management knowledge areas [37]. As noticed in the explored companies, projects where managers supported the development of relationships reported higher stakeholder satisfaction. On the other hand, projects where relationships were restricted, especially the informal ones, reported more tiresome micromanagement precautions. It is recommended thus that top management invests in activities that aim to invigorate both formal and informal bonds among project stakeholders (**Figure 5**).

Project managers must be engaged from the outset to participate in the generation of project visions. Traditional perspectives of project management restricted the role of project managers to planning and controlling the execution of downstream activities, which led to two-thirds of projects worldwide deemed as failures [38]. Keeping the project manager remote from the front end creates a gap between what is originally envisaged and what happens in reality. Modern and future project management is required to emphasise a social view where project managers are involved from early phases to reflect on project visions and link them to stakeholder needs, requirements and objectives to enhance their value accrual and guarantee their satisfaction.

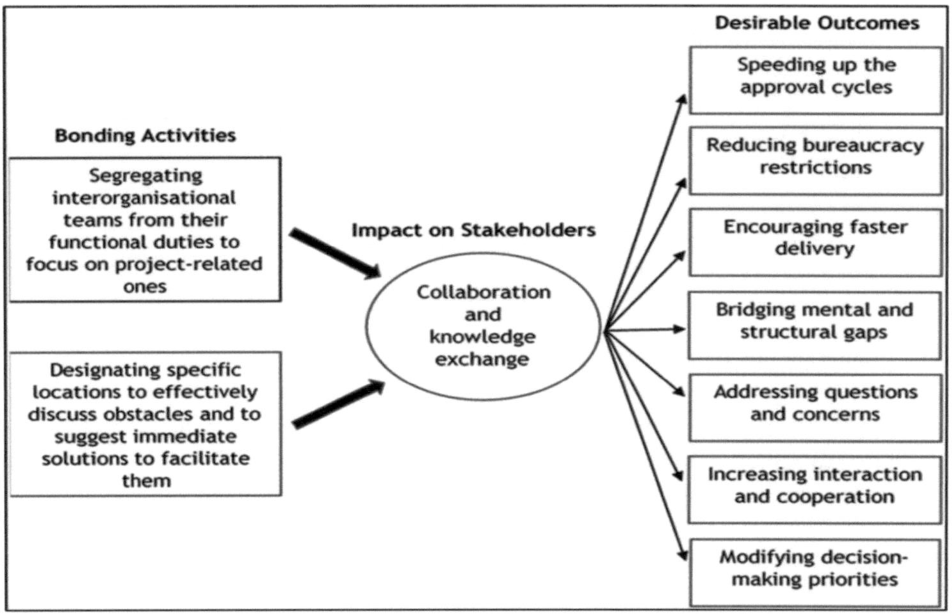


**Figure 5.**
*Bonding activities and their desirable outcomes.*

## 6. Conclusion

This paper employed a three-dimensional lens to explore the impact of social capital and networks on the value created for stakeholders in the front end of projects. The paper sought to develop a holistic understanding of the dynamisms that govern the use of social networks and resources to increase the probability of project ideas adoption. To do so, it linked the extant literature about social capital impact on organisational performance to the management of the front-end phase that is characterised with a highly fuzzy and explorative nature.

The central conclusion of the paper is the necessity of redirecting the efforts of project management researchers and practitioners from the basic notions of how to secure extra organisational resources to developing efficient ways of using what is available. This efficiency can only be generated in the minds of employees and stakeholders; thus, knowledge and social resources must be the focus. The ability of project stakeholders to collectively utilise their tacit and explicit knowledge is critical for modern project management. Having limited resources is a common project constraint that must trigger novel and creative concepts and outputs to allow organisations to achieve their sustainability and expansion goals.

Creating value in the front-end of projects is dependent on the willingness of stakeholders to utilise their social resources to reduce fuzziness. This requires managing both the internal and external network channels to encourage their collaboration. Similar insights are not new in the organisational theory, but are unclear in terms of the restraining dynamics in project management, particularly in that on the front end. The paper explored how social relationships are key in controlling interaction and collaboration within project networks and how they disseminate knowledge to provide a conventional context for decision-making. The paper also explained how these social relationships are tied to the variations in the power and positions of actors within project networks, which determines their access to knowledge, thus their importance and centrality for front-end stakeholder value optimisation.

Social network attributes decide the level of knowledge creation, exchange and exploitation, which affects stakeholders' perceptions of value. Project networks that have high interactions, strong relationships, intense communications and the right engagement of actors are more likely to develop creative and innovative ideas. The combination of these attributes constitutes the limits of using stakeholders' social capital resources, which are then moulded according to the unique circumstances and confidentiality of the project and the changes in the market dynamics of the parent organisations. This forms the basis of the ability of stakeholders to come out with a sophisticated project proposal and an agreed definition that reflects their needs and expectations and that is then perceived to be satisfying on all business levels.

## Abbreviations

| | |
|---|---|
| PM | project management |
| PMI | project management institution |
| APM | association for project management |
| SH | stakeholder |
| PJM | project manager |
| PPM | principal project manager |
| PO | project owner |
| PMO | project management office |
| PT | project team |
| PMBOK | project management body of knowledge |
| FE | front-end |
| SCT | social capital theory |
| SNA | social network analysis |
| CPM | critical path method |
| PERT | program evaluation review technique |

## Author details

Hakem Sharari
Department of Business Administration, Al-Ahliyya Amman University, Amman, Jordan

*Address all correspondence to: h.sharari@ammanu.edu.jo

## References


[1] Morris PWG. Reconstructing Project Management. Chichester, UK: John Wiley & Sons; 2013

[2] Aaltonen K, Kujala J, Havela L, Savage G. Stakeholder dynamics during the project front-end: the case of nuclear waste repository projects. Project Management Journal. 2015;**46**(6):15-41

[3] Edkins A, Geraldi J, Morris P, Smith A. Exploring the front-end of project management. Engineering Project Organization Journal. 2013;**3**(2): 71-85

[4] Sydow J, Braun T. Projects as temporary organizations: An agenda for further theorizing the interorganizational dimension. SSRN Electronic Journal. 2018;**36**(1):4-11

[5] Laursen M, Svejvig P. Taking stock of project value creation: a structured literature review with future directions for research and practice. International Journal of Project Management. 2016; **34**(4):736-747

[6] Sharari H, Paton RA, Smart A. Project fuzziness to project value: the role of social capital. VINE Journal of Information and Knowledge Management Systems. 2022 (ahead-of-print)

[7] Matinheikki J, Artto K, Peltokorpi A, Rajala R. Managing inter-organizational networks for value creation in the front-end of projects. International Journal of Project Management. 2016;**34**(7): 1226-1241

[8] Morris PWG. The Management of Projects. London, UK: T. Telford; 1994

[9] Hong P, Nahm AY, Doll WJ. The role of project target clarity in an uncertain project environment. International Journal of Operations and Production Management. 2004;**24**(2):1269-1291

[10] Artto K, Kulvik I, Poskela J, Turkulainen V. The integrative role of the project management office in the front end of innovation. International Journal of Project Management. 2011;**29**(4):408-421

[11] Nahapiet J, Ghoshal S. Social capital, intellectual capital, and the organizational advantage. Academy of Management Review. 1998;**23**(2):242-266

[12] Tsai W, Ghoshal S. Social capital and value creation: the role of intrafirm networks. Academy of Management Journal. 1998;**41**(4):464-476

[13] Krackhardt D, Stern R. Informal networks and organizational crises: an experimental simulation. Social Psychology Quarterly. 1988;**51**(2):123

[14] Inkpen A, Tsang E. Social capital, networks, and knowledge transfer. Academy of Management Review. 2005; **30**(1):146-165

[15] Jensen R, Szulanski G. Stickiness and the adaptation of organisational practices in cross-border knowledge transfers. Journal of International Business Studies. 2004;**35**(6):508-523

[16] Lin N. Building a network theory of social capital. In: Social Capital. New York: Routledge; 2017. pp. 3-28

[17] Bourdieu P. Forms of capital. In: Richards JC, editor. Handbook of Theory and Research for the Sociology of Education. New York: Greenwood Press; 1986. pp. 241-258

[18] Hackman J, Oldham G. Work Redesign. Reading, MA: Addison-Wesley; 1980

[19] Portes A. Social capital: Its origins and applications in modern sociology. Annual Review of Modern Sociology. 1998;**24**:1-24

[20] Field J. Social Capital. London: Routledge; 2003

[21] Kijkuit B, Van Den Ende J. The organizational life of an idea: integrating social network, creativity and decision-making perspectives. Journal of Management Studies. 2007;**44**(6): 863-882

[22] Perry-Smith J. Social yet creative: the role of social relationships in facilitating individual creativity. Academy of Management Journal. 2006;**49**(1):85-101

[23] Hansen M. The search-transfer problem: the role of weak ties in sharing knowledge across organisation subunits. Administrative Science Quarterly. 1999; **44**(1):82-111

[24] Stevens E. Fuzzy front-end learning strategies: Exploration of a high-tech company. Technovation. 2014;**34**(8): 431-440

[25] Denzin NL, Lincoln Y. Handbook of Qualitative Research. Thousand Oaks, CA: Sage Publications; 1994

[26] Patton MQ. Qualitative Evaluation and Research Methods. London: SAGE Publications; 1990

[27] Patton MQ. Qualitative Research and Evaluation Methods. London: SAGE Publications; 2002

[28] Morris T, Wood S. Testing the survey method: continuity and change in British industrial relations. Work Employment and Society. 1991;**5**(2):259-282

[29] Knights D, McCabe D. How would you measure something like that? Quality in a retail bank. Journal of Management Studies. 1997;**34**(3):371-388

[30] Bryman A, Bell E. Research Methods and Organisation Studies. London: Routledge; 2003

[31] Guest G, Bunce A, Johnson L. How many interviews are enough? An experiment with data saturation and variability. Field Methods. 2006;**18**(1): 59-82

[32] Tay I. To what extent should data saturation be used as a quality criterion in qualitative research. Pulse. 2014. Available from: www.linkedin.com/pulse/20140824092647-82509310-to-whatextent-should-data-saturation-be-used-as-a-quality-criterion-in-qualitative-research

[33] Harding J. Qualitative Data Analysis: from Start to Finish. London: SAGE Publications; 2018

[34] Corbin J, Strauss A. Basics of Qualitative Research: Techniques and Procedures for Developing Grounded Theory. Thousand Oaks, CA: SAGE Publications; 2008

[35] Saldaña J. The Coding Manual for Qualitative Researchers. London: SAGE Publications; 2015

[36] Bogdan RC, Biklen SK. Qualitative Research in Education: An Introduction to Theory and Methods. Boston, Mass: Pearson A&B; 2006

[37] Project Management Institute. A Guide to the Project Management Body of Knowledge (PMBOK® Guide - Sixth Edition). Newtown Square. 2017

[38] Project Management Institute. A Guide to the Project Management Body of Knowledge (PMBOK® Guide - Seventh Edition). Newtown Square. 2021

## Chapter 10

# Knowledge Management as a Prism to Better Distinguish Useful Forms Derived from or Inspired by Games or Play Activities

*Stéphane Goria*

## Abstract

Games, play and, by extension, gamification, or playification activities can be seen as sources of inspiration for the development of many and varied devices. The scientific literature on the subject and the tools, activities, or systems used are in full development and focus as much on the characteristics of the forms as on the characteristics of the components themselves. It therefore seemed appropriate and justified to link these uses to knowledge management. Indeed, each aspect of knowledge management can be associated with one or more categories of serious games, serious play, game with a purpose, game-derived, etc. Knowledge management can thus be used as a model for a meta-analysis of game-derived forms employed within organizations. It seems equally relevant to us to reflexively question the categories of jobs inspired by and derived from games, and to define their main characteristics, as contributions to the strands of knowledge management. A whole field of practice and study can thus be revealed at the intersection of those of knowledge management and forms of devices or professional tasks more or less inspired by games.

**Keywords:** serious game, game with a purpose, game for purpose, wargame, empathic game, agile game, serious play, serious gaming, gamification, gameful design, playful design, disengamement, knowledge acquisition, knowledge capitalization, knowledge creation, knowledge mapping, knowledge sharing

## 1. Introduction

The game has taken an important place in our societies. Its use can be purely recreational, but it can also be motivated by an additional utilitarian purpose, independent of leisure. It is within this context that we consider knowledge management in this chapter as a means of considering all these new types of jobs, more or less diverted or inspired by games. This perspective is not fundamentally original. We share it with other researchers [1–11]. However, these works only present a particular vision, an aspect, of what exists as forms inspired by play or games in connection with knowledge management, or propose a very quick review of the main existing categories. This chapter provides a more comprehensive overview. Thus, like other authors [12–17], we approach knowledge management by expressing it through five main components or sub-processes, which we group as follows: (A) identification and mapping of knowledge, (B) acquisition and updating of knowledge (present in the organization), (C) sharing and use of knowledge, (D) formalization and capitalization of knowledge, (E) creation and transfer of knowledge for innovation. As we progress, we discuss a variety of forms derived from games contributing to each of these processes. We cannot be exhaustive, as these forms are numerous and varied [18], but we aim to give you a sufficiently broad and varied overview to allow you to have a fairly comprehensive idea of the existing major categories. However, before addressing these categories, it seems necessary for us to define what a game can be and, by extension, a serious form derived from games.

## 2. Play and games characteristics

Games and play give rise to multiple proposals that draw more or less inspiration to solve problems and provide support that goes well beyond the playful sphere. In fact, to have a correct understanding of this field of applications, it seems important to quickly discuss the main characteristics of purely playful forms and then focus on serious gaming forms.

For at least 70 years, gaming activities have been perceived as distinct from non-gaming activities. We have a set of criteria to characterize them, inherited from Johan Huizinga [19] at the international level and from Roger Caillois [20] in a more Francophone context. According to these two authors, an activity can be qualified as a game if it meets the following conditions:

- it must be practiced freely by its players;
- its boundaries must be recognizable in spatial and temporal dimensions;
- from the players' point of view, it must be easily possible to distinguish a limited duration, that is, a playtime (at least, its beginning and end) and the boundaries of the space that accommodates it;
- the activity must be subject to accept and known rules by its players;
- it must be an escape from reality (be fictional).

These characteristics are common to all games/play and contribute to establishing the identity of each one. Roger Caillois added to Huizinga's characteristics the conditions of unproductivity and uncertainty in the course of the game or play. The unproductive nature means that the game itself does not produce anything. As for the unproductivity aspect, it requires that players cannot predict the entirety of the game's progression, including its duration. Moreover, Caillois also removed the requirement for the development of a feeling of tension and joy on the part of the players, which Huizinga had among his characteristics but did not find in games played seriously.

By proposing that the activity be unproductive rather than free (as initially proposed by Huizinga), Caillois incorporates the possibility of transferring goods from one player to another within the framework of a game [20]. The total amount of money involved in the game at the beginning must be the same at the end of the game. This allows for the inclusion of games such as Poker and other Casino games in this definition. However, in the case of Lotteries, there is a concern, as typically a portion of the money wagered is used to fund another activity (e.g., a charity). To still consider these activities as unproductive, it is possible to view the funding that motivates them as an entry fee that the player must pay to access a game, but this distorts Caillois's criterion of unproductivity slightly.

With these last two examples of games, the issue of the association between seriousness and play arises. According to Caillois, games can already be considered as serious forms of play in terms of concentration and involvement of at least some players regarding the amounts that can be won (or lost). Similarly, the contextual situation and the stakes involved can make the game much more serious than it should be. Let us recall, for example, the chess matches between Bobby Fischer and Boris Spassky or those of Garry Kasparov and Deep Blue.

For Huizinga, the perspective is slightly different; the playful nature is superior to seriousness and prevails over the latter. However, with these two authors, we remain within the framework of classical games, with the exception of certain cultural cases, such as religious ones (e.g., the case of the whirling dervishes).

But these two authors have avoided discussing other forms closely resembling games that have been regularly used for at least a few centuries, particularly by the military [21] or educators [22]. Thus, educational or simulation games (including wargames or kriegspiels) do not meet the majority of the criteria of Huizinga and Caillois to be qualified as games. Even if we set aside the criterion of unproductivity, considering that there will only be a transfer of information or knowledge, it seems challenging not to consider these games as unimposed (the teacher or military superior imposing to "play"). Similarly, it is difficult to argue that these games are fully distinct from real activities (even more so in the case of simulation games, including wargames).

We will delve into some of these forms of games designed for serious purposes in more detail. However, since we just talked about it, we need to already put into perspective what we mean by a serious objective. Indeed, this serious objective is relative to the person who has identified it and is trying to achieve it through play. It can be difficult to determine whether the situation falls under a form of serious play or not. For example, how would you qualify the situation of a parent who, to accomplish a task (serious objective) at home, encourages their somewhat unruly child to play on a console (playful context)?

From the perspective of the encouraging parent, the game is intended to achieve a serious objective (having a moment of peace to work). From the child's point of view, if the proposal is appealing to them, they at least feel they have the freedom to play.

It is therefore quite challenging to define what a game or play can be, and even more difficult to deduce what a serious game, a game-inspired structure, a serious playful activity, or a serious activity in the context of play is, etc. There have been attempts at synthesis, such as that of Wardaszko [23], from which we draw the fundamentals. In his doctoral thesis, Wardaszko identified 16 criteria to define a game based on about 10 definitions proposed by various experts in the field. However, in the table he produced, it is observed that only two criteria are in consensus or nearly so: (1) a game includes rules that guide and limit the players in what they can do, and (2) there is an objective or results to be achieved at the end of the game. However, these two criteria alone are not sufficient to qualify an activity or structure as a game, including serious games. Indeed, if we attempt a definition by reciprocal, there are far too many structures or activities that do not fall under the category of games (e.g., the development of a business project follows the rules, presents objectives, and results to achieve). Therefore, we adopt a third criterion to define a game, drawn from a French author and game specialist: Henriot [24]. Among his works, he had mentioned the problem of defining what a game or a game activity is, as the perception of what a game is also depends on culture, era, and thus the viewpoint. We adopt his criterion, which qualifies a (3) activity or a structure that resembles another recognized game as such.

Thus, the three Game criteria (G1, G2, and G3) used to qualify a game or a game activity are as follows: A game or activity must (G1) strongly resemble a form already recognized as a game or game activity, (G2) have rules guiding the players, and (G3) aim for an objective to be achieved that motivates or justifies, at least in part, the interest in playing it. In addition, we add four other Play criteria (P1, P2, P3, and P4) that reinforce the playful aspect more than they characterize it. We adopt as the first Play criterion the one from Huizinga, specifying that (P1) the activity is more game-like if it also creates a feeling of tension and joy among its players. We note, however, that this criterion is redundant since it reinforces the one of similarity to another game and is also quite difficult to assess (observation or questioning of players is required to determine it). Two Play criteria are borrowed from Caillois. Criterion (P2) concerns the uncertainty of the game's progression. It can justify the game itself (trial and error, exploration of possibilities, challenges to overcome...). It is understood that criteria (P1) and (P2) are closely related, as the uncertainty of an outcome itself creates a form of tension during the activity and potential joy in case of success, even partial. The criterion (P3) is that of play freedom, which we propose in the form of a corollary. In a serious context, there is play freedom if at least one non-playful alternative is offered to individuals to perform the same tasks or activities. Depending on the cases, non-players may not wish to participate in a serious game or a gamified activity [25], while in other cases, it is the players who may reject a form of serious game that they do not recognize, while non-players may appreciate this change [26]. By leaving the choice of engagement or non-engagement in a gamified activity or structure, we can involve all individuals. It also allows for alternating roles and limiting issues of fatigue related to the repetition of the same activities.

We thus have minimum criteria to define a game, while the level of seriousness that may or may not be associated with it depends on the context of game use and the engagement of the people participating, considered as players. Therefore, there are forms of serious games that are closer to pure ludic games and others that are more distant. Of course, there is a somewhat difficult boundary to place, beyond which the practice or structure considered cannot be classified as a game. We will also see when we apply this in a serious setting that it is preferable to add an (P4) criterion to the criteria already set out, so that the game is not a tool for manipulating people. Indeed, this would run counter to the ply principle itself.

## 3. Serious games, serious play, gamification, and others playful or gameful inspirations

The list of various game or play-inspired structures and activities to achieve a serious purpose is quite extensive. In this section, the most well-known and complementary ones will be presented to you.

### 3.1 Serious games

The expression serious game was used in the sense it is now attributed in a book dedicated to the subject published in 1970 by Clark Abt [27], but it took a few years and the development of serious video games for the term to be widely employed. However, the utility games discussed in Abt's book were not video games, which can be explained by the year of publication. Nevertheless, in the early 2000s, a sort of equivalence between serious games and serious video games was made. This is undoubtedly due to the success of video games since the 1970s and the relatively discreet development of other forms of serious games until the last 20 years. We will see that there are many forms of games related to knowledge management, and whether they are digital or not does not matter much. But before we establish a connection between forms of serious games and knowledge management sub-processes, let us first review some of the most well-known of these forms.

As mentioned earlier in this chapter, the field of education has been the most fruitful with learning or educational games (edutainment, Edugames, learning games). However, from the very beginning, serious games do not necessarily serve as a support for acquiring knowledge or exercising skills specific to a single discipline. Depending on the learning strategies implemented through games, the approach can be multidisciplinary, blending communication, informational, linguistic, managerial, and pedagogical skills [28]. Then, other categories of serious games have appeared, dedicated to training or exercise through simulation (exergames), advertising (advergames), information (newsgames), art (artgames), data collection (datagames), etc.

What these serious games have in common, in addition to the three fundamental criteria mentioned above, is that they are structures expressly designed as game structures (if the outcome is successful) so that the people using them find them as enjoyable as games, but with the complementary objective of achieving a serious goal by employing them (learning, improving, being informed, raising awareness, creating a work of art, ...). Most of these serious games have attempted to be appreciated and create a sense of joy among their players, without necessarily succeeding often. Of course, we must also include military serious games (wargames) and their practice (wargaming), dedicated to both training, exercise, and exploration of tactics or other possible choices. However, the designers of these latter forms have not attempted to make the gameplay fun; on the contrary, the military domain imposes seriousness in the very practice of a form of the game [29].

### 3.2 Games with a purpose

These forms of games have generated others, among which is the category of Games With A Purpose (GWAP), also known as Games For (A) Purpose. These games are a derivative of Luis von Ahn's invention of CAPTCHAS (for: Completely Automated Public Turing test to tell Computers and Humans Apart) [30]. CAPTCHAS are designed to engage and employ a large number of people through a digital interface to assist in performing tasks that are not easily automated. Therefore, they represent a form of crowdsourcing. Shortly after, the same author, along with Laura Dabbish, proposed small games inspired by CAPTCHAS for annotating, particularly images [31]. This category was called ESP games for ExtraSensory Perception games [32]. Following this proposal and the enthusiasm generated by this type of serious games, new names were suggested, such as 'game-based crowdsourcing' or 'crowdsourcing-based game,' but it seems that the term GWAP is now the most widely used.

In this context, most GWAPs are based on soliciting and employing a large number of 'players,' who may be more or less voluntary contributors [33]. The early GWAPs were based on crowdsourcing, which led to the development of other games following the same principle. However, we found that the crowdsourcing aspect was not a necessary characteristic to distinguish GWAPs from other serious games, especially since it is possible to create games to solve problems (and thus qualify as GWAPs) by involving only a small group of participants. Such forms may be referred to as micro-crowdsourcing [34] or swarm gaming [35].

There is another criterion that differentiates a GWAP from other serious games more easily. In the case of a GWAP, the 'players' are workers whose work primarily contributes to another recipient. In a 'classic' serious game, the player is the recipient and, therefore, the beneficiary of the game's contribution, which is not the case with a GWAP. However, GWAPs must still be distinguished from certain gamified structures developed to encourage people to perform tasks for others at a lower cost, which Ian Bogost [36] calls 'exploitationware.' Therefore, among serious games that include GWAPs, there is another criterion to meet to avoid classifying them as exploitationwares or games based on player deception. In a genuine GWAP, participants are clearly informed, before starting the game, about the use of data or other benefits derived from the activity of employing the GWAP and its direct beneficiaries. Given its importance, this criterion is added to the Play criteria mentioned above as (P4).

### 3.3 Empathic games and other related games

Another branch of serious games that is quite close to both purely recreational games and GWAPs is that of persuasive games, which were named as such by I. Bogost during the second half of the 2000s. These are games designed to convey a message and influence the people who play them in order to raise awareness or convince them to change their beliefs or behavior regarding a given situation presented in the 'game' [37]. In this sense, they can be considered serious games of the goal-oriented type, whose main objective is to achieve a change in belief among the 'players,' even if, strictly speaking, they function in the opposite direction of GWAPs (from the game to the crowd rather than from the crowd to the game). In this sense, they are social serious games, meaning that their dissemination primarily occurs *via* social networks [38]. This aspect made us realize that goal-oriented games, qualified as such by their creators, generally announce their serious intention before the game starts, which is not necessarily the case with persuasive games.

Persuasive games would be a kind of empathic games (empathy serious games/ empathic serious games), and Martine Mauriras-Bousquet's definition [39] regarding business role-playing games seems to correspond to them if we generalize the context: 'designed to help executives put themselves in the shoes of their subordinates, understand their problems, and see things from their point of view.' Forgotten for several decades, these games have been the subject of research again and reappeared under this name, shortly after the term expressive games. However, it seems that this expression is mainly used to evoke games that emotionally engage the player, as in the case of *The Walking Dead* (Telltale Games) presented as an empathic game by Caballero [40]. From this perspective, Heidi McDonald [41] also includes romance games in this category.

Expressive games would be serious empathic games. With empathic games, these games often share the common feature of encouraging players, through their mechanics, to reflect on sensitive subjects based on sentimental content [42]. They impose reflection on a problematic situation experienced by others, while non-expressive empathic games only offer an additional experience based on mechanisms involving emotional stimuli. In a very similar vein, we can also mention a specific expressive game, which are designed as recreational games but have the dual function of prompting players, through the experience offered through the game, to reflect on a real problematic situation [43]. From this perspective, expressive games are ludic empathic games, meaning that they are positioned in contrast to persuasive games, which are empathic serious games. The entire category of empathic games would fall between these two opposing concepts.

### 3.4 Serious play and serious gaming

We have just discussed various games designed to achieve a serious purpose in a more or less playful manner. However, it is not always necessary to create a game to blend playfulness and seriousness. It is possible to use an existing game or components of a game and associate them with a method of use to guide people in a purposeful use of originally playful components. Among these types of usage, the *Lego Serious Play* method is emblematic. Imagined in 1995, this method is initially based on the use of the famous Lego bricks combined with a metaphorical reasoning to allow people to share a vision of a problem, exchange viewpoints on a situation, etc. After difficult beginnings and multiple modifications, this method found success in the early 2000s [44]. Due to its success and the alternative it offers to the design of serious games, this method has given rise to many others (*Playmobil Pro*, *Business origami, Minecraft serious play*).

Although the expression may be ambiguous, some authors [45–47] prefer to use the term serious gaming rather than serious play to better distinguish it from the method using Lego bricks. In this sense, when we talk about serious gaming, it refers to utility activities that involve repurposing a game structure for serious purposes. However, we note that other authors prefer to use the term serious gaming to signify that it refers to practices of serious games [48–51], or even to a set of utilitarian uses of serious games or non-serious games [52]. Bouko and Alvarez [47] prefer to use the term serious diverting to refer to forms of serious play, but this terminological usage is limited only to the publications of these authors. We prefer to use the term serious play, which is more widely used and seems less problematic in terms of interpretation, as it directly relates to the activity of play. However, to better distinguish serious play from serious gaming as the practice of a serious game, we add the specific criterion that serious play requires a person to accompany the players as a facilitator (or even a referee) of the activity. This can be a participant who takes on this particular role, but in this case, their practice will be different from that of other participants, as they will guide and encourage them without directly participating in the reflections and choices of the other players.

### 3.5 Approaches combining serious game design and serious play

There is at least one form of practice that combines the design of serious games and serious play. We have already mentioned this one, which is quite ancient: wargaming. This activity, primarily conducted by military and diplomatic personnel, takes various forms. In one way or another, it involves having a game based on a map and reasoning, argumentation, movement, confrontation mechanisms, etc., presenting a specific situation and at least one objective for which the participants/players must reflect and provide at least one response. Depending on the problems and related needs, the activity varies. It may involve designing a dedicated game or simply adapting an existing game, which will lead to one or more game sessions. These sessions can take place in various formats, such as seminar wargames [53], course of action wargames [54], red teaming wargames [54], matrix games [55], depending on the intended purpose. In these cases, unless the objective is personnel training (where using a pre-existing game is possible), the design or adaptation of a game is the first part of a process aimed at addressing a specific problem, and the practical implementation (game activity) is the second part, thereby increasing the possibilities offered.

In terms of characteristic criteria for these forms, they are simulation games requiring a facilitator and a referee (it can be the same person), as well as the design of at least one scenario and a map representing a past, current, or potential situation as a starting point for the game, along with rules and mechanisms based on real data. Additionally, concerning the played sessions, they require a preparatory briefing phase for the players to respond effectively to the posed problem, and once the play activity is completed, it concludes with a debriefing phase to capitalize on knowledge and data generated from the play.

### 3.6 Partial or complete design of serious games or serious play

The design of serious games and other serious activities inspired by games can take various forms and achieve different objectives. The design of a serious game or play can itself be a method of learning (learning by serious game or play design) [56] and address other issues that we will discuss a little further. However, it is not always necessary to create a game from scratch or design a complete game structure or activity to achieve the desired goal.

If we consider the game activity, at least two expressions have emerged to describe this type of transformation: gamification [57, 58] and playful design [59]. Gamification aims to change people's attitude directly or indirectly by modifying the context in which they operate, through the integration of game design elements or elements reminiscent of the gaming universe, to make the work context more stimulating. When the context is changed to bring a more playful touch, some refer to it as structural gamification [60], but we find it simpler to call it contextual playful design since the structure of the work context is still modified. In these cases, the work itself is not changed, but it is associated with a gamified system that may be based, for example, on gaining or losing badges and/or experience points, progressing through virtual statuses, adding an esthetic veneer evoking the game, etc. These additions of contextual elements are supposed to create new interactions with reference to a game, a form of play, or partially imitating a gaming space. This transformation of the space can be more or less extensive. It can be limited to elements constituting the decor of a place, such as at the *Google Campus*, where the game is present through various esthetic reminders in the work environment, but without these elements directly affecting the work itself [61].

According to another inverted approach that could be considered a particular form of goal-oriented game, we can talk about gamification when the game is integrated into work, and playing contributes to better performance, better support for repetitive tasks, or maintaining a high level of attention [62]. In these cases, the integration of a game into a given situation changes its configuration and contributes to its improvement.

In an approach focused on the proper design of a structure by transforming it more or less using game elements, there is the gamification approach [59]. This also applies when designing a game structure or one that strongly evokes gaming and associating it with a work context to improve conditions or performance. This works equally well with digital and non-digital inputs. For instance, to raise awareness or support people in the practice of agile methods (such as project design and management methods like *Scrum*, *Kanban*, *DevOps*...), numerous agile games, whose names are associated with their context of use, have been proposed. Some are genuine serious games, while others are adaptations of serious play or pure games, and still others are more gamified structures. To achieve the same goal, there is a reverse approach to the design process called disengamement (this neologism was created by melding the terms disengagement and game). This involves using a game as a base and modifying it to adapt it to the goals [63]. If it is a simple contextualization without changing the nature of the game, as we mentioned earlier with the case of situational gamification and previously with serious play if the way of practicing the game structure is changed. If the game is slightly modified or adapted without major changes (the original game is still easily recognizable in terms of mechanics and esthetics), we can speak of serious modding [47]. If the disengamement process is carried out thoroughly, fundamental elements of the game are removed, non-playful components are added to adapt it to the desired objective, and the game mechanics may even completely disappear... If we follow this logic of design by transforming a game away from its nature, at the end of the process, we get a structure that is no longer playful, just as a gamification process taken to its limits results in the design of a game. Of course, in practice, these processes and their variants are often alternated to achieve the desired structure and test prototypes designed gradually.

## 4. Knowledge management and serious game or play

We have just reviewed various forms, more or less inspired by games or play, to achieve serious objectives. Now, we will approach them through the prism of knowledge management, more specifically, the five sub-processes presented in the introduction.

### 4.1 Knowledge spotting and mapping

Play or Games can greatly inspire organizations to identify and map the knowledge present within them. Firstly, although this applies to each process, the already employed Knowledge spotting and mapping tools and methods can be gamified or playfied. Indeed, gameful design and gamification work very well in offering alternative approaches to what already exists. We prefer to talk about alternative or complementary approaches because, as mentioned earlier (criterion s3), it is preferable for the game to be the participants free choice. Even when it involves partial transformation, it is better to consider two paths that are equivalent in terms of the personnel's choices. The first is the use of conventional tools and methods (i.e., without any link to games). The second path involves an approach evoking games while leading to the same purpose. If the goal is to populate a database, an ontology, or a map, there is no reason why both aspects (with or without ludic inspiration) should not be proposed.

If digital tools are used for this purpose, gamification can take the form of limited badges or points awarded to participants based on their number of contributions. These badges can also be used to recognize certain expertise within the organization [64]. With different approaches based on crowdsourcing or micro-crowdsourcing that question the available skills and expertise using CAPTCHAS or digital games with a purpose, the obtained responses regarding expertise-related questions can be cross-referenced to highlight the most consensual ones (perhaps less interesting, as they are known by a larger number of people) and the least frequently mentioned ones that deserve verification. This type of device can also be applied to the development of a knowledge ontology [65] or to maps constructed over time and regularly updated, similar to what is used by *Waze*, the road traffic tool, through voluntary participants [66]. Another possibility is to map user experience using a game of questions or a role-playing game based on different personas (one per card) [67]. It will then be possible, based on the produced map(s), to explore available or even missing skills and knowledge and to report on them. On the same principle, it is possible to create a map in the form of a wargame on a board, showing the strengths and weaknesses of a system or a product (based on an adaptation of a User Experience map and a list of fundamental parameters) [68].

### 4.2 Knowledge acquisition and update

Acquiring and updating knowledge can take various forms. Among these, there is the recruitment of new personnel. Thus, an approach that appeals to games, but which has also been one of the early successes of serious games, is recruitment assistance. Some games allow the identification of skills among numerous candidates. For example, *America's Army* was developed by the U.S. military from the core of a first-person shooter game, *Unreal Tournament* (developed by Epic Games and Digital Extremes), in the early 2000s. It significantly improved recruiting new recruits for many years [69]. Similarly, games in different forms can be used in human resources for attractiveness and candidate selection purposes, and it is now a commonly considered solution [70] both in physical and virtual settings.

Among the inspired forms that can contribute to recruitment, those based on crowdsourcing (gwap) are quite effective and adaptable to different contexts. For example, by involving numerous people, some more or less expert, and by cross-referencing their responses, it is possible to complement the existing data, estimating a date, a location [71], relevant keywords (we will return to this in the case of knowledge capitalization). Similarly, problem-solving by exploring multiple possibilities, drawing on the intuition and understanding of a crowd of people, can also be envisaged. One of the first successful games with a purpose, successfully implemented, this proposition is *Foldit* [72]. This game was developed from protein folding simulation software to identify efficient positions to combat viruses (including HIV and more recently, Covid-19). It found a solution within a few weeks that other forms of computer simulations had not been able to recognize. This game with a purpose has since inspired others, including *Eterna*, also dedicated to medical research, but there are numerous other application domains [73].

It is also possible to use a physical game, such as a card game like *Rummy of attributes*, where participants play in small groups (e.g., 3–6 people) to find common points between elements of the same nature represented on cards (projects, departments, products, locations, etc.). By recognizing common points or making connections with different elements that players recognize or are aware of, implicit elements can be easily collected [74]. By playing this game over time, new data may appear and complement those already in memory.

### 4.3 Knowledge sharing and utilization

A wide range of game-inspired approaches can facilitate knowledge sharing, so much so that we might consider there to be a specific category of play and games with a sharing purpose. But among these games and activities two sets are particularly prominent. Thus, the first set is strongly linked to the context of educational learning. Indeed, there is an enormous number of serious games dedicated to this purpose, to the extent that one might believe that the sole function of serious games is education. The literature about serious game for education topic is extensive, so we will not dwell on this aspect of knowledge sharing.

The second set is complementary to the first, i.e. to all other forms of knowledge sharing. It brings together various approaches, of which serious play seems to be the most prevalent. Indeed, the integration of gaming elements and tools with a method to guide participants toward a serious objective has been extensively developed in the last two decades, following the early success of the *Lego Serious Play* method. This method paved the way for knowledge sharing by facilitating group interactions around a table [4, 43]. The generic idea is to gather participants in groups of 4 to 8 around a table and follow the instructions of a facilitator. Participants then build structures based on metaphors to introduce themselves and often engage in ice-breaker activities to build trust within the group. They are then prompted to solve a problem and propose a representation or a solution, starting with an individual construction, which is later explained to the other members at the table. Finally, the participants collectively create a construction that represents the problem and/or a potential solution. We will revisit the contribution of this method to innovation later. By allowing individuals to express themselves differently and represent knowledge using toys or symbolic elements, this approach provides alternative ways to share knowledge. Similar methods based on origami [75], *Playmobil* figures and toys [76], or adaptations of digital games, such as *Minecraft* [77], have also been proposed and successfully used.

Of course, this is not entirely new. Mannequins were developed as early as the 1960s to train people in emergency procedures [78], and dolls have been used since the eighteenth century [79]. As we have seen, wargaming is also an ancient practice that facilitates knowledge sharing and utilization. Regarding knowledge sharing, we particularly emphasize the interest in the Pros vs. Cons matrix game method, which can easily be applied outside the military domain. In its basic form, this system is relatively simple. The facilitator asks participants or players gathered around a table to present logical arguments in the form of sequences of actions to be taken to solve a problem or face a situation [55]. Players can oppose each other (which is preferable for argument development). One player or team presents valid arguments in favor of a specific action (justifying its potential success), while others argue against that action (highlighting its potential failure or at least its limited chances of success). After a few exchanges around the table and possible arbitration by the referee, the player who argued in favor of the success of a sequence rolls 2 six-sided dice or 3 six-sided dice (the latter option seems preferable). To succeed in the sequence, the player must obtain a score higher than the average of the dice rolls, with a bonus or penalty depending on the number and value of arguments proposed and validated by the referee in favor (pros) and against (cons) during the preceding discussion (with 3 six-sided dice, the average score is 11, and if, for example, there are 3 arguments for and 2 arguments against, the player must roll a score of 12 or higher to succeed because of a + 1 bonus = 3 pros – 2 cons). This system is inspired by tabletop role-playing games, with the referee acting as the game master. Knowledge sharing occurs gradually throughout the process. It is desirable that action sequences be represented using figurines, drawings, or a chart to better track the evolution of events.

A lighter form that is suitable for planning is the agile game called *Planning poker* (or agile poker, scrum poker, etc.). Using a deck of cards, each with a different number from the Fibonacci sequence and color-coded into families, the players evaluate, for example, the time or complexity of a task by choosing one card from their deck and placing it face down in front of them. Then, all players simultaneously reveal their cards. Participants with the most extreme numbers justify their choices. Afterward, each player takes back their card and reevaluates the task. Depending on the approach, the average scores are calculated or attempts are made to reach a consensus [80].

As for knowledge utilization, the proposals are more limited but still exist. There are various forms of simulations, more or less game-like, that train individuals in tasks for which they already possess some theoretical knowledge but lack sufficient practical experience. Driving, flight, shooting, handling, sales, medical, and other simulators fall into this category [4, 81, 82]. These game-inspired forms are not limited to digital applications, as professional role-playing exercises, although requiring a facilitator, also represent another form of serious play. The origins of this approach date back to at least the works of Jean-Louis Moreno in 1946 and are still relevant today [83].

## 4.4 Knowledge formalization and capitalization

In principle, using games to formalize and capitalize knowledge may not seem easy. However, some game-inspired forms have been developed for this purpose, one of which is the design of serious games. Whether digital or physical, all serious games are forms of formalizing and capitalizing knowledge. The games designed in this way serve as models and choices of hypotheses and formalization, and it is advisable to keep track of them. Serious game/play design is also a very interesting activity when seeking to capitalize knowledge. This mode of design can also be applied to the development of analog games such as fresk workshops (the *climate fresk*, the *digital fresk*, the *circular economy fresk*...)[1]. Such a workshop is based on animation relying on the participants' reflection to reconstruct a sort of puzzle, which in its design requires a specific organization based on data organized in the form of a cause-and-effect diagram. These are persuasive games or persuasive play that, in their design framework, involve direct links with the knowledge they mobilize [84]. Similarly, the development of an empathic game (mentioned earlier) is a form of knowledge capitalization in itself, as the resulting game offers a simulation and sharing of a point of view on a situation by placing the player in the position of another person at a specific moment.

Another approach is to adapt/modify a serious game dedicated to learning, for example, to exploit it at a meta-knowledge level. The game then serves as a support for questions and annotations to better express certain learnings from the game [85]. It is no longer beginners who go through the game's stages, but experts capable of providing information on various elements. This is a two-level serious game format. In a somewhat similar approach, a tool or platform designed for knowledge capitalization (by acquiring practices subsequently transformed into virtual reality modeling, for example) can be adapted and gamified to complement the information thus acquired [86].

In terms of games specifically dedicated in their practice to knowledge capitalization, we complement this list with two agile games and a type of wargame.

[1] This is the first and best-known fresk; here are a few examples of sites and workshops dedicated to it: https://climatefresk.org, https://climateclarity.co.uk or https://www.greenofficeproject.com/climate-fresk.

Agile games are primarily intended to raise awareness, encourage, or support the implementation of agile methods. They include numerous games or game activities designed, adapted, or adapted for this purpose. Among all these games, those designed for the stage of an agile design process aimed at feedback (retrospective) are very interesting for knowledge capitalization. For example, games like *Speed boat* (or *Seal boat*) allow a team, via a graphic model (template) where the game consists of completing the parts, to provide a general update on the activities carried out, and the team members can together assess strengths, weaknesses, improvement opportunities, and problems that still need to be addressed [18]. Other agile games (*Retrospective bingo*, *Game of throne retrospective*, *Lego retrospective*, *Starfish*...) are dedicated to this team feedback and make a progress review more interesting and dynamic while addressing a number of questions that will bring out numerous knowledge that can be capitalized.

If one wishes to develop a complete sequence of knowledge acquisition, course of action wargames can be a good model for carrying out such a formula for a civil case. The principle of this type of wargame is quite simple in itself. An animator and referee leads participants to think together, either opposing or cooperating while being in competition, to solve a problem related to a situation. The game relies on a map on which elements are symbolized by locations, and results of actions are visualized. The participants develop a list of different possible courses of action (hence the name of this type of wargame), estimate them according to their risk of realization (success or failure and consequences in either case), and rank them based on a list of criteria (e.g., alignment with the set framework, feasibility of the intervention, its originality and distinction from other proposed actions). Then, the selected courses of action are played multiple times (in the form of matrix games, for example, as explained earlier) to complete the evaluation of each plan and gather all relevant information for the decisions to be made [87]. This type of game can also be used to analyze a past situation, the options available in relation to what was done and could have been done, to capitalize all this knowledge once argued, annotated, and proposed in an appropriate format for storage and future mobilization.

### 4.5 Knowledge creation and transfer to innovation

There are several serious forms inspired by play or games with the aim of contributing to knowledge creation or knowledge transfer directly contributing to an innovation process. Some of these forms are related to gamification or playification, respectively, involving the transformation of structures or non-playful activities by adding playful elements or even turning them into games.

Firstly, there are different creativity techniques and methods that have been transformed into game-like formats. One example is the *Ball toss brainstorming*, which is a simple brainstorming activity combined with a ball that players toss within a limited time to avoid elimination (each player must propose a new original idea when in possession of the ball). This technique can be supported by dedicated tools, such as the *Qball* [18], which is a foam ball containing a microphone that each participant uses to express their idea more clearly to others. Similarly, the *Gamitrization* gathers a set of tools from the TRIZ creativity method that have been transformed into a game [88]. Some of these tools are designed to introduce beginners to TRIZ but can also be used in creativity sessions. In a different way, the *Cubification* method proposes combining several selected characteristics to define a product and its market by forming different facets of a *Rubik's Cube* that each participant constructs themselves [89].

On the opposite end, some games like *Concept* or *Big Idea* can be adapted for use in brainstorming sessions [90, 91]. The board game *Concept* can be diverted to help express ideas only using elements to gain perspective on the problem posed. In the case of the card game *Big Idea*, players are required to combine different words and adjectives on the cards they are dealt to respond to the creativity problem.

Other tools and methods inspired by game structures and game activities can also be utilized. We have already mentioned the *Lego Serious Play* method, which also offers an application framework to support an innovation process [44]. Following the same principles (small groups of people gathered around a table with Lego bricks and other objects), this method involves first elaborating on one's vision of the problem or a potential solution, then sharing it with others (from one's table and then other tables), and finally co-constructing a relevant and original solution with the most advantages. Similarly, the wargames we previously discussed offer solutions for innovation and complement the innovation process [92]. For example, there is the technique of red teaming, which has two variants. The first, *red teaming wargame*, aims to encourage reconsideration of a system or situation by proposing radically different solutions and actions based on a standard situation. This method stimulates creative thinking by encouraging participants to think differently. The second method is the "red team method" used in information security, somewhat different and unfortunately, it can be confused with the former. The *red team* method is a devil's advocate method. It mobilizes a team that is assigned the objective of considering solutions to attack the existing system to identify its robustness and weaknesses [92]. Each weakness then requires reflection to be corrected and thus contribute to system improvement. Wargames also allow the simulation of the use of new technology, method, or doctrine to estimate its potential contribution. This can take the form of a matrix game (as explained earlier). This method, in addition to the standard wargame tools, only requires the production of descriptions of the envisaged technology, method, or doctrine. After several games are played, insights are drawn from the possibilities offered or not, their advantages and disadvantages, problematic or interesting situations, etc. This method can complement the prototyping process, with proposals from one method feeding the next implementation cycle of the other [93]. Finally, in a disengamement mode inspired by wargames, product confrontation cards [68], mentioned earlier, allow both visual mapping of strengths and weaknesses of competing products or technologies and, through matrix game-like reasoning or brainstorming, to consider the next generation to be developed by choosing to reinforce certain strengths or weaknesses.

## 5. Conclusions

It is quite challenging to review the major categories of play and game-inspired forms that can be applied to knowledge management. This chapter is an attempt to provide you with an overview and the keys to search for or develop solutions that will be most suitable for your needs. That is why we started this chapter by specifying how games and game activities can be defined by describing some of their distinct characteristics. Three main characteristics stand out regarding the proposed structure as a game, which must:

- (G1) strongly resemble a form already recognized as a game,
- (G2) have rules guiding the players,

- (G3) tend toward an objective to be achieved that motivates or justifies, at least in part, the interest in playing.

However, even though these characteristics are necessary, considering them alone can lead to a form of serious game that will not truly interest its audience and will ultimately be rejected. Thus, four other characteristics can help you achieve your serious objective through a form of Play. They require developing a proposition that should, as much as possible:

- (P1) evoke a feeling of tension and/or joy among its players,

- (P2) be partially uncertain in its unfolding,

- (P3) be voluntary, meaning it offers an alternative to those who do not want to play so that they can still achieve the same objective,

- (P4) before taking part in this kind of activity, clearly inform participants about how what is generated by the play will be used and who will benefit from it.

With these known characteristics, different forms inspired by games and used for serious purposes have been presented to help you better understand the differences between serious games, games with a purpose, empathic games, agile games, serious play, gamification, and disengagement. Indeed, those dedicated to knowledge management are no exception.

After describing these forms, we have discussed some of the possibilities they offer in the context of five knowledge management sub-processes. Thus, all stages of knowledge management can be associated with a form of play. The possibilities are endless and will continue to develop. If the categories presented are already numerous, it is likely that they will multiply, as this type of approach is experiencing a renaissance. Fifteen years ago, gamification was barely being proposed, and now it is part of the common vocabulary of many organizations.

Of course, this perspective can be reversed, and all serious or purely playful game forms can be analyzed from the point of view of knowledge management. We mentioned the case of games with a sharing purpose, which represent a substantial set of game-inspired solutions. In this way, both the implementation and operation of these devices can be studied from a knowledge management perspective. The same applies to the other sets of edutainment devices that we can build up and then analyze on the same model: games with an acquisition purpose, games with a capitalization purpose, game with mapping purpose, and games with a creation purpose. On the same principle, edutainment devices integrating several knowledge management sub-processes, such as wargaming practices, can be analyzed under the prism of a complete knowledge management process.

## Glossary

| | |
|---|---|
| Advergames | serious game dedicated to advertising, the most of time is a video game which by the game promotes a brand or a product. |

| | |
|---|---|
| Agile game | a game intended to introduce an agile method or to facilitate its implementation. |
| Agile method | method intended for small development teams (5–20 people) aimed at quickly proposing effective, functional solutions adapted to needs from successive iterations of the design process. Since the beginning of the 2000s, its methods have been based on the Manifesto for Agile Software Development. |
| Art game | an artistic production heavily inspired by video games or an artistic work that utilizes certain interactive mechanics and esthetic characteristics of games to better engage the audience. |
| Business origami | method proposed by the Hitachi Design Centre that uses numerous pieces of paper with illustrations and space to write for mapping an environment or problematic situation by pasting, folding and linking different pieces of paper. |
| CAPTCHA | means Completely Automated Public Turing test to tell Computers and Humans Apart. They are program developed to engage and employ a large number of people through a digital interface to assist in performing tasks that are not easily automated. |
| Concept | a boardgame, designed by Alain Rivollet and Gaëtan Beaujannot, published by Repos Production, based on the guess of words or expressions through the selection of icons by a placement of a few pawns on a board. |
| Course of action wargame (CoA wargame) | a kind of wargame or wargame using to consider a particular situation in order to determine most of the possibilities, including the best and the most risky. |
| Cubification | activity and methodology designed by Hélène Michel using the construction of an object evoking a Rubik's Cube, accompanying a generation of ideas and the creation of an argument aimed at imagining a new product or service as well as its strategic positioning from the combination of different aspects represented by small square vignettes of different colors organized on the model of the original Rubik's Cube. |
| Datagame | a kind of serious game dedicated to resolve a data collection problem. |
| Empathic game (empathy serious game or empathic serious game) | a kind of serious game designed to help people to understand the problems of other people by a particular point of view adoption proposed by the game. |
| ESP game (ExtraSensory Perception game) | a kind of serious game specially dedicated to document annotation. The player must find the same annotations for a document as a majority of people or/and an expert group. |

| | |
|---|---|
| Exergame | contraction of the terms exercise and game, it is a kind of (digital) device dedicated to training by a simulation exercise prosed as a game. |
| Exploitationware | term proposed by Ian Bogost to qualified a king of software which presents itself in the form of a game or by exploiting numerous attributes in order to motivate, or even manipulate, people to carry out work-like tasks. |
| Expressive game | a recreational game with a specific game play which as a goal to question the player about a problematic realistic situation presented in the game. |
| First-person shooter (fps) | a shooting video game in which the player directs and controls the movements of a single armed character, usually seen from behind, in order to use the latter's field of vision to shoot various enemies. |
| Game | a kind of structure allowing a play activity, which must at least strongly resemble a form already recognized as a game, have rules guiding the players, tend towards an objective to be achieved that motivates or justifies, at least in part, the interest in playing, and, as much as possible evoke a feeling of tension and/or joy among its players. |
| Game of throne retrospective | game whose purpose is to make the retrospective step, mandated by many agile methodologies, more enjoyable and methodical. |
| Game With A Purpose (GWAP) | a kind of serious game in which the recipient of the utilitarian results obtained via the game are not those who play it. These games are most often digital and based on a crowdsourcing approach, i.e. mobilizing a large number of contributors/players to solve a problem via the game. |
| Gamification | process of developing or partially transforming non-game devices by integrating numerous elements of game design to make them more attractive and engaging. |
| Gamified system | a system that has been designed or modified through a gamification process, i.e. even though it is not a game, elements of game design can be identified in its mechanics or aesthetics. |
| Gamitrization | a set of games to train or support the use of numerous TRIZ tools and methods. |
| Ice-breaker | an exercise or game designed to build cohesion and trust among a group of people who do not know each other. They are team-building and teamwork facilitation tools. |
| Kriegspiel | Historically, this is the best-known early form of map-based military wargaming devised in Prussia at the turn of the seventeenth entury. Nowadays, this name is used for a wargame on map, offered as a ready-to-use |

| | |
|---|---|
| | package, with a dedicated scenario and a rigid set of rules to simulate one or more groups of military action(s). |
| Lego Serious Play | a methodology for supporting reflection and group work based on Lego bricks and other Lego objects. It is available in a range of applications (team motivation, problem solving, innovation). |
| Matrix games | a game system imagined by Chris Engle in 1992 and inspired by tabletop role-playing games, which brings to wargaming a freedom of action and adaptation based above all on the players' relevant argumentation. |
| Minecraft serious play | a specific version of video game Minecraft dedicated to education and other serious problem solving, based on the game's universe and, most importantly, the possibilities offered by its mechanics of building using small cubes. |
| Newsgame | a serious video game designed to inform in the same spirit as a newspaper or newsflash. |
| Persona (user persona) | fictional character whose essential characteristics are displayed on a dedicated worksheet, the purpose of which is to represent an individual corresponding to a particular group of people associated with a design or innovation problem to be solved. |
| Play | often fun activity based on a set of rules called a game. |
| Playification | A process aimed at making an activity more enjoyable by incorporating game elements into it without altering its structure. |
| Playfied | the result of integrating playful considerations into the way you use or approach a non-playful structure without modifying it. For example, holding a work meeting using Lego bricks (Lego serious play method) does not change the nature of the meeting itself, nor its objective, nor necessarily the place where it takes place. |
| Playmobil Pro | a serious play methodology based on Playmobil toys. |
| Pros vs. Cons matrix game | a category of matrix game system that requires players on different sides of the argument to put forward arguments for and against the possibility or difficulty of carrying out an action. The estimated difference between the arguments Pros and Cons is then translated into a score that a dice roll must reach for the action to be carried out in the game round. |
| Qball | object shaped like a foam ball the size of a handball, containing a microphone and a speaker, which allows different people to safely pass it to one another and use it to speak and be heard clearly in a room. |
| Red teaming wargame | wargame aimed at developing a critical analysis, through the exploration of a system's flaws and/or the search for radically original but plausible approaches in the context of a real but simulated situation, all aimed |

| | |
|---|---|
| | at challenging a doctrine, a pre-established situation or strategic issue. |
| Role-playing game | a game in which each player embodies a single character (persona), with the exception of the player taking on the role of game master (narrator, animator and game referee) in an often imaginary world. The archetypal tabletop role-playing game is Dungeons & Dragons, while the archetypal online role-playing game is World of Warcraft. |
| Romance game | a king of video game with for main goal to establish a romantic relationship between the character pilot by the player and one or more of the non-player characters proposed in the game. |
| Retrospective bingo | game whose purpose is to make the retrospective step, mandated by many agile methodologies, more enjoyable and methodical. |
| Scrum | agile method dedicated do software development. |
| Seminar wargames | a game mode in which the game is played in the form of a seminar, bringing together a large number of people who give their opinions directly during the game or at the end of the game, via a specific questionnaire provided to them. |
| Serious game | a game that is played for a non-game purpose (work, learning, awareness-raising, information, etc.). It is a utilitarian game that can be digital as well as physical. The game serves as a medium for carrying out a task, the playful framework of which is supposed to make it easier or more motivating. |
| Serious gaming | the practice of serious games, or the hijacking for serious purposes of a game designed purely for leisure. |
| Serious play | professional practice following a precise methodology involving the use of games or game elements to carry out a serious task. The best-known such methodology is currently Lego serious play. |
| Speed boat (Seal boat) | A game whose purpose is to make the retrospective step, mandated by many agile methodologies, more enjoyable and methodical. |
| TRIZ | the theory of inventive problem solving is a set of creative tools and a Russian-based approach to solving technological innovation problems, using a formal methodology initially based on the analysis of a very large number of patents. |
| fresk workshops | the climate fresk, the digital fresk, the circular economy fresk. |
| Wargame | Simulation of a situation characterized by tension, crisis, or confrontation (usually military, but not necessarily) using a utilitarian game based on a scenario featuring complex interactions between several protagonists whose roles can be taken on by players. |

| | |
|---|---|
| Wargaming | professional use of wargame, i.e., the playing of a wargame(s) with the aim of answering a serious questions. |

## Author details

Stéphane Goria
Université de Lorraine, Crem, Nancy, France

*Address all correspondence to: stephane.goria@univ-lorraine.fr

## References

[1] Rinc S. Integrating gamification with knowledge management. In: Proceedings of the Management, Proceedings of the Knowledge and Learning - International Conference. Portoroz, Slovenia. Celje: ToKnowPress; 2014 pp. 997-1003

[2] Swacha J. Gamification in knowledge management: Motivating for knowledge sharing. Polish Journal of Management Studies. 2015;**12**(2):150-160

[3] Allal-Chérif O, Makhlouf M. Using serious games to manage knowledge: The SECI model perspective. Journal of Business Research. 2016;**69**(5):1539-1543. DOI: 10.1016/j.jbusres.2015.10.013

[4] Jensen CN. SERIOUS PLAY approaches for creating, sharing, and mobilizing tacit knowledge in cross-disciplinary settings [thesis]. Tempe: Arizona State University; 2017

[5] MacBryde JC, Dorfler V, Shpakova A. Changing the game: A case for gamifying knowledge management. World Journal of Science, Technology and Sustainable Development. 2017;**14**(2/3):1-17. DOI: 10.1108/WJSTSD-01-2017-0002

[6] Suh A, Wagner C. How gamification of an enterprise collaboration system increases knowledge contribution: An affordance approach. Journal of Knowledge Management. 2017;**21**(2):416-431. DOI: 10.1108/JKM-10-2016-0429

[7] Sampaio MC, Sousa MJ, Dionísio A. The use of gamification in knowledge management processes: A systematic literature review. Journal of Reviews on Global Economics. 2019;**8**:1662-1679. DOI: 10.6000/1929-7092.2019.08.150

[8] Friedrich J, Becker M, Kramer F, Wirth M, Schneider M. Incentive design and gamification for knowledge management. Journal of Business Research. 2020;**106**:341-352. DOI: 10.1016/j.jbusres.2019.02.009

[9] Marcão RP, Pestana G, Sousa MJ. Knowledge management and gamification in Pharma: An approach in pandemic times to develop product quality reviews. Electronic Journal of Knowledge Management. 2020;**18**(3):255-268. DOI: 10.34190/EJKM.18.03.005

[10] Galeano-Ospino S, Machuca-Villegas L, Gasca-Hurtado GP. Knowledge transfer in software development teams using gamification: A systematic literature review. In: New Perspectives in Software Engineering: Proceedings of the 9th International Conference on Software Process Improvement (CIMPS 2020). Cham: Springer International Publishing; 2021. pp. 115-130

[11] Ouriques L, Barbosa CE, Xexéo G. On the design of educational course of action wargaming. Developments in Business Simulation and Experiential Learning; Vol. 49. 2022. pp. 29-46

[12] Gold AH, Arvind Malhotra AHS. Knowledge management: An organizational capabilities perspective. Journal of Management Information Systems. 2021;**18**(1):185-214. DOI: 10.1080/07421222.2001.11045669

[13] Lee H, Choi B. Knowledge management enablers, processes, and organizational performance: An integrative view and empirical examination. Journal of Management Information Systems. 2003;**20**(1):179-228. DOI: 10.1080/07421222.2003.11045756

[14] Gholami MH, Asli MN, Nazari-Shirkouhi S, Noruzy A. Investigating the influence of knowledge management practices on organizational performance: An empirical study. Acta Polytechnica Hungarica. 2013;**10**(2):205-216

[15] Alyoubi B, Hoque MR, Alharbi I, Alyoubi A, Almazmomi N. Impact of knowledge management on employee work performance: Evidence from Saudi Arabia. The International Technology Management Review. 2018;**7**(1):13-24

[16] Chikhi I, Bouarfa H. Knowledge management process through a cloud computing based approach. In: Proceedings of the European Conference on Knowledge Management; 5-6 September; Lisbon, Portugal: Academic Conferences Ltd; 2019. pp. 238-247

[17] Stephen P. Effects of knowledge capture and acquisition practices on organizational performance. European Journal of Information and Knowledge Management. 2022;**1**(1):43-55. DOI: 10.47941/ejikm.854

[18] Goria S. A mapping of the kinds of work activities and other productive uses inspired by play or games. Journal of Games, Game Art, and Gamification. 2022;**7**(2):29-37. DOI: 10.21512/jggag.v7i2.8883

[19] Huizinga J. Homo Ludens: A Study of the Play-Element in Culture. London: Routledge; 2014

[20] Caillois R. Man, Play, and Games. Urbana: University of Illinois Press; 2001. 208 p

[21] Perla P. Wargaming and the cycle of research and learning. Scandinavian Journal of Military Studies. 2022;**5**(1): 197-208. DOI: 10.31374/sjms.124

[22] Hai AA, May H, Nawrotzki K, Prochner L, Valkanova Y. New education: An experimental era. In: Hai AA, May H, Nawrotzki K, Prochner L, Valkanova Y, editors. Reimagining Teaching in Early 20th Century Experimental Schools. Cham: Palgrave Macmillan; 2020. pp. 1-25

[23] Wardaszko M. Application of decision-making simulation games in teaching management skills [thesis]. Warsaw: Académie Leon Koźmiński; 2013

[24] Henriot J. Le jeu. Paris: Synonyme; 2020. 109 p

[25] Ros S, Gonzalez S, Robles A, Tobarra LL, Caminero A, Cano J. Analyzing students' self-perception of success and learning effectiveness using gamification in an online cybersecurity course. IEEE Access. 2020;**8**:97718-97728

[26] Kuindersma E, van der Pal J, van den Herik J, Plaat A. Voluntary play in serious games. In: Games and Learning Alliance: 4th International Conference, GALA 2015; December 9-11, 2015; Rome, Italy. Trier: dblp. 2016. pp. 131-140

[27] Abt C. Serious Games. New York: University Press of America; 1970. 176 p

[28] Popescu MM, Romero M, Usart M. Serious games for serious learning using SG for business, management and defence education. International Journal of Computer Science Research and Application. 2013;**3**(1):5-15

[29] Caffrey MB. On Wargaming: How Wargames Have Shaped History and How they May Shape the Future. Newport: Naval War College Press; 2019. 479 p

[30] von Ahn L, Blum M, Hopper NJ, Langford J. CAPTCHA: Using hard AI

problems for security. In: Proceedings of the International Conference on the Theory and Applications of Cryptographic Techniques. Berlin, Heidelberg: Springer; 2003. pp. 294-311

[31] von Ahn L, Dabbish L. Labeling images with a computer game. In: Proceedings of the SIGCHI Conference on Human factors in computing systems; Vienna, Austria; April. 2004. pp. 319-326

[32] Chen KT, Lin CW, Chen LJ, King I. Human computation games and optimization of their productivity. In: Usmani Z-U-H, editor. Web Intelligence and Intelligent Agents. London, UK, Rijeka, Croatia: InTech; 2010. pp. 289-304

[33] Mollick E, Werbach K. Gamification and the enterprise. In: Walz SP, Deterding S, editors. The Gameful World: Approaches; Issues, Applications. Cambridge: MIT Press; 2015. pp. 439-461

[34] Dai P, Lin CH, Weld DS. POMDP-based control of workflows for crowdsourcing. Artificial Intelligence. 2013;**202**:52-85. DOI: 10.1016/j.artint.2013.06.002

[35] Downes-Martin S. Swarm gaming approach to organizing in-stride games. In: Robinson M, Downes-Martin S, Connections US Wargaming Conference 2018 Working Group, editors. In-Stride Adjudication. Vol. 2018. Washington, DC: National Defense University. pp. 65-79

[36] Bogost I. Why gamification is bullshit. In: Walz SP, Deterding S, editors. The Gameful World: Approaches, Issues, Applications. Cambridge: MIT Press; 2014. pp. 65-79

[37] Bogost I. Persuasive Games: The Expressive Power of Videogames. Cambridge: MIT Press; 2007. 464 p

[38] Critelli M, Schwartz DI, Gold S. Serious social games: Designing a business simulation game. In: Proceedings of the 2012 IEEE International Games Innovation Conference; 7-9 September 2012; Held, Rochester. New York: IEEE; 2012. pp. 1-4

[39] Mauriras-Bousquet M. An educational technique of great potential: Simulation games. Prospects. 1974;**4**(4):555-578

[40] Caballero V. Empathic games are here to stay! In: What's Next, Presentation at the Game Developers Conference; March 17 – 21; San Francisco. London: informatech; 2014

[41] McDonald H. Are gamers ready for gay love? Improving romance in games. In: Kafai YB, Richard GT, Tynes BM, editors. Diversifying Barbie and Mortal Kombat: Intersectional Perspectives and Inclusive Design in Gaming. Carnegie Mellon: ETC Press; 2016. pp. 247-258

[42] dos Santos DB, Maciel C, Pereira VC, dos Santos NEP. Digital empathic games and their relation with mortality: Analysis of discussion forums. Lecture Notes in Computer Science. 2019;**1195**:307-319

[43] Genvo S. Defining and designing expressive games. Journal of Media Studies and Popular Culture. 2016;(special issue):90-106

[44] Blair S, Rillo M. Serious Work: How to Facilitate Meetings & Workshops Using the Lego Serious Play Method with Conscious Incompetence. New Delhi: ProMeet; 2016. 252 p

[45] Young MF, Slota S, Cutter AB, Jalette G, Mullin G, Lai B, et al. Our princess is in another castle: A review of trends in serious gaming for education. Review of Educational

Research. 2012;**82**(1):61-89. DOI: 10.3102/0034654312436980

[46] Bottino RM, Ott M, Tavella M. Serious gaming at school: Reflections on students' performance, engagement and motivation. International Journal of Game-Based Learning (IJGBL). 2014;**4**(1):21-36. DOI: 10.4018/IJGBL.2014010102

[47] Bouko C, Alvarez J. Serious gaming, serious modding and serious diverting... Are you serious?! In: Lindsey Joyce L, Quinn B, editors. Mapping the Digital: Cultures and Territories of Play. Leyde: Brill; 2016. pp. 101-113

[48] Knight JF, Carley S, Tregunna B, Jarvis S, Smithies R, de Freitas S, et al. Serious gaming technology in major incident triage training: A pragmatic controlled trial. Resuscitation. 2010;**81**(9):1175-1179. DOI: 10.1016/j.resuscitation.2010.03.042

[49] van Der Zee DJ, Holkenborg B, Robinson S. Conceptual modeling for simulation-based serious gaming. Decision Support Systems. 2012;**54**(1):33-45. DOI: 10.1016/j.dss.2012.03.006

[50] Laamarti F, Eid M, El Saddik A. An overview of serious games. International Journal of Computer Games Technology. 2014;**358152**:1-16. DOI: 10.1155/2014/358152

[51] Chang TP, Sherman JM, Gerard JM. Overview of serious gaming and virtual reality. In: Nestel D, Hui J, Kunkler K, Scerbo MW, Calhoun AW, editors. Healthcare Simulation Research. Cham: Springer; 2019. pp. 29-38

[52] Jenkins H, Camper B, Chisholm A, Grigsby N, Klopfer E, Osterweil S, et al. From serious games to serious gaming. Serious games: Mechanisms and effects. In: Ritterfeld U, Cody M, Vorderer P, editors. Serious Games: Mechanisms and Effects. London: Routledge; 2009. pp. 448-468

[53] Appleget J, Burks R, Cameron F. The Craft of Wargaming: A Detailed Planning Guide for Defense Planners and Analysts. Annapolis: Naval Institute Press; 2020

[54] United Kingdom Ministry of Defense. Development, Concepts and Doctrine Centre. Swindon: Wargaming Handbook, Development, Concepts and Doctrine Centre; 2017

[55] Curry J, Engle C, Perla P. The Matrix Games Handbook: Professional Applications from Education to Analysis and Wargaming. Keynsham: The History of Wargaming Project - John Curry Editions; 2022. 298 p

[56] Lépinard P. La ludopédagogie en école de management: Le cas du projet EdUTeam. Éducations. 2022;**6**(1):G1-G13

[57] Nicholson S. A user-centered theoretical framework for meaningful gamification. In: Proceedings of the gls 8.0 Conference: Games + Learning + Society; 12-13 June. Madison: ECT Press; 2012. pp. 223-229

[58] Márquez SE, Waern A, Márquez SL, López Recio D. Playification: The physeear case. In: Proceedings of the 2016 Annual Symposium on Computer-Human Interaction in Play: CHI PLAY Companion '16; October 16-17; Autin, Texas. New York: Association for Computing Machinery; 2016. pp. 376-388

[59] Deterding S, Dixon D, Khaled R, Lennart N. From game design elements to gamefulness: Defining "gamification". In: Proceedings of the 15th International Academic MindTrek Conference. New York, ACM New York: Envisioning Future Media Environments; 2011. pp. 9-15

[60] Kapp KM, Blair L, Mesch R. The Gamification of Learning and Instruction Fieldbook: Ideas into Practice. San Francisco: Wiley; 2014

[61] Zichermann G, Linder J. The Gamification Revolution: How Leaders Leverage Game Mechanics to Crush the Competition. New York: McGraw-Hill; 2013. 256 p

[62] Savignac E. The Gamification of Work: The Use of Games in the Workplace. John Wiley & Sons; 2017. 208 p

[63] Goria S. Les visualisations de données inspirées par le jeu et la conception par disengamement. Les Cahiers du Numérique. 2016;**12**(4):39-64

[64] Narayanan A. Gamification for Employee Engagement. Birmingham: Packt Publishing Ltd; 2014. 152 p

[65] Ziebarth S, Malzahn N, Hoppe HU. Matchballs–A multi-agent-system for ontology-based collaborative learning games. In: Proceedings of the Collaboration and Technology: 18th International Conference, CRIWG; September 16-19; Raesfeld, Germany. Springer Berlin Heidelberg; 2012. pp. 208-222

[66] Gómez-Barrón JP, Manso-Callejo MÁ, Alcarria R, Iturrioz T. Volunteered geographic information system design: Project and participation guidelines. ISPRS International Journal of Geo-Information. 2016;**5**(7):108. DOI: 10.3390/ijgi5070108

[67] Luchs MG, Swan S, Griffin A. Design Thinking: New Product Development Essentials from the PDMA. John Wiley & Sons; 2015. 464 p

[68] Goria S. How to adapt a tactical board wargame for marketing strategy identification. Journal of Intelligence Studies in Business. 2013;**2**(3):12-28

[69] Smith RD. Military Simulation & Serious Games: Where we Came from and Where we Are Going. Modelbenders Press; 2009. 412 p

[70] Kumar A, Sowdamini T, Manocha S, Pujari P. Gamification as a sustainable tool for HR managers. Acta Universitatis Bohemiae Meridionales. 2021;**24**(2):1-14

[71] Annad O, Bendaoud A, Goria S. Web information monitoring and crowdsourcing for promoting and enhancing the Algerian geoheritage. Arabian Journal of Geosciences. 2017;**10**:1-15

[72] Cooper S, Khatib F, Treuille A, Barbero J, Lee J, Beenen M, et al. Predicting protein structures with a multiplayer online game. Nature. 2010;**466**(7307):756-760

[73] Lafourcade M, Joubert A, Le Brun N. Games with a Purpose (GWAPS). London: John Wiley & Sons; 2015. 158 p

[74] Goria S. A deck of cards to help track design trends to assist the creation of new products. International Journal of Technology, Innovation and Management (IJTIM). 2022;**2**(2):1-17. DOI: 10.54489/ijtim.v2i2.78

[75] Fox D. Using the business origami technique to understand complex ecosystems. In: Judge TK, Neustaedter C, editors. Studying and Designing Technology for Domestic Life: Lessons from Home. Amsterdam: Morgan Kaufmann; 2014. pp. 93-110

[76] Trullemans S, Valadez JI. Collaborative sketching with tangibles: Let's stop soulless meetings. In: CHI Conference on Human Factors in Computing Systems Extended Abstracts; 29 April - 5 May; New Orleans, LA, USA.

New York: Association for Computing Machinery; 2022. pp. 1-3

[77] Ekaputra G, Lim C, Eng KI. Minecraft: A game as an education and scientific learning tool. In: Information Systems International Conference (ISICO); 2-4 December. Lisbon: International Assn for Development of the Information Society (IADIS); 2013. pp. 237-242

[78] Lang A, Bolls P, Potter RF, Kawahara K. The effects of production pacing and arousing content on the information processing of television messages. Journal of Broadcasting & Electronic Media. 1999;**43**(4):451-475. DOI: 10.1080/08838159909364504

[79] Gelbart NR. The king's Midwife: A History and Mystery of Madame du Coudray. Berkeley: University of California Press; 2023. 358 p

[80] Gandomani TJ, Faraji H, Radnejad M. Planning Poker in cost estimation in Agile methods: Averaging vs. Consensus. In: Proceedings of the 2019 5th Conference on Knowledge Based Engineering and Innovation (KBEI); 28 February 2019 - 01 March; Tehran, Iran. 2019. pp. 066-071. DOI: 10.1109/KBEI.2019.8734960

[81] Zhou Q, Bekebrede G, Mayer I, Warmerdam J, Knepflé M. The climate game: Connecting water management and spatial planning through simulation gaming? In: Bressers N, editor. Water Governance as Connective Capacity. Routledge; 2016. pp. 109-127

[82] Papadopoulou P, Chui KT, Daniela L, Lytras MD. Virtual and augmented reality in medical education and training: Innovative ways for transforming medical education in the 21st century. In: Lytras MD, Aljohani N, Daniela L, Visvizi A, editors. Cognitive Computing in Technology-Enhanced Learning. IGI Global; 2019. pp. 109-150

[83] Moreno JL. Psychodrama and group psychotherapy. Sociometry. 1946;**9**(2/3):249-253

[84] Kors MJL, Van der Spek ED, Schouten BA. A foundation for the persuasive gameplay experience. In: Proceedings of the 10th International Conference on the Foundations of Digital Games (FDG 2015); June 22-25. Pacific Grove: Foundations of Digital Games; 2015

[85] Carron T, Talbot S. Industrial knowledge assessment for capitalization purpose via learning techniques. World Applied Sciences Journal. 2014;**31**:28-35. DOI: 10.5829/idosi.wasj.2014.31.arsem.598

[86] Torres-Loredo JL, Palma-Ruiz JM, Saiz-Álvarez JM. Digital transformation of the Quadruple Helix: Technological management interrelations for sustainable innovation. In: Ratten V, editor. Entrepreneurship as Practice: Time for More Managerial Relevance. Singapore: Springer Nature Singapore; 2022. pp. 109-126

[87] Bullard JA. Breaking the Barrier between Operations and Intelligence [technical report, master's thesis]. Marine Corps University Quantico VA; 2017

[88] Hentschel C, Thurnes CM, Zeihsel F. GamiTRIZation–gamification for TRIZ education. In: Proceedings of the Automated Invention for Smart Industries: 18th International TRIZ Future Conference, TFC 2018; Strasbourg, France, October 29-31. Springer International Publishing; 2018, 2018. pp. 29-39

[89] Michel H. Gamification for Innovation: Cubification in Action

with Hélène Michel and Opopoï; Rapid Innovation in Digital Times [Internet]; 2016. Available from: https://nbry.wordpress.com/2016/09/12/gamification-for-innovation-cubification-in-action-with-helene-michel-and-opopoi/

[90] Goria S, Humbert P, Roussel B. Information, Knowledge and Agile Creativity. John Wiley & Sons; 2019

[91] Mercier M, Lubart T. The effects of board games on creative potential. The Journal of Creative Behavior. 2021;**55**(3):875-885. DOI: 10.1002/jocb.494

[92] Ackerman G, Clifford D. Red teaming and crisis preparedness. In: Oxford Research Encyclopedia of Politics. 2021

[93] Wong YH, Bae SJ, Bartels E, Smith BM. Next-Generation Wargaming for the U.S. Marine Corps: Recommended Courses of Action. Santa Monica, CA: RAND Corporation; 2019. 252 p

Chapter 11

# Knowledge Management in the Context of Toxicity Testing

*Audrey Sanctorum, Jan Maushagen, Sara Sepehri, Guillaume Vrijens, Joery De Kock, Tamara Vanhaecke, Olga De Troyer and Christophe Debruyne*

## Abstract

The chapter presents the knowledge management system, developed in the context of an interdisciplinary project called TOXIN, for the toxicity testing domain to facilitate the safety assessment of new cosmetic ingredients. Tools have been developed to capture existing knowledge captured in Safety Evaluation Opinions documents issued by the Scientific Committee on Consumer Safety in a knowledge graph, to enrich this knowledge with knowledge from other sources, and to access this knowledge efficiently. Ontologies and semantic technology are used to build the toxicological knowledge graph and its tools. The developed knowledge management system is based on the processes for creating, maintaining, and exploiting knowledge graphs defined in the Abstract Reference Architecture. The chapter discusses the approach followed for developing the knowledge management system, and the tools developed to support the different processes of the Abstract Reference Architecture. These tools include end-user tools, as well as more advanced tools for information technology experts.

**Keywords:** knowledge graph construction, knowledge consumption, knowledge graph enrichment, knowledge graph engineering, data lifting, quality assurance, domain ontology development, end-user development, toxicity testing, jigsaw metaphor

## 1. Introduction

Toxicology is a field of science investigating the potentially harmful effects of chemical compounds on living organisms, including humans. An important branch of toxicology is regulatory toxicology, in which chemical safety assessments are carried out in order to permit decisions towards the protection of health against adverse effects of chemical substances under their conditions of use [1]. Historically, animal testing has formed the basis for chemical safety assessment. Yet, scientific considerations and ethical constraints have driven a worldwide shift towards using animal-free methods for this purpose. This has been enforced by Regulation (EC) NO 1223/2009, imposing a full ban on animal testing in the cosmetics field, but also across other sectors, including pharmaceutical, food, and biocide industries, there is a tendency to address animal-free methods for safety evaluation. This has resulted in efforts to develop animal-free methods for evaluating the safety of chemicals, incorporating cell culturing and computational approaches. In general, there are four main approaches for toxicity testing:

1. *In vivo* toxicity testing involves exposing living animals to a substance to observe its effects on their health and behaviour.

2. *In vitro* toxicity testing involves conducting experiments on cells or tissues taken from a living organism. This method allows for more controlled conditions, as it eliminates the influence of other body systems on the effects of the substance being tested.

3. *In silico* toxicity testing involves using computer models to simulate the effects of a substance on a living organism and how a living organism interacts with a substance. This method relies on mathematical and statistical models and data from *in vivo* and *in vitro* studies to predict the toxic effects of a substance.

4. *In chemico* approaches aim to utilise an understanding of chemical reactivity to obtain insights regarding reactivity, aiding in the assessment of toxicity. Numerous experimental methods exist for assessing reactivity, and there is a growing trend of translating this information into computational (*in silico*) tools to streamline hazard identification. Whether obtained through experimentation or computation, the *in chemico* data should be incorporated into a strategic framework to support the decision-making process.

Although *in vitro*, *in silico*, and *in chemico* testing methods have made advances in supporting animal-free safety assessment of chemicals, in general, different types of methods are combined [2]. For instance, the *in vitro* approach can be complemented with computational approaches to gather, disclose (i.e. make available in a suitable form), and maintain (i.e. keep up to date) available toxicological information of chemical compounds to avoid redundant testing and/or to predict adverse effects of chemical compounds based on similarity. A wealth of data is available in the toxicological domain, but the available data is in a heterogeneous and varied format, including a diverse range of toxicological and risk assessment reports, regulatory standards, and guidelines. Manual searching through the different documents, reports, and data sources is current practice when information is required. This is a time-consuming process, and, in addition, aggregating knowledge and subsequently searching, analysing, and inferring implicit information from the integrated data is hard. Therefore, one challenge in this context is to provide tools for the efficient access, processing, and analysis of relevant data from the toxicological domain. Developing such tools is one of the objectives of the interdisciplinary project TOXIN[1].

TOXIN is developing a knowledge management system that gathers and organises all available toxicity data described in documents issued by the Scientific Committee

---

[1] https://ivtd.research.vub.be/irp-non-animal-methodologies-for-toxicity-testing-of-chemical-compouns-toxin-0

on Consumer Safety[2] about cosmetic ingredients listed as annexed II, III, IV, V, and VI under Regulation EC No 1223/2009. Each such document, called a Safety Evaluation Opinion, contains information about experiments (also called tests) of a chemical compound on e.g. laboratory animals, including information on the outcome of these tests, as well as the authors' opinions about the compound's toxicity. In TOXIN, semantic technology is adopted to build this toxicological knowledge management system. By using semantic technology, the information can be structured flexibly. This is because semantic technology represents and stores information using a graph data model, which is less rigid than the traditional relational model adopted in relational databases. This means that information can be added to entities as needed, avoiding complex data migration. Further, where the schema and data are "tightly coupled" in traditional relational databases, the graph data model in semantic databases is "schemaless"; the "schemas", which are called ontologies later on, are declared as facts themselves, and one can combine several such ontologies. Semantic technology allows us to express the semantics of the information, provides advanced querying mechanisms, and allows us to integrate diverse data from multiple sources into a coherent and meaningful *knowledge graph*. TOXIN's knowledge management system aims to support the non-animal hazard assessment[3] of cosmetic ingredients within the TOXIN project by providing as much knowledge as possible flexibly.

In this chapter, we present the approach followed for developing the knowledge management system, as well as the tools developed for it. The different tools support different processes for creating, maintaining, and exploiting knowledge graphs introduced in Ref. [3] by following the Abstract Reference Architecture (ARA). Two tools are provided for defining the knowledge graph of the knowledge management system and filling it with data: an end-user tool, based on the jigsaw metaphor, that allows the manual definition and filling of a knowledge graph by our subject matter experts (i.e. toxicologists), and a tool to automatically import toxicity data previously collected by the toxicologists from Safety Evaluation Opinions in spreadsheets into the knowledge graph. We also discuss integrating multiple other data sources from the field of toxicology into the TOXIN knowledge system to facilitate hazard assessment of new compounds by presenting the relationships integrating the different data sources to the toxicologists. Next, we discuss how we currently tackle aspects of the quality assurance of the knowledge graph. Furthermore, a search and query tool has been developed allowing toxicologists to explore and search in the knowledge graph. We also discuss how integrating the other data sources from the toxicological field can be used to answer questions formulated in the context of toxicity testing.

The chapter is organised as follows: Section 2 presents the background, i.e. introducing the concept of a knowledge graph, as well as the concepts of ontology and vocabulary. Next, the existing ARA framework for engineering knowledge graphs is presented. In Section 3, related work is discussed. Section 4 presents our approach towards knowledge management, and TOXIN's knowledge management system and the various tools developed so far are explained and demonstrated in Section 5. The chapter ends with conclusions and future work, which are presented in Section 6.

---

[2] https://health.ec.europa.eu/scientific-committees/scientific-committee-consumer-safety-sccs_en

[3] Hazard assessment, i.e., evaluating the intrinsic property of a molecule inducing toxicity out of the use context, is the first step of every safety assessment process.

## 2. Background

In this section, we provide the background of the work. We start by briefly explaining the concepts of a knowledge graph, an ontology, and a vocabulary. Thereafter, we present the ARA framework on which our knowledge management system is based.

### 2.1 Knowledge graph, ontology, and vocabulary

Knowledge graphs use the concept of a graph to describe knowledge of the real world. In graphs, knowledge is represented with nodes and edges where nodes represent entities for the real world and edges represent the relationships between entities [4]. An edge between two entities is called a triple. A triple is an ordered grouping of a subject, a predicate, and an object. A triple or set of triples can be seen as a directed edge-labelled graph called a data graph. A data graph may be identified by a name. Formally, such a named graph is represented by a pair $(n, G)$ where $G$ is a data graph and $n$ is the unique name (or "name") of the graph. One can also find the so-called *default graph*, which is the only graph without a name.

Graphs can be gathered into a graph dataset. A graph dataset is not composed of triples but rather by quadruples (or *quads*), as the name of the graph (if the graph has a name) is added to the triples: $<g,s,p,o>$ where g is the "name" of the graph and $<s,p,o>$ is the triple in the graph. Concretely, a knowledge graph is any graph dataset or combination of graph datasets.

The Resource Description Framework (RDF) [5] is a W3C-recommended abstract graph data model that allows representing data graphs. A set of triples expressed in RDF is called an RDF graph, which can be stored in a named graph.

An ontology can be (re)used or developed to specify which type of knowledge is stored in the knowledge graph [6]. An ontology describes concepts in a domain, the properties of the concepts, the relations between the concepts, and the domain rules that apply to them. In other words, an ontology aims to model a domain with as much precision as possible. In this way, the ontology can be used as a model for the knowledge to be stored, and the knowledge stored can be considered as an instantiation of the ontology [6, 7]. In this case, the knowledge graph is called an *ontology-based knowledge graph*. Using one or more ontologies to build a knowledge graph has the advantage of providing formal definitions of the knowledge that can be stored, its meaning, and possible restrictions on what can be stored. This not only provides an unambiguous description of the knowledge, but it also allows humans, as well as computers, to process the information and infer new knowledge. These ontologies are expressed in ontology languages, of which the Web Ontology Language (OWL) [8] is standardised by the W3C and supports complex reasoning tasks such as concept satisfiability checking (i.e. can a concept have instances?).

Not all knowledge graphs require expressive ontology languages, which come at additional computational costs. Another way to represent the semantics of the relationships within the data graph is using one or more *vocabularies*, which is a name given to lightweight ontologies. These ontologies are either built with a less expressive ontology language or restrict the use of a complex ontology language to those constructs deemed "light-weight". A vocabulary can be used to define class hierarchies, relation hierarchies, and relationships between classes. A vocabulary can be represented with RDF Schema (RDFS) [9]. RDFS is an extension of RDF. RDFS is meant to infer implicit information from explicit information. For instance, if a graph contains $< Garfield, is\ of\ type, Cat >$ and $< Cat, is\ a\ subclass\ of, Animal >$, then an RDFS reasoner can infer that $< Garfield, is\ of\ type, Animal >$. While already powerful and often used, it does not support complex reasoning tasks such as checking whether classes (e.g. *Cat*) can have instances or whether there are contradictions in the model or the data.

## 2.2 Ontology-based knowledge graph

As explained in the previous subsection, an ontology-based knowledge graph is a knowledge graph where one or more ontologies are used to define which type of knowledge can be stored in the knowledge graph [6].

Note that sometimes, the instances of the concepts and relationships defined in the ontology (i.e. the "real" data) are also considered as part of the ontology, removing the strict separation between model and data. However, we follow the approach proposed by Chasseray et al. in Ref. [7], where the distinction between model and "data" is kept: A knowledge graph is composed of a *domain ontology* and an *instantiated ontology*[4]. The domain ontology is used to specify the organisational structure of the knowledge graph, and as the name indicates, the instantiated ontology is an instantiation of the domain ontology containing the actual instances (i.e. data).

Furthermore, Chasseray et al. [7] combine ontologies with the OMG's Model-Driven Engineering (MDE) approach. MDE defines four modelling levels: data level, model level, meta-model level, and meta-metamodel level [10]. Following this MDE approach, three levels are considered for ontology modelling by Chasseray et al.: an instantiated ontology (i.e. the data level) is defined by a domain ontology (i.e. the model level), which is an instantiation of an *upper ontology* (i.e. the meta-model level), which defines the concepts and relationships needed to define domain ontologies. Note that the meta-metamodel level of MDE is not used in this approach. We show this three-levelled structure for an ontology-based knowledge graph in **Figure 1**.

## 2.3 Abstract reference architecture

In Ref. [3], the Abstract Reference Architecture (ARA) is introduced to define the main processes and tasks required during the life cycle of knowledge graphs. ARA consists of three layers: *Knowledge Acquisition and Integration Layer*, *Knowledge Storage Layer*, and *Knowledge Consumption Layer*, which correspond to the three major tasks related to using a knowledge graph in organisations: construction, storage, and consumption. See **Figure 2** for an illustration. Each of these tasks consists of sub-tasks:

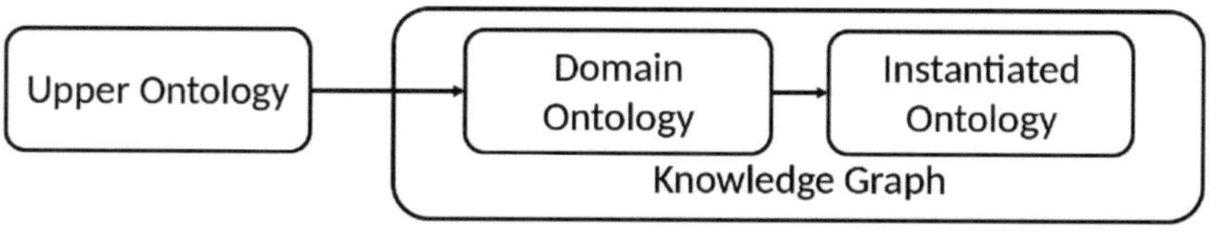


**Figure 1.**
*Ontology-based knowledge graph structure based on the Model-Driven Engineering (MDE) approach (adapted from [7]).*

[4] or a set of these when the knowledge graph is defined by more than one ontology

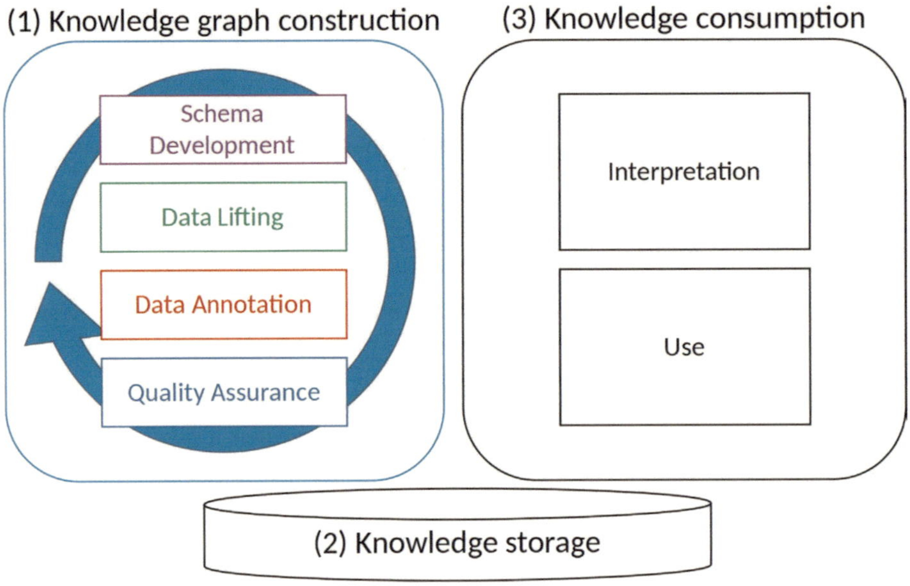


**Figure 2.**
*The architecture of a knowledge graph project depicting the various processes and tasks in knowledge graph engineering, based on Ref. [3].*

1. ARA distinguishes four sub-tasks in the Knowledge Acquisition and Integration Layer: *Schema Development*, *Data Lifting*, *Data Annotation*, and *Quality Assurance*. According to ARA, the first task is Schema Development (i.e. the development of the domain ontology). Data Lifting transforms raw data (e.g. stored in spreadsheets or classical databases) into semantic data. Data Annotation deals with linking and enriching the data with other relevant sources (e.g. other ontologies, knowledge graphs, vocabularies, or even classical databases), resulting in interlinked and contextualised semantic data. Quality assurance is about ensuring that the knowledge graph is of good quality, as one must rely on accurate data[5]. In **Figure 2**, one can see that the outcome of each of these activities informs the other. For instance, when the schema evolves, the transformation and integration of data into the knowledge graph may need to be updated.

2. The Knowledge Storage Layer deals with the storage of the knowledge graph. Two main architectural options are mentioned in Ref. [3]: (1) reusing existing data storage and providing mappings between the ontology and the data schemes of the existing storage and (2) using a graph-based data store.

3. The Knowledge Consumption Layer provides tools for interested parties to access the knowledge. Examples include search and querying tools.

[5] The difference between the two is that the former refers to mistakes (e.g. typos) and the latter to domain axioms not being respected (e.g. an instance cannot be an element of two disjoint classes).

## 3. Related work

### 3.1 Existing tools for supporting hazard assessment

Because the aim of the TOXIN knowledge system is to support the hazard assessment of new cosmetic ingredients, we first discuss existing tools in this context.

There are several approaches to hazard assessment, and various tools have been developed to support this process. One such tool is the OECD QSAR Toolbox [11], which is a software application that aims to classify chemicals based on their structural characteristics and potential toxic mechanisms of interaction. In this way, this toolbox can provide some support for hazard assessment.

COSMOS NG [12] is another tool and provides a database of toxicity opinions about several chemicals that can be used for hazard assessment. COSMOS NG also provides *in silico* tools for analysing toxicity data and, e.g. performing category formation. Compared to TOXIN, the datasets used are different, but even for the common ingredients, only oral exposure studies are included in COSMOS NG and used for *in silico* predictions, such as DNA binding or physicochemical properties. TOXIN is currently based on mainly *in vivo*-based hazard assessment with extra input from *in silico* testing (from the OECD QSAR toolbox). Therefore, it can be used to analyse how *in vivo* effects are related to the function or the structure of the ingredients.

VEGA HUB[6] includes several *in silico* models for hazard assessment, which can be freely downloaded. It predicts several toxicity endpoints, such as liver toxicity, skin sensitisation, carcinogenicity, and endocrine disruption. Another software available on VEGA HUB is Vermeer Cosmolife, which has the particularity to incorporate the context of use (called exposure scenario) and, therefore, can be used also for risk assessment.

There are other web applications available providing information for a more accurate and animal-free hazard assessment with a focus on one single endpoint, e.g. Vienna Livertox workspace[7], or on multiple endpoints, e.g. SApredictor[8] and ICE[9].

In a broader context, there is a growing interest in developing standardised vocabularies and ontologies that can be used to represent data about different toxicity tests efficiently [13]. The OpenTox initiative [14] aims to provide a framework for integrating and analysing diverse data sources using an ontology to improve the predictability of toxicology models and support decision-making in chemical safety assessment.

Tox21 [15] is a research program that seeks to identify new mechanisms of chemical activity in cells and use this information to prioritise untested chemicals for further evaluation and to develop more accurate predictive models of human response to toxic substances. One purpose is to provide a screening tool that would quickly identify potential hazards amongst a long list of potentially toxic compounds.

The work conducted in TOXIN has similarities with the previously mentioned initiatives. However, it is different in the sense that the main aim of our knowledge management system is to have a tool that can support toxicologists in the *in vitro* toxicity testing of cosmetic compounds by providing reliable and accurate existing

---

6 https://www.vegahub.eu/portfolio-types/in-silico-models/

7 https://livertox.univie.ac.at/

8 http://www.sapredictor.cn/index.php

9 https://ice.ntp.niehs.nih.gov/

information relevant for hazard assessment. In this way, it is more limited in its scope than the work conducted in Tox21. The OECD toolbox is currently used in TOXIN in the querying tool to provide a Hazard Evaluation Support System (HESS) for repeated dose toxicity studies using toxicological categories within the applicability domain of the tool. The *in silico* HESS predictions add value to the hazard assessment by pointing to or against a specific type of toxicity based on the structure of the chemicals.

### 3.2 Work on linking data related to toxicology

Numerous studies focused on linking data related to toxicology: Ref. [16] focuses on a comprehensive map of disease-symptom relations, Ref. [17] presents a method for representing the organisation of human cellular processes in a network and mapping diseases onto this network, and Ref. [18] provides an overview of existing work on integrating genes, pathways, and phenotypes to understand the effects of gene mutations better. While these studies are valuable contributions to the toxicology domain, they are specific. Moreover, their approaches may not necessarily apply to the broader task of integrating different available data sources.

## 4. Approach

As already explained in the introduction, our approach to knowledge management and the tools developed for it are based on the Abstract Reference Architecture (ARA).

**Figure 3** provides an overview of the tasks defined for our knowledge management system. As described by ARA, the process starts with the Knowledge Graph Construction process that consists of four tasks: Ontology Development, Data Lifting, Data Annotation & Enrichment, and Quality Assurance.

Ontology Development is concerned with developing the knowledge graph's schema, which is done by means of an ontology, created with an ontology language.

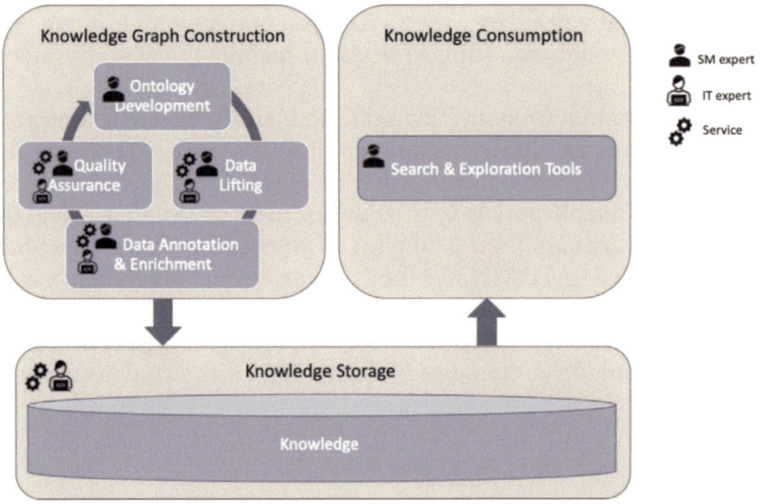


**Figure 3.**
*TOXIN's knowledge Management approach adapted from Ref. [19].*

As already indicated, we follow [6, 7] in the sense that a knowledge graph is the combination of a schema (i.e. an ontology) and an instantiation of that ontology (i.e. the data).

The term data lifting is used in ARA to denote the activities related to populating the knowledge graph. We have foreseen different ways to populate the knowledge graph in our knowledge management system. Subject matter experts can enter data manually. However, importing data from non-RDF sources, i.e. from spreadsheets, is also possible.

In ARA, Data Annotation comprises the activities of linking concepts and data with other relevant sources (e.g. other ontologies, knowledge graphs, vocabularies, or even classical databases), resulting in interlinked semantic data. We have called this task "Data Annotation & Enrichment" to better emphasise that data annotation also includes linking the data to existing sources. Some data annotation activities can be done manually by subject matter experts, but linking for the purpose of enrichment can be more complicated and may need the help of IT experts, although tools can also be developed for (semi-) automatic data annotation & enrichment.

Quality assurance is about ensuring that no mistakes are introduced into the knowledge graph and its ontology. This is a complex issue. In general, it concerns two aspects [20]: (1) the question of whether the knowledge graph has been built correctly, i.e. according to the requirements, and (2) the question of whether the right knowledge graph has been built, i.e. does the ontology correctly reflect the domain and does it contain correct data? Some quality control can be performed by subject matter experts, more technical aspects can be controlled by IT experts, but manual quality control is time-intensive. Tools could be helpful in this respect.

The Knowledge Storage process deals with the storage of the knowledge graph. In this process, we decide how to store and service the data to the various applications built on top of this knowledge graph. Since we build a knowledge graph with semantic technologies (i.e. RDF as the graph data model and Semantic Web ontology languages), we use a triplestore. A triplestore is a name commonly given to RDF graph databases.

The Knowledge Consumption provides query, search, & exploration functionality.

For the tools, we have followed an end-user approach as much as possible [19]. This is done because the direct use of semantic technology is often complicated for subject matter experts who are not technologically skilled. IT experts can be called in, but for specialised domains, such as the toxicology domain, it may take a long time before IT experts have familiarised themselves with the domain. In addition, an IT expert needs to stay available for the complete lifetime of the knowledge management system as knowledge systems tend to evolve over time, e.g. new properties, relationships, and concepts may be needed, and new data must be added. Furthermore, during the Knowledge Consumption process, the assistance of IT experts may be needed, e.g. for the formulation of (new) queries or for the development of (new) reasoning support. To avoid being largely or completely dependent on IT experts, we developed end-user tools where possible. This means that subject matter experts who are not skilled in Computer Science (in our case, toxicologists) should be able to use these tools with some minimal training. Ideally, all tasks in ARA should be accessible to subject matter experts; however, this seems not feasible for some tasks. In particular, automatic Data Lifting, automatic Data Annotation & Enrichment, Quality Assurance, and Knowledge Storage may require the assistance of IT experts. For the ontology development and the manual data input, we used the jigsaw metaphor [21]. The purpose of using this metaphor was to hide the technicalities of the semantic technology.

In **Figure 3**, three different icons are used to indicate who can perform the tasks. If a subject matter (SM) expert can perform the task, the SM expert icon is used, for instance, an SM expert can query the knowledge storage. The IT expert icon indicates that an IT expert should perform the task or at least be involved. The service icon is used to indicate that a (part of a) task can be done automatically. For instance, Data Lifting, Data Annotation & Enrichment and Quality Assurance have all three icons meaning that these tasks can be partially done by subject matter experts, partially by IT experts, and partially automated.

## 5. TOXIN's knowledge management system

We present the tools developed for the knowledge management system of TOXIN in this section. Recall that the ultimate goal of this knowledge management system is to support toxicologists in the hazard assessment of new compounds by bringing together multiple sources of available toxicological information into a knowledge graph and allowing them to query and search the graph.

The first aim was to gather information about toxicity tests, described in documents dossiers, called Safety Evaluation Opinions, issued by the Scientific Committee on Consumer Safety (SCCS) about cosmetic ingredients in a knowledge graph. Each dossier contains information about experiments (also called tests) of a compound mainly conducted on laboratory animals. The information includes the quantity of the compound tested, how it was inoculated, the species on which the compound was tested, and so on. The dossiers also include information on the outcome of these tests, as well as the authors' opinions about the compound's toxicity. The data contained in these dossiers are stored in an ontology-based knowledge graph to provide more efficient access to this data for toxicologists.

The second aim is to enrich this knowledge graph with information from other relevant sources in the toxicology domain.

Because the development of the knowledge management system is based on ARA, we describe the tool support for the different tasks in ARA described in Section 4.

### 5.1 Ontology development support

While ontology development is one of the tasks within our approach, we want to emphasise that the purpose of this step is not to allow toxicologists to create full-fledged domain ontology but to set up an ontology-based knowledge graph, where the role of the ontology is to define the organisational structure of the knowledge graph. The ontology that needs to be developed corresponds more with a vocabulary rather than a highly axiomatised ontology. Therefore, the expressiveness of the developed tool is kept limited with the aim to curb the learning curve for the toxicologists.

The tool developed for defining a domain ontology is a web-based application built on top of Apache Jena. The jigsaw metaphor [21], used in the tool to hide the technicalities of the semantic technology used, is implemented via the Google Blockly JavaScript library. The tool is not limited to the toxicology domain, but can also be used for other domains to define the ontology for an ontology-based knowledge graph. It is described in detail in [19, 22]. Here, we provide a short description to show the reader how the tool is used to develop the ontology of TOXIN's knowledge management system.

*DOI: http://dx.doi.org/10.5772/intechopen.1002341*

A predefined jigsaw block is provided to allow toxicologists to define the domain concepts in the ontology by themselves. In this way, toxicologists can easily define the domain concepts for which they will maintain information in the knowledge graph. An example of such a domain concept is "Repeated Dose Toxicity", which is used extensively in Safety Evaluation Opinions. **Figure 4** shows the web page for defining this domain concept. On the left-hand side of the page, one can see the predefined jigsaw block (i.e. top-level blue block "Domain Concept") that allows specifying the domain concept. Properties can be added by dragging and dropping the empty *Property* block from the *Custom Properties* tab in the menu at the left and filling the slots. Properties have a name, a value type, and an optional default value. In the example, the first property of the domain concept is named "OECD test nr" with value type "number" and no default value. Note that we also have the *Default Properties* tab in the left sidebar menu, which provides predefined blocks for recurring properties, such as the property "year". Re-using these recurring property blocks will improve the consistency of the ontology (as the recurring properties will always be defined in the same way) and speed up the specification process.

A domain concept can be composed of other domain concepts. In **Figure 4**, we see that the toxicologist specified that the *Repeated Dose Toxicity* concept is further composed of the *endpoints of repeated dose toxicity*, the *test method of repeated dose toxicity,* and the *reliability of test repeated dose toxicity* concept. This is shown in the blue Domain Concept block under the "Composed of" field. The "Composed of" dropdown allows adding other composing concepts. The dropdown "Is subconcept of" is used to indicate that a concept is a sub-concept of another concept. This can be used to introduce hierarchies between concepts. The ontology development process generally goes as follows (see **Figure 5**). The toxicologists use general jigsaw blocks to create the domain ontology, i.e. to define the domain concepts and their relationships needed for the knowledge graph. For each defined domain concept, a domain-specific jigsaw block will be generated. These generated jigsaw blocks can then, in turn, be used later on by toxicologists to compose and fill the knowledge graph (explained in the next

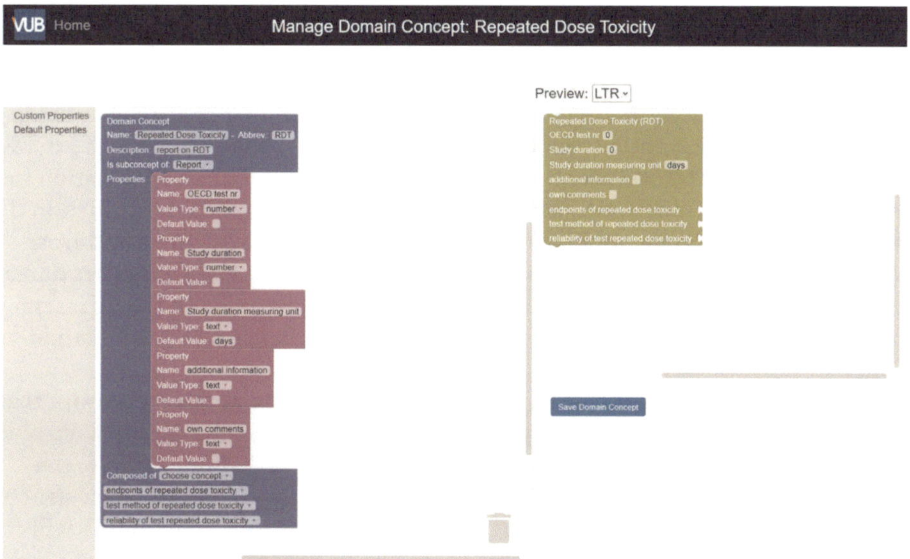


**Figure 4.**
*Screenshot of the domain concept definition page.*

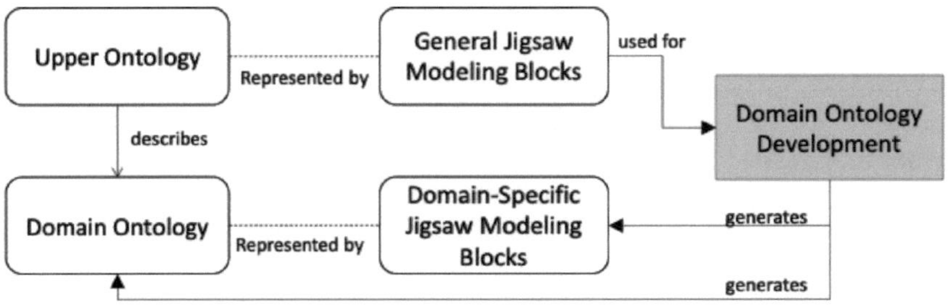


**Figure 5.**
*Ontology Development Process Using the Jigsaw Metaphor (taken from [19]).*

section (Section 5.2.1)). On the right in **Figure 4**, a preview of the generated jigsaw block for the domain concept defined on the left is given. In this case, the jigsaw block contains three puzzle connectors on the right side, one for each composing concept, and five slots, one for each property.

## 5.2 Data lifting support

The current purpose of the Data Lifting task of the TOXIN knowledge management system is to capture, in the knowledge graph, information about *in vivo* tests described in Safety Evaluation Opinions issued by the Scientific Committee on Consumer Safety (SCCS) about cosmetic ingredients.

### *5.2.1 Manual data lifting*

The first way to do this is by manually entering the information while reading a Safety Evaluation Opinion. For this, a toxicologist can use the domain-specific jigsaw blocks generated for the different domain concepts defined in the ontology. For example, when a toxicologist wants to enter the information from a particular Safety Evaluation Opinion document, they use the domain-specific jigsaw blocks created during the Ontology Development Process for Safety Evaluation Opinions (described in the previous section) to compose a so-called *dossier* (representing the opinion). They do so by connecting the relevant puzzle blocks and filling in the value fields in the blocks (see **Figure 6** for a (partial) example dossier). The jigsaw blocks can only be composed in a restricted way (i.e. as defined in the ontology) and validation for data fields is provided. **Figure 6**, for example, shows how a toxicologist filled in the dossier on "Tetrabromophenol Blue" by adding the report block "Repeated Dose Toxicity" block (created as shown in **Figure 4**) and connecting it with other domain concepts to complete the report. After that, the toxicologist filled in the different property values corresponding to the information found in the safety evaluation opinion[10].

In order to save time during the manual entering of data and also to ensure that similar data is always entered in the same way, the tool allows the user to save block structures so that they can be reused in multiple dossiers as is. For example, the "Repeated Dose Toxicity" block shown in **Figure 6** could be saved as a block structure. Then this block and all its sub-components (i.e. blocks attached to its right) will appear in the tab "saved block structures" depicted in **Figure 7**. These saved block

[10] https://health.ec.europa.eu/system/files/2021-08/sccs_o_232_0.pdf

**Figure 6.**
*Jigsaw Block composed for the dossier "Tetrabromophenol Blue".*

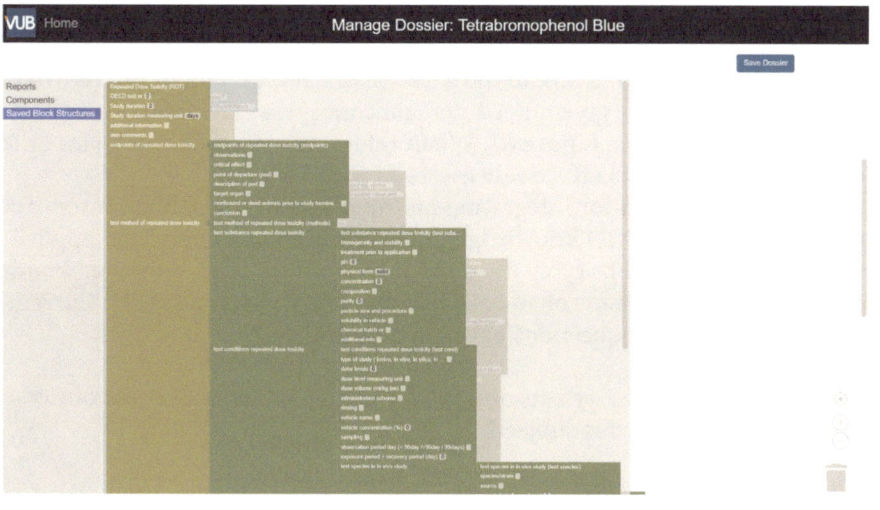


**Figure 7.**
*Screenshot of the dossier creation page's saved block structure tab.*

structures can be dragged and dropped as a whole, which saves time when composing another dossier.

### *5.2.2 Automatic data lifting*

In the past, the toxicologists of the TOXIN project used spreadsheets to structure and store information from Safety Evaluation Opinions. Because a considerable amount of time was spent on creating these spreadsheets, it was decided to develop a tool to import the data into the knowledge graph automatically.

We have used R2RML to transform the spreadsheets into RDF. R2RML is a W3C Recommendation for transforming relational data into RDF. Although spreadsheets are not relational databases, once stored as comma-separated values (CSV) files, they can be considered as containing relational data (i.e. rows with attributes). R2RML engines (and dialects) such as RML [23] and R2RML-F [24] provide support for CSV files. We have chosen to adopt R2RML-F as this particular engine loads the CSV files into an in-memory relational database, which allows manipulating the data in the records with SQL prior to generating RDF.

The only requirement is that the CSV files are well-formed (e.g. the first row contains the names of attributes and no duplicates are allowed). This requirement is ensured by the people curating the spreadsheets. The advantage of using R2RML is that when new spreadsheets need to be transformed into RDF, one only needs to specify new R2RML mappings (which can be done by an IT expert). So far, data from 93 scientific opinions dealing with 88 different cosmetic ingredients, published between 2009 and 2019 by SCCS, were imported this way.

### 5.3 Data annotation and enrichment support

The current purpose of the task is to facilitate access to relevant toxicological data and provide answers to specific questions that the toxicologists formulated (see below). In a later stage, the annotations and enrichment could be used for AI-based reasoning.

First, simple manual data annotation is possible while defining the ontology and entering data. For a dossier, a link to the Safety Evaluation Opinion file for which the dossier is created should be given. For a domain concept, an IRI referring to a relevant source can be provided (see **Figure 8**). When references to other ontologies or RDF datasets are provided, users effectively create Linked Data[11].

Furthermore, a method for integrating multiple toxicological data sources and linking them with the TOXIN knowledge graph has been developed and applied [25]. The method starts with identifying the desired capabilities of the enriched knowledge management system by means of so-called Competency Questions [26]. Currently, the following competency questions have been formulated:

1. Knowing some adverse effects observed in a subject, what diseases or toxic processes may affect this subject?

2. Which biological processes or pathways are affected by a certain disease?

3. The functioning of what gene or protein is impaired by some toxic process?

These questions helped to select the potential sources for the enrichment. In collaboration with the toxicologists, the following sources were selected: TXPO [27], OGG [28], Uniprot [29], Reactome [30], Kegg [31], and CTD [32]. We furthermore identified the Gene Ontology (GO) [33] and Gene Ontology Causal Activity Modelling

[11] Linked Data is an initiative in which one published RDF data according to specific best practices that result in interconnected data stored on different servers; a Web of data.

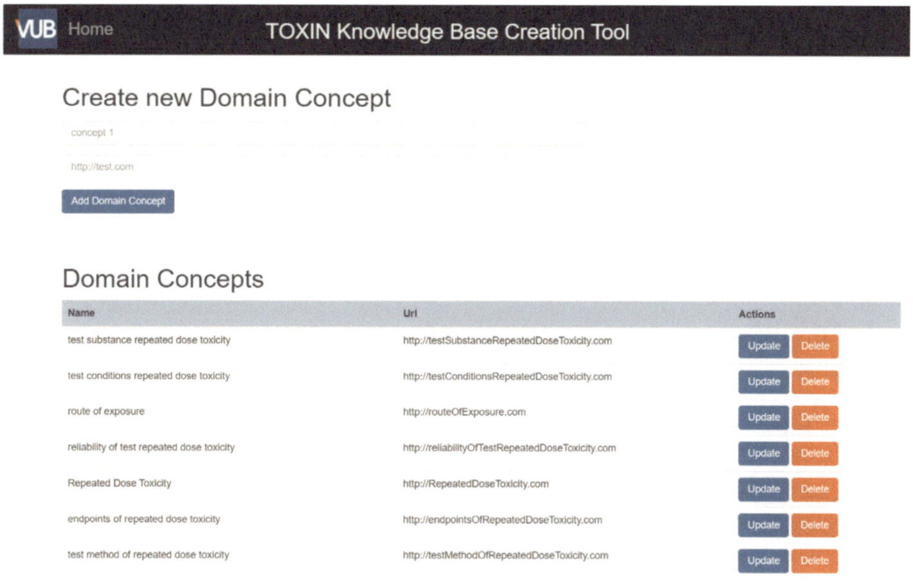


**Figure 8.**
*Web page for domain concept creation and modification showing IRIs to related sources.*

(GO-CAM) [34]. GO is a comprehensive and structured data source that classifies and describes genes and gene products based on their biological functions, cellular locations, and molecular activities. GO is a resource that many of the other initiatives reference in their data.

The ToXic Process Ontology (TXPO) is an ontology designed to represent causal relationships between toxic processes. Its purpose is to clarify the toxicological mechanisms from latent to toxic manifestations in order to help in drug development. Similar to TOXIN, their current focus is on the liver, as it has been identified as one of the most affected organs upon oral administration of cosmetic ingredients to animals [35].

TXPO contains a set of human genes that are imported from the Ontology of Genes and Genomes (OGG). This ontology focuses on offering classes and relationships to represent genes and genomes in different organisms. TXPO only imports the genes related to human organisms. TXPO also contains entities and relationships from the Gene Ontology (GO) [33]. The goal of this ontology is to represent the functions of genes. To create relationships between a toxic process and the genes or proteins affected by this process, GO is the perfect intermediate. Some links already exist in TXPO between a toxic process and the natural processes that it affects. For this, GO annotations are used that represent the link between a GO term, i.e. a biological role and a gene product (gene or protein) that assumes this role in the organism. Each annotation is associated with a proof, which has a weight representing the confidence in the annotation. We considered the integration of annotations from two sources: OGG and from the gene ontology resource[12]. This resource regroups annotations made for a large variety of species and from several different sources. We chose to integrate only human gene products from UniProt.

---

12 http://geneontology.org

GO-CAM is developed by the GO community and is a modelling approach that builds upon GO. GO-CAM introduces models to connect GO annotations to represent causal relationships between gene products and biological processes, providing a more detailed and explicit representation of molecular events. The GO-CAM approach allows for the representation of specific regulatory interactions and signalling pathways, enabling researchers to analyse and interpret biological data in a more precise and context-dependent manner. For example, a GO-CAM model could show that the hyper-function of a biological process positively regulates another process. These relationships allow toxicologists to track a toxic effect from its starting point to all the other elements that are indirectly affected. GO-CAM is thus an interesting resource to represent the different relationships between biological processes.

Reactome and Kegg are two well-known pathways repositories. To integrate pathways from both repositories, we used associations from the Comparative Toxicogenomics Database (CTD). CTD combines biological data by manually curating and linking information from published literature. It offers several files containing the relationships between different biological entities, and for TOXIN, we used the disease pathway association file.

To perform the integration of (parts of) the different sources, we defined an upper structure, which is based on the TXPO ontology that has been developed to be used as a structure to build ontology-based knowledge graphs. While TXPO offers a set of classes and axioms, i.e. an ontology, we wanted to use the identifiers of these classes as individuals. Luckily, using semantic technology allows us to reuse these identifiers in a different ontology—our upper structure.

For the integration, we have chosen to maintain the original IRIs to uniquely identify the resources they describe and maintain the authority of the original sources. However, for the additional links and entities created for the integration, we have designed our own named graphs to describe them. This choice allows us to clearly distinguish between original resources and those added as part of the integration. This architecture is illustrated in **Figure 9**.

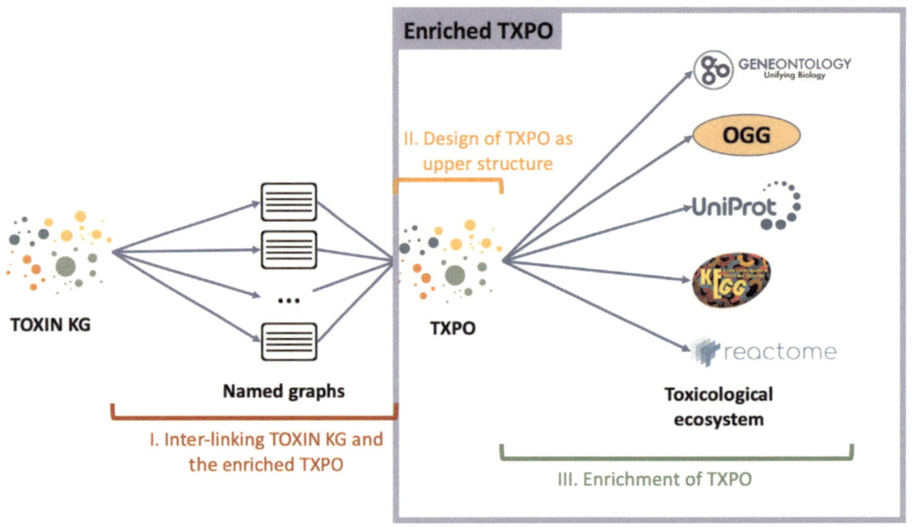


**Figure 9.**
*Schema of TEKG with the relations between TOXIN KG and the enriched TXPO.*

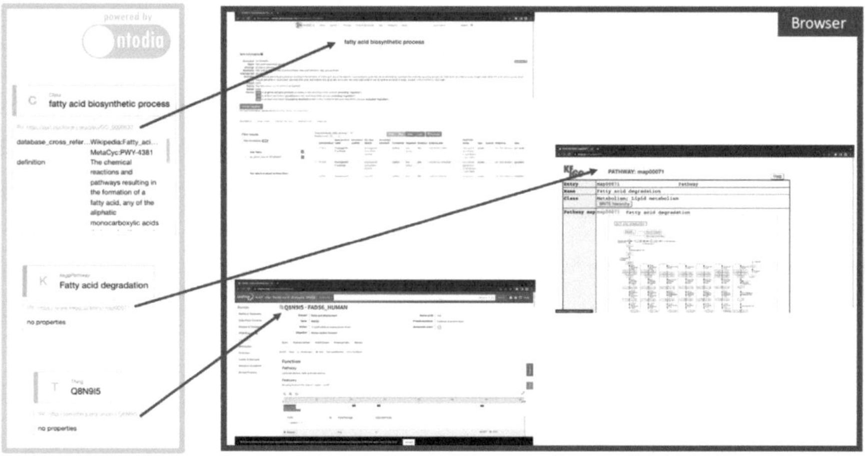


**Figure 10.**
*Illustration of the possibility of accessing the external sources from which data was integrated through the IRIs.*

The decision to retain the authoritative resources' IRI whenever possible allows access to additional information about entities in the knowledge graph from the original data source. An example of this can be seen in **Figure 10**. On the left of the figure, we can see three entities of the enriched knowledge graph represented with Ontodia (see Section 5.6 for more details about Ontodia). When the IRIs of these entities are visited, e.g. by clicking on them and loading the resource in a Web browser, the resources on the right of the image appear. This illustrates that we can access the source data through the IRI representing an entity. In other words, not only are the resources conceptually integrated, we even have "integrated" systems thanks to the distributed graph data model offered by RDF.

Concerning the linking of the TOXIN knowledge graph and the enriched TXPO, two kinds of links can be made. Firstly, direct links can be made between an effect observed in a dossier and the same effect present in the enriched TXPO. Secondly, from the observations and the conclusions in a dossier, a domain expert (who has the knowledge to infer the toxic effects from the observations) can infer "indirect" links between the dossier and the toxic effects or diseases that affect the test animal. There is no absolute knowledge about how to link some observations and a toxic effect, and errors can occur. Therefore, the links are stored in different named graphs. Each graph corresponds to an individual, a group, or a particular knowledge responsible for defining the links that it contains. In this way, it is possible to query only some of these links depending on who made them and on what ground. This type of linking is a manual process. Another approach is to create these links automatically. For the direct links, it is straightforward. The task is to infer the relations owl:sameAs between the TOXIN knowledge graph and the enriched TXPO, and tools exist to find these relations, such as Silk [36] and Alignment API [37]. Concerning the "indirect" links, some rule-based mechanisms could be put in place. This is subject to future work.

### 5.4 Quality assurance support

Currently, the support for quality assurance is limited in our tool to manual quality checking and the validation of the structure of the data in the knowledge graph by means of SHACL shapes. With SHACL [38], a W3C Recommendation, one can validate RDF graphs, i.e. one can validate the structure of triples in a Closed World Setting. SHACL provides a set of "core" constructs for declaring rules (value- and data type checking, cardinality, value ranges, comparisons, ... which can be combined with a set of logical operators). Validating the knowledge graph with SHACL is especially valuable in the case of the automatic import of the spreadsheets' data. A SHACL shape is a subset of an RDF graph, which can be declared, and to which one can add constraints.

Because we cannot expect that toxicologists can formulate constraints in SHACL, we looked for an approach by which the SHACL shapes and constraints can be generated. How this is achieved is explained in [19].

### 5.5 Knowledge storage

While quite a few triplestores are available (both free, commercial, and free for research purposes), we have adopted Apache Fuseki[13] for managing the storage of triples, named graphs, and SPARQL endpoints. The ontology is stored in one named graph. The data that have been lifted are stored in another. Data that have been integrated from other sources with the enrichment scripts are also stored in dedicated named graphs. This allows us to separate the ontology and the data, and to ensure that data from various sources (and possibly with different interpretations) are not mixed up.

### 5.6 Knowledge consumption support

Knowledge consumption concerns the access and use of the knowledge graph by end-users. The primary use of TOXIN's knowledge graph is to provide liver-specific toxicological information. For this purpose, a web tool has been developed that allows one to search TOXIN's knowledge graph from two perspectives; from the perspective of chemical compounds and from the perspective of health effects.

In the first perspective, one can search the knowledge graph for dossiers (i.e. Safety Evaluation Opinions) about specific compounds by means of the CAS number, INCI name, or SMILES string of the compound. For example, HC Yellow n° 2 can be found using the INCI name "HC Yellow n° 2", the CAS no 4926-55-0, or the SMILES string "C1 = CC=C(C(=C1)NCCO)[N+](=O)[O-]". As a result, a summary of information on the searched compound is given; an interface to the OECD QSAR toolbox is provided to select information from this toolbox for the compound, e.g. the Hazard Evaluation Support System (HESS) *in silico* prediction; and a list of the dossiers (i.e. opinions) that deal with the compound. The dossiers are grouped by the endpoints (acute toxicity, repeated dose toxicity, skin sensitisation, mutagenicity, and carcinogenicity). Clicking on such a dossier will show the information stored for the dossier, such as the OECD guideline number, dose levels, and GLP compliance. The UI for this perspective is shown in **Figure 11**.

In the second perspective, the user can search for compounds with dossiers mentioning a specific toxicological outcome by selecting a health endpoint. For the moment, the endpoints acute toxicity, repeated dose toxicity, and toxicokinetics are supported by the tool. As a result, in the "compound view" all relevant dossiers ordered by compound are listed (see **Figure 12** below); the "Opinions view" lists the relevant dossiers (i.e. opinions) directly (similar to the bottom part of **Figure 11**).

[13] https://jena.apache.org/documentation/fuseki2/

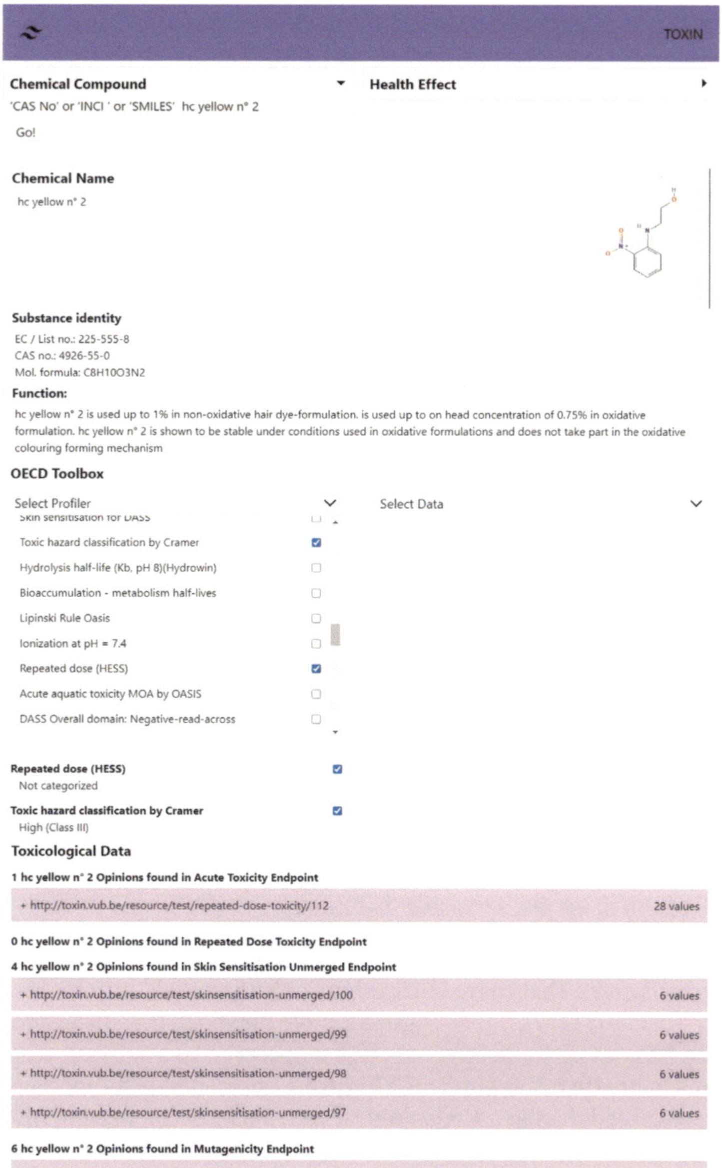


**Figure 11.**
*Partial screenshot of the search result of the chemical compound "HC Yellow n° 2".*

The user can easily filter the output by the type of test conducted (*in vivo* and/or *in vitro*) and by whether OECD guidelines were employed. Moreover, extended filters can search for values in certain parts coming from the opinions. The UI for this perspective is shown in **Figure 12** for the "Repeated dose toxicity" health effect.

A dedicated tool for querying and searching the enriched Knowledge graph described in Section 5.3 has yet to be developed, but an existing tool, Ontodia [39], has been used to show that the competency questions formulated by the toxicologists can be answered. Ontodia is a tool allowing one to visually explore a triple-based

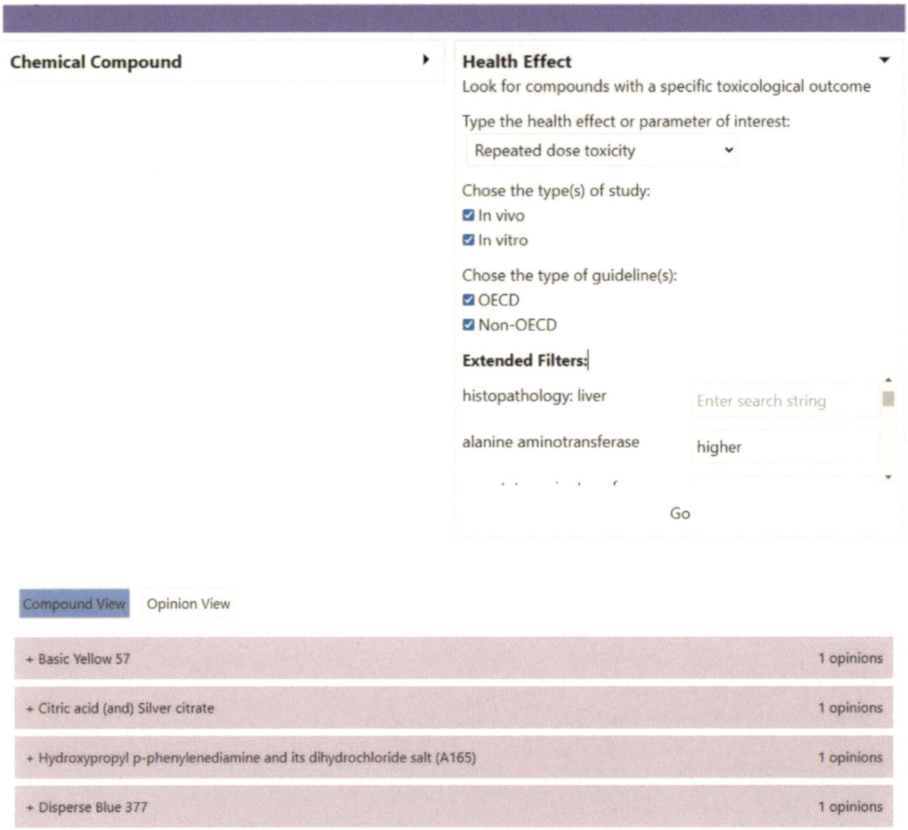


**Figure 12.**
*Screenshot of the search by Health Effect: "Repeated Dose Toxicity".*

knowledge graph using diagrams and faceted browsing, providing a way to navigate knowledge graphs (note that there exist other tools that could also be used for this purpose, such as WebVOWL[14]). In **Figure 13**, we illustrate the answer to the competency question "Knowing some adverse effects observed in a subject, what diseases or toxic processes may affect this subject?" **Figure 13** presents different adverse effects that could be observed during a toxicological test, such as "Increasing blood ALP concentration". These adverse effects are linked to toxic courses or diseases with the predicates "has part" and "has context". These predicates allow one to query all the toxic courses for which an adverse effect could be observed. Moreover, relationships between toxic processes are represented. However, it not only allows for finding toxic processes related to an adverse outcome, but it also allows for the examination of the relationships between adverse effects, toxic effects, toxic courses, and diseases.

## 6. Conclusions

In this chapter, we presented the knowledge management system developed in the TOXIN project to support toxicologists in the animal-free hazard assessment of new

[14] http://vowl.visualdataweb.org/webvowl.html

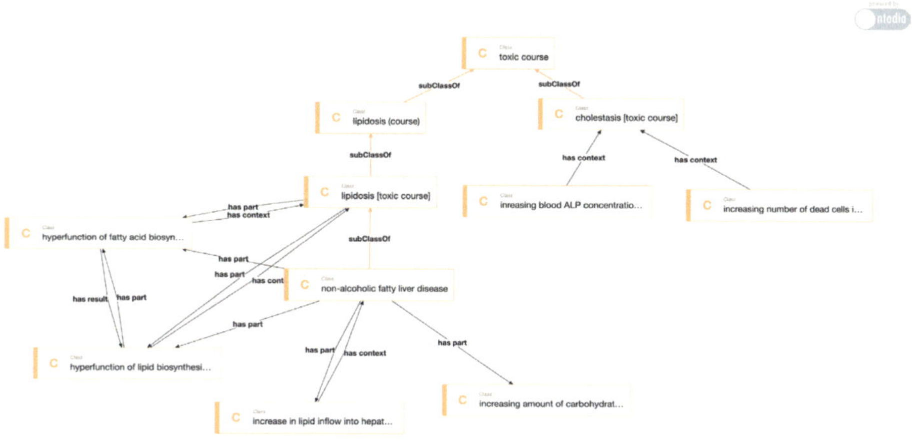


**Figure 13.**
*Illustration of how the enriched knowledge graph can be used to answer the competency question "Knowing some adverse effects observed in a subject, what diseases or toxic processes may affect this subject?".*

cosmetic compounds. The developed knowledge management system is based on the tasks defined for creating, maintaining, and exploiting knowledge graphs in the Abstract Reference Architecture (ARA), which defines the main processes and tasks required during the life cycle of knowledge graphs. The knowledge system is developed as a knowledge graph by means of semantic technology, and tools were developed for the following ARA tasks: the Ontology Development, Data Lifting, Data Annotation & Enrichment, Quality Assurance, and Knowledge Consumption.

In addition, special attention has been paid to the fact that subject matter experts, i.e. toxicologists, should be able to perform most of the tasks by themselves. Where possible, the tools shield the non-IT users as much as possible from the technical aspects of the technology used and they are able to use these tools with some minimal training. For the tasks for which this was impossible, automatic tools were developed where possible.

The different developed tools have been described. Two tools are provided for defining the knowledge graph and populating it with data. First, we have developed an end-user tool, based on the jigsaw metaphor, that allows the manual definition and population of a knowledge graph by toxicologists. In addition, we developed a tool to automatically import toxicity data previously collected by the subject matter experts in spreadsheets into the knowledge graph. A search and query tool has been developed that allows toxicologists to explore and search in the knowledge graph by means of a simple web-based user interface and without the need to use the technical query language SPARQL. Furthermore, we integrated multiple data sources from the field of toxicology into the TOXIN knowledge graph to further support the hazard assessment of new compounds. For exploring this enriched knowledge graph, an existing tool, i.e. Ontodia, is currently used. Finally, we investigated an approach to deal with some aspects of the quality assurance of the knowledge graph.

For future work, we are considering the use of Natural Language Processing (NLP) techniques for different tasks. We observed that relying solely on text matching for searching in the knowledge graph is insufficient, especially when seeking knowledge from diverse sources. For example, if a toxicologist wants to know which chemical compounds raise the value of a particular observation, they might search using the term "increase", however, given that different terminology is used to describe this effect, such as "growth" or "change", they will miss a few search results. In addition, sometimes results of tests are entered all together as one large text block rather than as separate results. Sometimes a value was even considered as a concept or the other way around when entering the knowledge, which means that searching should not be limited to the values of properties but also the names of concepts and properties should be considered.

Last but not least, other future work concerns the addition of a data provenance layer [40] to our knowledge graph, which will allow to trace who has added which information and when.

## Acknowledgements

The TOXIN project is financially supported by Vrije Universiteit Brussel under Grant IRP19.

Some funding came from Cosmetics Europe and the European Chemical Industry Council (CEFIC).

The research of Audrey Sanctorum has been funded by an FWO Postdoc Fellowship (1276721 N) of the Research Foundation Flanders.

## Acronyms

| | |
|---|---|
| ALP | alkaline phosphatase |
| ARA | abstract reference architecture |
| CAS | chemical abstracts service |
| CTD | comparative toxicogenomics database |
| CVS | comma-separated values |
| EC | European Commission |
| GLP | good laboratory practice (GLP) |
| GO | gene ontology |
| GO-CAM | gene ontology causal activity modelling |
| HESS | hazard evaluation support system |
| INCI | International nomenclature cosmetic ingredients |
| IRI | Internationalised resource identifier |
| IT | Information technology |
| MDE | model-driven engineering |
| NLP | natural language processing |
| OECD | organisation for economic co-operation and development |
| OGG | ontology of genes and genomes |
| OMG | object management group |
| OWL | web ontology language |
| R2RML | relational database to RDF mapping language |
| R2RML-F | extension of R2RML |
| RDF | resource description framework |
| RDFS | resource description framework schema |
| RML | RDF mapping language |
| SCCS | scientific committee on consumer safety |

*DOI: http://dx.doi.org/10.5772/intechopen.1002341*

| | |
|---|---|
| SHACL | shapes constraint language |
| SM | subject matter |
| SMILES | simplified molecular-input line-entry specification |
| SPARQL | standard query language and protocol for RDF triplestores |
| SQL | structured query language |
| TOXIN | non-animal methodologies for toxicity testing of chemical compounds |
| TXPO | toxic process ontology |
| UI | user interface |
| W3C | world wide web consortium |

## Author details

Audrey Sanctorum[1*], Jan Maushagen[1,2], Sara Sepehri[2], Guillaume Vrijens[3], Joery De Kock[2], Tamara Vanhaecke[2], Olga De Troyer[1] and Christophe Debruyne[3]

1 WISE Lab, Vrije Universiteit Brussel, Brussels, Belgium

2 Research Group of In Vitro Toxicology and Dermato-Cosmetology (IVTD), Vrije Universiteit Brussel, Brussels, Belgium

3 Montefiore Institute, University of Liège, Liège, Belgium

*Address all correspondence to: audrey.sanctorum@vub.be

## References

[1] Ball N, Bars R, Botham PA, Cuciureanu A, Cronin MTD, Doe JE, et al. A framework for chemical safety assessment incorporating new approach methodologies within REACH. Archives of Toxicology. 2022;**96**(3): 743-766

[2] Rajpoot K, Desai N, Koppisetti H, Tekade M, Sharma MC, Behera SK, et al. Chapter 14 - In silico methods for the prediction of drug toxicity. In: Pharmacokinetics and Toxicokinetic Considerations, Vol. 2 of Advances in Pharmaceutical Product Development and Research. Cambridge, Massachusetts, USA: Academic Press; 2022. pp. 357-383

[3] Denaux R, Ren Y, Villazón-Terrazas B, Alexopoulos P, Faraotti A, Honghan W. Knowledge architecture for organisations. In: Pan JZ, Vetere G, Gómez-Pérez JM, Honghan W, editors. Exploiting Linked Data and Knowledge Graphs in Large Organisations. Cham, Switzerland: Springer; 2017. pp. 57-84

[4] Hogan A, Blomqvist E, Cochez M, d'Amato C, de Melo G, Gutiérrez C, et al. Knowledge Graphs. Number 22 in Synthesis Lectures on Data, Semantics, and Knowledge. Switzerland: Springer; 2021

[5] Wood D, Cyganiak R, Lanthaler M. RDF 1.1 Concepts and Abstract Syntax. W3C Recommendation. USA: W3C; 2014. Availabale form: https://www.w3.org/TR/2014/REC-rdf11-concepts-20140225/

[6] Hepp M. Ontologies: State of the art, business potential, and grand challenges. In: Hepp M, De Leenheer P, de Moor A, Sure Y, editors. Ontology Management, Semantic Web, Semantic Web Services, and Business Applications, Vol. 7 of Semantic Web and Beyond: Computing for Human Experience. Boston, MA, USA: Springer; 2008. pp. 3-22

[7] Chasseray Y, Barthe-Delanoë A-M, Négny S, Le Lann J-M. A generic metamodel for data extraction and generic ontology population. Journal of Information Science. 2021;**48**(6):838-856. DOI: 10.1177/0165551521989641

[8] W3C OWL Working Group. OWL 2 Web Ontology Language Document Overview. W3C Recommendation. USA: W3C, Word Wide Web Consortium; 2012. Available form: https://www.w3.org/TR/2012/REC-owl2-overview-20121211/

[9] Guha R, Brickley D. RDF Schema 1.1. W3C Recommendation, W3C; 2014

[10] Colomb RM, Raymond K, Hart L, Emery P, Welty C, Xie GT, et al. The object management group ontology definition metamodel. In: Ontologies for Software Engineering and Software Technology. Berlin, Heidelberg: Springer; 2006. pp. 217-247

[11] Dimitrov SD, Diderich R, Sobanski T, Pavlov TS, Chankov GV, Chapkanov AS, et al. QSAR Toolbox - workflow and major functionalities. SAR and QSAR in Environmental Research. 2016;**27**:203-219

[12] Yang C, Cronin MTD, Arvidson KB, Bienfait B, Enoch SJ, Heldreth B, et al. COSMOS next generation – A public knowledge base leveraging chemical and biological data to support the regulatory assessment of chemicals. Computational Toxicology. 2021;**19**:100175

[13] Hardy B, Apic G, Carthew P, Clark D, Cook D, Dix I, et al. Toxicology

ontology perspectives. ALTEX. Alternatives zu Tierexperimenten. 2012; **29**(2):139-156

[14] Tcheremenskaia O, Benigni R, Nikolova I, Jeliazkova N, Escher S, Batke M, et al. OpenTox predictive toxicology framework: Toxicological ontology and semantic media wiki-based OpenToxipedia. Journal of Biomedical Semantics. 2012;**3**(Suppl 1):S7

[15] Thomas RS, Paules RS, Simeonov A, Fitzpatrick SC, Crofton KM, Casey WM, et al. The US Federal Tox21 Program: A strategic and operational plan for continued leadership. ALTEX - Alternatives to animal experimentation. 2018;**35**(2):163-168

[16] Zhou X, Menche J, Barabási A-L, Sharma A. Human symptoms–disease network. Nature Communications. 2014; **5**(1):1-10

[17] Stoney R, Robertson DL, Nenadic G, Schwartz J-M. Mapping biological process relationships and disease perturbations within a pathway network. npj Systems Biology and Applications. 2018;**4**(1):22

[18] Papatheodorou I, Oellrich A, Smedley D. Linking gene expression to phenotypes via pathway information. Journal of Biomedical Semantics. 2015; **6**(1):17

[19] Sanctorum A, Riggio J, Maushagen J, Sepehri S, Arnesdotter E, Delagrange M, et al. End-user engineering of ontology-based knowledge bases. Behaviour & Information Technology. 2022;**41**(9): 1811-1829

[20] Vrandecic D. Ontology evaluation. In: Staab S, Studer R, editors. Handbook on Ontologies, International Handbooks on Information Systems. Berlin, Heidelberg: Springer-Verlag; 2009. pp. 293-313

[21] Gozzi R. The jigsaw puzzle as a metaphor for knowledge. ETC: A Review of General Semantics. 1996;**53**(4): 447-451

[22] Sanctorum A, Riggio J, Sepehri S, Arnesdotter E, Vanhaecke T, De Troyer O. A Jigsaw-based end-user tool for the development of ontology-based knowledge bases. In: Fogli D, Tetteroo D, Barricelli BR, Borsci S, Markopoulos P, Papadopoulos GA, editors. Proceedings of IS-EUD 2021, 8th International Symposium on End-User Development, Vol. 12724 of Lecture Notes in Computer Science. Cham, Switzerland: Springer; July 2021. pp. 169-184

[23] Dimou A, Sande MV, Colpaert P, Verborgh R, Mannens E, Van de Walle R. RML: A generic language for integrated RDF mappings of heterogeneous data. In: Bizer C, Heath T, Auer S, Berners-Lee T, editors. Proceedings of the Workshop on Linked Data on the Web co-located with the 23rd International World Wide Web Conference (WWW 2014), Seoul, Korea, April 8, 2014. Vol. 1184 of CEUR Workshop Proceedings. Aachen, Germany: CEUR-WS.org; 2014

[24] Debruyne C, O'Sullivan D. R2RML-F: towards sharing and executing domain logic in R2RML mappings. In: Auer S, Berners-Lee T, Bizer C, Heath T, editors. Proceedings of the Workshop on Linked Data on the Web, LDOW 2016, co-located with 25th International World Wide Web Conference (WWW 2016), Vol. 1593 of CEUR Workshop Proceedings. Aachen, Germany: CEUR-WS.org; 2016

[25] Vrijens G. Knowledge graph construction to facilitate chemical compound hazard assessment in the toxin project. [Master's thesis] School of

Engineering and Computer Science - University of Liège. 2023

[26] Grüninger M, Fox MS. The Role of Competency Questions in Enterprise Engineering. Boston, MA: Springer US; 1995. pp. 22-31

[27] Yamagata Y, Yamada H. Ontological approach to the knowledge systematization of a toxic process and toxic course representation framework for early drug risk management. Scientific Reports. 2020;**10**:14581

[28] He Y, Liu Y, Zhao B. OGG: A biological ontology for representing genes and genomes in specific organisms. In: The 2014 International Conference on Biomedical Ontologies (ICBO 2014): October 8-9, 2014; Houston, TX, USA. CEUR Workshop Proceedings. Aachen, Germany: CEUR-WS.org; 2014. pp. 13-20

[29] The UniProt Consortium. UniProt: the universal protein knowledgebase in 2021. Nucleic Acids Research. 2021;**49** (D1):D480-D489

[30] Matthews L, Gopinath G, Gillespie M, Caudy M, Croft D, de Bono B, et al. Reactome knowledgebase of human biological pathways and processes. Nucleic Acids Research. 2008;**37**:D619-D622

[31] Kanehisa M, Furumichi M, Tanabe M, Sato Y, Morishima K. KEGG: new perspectives on genomes, pathways, diseases and drugs. Nucleic Acids Research. 2016;**45**(D1):D353-D361

[32] Davis AP, Murphy CG, Saraceni-Richards CA, Rosenstein MC, Wiegers TC, Mattingly CJ. Comparative toxicogenomics database: A knowledgebase and discovery tool for chemical-gene-disease networks. Nucleic Acids Research. 2022;**37**:D786-D792

[33] Ashburner M, Ball CA, Blake JA, Botstein D, Butler H, Cherry JM, et al. Gene ontology: Tool for the unification of biology. The Gene Ontology Consortium. Nature genetics. 2000;**25**:25-29

[34] Thomas P, Hill D, Mi H, Osumi-Sutherland D, Auken K, Carbon S, et al. Gene Ontology Causal Activity Modeling (GO-CAM) moves beyond GO annotations to structured descriptions of biological functions and systems. Nature Genetics. 2019;**51**:1429-1433

[35] Gustafson E, Debruyne C, De Troyer O, Rogiers V, Vinken M, Vanhaecke T. Screening of Repeated Dose Toxicity Data in Safety Evaluation Reports of Cosmetic Ingredients Issued by the Scientific Committee on Consumer Safety Between 2009 and 2019. Archives of Toxicology. 2020; **94**(11):3723-3735

[36] Volz J, Bizer C, Gaedke M, Kobilarov G. Silk - A link discovery framework for the web of data. In: Proceedings of the WWW2009 Workshop on Linked Data on the Web, LDOW 2009, Madrid, Spain, April 20, 2009, Volume 538 of CEUR Workshop Proceedings. Aachen, Germany: CEUR-WS.org; 2009

[37] David J, Euzenat J, Scharffe F, Trojahn C. The Alignment API 4.0. Semantic Web. 2011;**2**:3-10

[38] Knublauch H, Kontokostas D. Shapes Constraint Language (SHACL). W3C Recommendation. USA: W3C; 2017. Available from: https://www.w3.org/TR/shacl/

[39] Mouromtsev D, Pavlov DS, Emelyanov Y, Morozov AV, Razdyakonov DS, Galkin M. The simple web-based tool for visualization and sharing of semantic data and ontologies. In: Villata S, Pan JZ, Dragoni M, editors.

Proceedings of the ISWC 2015 Posters & Demonstrations Track co-located with the 14th International Semantic Web Conference (ISWC-2015), Bethlehem, PA, USA, October 11, 2015, Vol. 1486 of CEUR Workshop Proceedings. Aachen, Germany: CEUR-WS.org; 2015

[40] Gupta A. Data provenance. In: Liu L, Tamer Özsu M, editors. Encyclopedia of Database Systems. New York, NY: Springer; 2009. p. 608

Chapter 12

# Knowledge Management for the Marine Energy Industry: PRIMRE

*Jonathan Whiting, Cesar Ricardo Castillo, Jon Weers, Katie Peterson, Will Peplinski, Kelley Ruehl, Andrea Copping, Megan Anderson, Fadia Ticona Rollano, Nicholas Gilroy, Paul Susmarski, Lysel Garavelli, Hanna Fields, Hayley Farr and Sean Morris*

## Abstract

Marine energy involves capturing power from ocean currents and waves, and natural gradients of temperature and salinity. In nearly 20 years of modern development, the industry has generated considerable knowledge around resource assessment, site selection, technology design, manufacturing, testing, environmental effects, and standardization. The Portal and Repository for Information on Marine Renewable Energy integrates and connects marine energy knowledge hubs into a comprehensive and connected knowledge ecosystem with the goal of progressing the industry. The seven knowledge hubs include the Marine and Hydrokinetic Data Repository for datasets, Tethys and Tethys Engineering for environmental and technical documents, Marine Energy Projects Database for deployment activities, Marine Energy Software for software, Marine Energy Atlas for geospatial data, and Telesto for development guidance. At an early tumultuous time in the industry, these knowledge management systems organize vocabularies, retain important early lessons from developers, guide research activities internationally, inform permitting decisions for regulators, and provide authoritative sources of information for the public.

**Keywords:** marine energy, wave energy, tidal energy, knowledge hub, data, environmental effects, engineering, software, projects, geospatial, guidance

## 1. Introduction

The marine environment contains vast amounts of energy in the movement of waves and currents, and in natural gradients in temperature and salinity, which can be harnessed to provide power. Marine energy (also known as ocean energy, marine renewable energy, and marine and hydrokinetic energy) has significant potential to contribute predictable renewable energy to meet rising energy demands, enhance grid resiliency, and meet climate change goals [1]. Each marine energy resource is harvested by a different type of device that optimizes the type of energy, its periodicity, and the scale of the resource.

Waves are generated by wind passing over the ocean surface and friction causing wave crests to form. The wave climate is determined by local wind waves and swells caused by distant storms that can propagate great distances. The global wave power potential is estimated at around 29,500 TWh per year [2], mainly centralized in two westerly zones along the 40–60° latitude bands in both hemispheres [3]. This amount of power is approximate to present global power consumption, though realistic energy extraction is quite variable and is constrained by cost, conversion efficiencies, energy diffusion, and conflicting ocean use. Wave energy is being extracted using a variety of wave energy converters (WECs): point absorber, oscillating water column, attenuator, pressure differential, oscillating wave surge converter, or overtopping device (**Figure 1**). The wave energy industry is in the early stages of development and has few large or long-term deployments on record, though there is substantial research focused on unlocking wave energy developments.

Currents consist of movement of water in the oceans and exist as tidal currents and persistent ocean currents, which can be harvested for energy. In addition, the open flow of large rivers can also be harnessed for energy generation. Tides are driven by the gravitational pull of the moon and sun, as well as the rotation of the Earth and achieve fast speeds through flow concentration at land constrictions. Large-scale persistent ocean currents, such as the Gulf Stream, are driven by winds, the Coriolis effect, density gradients, and interactions with the continental shelves. Rivers are a byproduct of the water cycle and gravity, as runoff from precipitation moves from higher elevations towards oceans or basins. Approaches that completely restrict flow, such as dams and tidal barrages, are not considered as marine energy. The global tidal power potential is estimated at around 1200 TWh per year [4], concentrated at inlets and channels where the landmass constricts flow, though realistic energy extraction is significantly less. Current energy is being extracted in a variety of forms: axial flow turbine, cross flow turbine, tidal kite, Archimedes screw, or oscillating hydrofoil (**Figure 2**). The global tidal energy industry is more developed than that of wave energy, with more technology convergence on axial and cross flow turbines, some longer-term deployments, and the first commercial arrays coming online [5]. The high energy and often murky waters in tidal areas challenge the survivability and lead to high costs of deployment and operations [6].

**Figure 1.**
*Examples of wave energy converters tested around the world. Pictured from left to right are Mocean Energy's Blue X attenuator deployed in the United Kingdom, Eco Wave Power's point absorbers deployed in Israel, and Azura Wave Energy's point absorber deployed in the United States.*

**Figure 2.**
*Examples of tidal energy turbines tested around the world. Pictured from left to right are Andritz Hydro's HS1500 in the United Kingdom, Orbital Marine Power's $O_2$ in the United Kingdom, and Verdant Power's Gen5 KHPS in the United States.*

Ocean thermal energy conversion (OTEC) involves harnessing energy from the difference in temperatures between warm upper layers and cold deep layers at about 800–1000 m depth [7]. Heat is accumulated in the ocean's surface by solar irradiance, warming the surface waters in the tropics. The global thermal power potential is estimated at 34,500 TWh per year [8], concentrated between 30° north and south latitudes where the differential between the surface water and deep-water temperatures are at least 20°C. All the existing OTEC technologies use heat exchanges in conjunction with systems that use seawater or a working fluid for power conversion. Several OTEC demonstration projects have been deployed around the world (**Figure 3**) and the technology is emerging as a viable means of baseload power production, as well as providing ancillary services for freshwater desalination, fertilizing seaweed production, and seawater air conditioning. High capital costs have prevented commercial scale deployment of OTEC to date, reflecting the large size of the piping and plant systems.

**Figure 3.**
*Examples of OTEC demonstration projects around the world. Pictured from left to right are the Makai Ocean Engineering plant in Hawaii, United States, and the Okinawa Prefecture OTEC Demonstration Facility in Okinawa, Japan. Facility in Okinawa, Japan. Photo provided by Okinawa Prefectural Government, Industrial Policy Division.*

Salinity gradient generation involves extracting energy from the chemical potential between saltwater and freshwater, using pressure across semi-permeable membranes or ion-exchange membranes [9]. There is an estimated 1650 TWh per year [10] of technical potential power generation, concentrated at locations where large rivers flow into seawater. This technology has limited deployments [5] and is still the subject of considerable research and development before widespread commercial deployments will become feasible.

Internationally, the development of marine energy technologies has taken place largely over the past two decades. As an emerging field, information on marine energy has been distributed in many formats and locations, and critical lessons learned from early deployments may have been lost as early pioneering companies were liquidated or merged [11]. The natural progression of the industry has led to the development of several knowledge management systems around the world.

The value proposition for these knowledge management systems is to support the efficient advancement of the industry. Knowledge ultimately creates the foundation on which new advancements are rooted. Learning from existing efforts yields better efficiency by preventing the duplication of activities. Knowledge must be well archived to assess knowledge gaps that inform future targeted research, and widely accessible for multiple audiences. Dissemination of knowledge may also generate important financial investments as investors gain a clearer picture of activities. Creating authoritative sources of knowledge may also prevent the spread of misinformation among the public. Finally, knowledge management systems and the networks they support encourage partnerships and collaboration.

Within the United States, early knowledge management systems funded by the U.S. Department of Energy's (DOE) Water Power Technologies Office (WPTO) included Tethys and the Marine and Hydrokinetic Data Repository (MHKDR). Tethys was developed in 2009 and collects documents on the environmental effects of marine energy, while MHKDR was developed in 2015 and stores marine energy datasets generated from WPTO-funded research and development activities. Many smaller resources and online tools were also created at that time but were scattered among various websites. In 2018, WPTO funded three national laboratories – Pacific Northwest National Laboratory (PNNL), National Renewable Energy Laboratory (NREL), and Sandia National Laboratories (SNL) – to develop a system that would coordinate these databases and future databases into a single system known as the Portal and Repository for Information on Marine Renewable Energy (PRIMRE). This chapter will describe this effort to coordinate databases and knowledge across the developing marine energy industry.

## 2. Portal and repository for information on marine renewable energy

As the concept for PRIMRE (https://primre.org) was developed, the team considered that knowledge hubs like Tethys and MHKDR hosted very different types of data and information and had intentionally unique designs. These differences precluded combining the existing as well as future knowledge hubs into a single database. Rather, PRIMRE was envisioned to aggregate and combine different knowledge hubs under a single banner with strong internal connections, while allowing each to retain a unique identity, thereby valuing flexibility over conformity. A gap analysis was conducted to design and determine the content for five additional knowledge hubs: Tethys Engineering, Marine Energy Projects Database, Marine Energy Software,

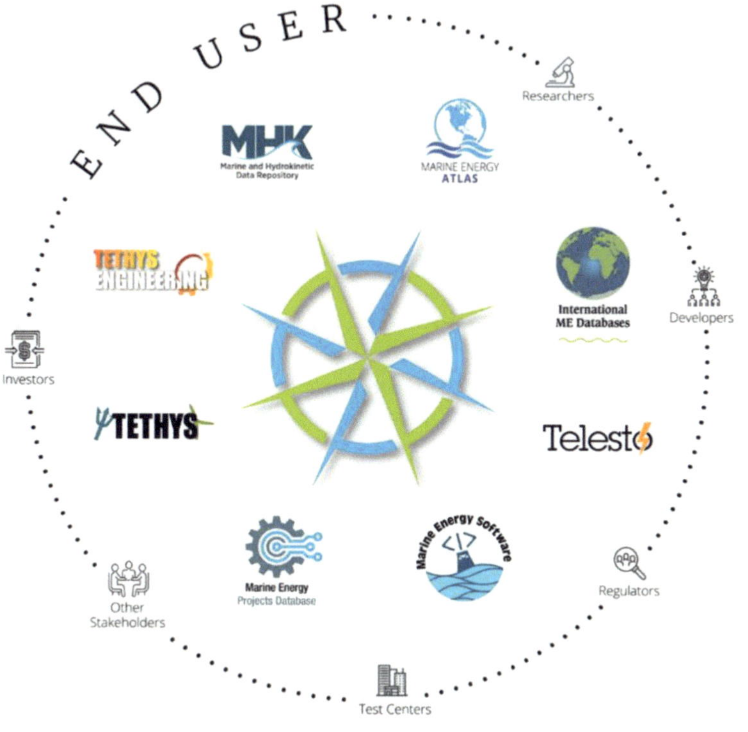


**Figure 4.**
*Diagram of the PRIMRE system, indicating the seven knowledge hubs and the end users that are targeted by the information.*

Marine Energy Atlas, and Telesto. These seven knowledge hubs form the ecosystem of PRIMRE (**Figure 4**) and will be described in more detail below. Interconnectivity between the databases was designed as a single aggregate search in PRIMRE, powered by a published metadata standard [12] and uniform Application Programming Interface (API) exchanges.

## 2.1 Design theory

The grand vision for PRIMRE was to create a coordinated ecosystem of industry-specific knowledge to overcome information barriers for research, development, and testing to progress the marine energy industry. Each knowledge hub houses a different format of information including data, documents, deployment activities, software, resource mapping, and testing guidance. PRIMRE acts as an umbrella that aggregates the knowledge hubs through a centralized search, while also including high-level information such as an events calendar, webinars, tutorials on marine energy, and educational resources. PRIMRE's goal is to house all relevant types of information in an appropriate location within the knowledge ecosystem. PRIMRE addresses challenges that exist around the difficulty in obtaining information that supports an emerging industry's existing data constructs. Information availability challenges are overcome by encouraging information to be made public, centralizing the information into a one-stop search, providing data and terminology standardization, and cataloging information to make it more discoverable and accessible.

The development of PRIMRE and its knowledge hubs is guided by regular user reviews and a steering committee. On a rotating basis, two knowledge hubs are reviewed each year with short surveys that encourage users to interact with and comment on specific aspects of the website, while their responses remain anonymous. Feedback is compiled into a report and action items are identified that guide development activities. Guidance is also provided by the steering committee that is composed of non-affiliated marine energy experts across industry, universities, test centers, and government agencies. This group meets regularly for updates on PRIMRE activities and provides guidance on critical needs for the marine energy community to the PRIMRE team.

The primary guiding principle reflected in the architecture of PRIMRE is to follow the FAIR data principles [13], making data and information findable, accessible, interoperable, and reusable. FAIR principles are common among data management practitioners, but it has also been applied to general knowledge management. Specifically, PRIMRE is designed to support the FAIR principles:

- **Findable**: PRIMRE follows a semantic structure with descriptive metadata that supports queries and machine readability. Significant focus is placed on search engine optimization and direct outreach to stakeholders. An example of structural enhancements to support findability was the creation of "signature projects", which collate information related to complex projects where information is decentralized. Signature projects are organizational constructs that aggregate information across all the knowledge hubs.

- **Accessible**: All PRIMRE content is free and available to the public, except for some proprietary data that are subject to moratoriums for a period. For all aspects of PRIMRE other than content editing, account login walls are intentionally avoided to reduce barriers that lead to information siloing and limit search engine archival.

- **Interoperable**: PRIMRE created a simplified metadata schema based on the U.S. Project Open Data [14] which allows standardized APIs to exchange metadata between the knowledge hubs and with external databases. Several PRIMRE taxonomies are controlled for consistency, drawing on international standards such as the IEC TC 114 [15].

- **Reusable**: PRIMRE content is always referenced to the appropriate source material, by either serving data with associated reports or deep-linking to authoritative source material such as a developer website. All methodologies for content collection and curation, data processing, and frameworks are made openly available through documentation.

### 2.2 In practice

While PRIMRE was originally envisioned to tie together existing knowledge hubs, it became apparent that the formats for many data and information sources pertinent to marine energy did not fit into existing knowledge hubs, requiring the creation of new ones. This led the PRIMRE team to create Tethys Engineering, Marine Energy Software, Telesto, Marine Energy Projects Database, and Marine Energy Atlas. Some knowledge hubs effectively live as subdomains under PRIMRE, but each holds a unique identity, structure, and purpose. This structure recognizes the value of content-specific design and branding to create a better user experience. For example, Marine Energy Software can create unique integrations with GitHub that show live statistics on recent code releases, and the Marine Energy Projects Database can generate live graphics that describe marine energy deployments. The user experience is tailored to the information within each knowledge hub, but users do not need to distinguish between knowledge hubs to find the information and can access all information through the PRIMRE aggregated search. By branding each knowledge hubs as PRIMRE, the system connectivity is underscored.

Collating large amounts of marine energy-specific knowledge in one location allows for the creation of products that analyze and leverage the information. PRIMRE is working towards developing "value-added products" that capitalize upon PRIMRE's centralized access to standardized, interoperable data sets to provide insights into industry trends, promote multi-sector analyses, and further advance marine energy research.

In the spirit of accessibility and discoverability, the PRIMRE team actively engages with the community including the marine energy industry, researchers, and other stakeholders. Activities such as search engine optimization, social media engagement, email newsletters, and introductory videos are used to raise general awareness of PRIMRE and marine energy at large. PRIMRE also practices targeted outreach including presentations at marine energy conferences, meetings with marine energy research and industry organizations, webinars, workshops, and more. These outreach activities are directed at enhancing the impact of knowledge management under PRIMRE. While many users may stumble across content in PRIMRE from search engines and are not aware of the broader framework, communicating the integrity of the system builds trust within the marine energy community, prevents duplication of effort with other knowledge management systems, and serves as a model for knowledge sharing around the world.

The knowledge contained in PRIMRE is generally technical in nature, but PRIMRE distills the information for audiences who may be less familiar with the industry. A "marine energy basics" section was created with introductory information about marine energy, including animations that demonstrate common technology types, always linked to more technical resources on knowledge hubs. Educational audiences have also been considered through directed educational resources, ranging from coloring books for children to job postings and educational programs for university and graduate students. Content is often simplified into one-page handouts for better accessibility.

PRIMRE is a platform and resource connecting the marine energy community. PRIMRE maintains an events calendar that tracks marine energy conferences, workshops, and webinars around the world. A bi-weekly newsletter called the PRIMRE Blast highlights funding opportunities, job opportunities, industry news highlights, and new content from the knowledge hubs. PRIMRE also frequently engages with other marine energy knowledge management systems around the world, including through an annual international workshop on data sharing [16].

### 2.3 Next steps

The PRIMRE knowledge hubs are continuously being updated and may undergo redesigns to improve information organization. The current foci are on reorganizing Telesto around a simulated marine energy development pathway; merging two separate components of Marine Energy Software; enhancing marine energy data pipelines and data lake architectures within MHKDR; and incorporating international GIS data into the Marine Energy Atlas. Each of these improvements are detailed in the later sections of this chapter. Future improvements will be driven by PRIMRE's DOE sponsors and the needs of the marine energy community.

The PRIMRE team is continuously pursuing API exchanges between knowledge hubs and advocates for API development within related marine energy knowledge repositories around the world. PRIMRE is exploring the integration of large language models (LLMs) based on recent commercial artificial intelligence releases, to develop a reliable and accurate chatbot around marine energy information, further encouraging accessibility for the public.

## 3. MHK data repository

MHKDR (https://mhkdr.openei.org/) was developed using a data management and dissemination platform designed by NREL to make data generated from DOE-funded marine energy research and development efforts available to the public. MHKDR protects DOE's investment in research and development by preserving and providing access to data, disseminating its data catalog to a network of data sharing partners (**Figure 5**), supplying context and metadata to search engines, and by disseminating the findings from DOE marine energy projects to relevant communities so they may build upon the knowledge and experience gained, avoid duplication of effort, reduce costs and risks associated with marine energy development, and accelerate the rate of innovation in renewable energy. MHKDR was built upon lessons learned from other data repositories and the technologies used to implement them, however, it was the first repository of its kind to be hosted in the cloud. The move to cloud hosting aligned with the primary goal of MHKDR, which is to make DOE-funded marine energy data universally accessible. In addition to a cloud-based

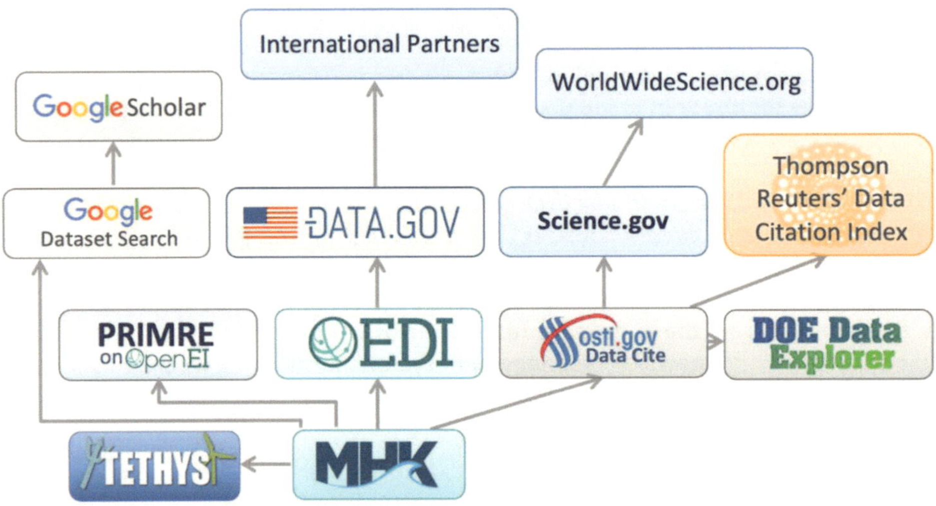


**Figure 5.**
*Diagram of MHKDR's network of data sharing partners. Metadata from the MHKDR data catalog is automatically shared with each of the sites above, allowing users of those sites to access data from MHKDR and PRIMRE systems.*

architecture, data standardization was also critical to laying the foundation for the development of marine energy data lakes. However, the practice of standardizing marine energy research data deviated significantly from initial concepts.

### 3.1 Design theory

The ultimate goal of PRIMRE's cloud-accessible marine energy data lake is to provide universal access to marine energy data. The PRIMRE team realized early on that high-impact, big data sets like DOE's U.S. Wave high resolution hindcast data [17] were inaccessible to many. Despite being publicly accessible, the 28 TB dataset (as of June 2023) simply could not be downloaded, stored, or utilized effectively by organizations that did not possess the high-performance computing and big data storage capabilities required to do so. The sheer size of the data inadvertently limited its availability to only those institutions endowed with the means to utilize it, typically: national laboratories, larger universities, and big corporations. By allowing free data processing directly on the cloud, DOE and the PRIMRE team could open access to big data like the U.S. Wave dataset to anyone, opening the doors for collaboration with smaller universities, high schools, start-up companies, local communities, and other sources of innovation.

MHKDR contains hundreds of datasets from many different research and development projects. To make data more interoperable and to support the development of a marine energy data lake, several data standards were developed and advertised to the marine energy community. The data models, or "content models" as they are called on MHKDR (https://mhkdr.openei.org/models/), are spreadsheet-based templates designed to create homogenous data submissions from a curated list of specific data topics. Data submitters were instructed to translate their data into these spreadsheet models prior to submission. In theory, the data submitters would accommodate the data translation exercise as part of their normal data submission workflow because of the inherent value in interoperable data and their contractual obligation as DOE funds recipients, which required them to do so. And because MHKDR was both in control of the standardization format as well as the sole recipient of that format, the data standardization process would be easy to automate. The spreadsheet-based data models were meticulously crafted and then locked down prior to being made available for download. Automated scripts were added to MHKDR that would recognize content models upon submission and process them, adding their data to a central data lake. The spreadsheet-based structure of the content models would lend itself nicely to a centralized, SQL-based data lake.

### 3.2 In practice

In practice, MHKDR content models had an extremely low adoption rate. Data translation is time consuming and expensive, especially for non-data scientists. Project data rarely occurs in tabular format and often requires complicated, multistep conversions to be compatible with the content models.

The assumption that project teams would translate their own research data into standardized formats was fundamentally flawed. Even if required to do so on condition of receipt of funding, most research and development projects are focused on solving their fundamental research questions. Almost all project resources are allocated towards meeting this goal and data acquisition is no exception. Data are collected and organized within the project scope with little regard for extended use beyond the project. Little to no time or budget is allocated for data standardization, contextualization, or dissemination beyond project team members. Even if such allocations were planned, many projects lack data scientists or other supporting staff to help with lengthy or difficult data translations. Lastly, project resources are finite. Deadlines and unforeseen costs exacerbate project resources and ensure that they are only spent on critical tasks. In the end, most projects simply submit the data they have, in whatever state (organized or not) that the data exist in at the end of the project.

Complicating matters, many critical marine energy datasets are not tabular and are simply not compatible with spreadsheet-based data models. Wave data, such as the data featured in the U.S. Wave dataset, are multi-dimensional time-series data that include information on height, period, shape, direction, and more. These data are best stored and queried in high-performance computer and cloud optimized data storage formats. Other datasets on MHKDR are best served in industry standard formats such as video files, seismic data, or 3D modeling formats. Converting these formats to a tabular data standard would essentially render them useless to industry. To preserve the utility of these datasets, the PRIMRE team realized they must be made available in industry standard formats, even if data model standard formats are more efficient or more interoperable.

### 3.3 Next steps

To address both issues, the PRIMRE team has developed a marine energy data pipeline and integrated it with MHKDR. The Marine Energy Data Pipeline automatically recognizes select data submitted to MHKDR and translates it into standardized formats prior to making the data publicly available. This allows researchers to submit data in the format it was generated, directly from instrument or modeling software. The originally submitted data are preserved for accountability and scientific posterity and presented alongside the translated data so that users of the data have easy access to both formats. The data pipeline process shifts the burden of data translation from the project research teams to an MHKDR data curation team, this way PRIMRE has made the standardization of DOE-funded research data more efficient. Data scientists working for MHKDR, trained in data translation and cloud optimization, can do the heavy lifting, while project researchers can focus on their primary tasks, reserving more funds for research and development in marine energy. As a result, MHKDR's new data standardization policy enables researchers to submit data in any format and data scientists working for PRIMRE will optimize its utility. The increased burden to the PRIMRE team is more economical for DOE as the dozens of individual project teams no longer need access to a data scientist, resulting in program-wide cost savings.

The PRIMRE and MHKDR teams are working together to continue to develop marine energy data pipelines, to automate the standardization and interoperability of marine energy data, and to make those data universally accessible in the cloud.

## 4. Tethys and Tethys engineering

Tethys and Tethys Engineering are separate knowledge hubs, which share the same content types and design frameworks and will therefore be described together for simplicity. Tethys (https://tethys.pnnl.gov) was developed in 2010 and contains a comprehensive collection of international journal articles, technical reports, and other documents on the environmental effects of marine energy and wind energy. Tethys Engineering (https://tethys-engineering.pnnl.gov) was developed in 2019 and contains international documents on the technical, engineering, and economics aspects of marine energy development and operation. Together, these knowledge hubs cover all topical marine energy areas, providing a fundamental and trustworthy source of information in the form of technical and scientific documents.

### 4.1 Design theory

The goal of both Tethys knowledge hubs is to aggregate decentralized information into a marine energy-specific repository that serves as an authoritative source for information to inform research gaps analysis, supporting permitting and regulatory decision-making, note engineering advancements, and preserve the history of data and information collection in an emerging science and industry. Scientific and technical documents are the most fundamental and trusted sources of information, including peer-reviewed journal articles, technical reports, conference papers, books, theses, and more. Identification of recent scientific publications is important for building trust that the knowledge hub is comprehensive. Aggregating and organizing these documents form the basis of knowledge on which research synthesis can be developed, as well as providing an information base that can be shared with an emerging industry.

Knowledge collection provides more value when it can be reviewed and synthesized to inform future recommendations for research and development. Progressing the marine energy industry requires that devices be deployed in the ocean, under the auspices of national and regional regulatory requirements. Regulators are tasked with assessing environmental risk of new proposed developments and need a body of research or experiences to support their decisions. The Tethys knowledge bases provide comprehensive and organized information that fits those needs. Similarly, Tethys Engineering provides reliable information that supports the design, prototyping, testing, and development of marine energy devices, considering harsh ocean conditions that challenge survivability, as well as optimizing the energy capture in a cost-effective manner.

The two Tethys knowledge bases act as a platform for disseminating and engaging with the marine energy industry and research community to enable the development pathway and meet regulatory standards. Beyond standard search engine optimization practices, knowledge hubs should perform active outreach and dissemination to a wide variety of end users. This same philosophy has been adopted by PRIMRE, but many of the tactics were identified and refined by Tethys.

### 4.2 In practice

Both Tethys websites are developed on Drupal [18], an open-source knowledge management system. Drupal provides a robust framework with community-generated modules to allow customization, integration support with other online tools, and ongoing support for security updates. This flexibility supported Tethys as it expanded over time to include additional features such as a marine energy events calendar, bi-weekly newsletter, webinar archive, interactive tools, export APIs, and more. Development of the Tethys knowledge bases follows an agile scrum methodology, drawing on experience and specialties distributed among a team of developers under the direction of a domain-knowledgeable product owner.

Content management is an important aspect of knowledge management and becomes essential when the expectation is that content is required to be comprehensive and up to date. Tethys originally explored automated web crawling methods for content collection, but the approach was quickly abandoned as crawlers struggled to read unstructured gray literature and fell short of expectations around identification of relevant content and proper tagging. Tethys has adopted a manual approach, employing a team of early-career researchers trained in appropriate entry and tagging, with oversight including refining of tags [11]. User reviews are conducted annually, soliciting user input on the comprehensiveness of the content, the functionality of each site, and identification of missing seminal documents. The continued engagement of a core group of researchers and other stakeholders support the usefulness and comprehensive content of the Tethys knowledge hubs. The collection is kept up to date by following domain-specific distribution lists and collecting input from members of the community. The relative youth of the marine energy industry assures that nearly all content is digital and can be made available, pending copyright laws. The Tethys websites exclusively contain documents that can be accessed with a link or with an uploaded file, so there are no references to documents that cannot be found. Tethys is unique in that it supports two domain spaces: marine energy and wind energy. As such, there are filters and divisions woven throughout the knowledge hub to allow users to choose content matching their interests.

To support information synthesis, Tethys is the serving platform for several international collaborations, including a task under the International Energy Agency's Technology Collaboration Ocean Energy System's Environmental (OES-Environmental) task and the International Energy Agency Wind Committee's (WREN) task. These groups leverage existing information to generate extensive synthesis reports that characterize the state of science for the industry (e.g., [19]), while also distilling the key information into illustrated digestible summaries for a less technical audience. International working groups spear-headed the creation of tools like the management measures tool (https://tethys.pnnl.gov/management-measures). Tethys Engineering was created more recently and is not currently the platform supporting international working groups or synthesis efforts, so that the impact cannot be evaluated as well in terms of number of users, name recognition, and references. This further highlights the importance of synthesis.

Tethys pioneers many forms of outreach and has achieved international name recognition, substantial visitors, and unanimous support and trust from the marine energy community. Tethys is technical by nature but attempts to distill information with the creation of illustrated summaries that focus on specific environmental interactions (e.g., collision risk of animals with turbine blades), while providing links to supporting documents as citations. An entire suite of educational materials has been created for students from primary school through college, including coloring pages and age-specific webinars (https://tethys.pnnl.gov/marine-renewable-energy-educational-resources). The team manages a mailing list to send new publications and industry announcements to nearly 3300 subscribers, effectively providing push notifications of content rather than waiting passively for users to search for content on Tethys. Significant effort goes into search engine optimization including crafting accurate and detailed metadata descriptions, exchanging links with other authoritative websites, improving speed and accessibility metrics, submitting a sitemap, and remaining stable and authoritative over a long time.

### 4.3 Next steps

With separate sponsors funding the wind energy and marine energy sides of Tethys, there are positive iterative improvements made by each respective sponsor that draws on the experience of the other. An example was the creation of the management measures tool for marine energy which catalogs environmental management and mitigation techniques available to developers; wind energy sponsors requested a similar tool but geared more towards a catalog of active monitoring technologies rather than methodologies, and several innovative features were replicated on the marine energy management measures tool.

Tethys Engineering lacks some community support compared to Tethys and is more often grouped under the banner of PRIMRE, but it may benefit from engagement with international working groups that can actively perform synthesis of the content. Leveraging PRIMRE-developed API schemas, Tethys content can be searched from Tethys Engineering and vice versa to make a seamless connection between the databases. This is aided by the two sites having identical frameworks, differing only in content scope.

Both Tethys knowledge hubs are expected to continue steadily increasing in content and functionality, remaining as backbones of information to support the advancement of the marine energy industry. User reviews, direct feedback from the community, and active engagement with researchers, regulators, and marine energy device developers guide new website development activities. Requests are from external knowledge hubs wishing to ingest Tethys or Tethys Engineering content into their websites becoming increasingly common. The Tethys and Tethys Engineering project teams are keen to support these requests to reduce redundant creation of competing knowledge repositories.

## 5. Marine energy projects database

The Marine Energy Projects Database (https://primre.org/Projects_Database) originated in 2018 with a U.S. DOE compilation of international planned, ongoing, and completed marine energy deployments. The list was restructured, expanded, and converted to a PRIMRE knowledge hub, launching in 2022. The Marine Energy Projects Database contains international information about marine energy projects, test sites, devices, and organizations engaged in marine energy development. The intent of the knowledge base is to support a range of users through transparency of information, including investors in understanding industry trends to guide investment decisions, researchers identifying knowledge gaps, regulators finding comparable deployments and forecasting industry growth, marine energy developers in communicating progress and seeking collaborators, and the public.

### 5.1 Design theory

The Marine Energy Projects Database is designed with a semantic structure that clearly defines taxonomies, relationships between content, and supports efficient querying of content. For example, a device is linked to projects and test sites where the device has been deployed, as well as to the manufacturer's organization page. A semantic structure provides a natural way for users to explore the content, supporting intuitively filterable searches as well as natural page progression through content. Live graphs convey statistics to communicate industry trends.

Content curation is designed to be open to the public so that developers can add or update their own entries through simple form submissions. This creates transparency and allows users to take ownership of their content if they wish. However, with the realistic expectation that the public alone will not create comprehensive and up-to-date content, a trained team of content curators review and add content on a regular basis.

### 5.2 In practice

The Marine Energy Projects Database is created on Semantic Mediawiki [20], within a subdomain of PRIMRE. It was designed with two different methods of exploring the system. The landing page is a faceted search that adds results matching keywords and limits results based on facet filters. This user-friendly and familiar interface allows the user to explore the entire database but is somewhat limited by only returning views for a subset of the content, as well as creating some inconsistency between different content types. The second method of exploration includes a searchable and sortable table view for each content type, highlighting key relevant fields for specific content types. Content-specific views also support live graphs with statistics on industry trends. Providing both query options allow for the user to choose the pathway most suited for the use case of interest.

Creating a highly interconnected database required a mapping exercise to identify how content is related to each other, including directionality of relationships and inheritance of properties. For example, a project should identify related devices but should inherit a technology type from the device. Queries become complex when mapping both directions and chaining relationships, but they enable a natural experience when exploring content. For example, searching for an organization that creates a device will return a listing of marine energy projects where the device was deployed.

Collection of content is uniquely challenging in a dynamic and emerging industry like marine energy, at times resulting in poorly documented or accessible information. Content entry is primarily conducted by a team of trained entry-level researchers with top-down supervision, documented search methodologies, and internal tracking mechanisms. The content team originally focused on updating the original list of deployments to match the expanded schema of information fields. Organizations were systematically updated from company websites and other online sources such as social media, while associated devices, projects, and test sites were flagged for updates. New content is discovered by following news releases from industry distribution lists and government funding announcements and by community suggestions, often from device developers.

### 5.3 Next steps

Outreach efforts will continue to seek buy-in from developers and manufacturers to begin updating their own content, while the PRIMRE team will continue to update content. Information about projects and organizations are rather fundamental to the industry, and other areas of PRIMRE collect similar information from various sources. One major next step will be using APIs to exchange the data with other knowledge hubs to reduce duplication. An example is that the Marine Energy Atlas receives project information from international sources and therefore has a subset of projects listed in the Marine Energy Projects Database, so workflows are being created so that the international sources feed directly into the Marine Energy Projects Database, which can be imported into the Marine Energy Atlas.

## 6. Marine energy software

The Marine Energy Software knowledge hub (https://primre.org/Software) is a collection of commercial and open-access software relevant to marine energy that was launched in 2020. This knowledge hub contains a variety of software packages used by the marine energy community to aid in analyses across the scope of marine energy such as engineering and technical design, operations and maintenance, environmental assessment, economics and performance metrics, optimization, and data analytics and visualization. While the marine energy industry calls for a breadth of analyses to be performed, the members of the community often have a more focused line of expertise, and this makes it difficult to know what software tools are available to perform other aspects of the marine energy projects that fall outside of their line of expertise. This created a need for developing a collection of the software tools that are used by the marine energy community to accelerate industry development and identify gaps where the availability of software is lacking or underrepresented. This need led to the development of the Marine Energy Software knowledge hub. Currently, this knowledge hub is split between the Code Hub and Code Catalog with each developed around the familiarity and expectations of their respective target audiences.

### 6.1 Design theory

The main goal of the Marine Energy Software knowledge hub is to provide a space where relevant marine energy software and content about the software is aggregated and available for universal access. This goal called for the Marine Energy Software pages to be hosted on public web platforms. Moreover, an aspect of this universal access goal is to provide relevant information that will aid decision-making around adoption of individual and/or suites of software. Relevant information to display is based on target audiences, because some intended users rely on open-source software while others are more comfortable using commercial software. Users of open-source software have typically become accustomed to using version-control systems for software development such as GitHub and GitLab when it comes to searching and browsing open-source software packages that they can adopt. This is because these platforms not only allow the software development to be controlled, but they also allow the potential user to understand how well maintained the open-source software is and the depth of the adoption among users. This differs from users of commercial software in that they are more likely to use catalogs that compare software packages that were developed for specific purposes and do not necessarily rely on understanding how the software is maintained. This difference in the target audience called for two separate resources to be developed.

Another goal of the Marine Energy Software Knowledge Hub was to allow developers to easily maintain content. This is because the marine energy space is constantly evolving with new needs and software development to address these needs. Thus, Marine Energy Software was designed to allow new software or new versions of existing software to be easily incorporated into each resource. Moreover, the ability for users to also add software was incorporated to allow the community to also contribute to what is found within the knowledge hub.

### 6.2 In practice

Marine Energy Software is split between the Code Hub and Code Catalog. The Code Catalog was developed using Semantic MediaWiki [20] within a subdomain of PRIMRE and it is composed of results following a standard template of relevant information for open-sourced and commercially available software within the resource. The search page has facets that can filter results within the catalog by price, commercially available or open-source, license and development status, and relevant marine energy technology types. Users can register their software to be included in the Marine Energy Software knowledge hub using a standard submission form.

The Code Hub is hosted outside of PRIMRE on a site that was developed using the React framework and it is composed of a GitHub software collection. Only open-source software is currently included within the Code Hub. The Code Hub features automatic pulls from the GitHub repositories for all open-source software to feature new releases on the landing page, so users are made aware of new software releases. Users can navigate and browse the Code Hub with the search bar or filtering by facets. Like the Code Catalog, Code Hub results provide metadata on open-source license type, marine energy technology type, and the domain-specific use for the software. The Code Hub also provides metadata and metrics that are relevant to software development, such as maintenance and adoption by the user community. Users can add their open-source software to the Code Hub by using the same standard submission form that is used by the Code Catalog.

### 6.3 Next steps

A user review in 2021 revealed that there was confusion over whether to use the Code Hub or Code Catalog to find relevant software of interest. To streamline and unify access to the software and software content, the Code Hub and the Code Catalog will be combined into one resource. When users search through the reorganized Code Hub, the content and schema from the Code Catalog will be combined with the existing Code Hub repository content. This improvement eliminates confusion and reduces knowledge hub maintenance costs. User reviews will continue to identify development priorities and new content, so that the knowledge hub will continue to grow with the marine energy community.

## 7. Marine energy atlas

The Marine Energy Atlas (https://maps.nrel.gov/marine-energy-atlas/) is an interactive, open-access web application that allows users to visualize, analyze and download spatial data related to the marine energy industry. The overarching goal of the application is to make it easy for different stakeholders to access data that can help them plan for marine energy projects, whether for device design or project siting. The datasets on the Marine Energy Atlas can be queried and downloaded, and the application features an in-app processing tool that performs easy analyses within an internet browser. The back-end architecture of the Marine Energy Atlas is the Visualization Analysis Design Research (VADR) system, which has a "future-proof" structure with the potential for adding new layers, updating data, and adding in-app processing tools.

### 7.1 Design theory

The Marine Energy Atlas is primarily an interactive map viewer. Multiple layers can be visualized on the map at the same time. The layers are organized by dataset in the Data Library, which is easily searchable, and users can browse tags to further narrow down layers of interest. Through the legend panel, layers can be elevated, removed, and opacity can be changed so that overlapping layers are still viewable. With the layers on the map, the user can quickly query the layers using the tools on the map, either via a coordinate or shape. Querying through the application allows the user to quickly identify areas of interest without needing to download the entire datasets while also allowing them to inform their interrogation if the dataset is downloaded.

The VADR system on which the Marine Energy Atlas is built is a monolithic code repository that allows for the shared maintenance of the Marine Energy Atlas codebase. It has been designed with modularity in mind, with Docker images being the primary deployment architecture to better support updating and maintaining applications. Improvements made to other parts of the repository allow for the Marine Energy Atlas to benefit without any additional cost. VADR utilizes a Continuous Integration/Continuous Delivery pipeline to permit seamless deployments and updates to the AWS infrastructure that backs the Marine Energy Atlas and other applications. Marine Energy Atlas and all VADR applications are built with modern tools and libraries that are actively maintained to allow for ease of maintenance.

### 7.2 In practice

Resource assessments of U.S.-based marine and hydrokinetic resources are the featured data layers on the Marine Energy Atlas. The U.S. DOE WPTO Wave Hindcast Dataset (https://www.nrel.gov/water/wave-hindcast-dataset.html) contains the highest-resolution time-series data on wave attributes in U.S. waters. The six variables are defined by the International Electrotechnical Commission Technical Commission 114 wave resource assessment technical specification [21], are available in a spatial resolution as fine as 100 to 200 meters in shallow water and a three-hour time step, and span from 1979 to 2020. The Marine Energy Atlas also contains resource data on ocean currents, temperature, salinity, tidal and river currents, and links to buoys that collect real-time wave data.

The Marine Energy Atlas also contains non-resource spatial data that helps stakeholders approach other facets of project planning. Through a partnership with OES, international layers were added to the Marine Energy Atlas. The new data feature locations of marine energy projects at different stages, as well as the locations of marine energy test facilities. Other new layers include spatial data on ports, population density, marine protected area shapefiles, and bathymetry.

The Capacity Factor Tool is an in-app processing tool that allows users to create capacity factor maps for a specific wave energy converter. The capacity factor is a calculation that represents the ratio of the actual time-averaged power generation to the maximum possible power generation of a particular device. This quantity is key for estimating the power output of devices that utilize intermittent energy sources, such as waves, as that device will not always be operating at peak performance. In the Marine Energy Atlas's Capacity Factor Tool, users can upload a power matrix that reflects their wave energy converter. The tool uses the significant wave height from the WPTO Wave Hindcast Dataset and the uploaded power matrix to generate a capacity factor map, based on underlying calculations and previously determined joint probability distributions. The results are generated in minutes, thanks to these optimized underlying calculations.

### 7.3 Next steps

The Marine Energy Atlas will continue adding spatial layers beyond resource assessments to aid in project siting and planning. Additionally, development of new in-app processing tools will further the utility of these layers by allowing users to perform geospatial analyses and interact with the data, without downloading data.

## 8. Telesto

Telesto (https://primre.org/Telesto) is a collection of wiki-based information pages and databases that was developed using Semantic MediaWiki [20] under a subdomain of PRIMRE. Telesto was initially developed in 2020 as a collection of databases and wiki-based guidance for technical information on marine energy that would be developed, curated, and maintained by the community. Some initial pages were created for marine energy measurement and testing guidance, as well as a sensor and instrumentation database and a testing facilities database. This type of information was useful for the community, but it lacked other relevant information such as regulation and permitting, resource characterization, and industrial materials. Moreover, the community engagement with Telesto slowed after the initial development phase and much of the information contained within Telesto became outdated, resulting in a poorly integrated and maintained set of web pages that needed reorganization. In 2023, Telesto was reorganized around the theme of providing information relevant to the stages of marine energy development.

### 8.1 Design theory

The reorganization of Telesto required a new central theme and design. The breadth of relevant information not already captured in one of the PRIMRE Knowledge Hubs meant that the reorganization should incorporate content that was dispersed across PRIMRE while allowing for flexibility in how the content was structured (e.g., wiki or database). Review of existing information led to a reorganization under the theme of a project timeline. The reorganization creates a landing page that links to five sub-pages of content organized by the stages of marine energy development: Planning, Design and Build, Testing and Measurement, Deployment, and Decommissioning. These stages also appear on a horizontal navigation bar that links all pages within Telesto to a specific development stage. This organization allows links to content from other Knowledge Hubs and other PRIMRE organizational schemes (e.g., Signature Projects, Marine Energy Basics), integrating the entire PRIMRE site and bringing greater attention to some content, like international standards. It also provides a home for some content which have had no well-defined home but are frequently used by the marine energy community.

### 8.2 In practice

Telesto content were organized under the new theme and linked accordingly. Some topics were found to span the entire development life cycle and were highlighted with separate pages: Lessons Learned; Performance Metrics; Economics; and Compliance. This creates multiple levels of visibility for finding this content, either through dedicated pages or the development life cycle themes.

With respect to design, the initial reorganization effort for Telesto visualized a somewhat linear timeline. An initial review of this design from the marine energy community pointed out that technology development in any field tends to be an iterative process of design and testing, sub-scale construction and deployments, followed by additional design and testing until a full-scale deployment may be considered possible. The Telesto reorganization pivoted away from the idea of a timeline and more towards the idea of a design pathway. Pathways can be non-linear but hopefully lead to a destination (e.g., full-scale deployment).

### 8.3 Next steps

The Telesto reorganization is identifying new locations for content. Although requests for new Telesto content (e.g., data/information from projects, marine energy tools and applications) regularly arise, a formal process has been designed to incorporate new future requests. Unlike all the other knowledge hubs, Telesto is the only unstructured, non-semantic database, and plays an important role of aggregating information and resources under this new cohesive theme.

## 9. Conclusion

PRIMRE is an expansive network of knowledge hubs focused on the emerging marine energy industry. Seven unique knowledge hubs represent different content scopes and formats that are connected by a centralized search. The scope encompasses comprehensive of authoritative information and data about the marine energy industry. Content is gathered from around the world except for datasets in MHKDR and the Marine Energy Atlas because of data mortgage limitations. While the marine energy industry is still progressing towards commercialization, this framework sets the stage for organized and efficient growth of the industry through accessible information about relevant technical, environmental, and socio-economic research and development.

Design and implementation of PRIMRE was not without challenges. The following list highlights lessons learned during the knowledge management process:

1. **Branding:** Naming conventions are bound to change with emerging technical domains. A great example is that the U.S. originally referred to this industry as "marine and hydrokinetic energy" to encompass riverine technology, before shifting towards "marine renewable energy" to match international conventions while distinguishing from non-renewable offshore energy, before ending at "marine energy" for brevity. This resulted in some database name changes along the way, though MHKDR and PRIMRE were not renamed because of established branding.

2. **Documenting procedures:** Over five years, PRIMRE has lost several key staff that were vital to the project, leading to setbacks. This raises the importance of documenting procedures and building redundancy for activities and capabilities.

3. **Multidisciplinary team:** The PRIMRE team is composed of software developers, domain experts for engineering and environmental effects, and communications and outreach professionals. Domain diversity supports successful decision-making and project direction.

4. **Sponsor support:** The U.S. Department of Energy provides more than just financial support, also providing encouragement that funding recipients contribute content, connections with international groups like Ocean Energy Systems, and legitimization of the activities.

5. **Continuous funding:** Knowledge management cannot be set up and forgotten, or the initial investment is meaningless. It requires active investment to maintain online security and development, ensure that content is recent, and to engage in outreach. The expenses often lead private companies to monetize the information, but public funding supports the accessibility and stability of collected information.

6. **Active outreach:** With all the time and money that goes into knowledge management, from architecting the system to collecting and curating the content, the goal is that the target audience is aware of and using the system. This highlights the importance of performing search engine optimization, attending industry conferences, connecting with other domain-specific networks, generating educational materials, and hosting online events to drive additional impact.

Measuring the impact of knowledge management is challenging. Web analytics can provide counts of visitors and pageviews, which gives a measure of exposure that can be influenced by global awareness or interest in the topic. During the last year, all the knowledge hubs cumulatively received over 800,000 pageviews from 250,000 visitors. PRIMRE tracks usage metrics for each knowledge hub independently and reports on these metrics annually, demonstrating continued growth. Though it is difficult to know whether to attribute this growth to an increase in content, enhanced search engine optimization, or general growing interest in marine energy. A more subjective way to measure impact is through informal comments made by key members of the marine energy community at industry events. Most of the U.S. and international communities are aware of PRIMRE and provide overwhelmingly positive feedback as to the functionality and utility of the information. Anonymous feedback is also requested from the community each year through rotating user review surveys.

An emerging industry like marine energy is a fascinating setting to practice knowledge management because the knowledge hubs are built from the ground up without competing entities. This can be juxtaposed against the offshore wind energy industry, which is a comparable renewable energy industry, but one that is commercialized as a competitive grid-scale energy source. While there are some quality knowledge hubs supporting offshore wind, it is common for there to be less connectivity between efforts, paid membership requirements to access information, and significant gaps in knowledge (e.g., many countries lacking data repositories). These factors are believed to negatively contribute to public opinion of offshore wind energy. By comparison, setting up a robust and transparent network of databases at the start of commercialization may support transparency and combat misinformation. Time will tell how impactful the PRIMRE knowledge management will be as the marine energy industry progresses towards commercialization.

## Funding statement

The National Renewable Energy Laboratory is a national laboratory of the U.S. Department of Energy, Office of Energy Efficiency and Renewable Energy, operated by the Alliance for Sustainable Energy, LLC. under contract No. DE-AC36-08GO28308. Pacific Northwest National Laboratory is operated by Battelle for the U.S. Department of Energy under contract DE-AC05-76RL01830. Sandia National Laboratories is a multisession laboratory managed and operated by National Technology & Engineering Solutions of Sandia, LLC, a wholly owned subsidiary of Honeywell International Inc., for the U.S. Department of Energy's National Nuclear Security Administration under contract DE-NA0003525.

## Nomenclature list

| | |
|---|---|
| API | application programming interface |
| DOE | department of energy |
| LLM | large language model |
| MHKDR | Marine and Hydrokinetic Data Repository |
| NREL | National Renewable Energy Laboratory |
| OES | Ocean Energy Systems |
| OTEC | Ocean Thermal Energy Conversion |
| PNNL | Pacific Northwest National Laboratory |
| PRIMRE | Portal and Repository for Marine Renewable Energy |
| SNL | Sandia National Laboratories |
| TWh | Terawatt-hour |
| VADR | Visualization analysis design research |
| WEC | wave energy converter |
| WPTO | Water Power Technologies Office |
| WREN | Working Together to Resolve Environmental Effects of Wind Energy |

## Author details

Jonathan Whiting[1*], Cesar Ricardo Castillo[2], Jon Weers[3], Katie Peterson[3], Will Peplinski[2], Kelley Ruehl[2], Andrea Copping[1], Megan Anderson[2], Fadia Ticona Rollano[1], Nicholas Gilroy[3], Paul Susmarski[3], Lysel Garavelli[1], Hanna Fields[3], Hayley Farr[1] and Sean Morris[3]

1 Pacific Northwest National Laboratory, Seattle, United States

2 Sandia National Laboratories, Albuquerque, United States

3 National Renewable Energy Laboratory, Golden, United States

*Address all correspondence to: jonathan.whiting@pnnl.gov

## References

[1] International Renewable Energy Agency (IRENA). Scaling up investments in ocean energy technologies: A brief from the IRENA Collaborative Framework on Ocean Energy and Offshore Renewables. 2023; 31

[2] Rusu E, Onea F. A review of the technologies for wave energy extraction. Clean Energy. 2018;**2**:10-19. DOI: 10.1093/ce/zky003

[3] Cao C, Chen G, Qian C, Shang J. Spatiotemporal variability and climate teleconnections of global ocean wave power. Frontiers in Marine Science. 2022;**9**:900950. DOI: 10.3389/fmars.2022.900950

[4] International Renewable Energy Agency (IRENA). Innovation Outlook: Ocean Energy Technologies. 2020; 112

[5] Ocean Energy Systems (OES). Annual Report: An Overview of Ocean Energy Activities in 2022. 2022; 228

[6] Clark C, DuPont B. Reliability-based design optimization in offshore renewable energy systems. Renewable and Sustainable Energy Reviews. 2018;**97**:390-400. DOI: 10.1016/j.rser.2018.08.030

[7] Vega LA. Ocean thermal energy conversion. In: Meyers RA, editor. Encyclopedia of Sustainability Science and Technology. New York, NY: Springer; 2012. DOI: 10.1007/978-1-4419-0851-3_695

[8] Nihous G. A preliminary assessment of ocean thermal energy conversion resources. Journal of Energy Resources Technology. 2007;**129**:10-17. DOI: 10.1115/1.2424965

[9] Hsu WS, Preet A, Lin TY, Lin TE. Miniaturized salinity gradient energy harvesting devices. Molecules. 2021;**26**(18):5469. DOI: 10.3390/molecules26185469

[10] Scråmestø OS, Skilhagen SE, Nielsen WK. Power production based on osmotic pressure. In: Waterpower XVI; July 27-30, 2009. Spokane; 2009

[11] Whiting J, Copping A, Freeman M, Woodbury A. Tethys knowledge management system: Working to advance the marine renewable energy industry. International Marine Energy Journal. 2019;**2**:29-38. DOI: 10.36688/imej.2.29-38

[12] Portal and Repository for Marine Renewable Energy (PRIMRE). PRIMRE Developer Documents: Metadata Schema [Internet]. 2023. Available from: https://primre.org/Developer_Documents#appendB [Accessed: July 1, 2023]

[13] Wilkinson M, Dumontier M, Aalbersberg I, Appleton G, Axton A, Baak A, et al. The FAIR guiding principles for scientific data management and stewardship. Scientific Data. 2016;**3**:160018. DOI: 10.1038/sdata.2016.18

[14] DCAT-US Schema v1.1 (Project Open Data Metadata Schema) [Internet]. 2014. Available from: https://resources.data.gov/resources/dcat-us/ [Accessed: June 1, 2023]

[15] International Electrotechnical Commission (IEC). TC114 Marine Energy – Wave, Tidal and other water current converters – Part 1: Vocabulary. 2020

[16] Copping A, Weers J, Ruehl K, Farr H. International Workshop on Marine Energy Data Sharing: Workshop Report2021. p. 15

[17] Yang Z, Neary V, Kilcher L. High resolution ocean surface wave Hindcast (US Wave) data. United States; 2020. 10.15473/1647329

[18] Drupal [Internet]. 2009. Available from: https://www.drupal.org/ [Accessed May 05, 2023]

[19] Copping AE, Hemery LG. OES-Environmental 2020 State of the science report: Environmental effects of marine renewable energy development around the world. Report for Ocean Energy Systems (OES). 2020; 327. 10.2172/1632878

[20] Semantic Mediawiki [Internet]. 2005. Available from: https://www.semantic-mediawiki.org/wiki/Semantic_MediaWiki [Accessed: June 1, 2023]

[21] International Electrotechnical Commission (IEC). TC114 Marine Energy –Wave, Tidal and other water current converters – Part 101: Wave Resource Assessment. 2023

Chapter 13

# Effect of the Different Types and Structures of Communities of Practice on Learning: A Case Study of an Education Service Company

*Yuichi Matsumoto*


## Abstract

Although communities of practice (CoPs) are known to facilitate learning, boundary crossing, and knowledge creation, these effects have not been examined according to different structures in the extant literature. Thus, this chapter presents an exploratory study on how the establishment of various types and structures of communities affects the effectiveness of an individual's learning and boundary crossing. This was an exploratory qualitative case study of an educational service company, in which data were collected using face-to-face semi-structured interviews and participative observations. Using a case study, we classified CoPs into two types based on their size and frequency of interactions: interaction and networking communities. We also conceptualized four learning styles in CoPs and investigated the relationship between the two types of communities and the four learning styles derived from previous research. We found that the CoPs examined in this study interacted with each other (through learners' multiple affiliations with various communities) to form multilayered structures, which present advantages such as the possibility of high-level learning through multifaceted and circular learning, and the ability to build networks among communities. Therefore, we conclude that multilayered CoPs structures are effective in enhancing all four learning styles.


**Keywords:** communities of practice (CoPs), legitimate peripheral participation, multifaceted learning, boundary-crossing learning, circular learning

## 1. Introduction

Communities of practice (CoPs) [1–4] are known to facilitate learning, boundary crossing, and knowledge creation. However, despite such diverse outcomes, extant literature does not discuss these effects considering CoP types and structures. Several studies have discussed the need to expand the definition of CoPs (e.g., [5, 6]); however, the fragmentation of the concept has only led to confusion rather than moving the discussion forward. To help elucidate this matter, we conducted an exploratory study of how establishing different types and structures of CoPs [1–4] affects individual learning and boundary crossing based on a case study of an educational service company, the results of which are presented in this chapter. Specifically, we examined how the multilayered structure of CoPs facilitated learning. Here, we attempt to organize the concept of CoPs and divide it into two broad types. We then conduct a case study to uncover and discuss how these two types of CoPs should be constructed and managed.

## 2. Previous researches

### 2.1 The concept of communities of practice

CoPs are defined as "groups of people who share a concern, a set of problems, or a passion about a topic, and who deepen their knowledge and expertise in this area by interacting on an ongoing basis" [4]. However, the content of the CoPs concept varies widely, and the usage of this term is diverse [7]. This is because previous studies relied on one of four representative studies (i.e., [1–4]), between which there were differences in the content (**Table 1**).

### 2.2 The tradeoffs between scale and frequency, level of learning

The conceptual diversity described above limits the development of CoPs, thus we must discuss the expansion of this concept. To address the diversity of the concept, this section focuses on size. CoPs have been proposed as primarily small places of work where members frequently interact through their practices as their style of learning [1]. Other studies have also noted the importance of learning based on interactions [9, 10]. However, another style of learning exists, in which people meet and acquire new knowledge and information through communication across workplace boundaries [11]. In this type of learning, the CoP is primarily large and infrequent, and connections and knowledge are created through boundary crossing [12, 13]. In previous studies, there has been conceptual confusion between small, frequently interacting CoPs and large, infrequent, boundary-crossing CoPs. In this chapter, we discuss how CoPs can be used more effectively by classifying them into two types.

Another issue involves high- and low-level learning. Meta-level learning has been discussed in, for example, single- and double-loop learning [14] and higher-level learning [15] studies; however, all of these studies were conducted at the organizational level and have not been discussed even at the individual level [16]. CoPs are suitable for lower-order learning, where knowledge, skills, and information are acquired, but not for higher-level learning, where existing beliefs and values behind knowledge and skills are transformed [17]. However, this is derived from a static view of the concept of a CoP, and other studies (e.g., [18]) suggest that even in a CoP, it is possible to trigger transformative learning, which leads to a change in values and perspectives [19, 20]. In this study, we examined the classification of these two types of CoPs.

### 2.3 Four learning styles

It is useful to consider that the two types of CoPs are not only different in size and frequency, but also in the learning styles therein. Separating them into categories would be futile if their learning styles were the same, even if their size and frequency

| | Lave and Wenger [1] | Brown and Duguid [2] | Wenger [3] | Wenger et al. [4] |
|---|---|---|---|---|
| Can we create a CoP? | Embedded in social and historical context (already exists) | Finding and discovering CoPs within organizations | Co-exists with and found from organization | To be able to make and cultivate |
| Reproduction of CoPs | Through a common process to advance identity construction and learning | Not discussed | Reproduced by participation, embodiment, and design | Discussed in their development model |
| Operation and management | Not discussed | Not discussed | Mutual construction in each member's practice | Discussed its importance and methods |
| Main purpose | Learning and skills transfer (practice and work in the community as well) | Understanding work, learning, and innovation from non-canonical view | Creating meaning and learning through identity construction by practice | Creating, storing, updating, and sharing knowledge |
| Elements | Communities, practice | Communities, practice | Communities, practice | Domain, community, and practice |
| Contents of members' practices | Fulfilling participation in the community | Learning by practice (understanding work and innovation) from non-canonical view | Participation and reification in the dimensions of mutual engagement, joint enterprise, and shared repertoires | Increasing knowledge in the domain |
| What guides learning? | Curriculum of learning and curriculum of education | Promoting membership and access to the CoPs as well as storytelling, collaboration, and social construction | Practices that guide learning (participation and reification, emergence, modes of belonging, local and global) | Domain |
| Boundary crossing | Relationships that transcend boundaries are CoPs | CoPs across organizational boundaries | Practices such as boundary objects and brokering lead boundary crossing | CoPs across organizational boundaries |
| Memberships | From newcomers to experts | From newcomers to experts | Formed through participation and reification | Coordinator, core members, active members, and peripheral members |
| Member instructorship | Not discussed | Not discussed | Not discussed | Instructorship of coordinator is important |
| Identity | Construction of learner's identities progresses simultaneously with participation | Practical-based view transforms organizational identity | Guided by participation and non-participation | CoP is a "home of identity" |

| | Lave and Wenger [1] | Brown and Duguid [2] | Wenger [3] | Wenger et al. [4] |
|---|---|---|---|---|
| Relationship between CoPs and organizations | Close to identical, but not the same | Distinguish between formal organizations and CoPs; the relationship between the two is important | Separate but overlapping | Distinguishes between formal organizations and CoPs, and presents the concepts of double-knit organizations |
| Horizontal relationships among CoPs | Peripheral legitimacy is the nexus between CoPs | Perceiving the organization as a set of CoPs can solve the problems of the organization | Suggesting the constellation of practice as the collection of CoPs | Suggesting distributed CoPs |
| Multilayered relationships among CoPs | Participation at multiple levels inevitably accompanies membership in a CoP | Assumes an aggregation of CoPs linking each other | Constellation is a connotation of CoP | Assumes multilayered nature with sub-communities |

**Table 1.**
*Conceptual comparison among CoPs in the four representative studies. Source: Matsumoto [8].*

were different. The basic learning styles of CoPs have been presented in the previously mentioned four major studies. In this section, we organize and summarize them as the four learning styles described below.

### *2.3.1 Legitimate peripheral participation*

Derived from Lave and Wenger [1], the legitimate peripheral participation learning style involves the sharing and creation of knowledge and skills through interactions among members of a CoP [1]. This style has been proposed as a learning method for newcomers to acquire knowledge and skills by fully participating in the CoP through sociocultural practices. The basic idea of legitimate peripheral participation is that new members acquire the skills of the community from existing members and develop their identities through participation [21] while becoming members of the CoP. The acquisition and creation of knowledge and skills from existing members are thought to be the primary learning style [22]. Regarding the level of learning, it is lower-level learning [17]. Legitimate peripheral participation and CoPs are inseparable, but this concept assumes a static and stable concept of CoP. Learning through legitimate peripheral participation is suitable for small communities [23] and difficult in CoPs that are large and have infrequent interactions, such as those with many subsequent boundary crossings [24] and online CoPs [25].

### *2.3.2 Multifaceted learning*

Multifaceted learning, derived from Brown and Duguid [2], involves acquisition of diverse knowledge and skills. This is a higher-level learning style based on the comparison between canonical and non-canonical knowledge [3]. There is often a divergence between knowledge believed to be correct in the field (canonical knowledge) and practice-based or field knowledge (non-canonical knowledge), and this difference leads to learning [3, 26] that enhances CoPs [27]. That is, using this difference helps CoP members to understand work and innovation. Moreover, this learning style incorporates values and perspectives, as well as diverse knowledge and skills acquisition in the workplace [28], public health practice [29], public office [30], and society [31].

#### *2.3.3 Boundary-crossing learning*

This learning style, derived from Wenger [3], involves acquiring, sharing, and creating skills and knowledge through network interactions, that is, through interacting with external communities and their members [32]. CoPs link local human resources and knowledge [4], and the creation of human networks can be used to increase the total amount of knowledge available [33], distribute knowledge, maintain and improve its quality, and create knowledge through interactions [34], thus boundary-crossing learning is characteristic of CoPs. This style is mainly low-level learning, but sometimes, high-level learning occurs. Boundary crossing enhances collaborative learning in CoPs in three ways. First, boundary-crossing activities increase members' diversity [35] to facilitate collaborative knowledge creation through multiple viewpoints. Second, boundary crossing encourages members to compare their experiences, knowledge, and selves, thereby facilitating new insights and knowledge. CoPs enhance this type of knowledge creation, leading to knowledge sharing [36], information gathering [37], problem-solving [38, 39], and personal career design [40, 41]. Third, boundary crossing enhances higher-level learning by, for example, generating meaning [3], emphasizing the value of work [42], promoting the understanding of members' identities [19], and enhancing lower-level learning, including through knowledge sharing. It is possible to resolve contradictions and enhance activities by spontaneously establishing CoPs and facilitating boundary crossing. This style of learning is enhanced by extensive boundary crossing and the ability to interact with many people. Large CoPs created by social events, even if infrequent, are also effective. However, the learning effect of boundary crossing is weak when practiced with a fixed group of people.

#### *2.3.4 Circular learning*

Derived from Wenger et al. [4], circular learning is argued to be based on members of a CoP that are also members of formal organizations, and that this multimembership creates a cycle of learning. It is mainly a low-level learning style, but sometimes high-level learning occurs. The members bring their experiences and knowledge to the CoP, discuss, generalize, or document them, obtain support for problem-solving, and then apply them to real problems at their respective organizations. Multimembership is an important aspect of CoPs [42, 43]. The learning cycle between CoPs and organizations is effective [34, 44] not only for sharing knowledge [45], but also for generating transformative learning [41, 46].

We summarized the above four learning style in **Table 2**.

We considered these four learning styles to be effective in CoPs' learning and examined how these learning styles relate to different types of CoPs and how they are constructed and operated. To this effect, we conducted a case study of an educational service company as described below.

| Research | Lave and Wenger [1] | Brown and Duguid [2] | Wenger [3] | Wenger et al. [4] |
|---|---|---|---|---|
| Names and methods of learning styles | Legitimate peripheral participation | Multidisciplinary learning | Boundary-crossing learning | Circular learning |
| | Learning through full participation and interaction within the CoP for knowledge acquisition | Learning from the differences between canonical and non-canonical knowledge to transform values and perspectives among organizations and CoPs | Crossing the various boundaries of organizations and CoPs to acquire knowledge and relationships with those outside the CoP | Learning through moving between one's organization and CoP to discuss and confirm knowledge and skills |

**Table 2.**
*Learning processes derived from four representative studies.*

## 3. Methods

### 3.1 Research sites

To clarify learning in CoPs, we conducted a case study based on the data collected using qualitative methods. This was a single case study based on Yin's work [47], and we selected Kumon Ltd. as the research site. Kumon is a company that provides education services for children, franchises Kumon-style classrooms, and supports children's learning. We selected this company because it was suitable for a single case study that met all three of the following criteria: (1) the case is definitive, (2) the case is extreme and unique, and (3) the subject is a new fact [47]. Further, we selected Kumon because it enhanced diverse learning based on CoPs. Specifically, in Kumon, instructors teach children in Kumon-style classrooms using common teaching materials and form CoPs with learners and support staff in each classroom. Similarly, instructors participate in many CoPs to improve their teaching skills. The CoPs in this study meet the definition by Wenger et al. [4] and are adequate for discussing the relationship between the two types of CoPs, the four learning styles, and better management methods, consistent with the purpose of this study.

In addition, Kumon has various learning communities such as those formed through their "district meetings" at the district level and "courses" led by Kumon at the national level. Nevertheless, this chapter focuses on the following four CoPs that are more autonomously constructed and operated by instructors and have a multi-layered structure: seminars and voluntary institutes in which instructors participate, seminars and voluntary institutes organized by instructors, mentor seminars, and instructors' research conferences. Although studies dealing with multilayered structures exist, such as the study by Wenger et al. [4] focusing on global CoP, Kumon's case is characterized not only by its inclusive scale but also by the construction of a multilayered structure based on proficiency level. We believe that this study will present new findings in existing studies.

### 3.2 Research method

Two survey methods were used to collect the case study data: interviews and participative observations.

Seven instructors who were teaching at Kumon with 10–30 years of work experience were selected as interviewees. As per our request, they were selected by the Kumon HRM staff after explaining the purpose of the study. The interviews were conducted face-to-face for one and a half hours using, a semi-structured form [48] and the protocols were recorded using an IC recorder and transcribed by the author. Kumon officers were sometimes interviewed and provided supplementary explanations as needed. In addition, we observed the actual instructions in some classrooms.

The participative observation survey was conducted with the cooperation of Kumon, wherein we observed two events sponsored by Kumon: the Kumon instructors' research conference and the mentor seminar. At the instructors' research conference, we participated in discussions of theme meetings and took notes, while at the mentor seminar, we simply observed their discussions and took notes. Subsequently, we got documents about Conference from Kumon. These observations were then used to construct a case study.

## 4. Case study

### 4.1 Overview of Kumon

Kumon Institute of Education Co., Ltd. was established in 1962. They developed original learning materials and managed classrooms nationwide to teach mathematics, English, and Japanese as well as French, German, and calligraphy.

Kumon operates 23,700 franchised Kumon-style classrooms (for mathematics and arithmetic, English, and Japanese) at 115 office location across Japan (as of March 2023). Kumon's classrooms are operated twice a week for approximately 5 hours per day. In their classrooms, students tackle their original educational materials independently, and instructors (teachers) support individualized learning activities. Homework is assigned each time and students are expected to complete it at home and bring it to the next class. Each instructor manages their own classroom with Kumon's support through a franchise system. Instructors, mainly women, begin operating their own classrooms after training. Each Kumon classroom is supervised by a regional office, and the Kumon staff provide support for their classroom operations. One Kumon staff member supported approximately 50 instructors.

Kumon education emphasizes "high basic literacy," "self-affirmation," and "independent learning ability" to help students acquire the "zest for life." The features of the Kumon educational method can be summarized into four points: individualized learning, self-directed learning, small-step materials, and operations by instructors and staff. First, regarding individualized learning, teachers use materials that correspond to each student's academic ability. Even if all students are of the same age and grade, there may be differences in their abilities. This individualized attention on the students in turn improves each student's academic ability significantly. Another feature of their individualized learning is starting with the materials level, where students are sure to score full marks, and graduating to higher-level materials step by step. By guiding students to get full marks on their educational material, instructors and staff can foster their confidence and self-affirmation, thereby increasing their motivation to learn. Improvements in the students' academic skills encourage them to try materials at a higher level, regardless of their age or grade. It is thus common for students to study at a higher level in Kumon; for example, some third-grade students study at the fifth or sixth grade level of elementary school.

Second, self-directed learning means that Kumon does not conduct one-way education as in school education. In the Kumon classroom, each student works on his or her own material, solving problems independently and listening to the instructors' and staff's guidance. Third, they use small-step materials, which means the content's difficulty level gradually increases from easy to advanced. Kumon's teaching materials are created using the expertise gained over Kumon's long history and are improved daily based on feedback from the classroom. This means that students can solve the material that is adequate for them, and small increments in their level ensure that their academic skills are effectively established.

The fourth factor is the guidance of the instructors and staff. Instructors and staff are indispensable for monitoring each student's progress and supporting their learning. The instructors/staff members are aware of the students' abilities and provide them with adequate materials. They do not move on when the student is not ready; they provide them with lower-level materials to tackle and only allow them to progress to higher-level materials when they have the academic literacy and desire to advance. This plays an important role for instructors and staff, who can objectively look at students. Recognizing, praising, and encouraging students' efforts is essential for fostering self-directed and positive learning attitudes. Each of these four features influences the others and creates a synergistic effect. When instructors accurately understand materials that have been refined over Kumon's long history and use them appropriately in the classroom, teaching methods based on the four aforementioned characteristics can be implemented.

We found that Kumon instructors learned from many experiences under the company concept of "learning from children" in their own classrooms, and at the same time, they are members of diverse CoPs wherein they obtain information that helps them improve their skills in and motivation for teaching and classroom management. As discussed below, the results of these CoPs have been highly positive and we believe that there is a strong relationship between learning activities and teaching performance. Furthermore, Kumon has a mechanism for forming a CoP and expanding boundaries among instructors, which we discuss later in this chapter.

### 4.2 Kumon's instructor support

How does Kumon support instructors? Kumon classrooms in each region are supervised by a branch office. For example, the Nishinomiya Office oversees the classrooms in Nishinomiya City, Hyogo Prefecture. The branch office controls the classes in the region, and instructors visit the office to pick up teaching materials for their classrooms. Instructors can easily meet the staff at the office and ask for advice on their problems. The offices are grouped into "areas" according to the wider region. The Nishinomiya Office is located in the Kansai area. Various activities are conducted within the region, offices, and areas.

The Kumon organization has a development department that is responsible for communicating about how to use Kumon's teaching materials. They conduct lectures to transfer business knowledge and develop tools that facilitate learning. Alongside the instructional department, they also promote classroom development by improving instructors' skills and training them. The department also publishes a magazine that provides information to instructors.

Kumon staff manage 50–60 instructors. They work with instructors to determine how classrooms should be managed. Just as a teacher understands their student, staff understand the teachers' strengths and weaknesses and guide them appropriately on how to overcome and improve their weaknesses. This guidance is important and affects the success or failure of classroom management.

Undoubtedly, the greatest source of the excellent results produced by Kumon is the instructors' interactions and shared learning activities and the professional development that they obtain from them. As of March 31, 2014, Kumon had consolidated sales of 86,446 million yen, ordinary income of 10,773 million yen, and 4038 employees throughout the group. In addition to 85 locations nationwide, Kumon has regional headquarters in North America, South America, Asia and Oceania, China, Europe, and Africa, and is actively developing its business in 47 countries and regions worldwide. In Japan alone, the company had 1.46 million learners (total number of learners in all subjects) in 16,500 classrooms as of March 31, 2014. The company manages these classrooms with 14,600 instructors. Overseas, there are 8400 classrooms with 2.81 million learners (total number of learners in all subjects) and 7400 instructors, and is attracting attention both domestically and internationally as a universal business model.

However, the development of instructors at Kumon is achieved through the autonomous learning of the instructors themselves, not only through the Kumon Method of Education. This is also supported by learning based on various types of CoPs that instructors spontaneously establish through Kumon. Kumon contains a system that activates the building of CoPs and learning based on these. This is the most important factor that enables Kumon to continue to develop instructors who make the most of the Kumon method and materials to steadily improve student performance.

In the following section, the CoPs formed by Kumon instructors are described in detail based on the authors' research.

### 4.3 Kumon instructors' CoPs

There are four types of Kumon CoPs discussed in this chapter: (1) "seminars" that Kumon instructors spontaneously conduct, (2) "small-group seminars" coordinated by Kumon, (3) "mentor seminars" conducted by skilled instructors, and (4) "instructors' research conferences" held at the national level. Kumon has a system in which these CoPs, which differ in size, frequency, and spontaneity, are formed and operated, and they have a synergistic effect. This has improved the instructors' teaching skills.

#### *4.3.1 "Seminars" in which instructors participate*

New instructors, who have just opened their own classrooms after receiving Kumon training, typically do not have sufficient previous experience, either as teachers or managers of their own classrooms. Therefore, they must rely on Kumon materials and support staff to manage their classrooms through trial and error. However, the instructors must manage their classrooms independently, which is challenging task.

Consequently, instructors actively participate in "seminars" to share their teaching and management knowledge in order to improve student performance and increase the number of self-motivated learners. These seminars primarily aim to explore and share teaching and management skills. They take place on days when classes are not held and are attended by approximately 20–30 instructors. The seminars are coordinated and managed by experienced instructors. Seminars authorized by Kumon are accredited: Kumon requires instructors to participate in them and submit reports thereafter, and they earn credits for their participation.

It is important for Kumon staff to use seminars for instructor development. Depending on the instructors' need to improve their abilities, staff members introduce and encourage instructors to participate in these seminars. This is because these seminars present many teaching examples and data that can help instructors develop their own skills. Many instructors have their own instructional data. Second, it is meaningful for instructors to learn from other instructors, not only teaching skills, but also classroom management, career design, and how balancing work and family life. Therefore, it is essential for the Kumon staff to guide instructors to appropriate seminars while considering their individual characteristics and the nature of each seminar.

During seminars, the instructors hold lively discussions on issues such as day-to-day classroom management and effective teaching methods, providing their own examples as they discuss. Even instructors attending for the first time can immediately engage in discussions. Instructors not only share the same topics but also use common Kumon teaching materials, with which they are deeply familiar. For example, if someone says, "In the second question of the Japanese B-1 material...," all the other instructors immediately understand the question and answer it with their own teaching examples. Such interactions allow them to engage in more detailed discussions and skills sharing.

For new instructors in particular, it is very important that senior instructors play the role of mentors in seminars. This is a valuable opportunity for them to solve their problems. Experienced instructors can provide varied advice, from confirming their teaching expertise to solving problems related to students who are not improving, classroom management, teaching careers, and personal concerns. After attending such seminars, new instructors often regret why they had not started participating in seminars sooner.

As instructors gain experience and proficiency in teaching, Kumon often asks them to manage their seminars. The instructors share their knowledge and skills in teaching and classroom management with the participants based on their own experiences. At first, some instructors hesitate to manage seminars, but they understand the significance of sharing their teaching skills and passing on what they have learned from senior instructors, and they accept their roles. It is common for proficient instructors to take over seminars from senior instructors or manage seminars themselves while continuing to participate in seminars to learn.

Kumon's staff prepare seminars by arranging the venue, but they do not engage in seminars unless instructors ask them to maintain their spontaneity. This differentiates them from "small-group seminars," which we discuss next.

### *4.3.2 "Small-group seminars" conducted by Kumon*

Small-group seminars are CoPs coordinated by Kumon; the organization also creates its learning content. They are different from the previously discussed seminars, for which spontaneity is important. However, they are the same in that they both aim to equip instructors with good teaching skills. The background of the small-group seminar system promotes more interactive learning between Kumon and the instructors and encourages the application of learned skills and knowledge in the classrooms. Kumon ensures that instructors acquire the teaching skills that the organization has accumulated over the years.

Another characteristic that differentiates small-group seminars from seminars is that, in the former, the Kumon staff provide the lecturers and are in charge of the seminars. They lecture using the same textbook and slide materials, not only to standardize the teaching content but also to stimulate learning among staff.

Five to six instructors participated in each small-group seminar, which Kumon emphasized during the design of the system. The rationale for this is that if there are too many instructors participating, some of them might not speak up or may become too reserved, while having too few participants might make interaction between them difficult. Currently, instructors study one theme over 3 months in three sessions.

The venue for the small-group seminars is primarily the branch office. Typically, two to three small-group seminars can be held simultaneously. Even if one branch office has sufficient meeting rooms to hold each seminar in a separate room, they would rather hold several seminars in a large room simultaneously. This is intended to increase the interaction between small groups and raise instructors' competitive awareness. Additionally, each branch office is equipped with desks, chairs, computers, and displays that can be used in small-group seminars. By providing the same equipment at all offices nationwide, they create an environment in which learning can begin immediately, eliminating unnecessary hassles for the Kumon staff. The standardization of hardware and software shows Kumon's enthusiasm for small-group seminars and the importance of interaction among instructors in the activities of the CoP.

Instructors who wish to participate in small-group seminars can do so by applying to branch offices in their areas. Kumon assigns five or six members who will attend the seminar, some of which are veterans, while others are newcomers. The learning activities are facilitated by staff, and instructors present and discuss their own cases. This allows new instructors to ask questions and expert instructors to get to know the newcomers and train them based on their individual needs.

Small-group seminars have a significant impact on the professional growth of the Kumon staff. Before these seminars were established, the consulting staff had to create their own content, which led to difficulties in ensuring uniformity. By standardizing the content, it became easier to compare different methods of teaching the same content. It became clear how the facilitation of small-group seminars differed among staff members and what they needed to learn. Learning among consulting professionals became more active, and newcomers were able to acquire knowledge and skills more efficiently by observing expert staff seminars. A multilayered CoPs were also been established as a result of joint learning among several offices within an area or the presentation and sharing of best practices at the national level, beyond the boundaries of the office.

The characteristic of small-group seminars is that standardized content is learned by a CoP that emphasizes small-group interaction; however, when compared to seminars that are spontaneously constructed by instructors, it is clear that the two CoPs have different characteristics. Kumon's system of equipping instructors with teaching skills allows different CoPs to coexist and interact with each other. It is a combination of the two CoPs described below that facilitates learning.

#### *4.3.3 "Mentor seminars" with skilled instructors*

Kumon has several systems that support those who have only been teaching for a short period. One of these is the "Instructor Advisor" system, in which senior instructors mentor first-year instructors. There are events called the mentor seminars that bring together mentoring instructors and instructors involved in the management of the seminar. The unique feature of this event is that the participating instructors are limited to those who are highly successful, not only in their teaching skills but also in classroom management. In other words, these seminars are CoPs for accomplished teachers.

Mentor seminars are held regularly and are led by highly skilled instructors who have worked for many years; their purpose is to improve the skills and management performance of both instructors and the branch office. Many of these highly skilled instructors are well known, not only at the regional level, but also at the area and national levels. The opportunity to meet and hear from such instructors is valuable for those who have attained a certain level of proficiency.

There are three reasons why instructors participate in mentor seminars. The first reason is the same as the incentive to participate in selective training in companies. In other words, participation in a mentor seminar means that one's teaching skills and classroom management results are recognized by Kumon. The second reason is the opportunity to meet and learn from highly skilled veteran instructors, who are good role models for instructors. This opportunity is both a badge of merit to the instructors for their teaching skills and classroom management efforts and a strong incentive to participate. Third, there is an opportunity to interact with other proficient instructors. As they become more proficient in their teaching skills, some instructors may wish to further develop themselves in a higher-level CoP. However, such opportunities are not easy to access, especially in rural areas, where there are few classrooms. However, mentor seminars, which are CoPs in their own right, make such opportunities more accessible since they facilitate interactions with instructors of certain proficiency levels. Further, they provide a platform on which networks among proficient instructors can expand, which can then be filtered down to seminars and small-group seminars.

The mentor seminar that the author observed was attended by approximately 200 of the most proficient instructors in the area. After the opening greeting, there was an opportunity to ask participants to present recent examples of their work achievements. Presenters had been pre-selected, and perceived as honors. The highly skilled instructors provided feedback on the presentations and praised the presenters' efforts and ingenuity, and all the participants applauded them. After the presentations, a group discussion of the content of the presentations was held for approximately 20 minutes. Proficient instructors sat near each other at their desks and discussed their case studies and experiences. The instructors were distributed such that they were not clustered with those from nearby offices, allowing for networking among the instructors. Highly proficient and experienced instructors presented discussion topics such as "changing the mindset of instructors," which evoked lively discussions. Several participants reported on the results of these discussions. Some instructors reported that they realized the high quality of the mentor seminars and the stimulation that came with them. The Kumon staff members also participated and were tasked with helping the instructors that they were in charge to build their networks and inspire them to grow. They asked the mentors to support them in doing so.

During the final question-and-answer period, the high-skilled instructors provided advice on specific issues related to seminar management one after another from the perspective of Kumon's local-level long-term development plans. Thereafter, some of the instructors expressed the significance of participating in these seminars to me, explaining that in their area, there are no other proficient instructors, hindering their ability to learn together. They expressed that meeting and hearing the highly skilled instructors motivated them.

### 4.3.4 National-level "instructors' research conferences"

Instructors' research conferences are Kumon's largest CoPs as they gather instructors from all over Japan at a large venue once a year to present and share research results.

At the conference that the author observed, at first, breakout sessions were conducted to present teaching methods. Divided by subject and purpose, instructors presented effective teaching methods that have been studied in seminars. As only highly successful teaching methods that have passed the screening process can be presented at such conferences, these presentations and the methods taught therein were important for the instructors to grasp. Some instructors aimed for seminars where they hosted presentations and sought to develop their abilities and confidence by recruiting younger instructors.

The presentations we observed concerned teaching methods for Japanese language materials and learners, who explained the areas with which students tended to struggle, methods that had been effective in helping them overcome these obstacles, and ways to use existing methods to solve specific problems with the materials. Instructors listened attentively and took notes on the teaching methods.

In another room, there was a breakout session in which instructors with short teaching careers and senior instructors met and presented their experiences. The presenters explained how they overcame specific problems and concerns, such as how they established their classrooms and balanced their family lives in the early years of their careers. Afterward, there was time for the instructors to interact with each other. Communication between instructors with short careers allowed them to share their concerns. The new instructors listened attentively to the seniors' experiences. Because new instructors who have just opened their own classrooms typically do not have many opportunities to network with other instructors, it is very important to provide forums such as these for them.

After the seminar, a plenary session was held in a large hall, where all the participating instructors gathered. During the plenary session, Kumon explained its history and future strategies, and awarded instructors with long careers. The instructors aspired to receive such awards in the future, so they listened attentively to the veteran instructors' award speeches. The subsequent reception was said to be an opportunity for networking among the instructors.

In summary, these instructors' research conferences are CoPs open to all instructors. These are platforms for presenting and sharing teaching methods. By bringing together diverse groups of instructors, the conferences provide exposure to various perspectives. In addition, the conferences are CoPs that promote networking beyond the boundaries of districts, areas, and seminars. Even if the conferences are held only once a year, this networking provides opportunities to participate in new seminars and independent study groups, further promoting learning within the district or area.

The multilayered structure of the CoPs addressed in this study is summarized in **Figure 1**.

Based on the above examples, the next section discusses the relationship between the structure of CoPs and learning styles, as well as the interaction between CoPs.

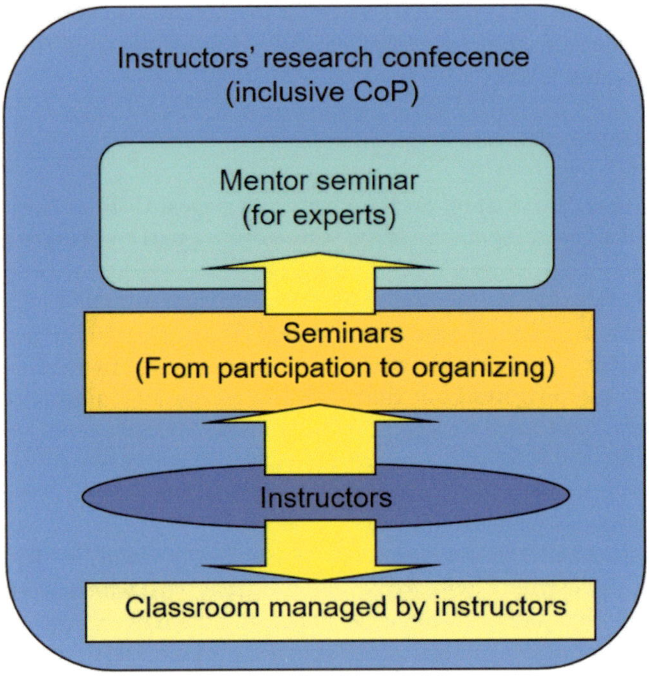


**Figure 1.**
*Layered structure of CoPs in Kumon.*

## 5. Discussion

### 5.1 Types of CoPs and learning styles

We classified the Kumon CoPs in the case studies according to the dimensions of their characteristics, which differ in terms of size, frequency of meetings, and learning activities. The results are presented in **Table 3** below.

The first classification characteristic is the frequency of meetings. Seminars and small-group seminars were classified as "interaction CoPs," in which participants gather frequently for study, while mentor seminars and instructors' research conferences were classified as "networking CoPs," held approximately once a year. The next dimension relates to the purpose of learning activities. Although the main purpose of all CoPs is learning and development, the seminars and small-group seminars are interactional, the main purpose of which is to discuss and develop teaching methods with a certain number of members, whereas mentor seminars and instructors' research conferences are based on exchange, in which the main purpose is to promote human exchange and learning. Mentor seminars and instructors' research conferences are networking-based events, of which the promotion of human communication is an important objective, in addition to learning. Thus, the four CoPs examined in this study can be classified into two main types: instruction and networking CoPs.

Concerning learning styles, seminars and small-group seminars, which were categorized as instructional CoPs, were conducted to improve teaching skills based on legitimate peripheral participation. Seminars are the lowest-level platform for

| CoPs/dimension | Seminar | Small-group seminar | Mentor seminar | Instructors' research conference |
|---|---|---|---|---|
| Learning activity and purpose | Discussion and consultation among instructors, presentation of case studies | Discussions among instructors, advice to newcomers | Discussions and networking among skilled instructors | Research presentations and viewing, interaction with other instructors |
| Scale | Small (20–30 people) | Small (5–6 persons) | Medium (about 200 people) | Large (about 3000 people) |
| Life span | Long (no expiration date) | Short (3 months) | Temporary | Temporary |
| Frequency | Frequent (1 per week to 1 per month) | Frequent (once a month) | About once a year | Once a year |
| Homogeneity | Homogeneous | Homogeneous | Heterogeneous | Heterogeneous |
| Boundary crossing | Within the boundaries | Within the boundaries | Cross-boundary | Cross-boundary |
| Spontaneity | Spontaneous | Intentional | Spontaneous | Intentional |
| Institutionalization | Freedom | Institutionalized | Freedom | Institutionalized |
| Connection | Horizontal | Horizontal | Vertical | Vertical |
| Learning style | Legitimate peripheral participation Circular learning multifaceted learning | Legitimate peripheral participation Circular learning | Boundary-crossing learning multifaceted learning | Boundary-crossing learning multifaceted learning |

**Table 3.**
*Four CoPs in Kumon.*

new instructors and beginners to deepen their participation in the community by presenting and discussing examples from their classrooms. Eventually, accomplished instructors will be able to guide them as successors and help them become accomplished instructors themselves through these seminars and workshops. The frequency of these activities promotes circular learning; that is, the strength of seminars and small-group seminars is that participants practice what they have learned in their classrooms and present the results to the CoP for further discussion. Multifaceted learning is also characteristic of these activities as evidenced by the participants comparing the seminars/independent studies with the methods used in classrooms and manuals.

However, in the case of mentor seminars and instructors' research conferences, which are categorized as networking CoPs, legitimate peripheral participation is unlikely to occur because they are held irregularly and infrequently. Furthermore, because of this infrequency (being held far apart), frequent circular learning is unlikely. Instead, mentor seminars and instructor research conferences enable boundary-crossing learning outside the community through various encounters. At mentor seminars, networks of high-achieving, high-level mentors are established at once, and at instructors' research conferences, broad networks of mentors interested in teaching methods and exchange meetings for newcomers are created, from which knowledge and skills are acquired. Participation in these networks promotes multifaceted learning by comparing oneself and one's skills from various perspectives (from newcomers to veterans, and from seasoned instructors to novices) and learning from the differences.

In summary, we have classified these CoPs into instructional CoPs, in which legitimate peripheral participation and circular learning are the main learning styles and proficiency is achieved through regular learning activities; and networking CoPs, in which boundary-crossing learning is the main learning style. Compared to instructional CoPs, networking CoPs are less effective in deepening skills and knowledge through continuous interactions. Instead, networking CoPs can create an environment that leads to the formation and participation of new CoPs, increasing the potential total amount of knowledge exchanged as well as the knowledge and skills gained through out-of-community learning.

Multifaceted learning occurred for both CoP types. If multifaceted learning is divided into (1) acquiring diverse knowledge and perspectives and (2) learning by finding differences through comparison, it can be said that (1) interaction and (2) networking CoPs are effective for promoting learning. Membership in both types of CoPs (multimembership between the two) leads to further multifaceted learning. Thus, the two types of CoPs are complementary and promote the four types of learning.

### 5.2 Interaction between multilayered CoPs

Next, we discuss the interactions between CoPs. The CoPs of Kumon instructors that we examined in this study have a multilayered structure. Thus here, we ask the question "What effect does a multilayered structure rather than parallel CoPs have on learning, as in the case of Kumon?" From the learning perspective, we found that the advantages that can be derived from the multiple affiliations of CoPs include the possibility of higher-level learning through multifaceted and circular learning and the ability to build networks among the CoPs. In addition, the case study suggests that the concept of multilayeredness takes two forms: (1) multilayeredness encompassing multiple CoPs, such as the relationship between instructors' research conferences (national) and seminars (local), and (2) multilayeredness according to the level of proficiency in elementary, junior high, and high schools. The Kumon case is characterized by the inclusion of these two layers within its structure. In other words, from the instructor's perspective, there is a multilayered structure according to proficiency that consists of the seminars and voluntary institutes that they participate in or host, the mentor seminars where those proficient in these seminars gather, and the national instructor's research conferences.

This multilayered structure enables instructors, who are learners in this case, to choose CoPs according to their proficiency level. In this case, after becoming proficient, the instructor learners graduate from being participants to being organizers and then to being participants in mentor seminars where other proficient learners can discuss and stimulate each other. Likewise, an inclusive CoP (i.e., instructors' research conferences) in which anyone can participate and interact with many people makes it possible to build a boundary-crossing network and learn. The multilayered structure of CoPs facilitates learning across community boundaries and the resettlement of communities according to their level of proficiency.

## 6. Conclusion

This chapter presents a case study through which we examined the impact of CoPs on learning. We found that the four types of learning in CoPs are achieved through participation in two types of CoPs—instructional and networking—and that a multilayered structure based on the dual multilayeredness of proficiency and inclusiveness promotes proficiency and network building. The following is a description of the theoretical contributions, practical implications, and limitations of this study and its results.

The first theoretical contribution is the derivation of the two types of CoPs based on their characteristics and learning activities. Second, this study relates these CoP types to learning style. The four learning styles proposed in this study were derived from the interaction between the two types of CoPs, which is a result of learners establishing and becoming members of these two types of CoPs. Third, it highlights the significance of the multilayered nature of CoPs based on proficiency levels. Existing studies (e.g., [4]) on global CoPs have focused on the function of inclusion and links between subordinate communities; however, in this study, learners also moved to higher communities in accordance with their proficiency levels. The dual multilayeredness of proficiency and inclusivity facilitates learning across the boundaries of CoPs in two ways: network expansion and movement between communities according to proficiency level. It facilitates learning activities not only between CoPs but also between organizations and CoPs, and the layered structure of CoPs according to proficiency is more effective in building many CoPs within a company and involving organizational members [2, 4]. Therefore, constructing a multilayered CoP structure that promotes boundary-crossing learning between formal organizations can provide a useful perspective on organizational learning.

The first practical implication is the significance of establishing and being a member of these two types of CoPs. By belonging to either the interaction type or the networking type, or both, it is possible to avoid the stagnation of learning, such as ending up in informal gatherings or not becoming proficient, even though exchanges are expanding. Establishing inclusive CoPs is beneficial beyond connections between CoPs. Secondly, we recommend establishing a multilayered structure for CoPs. Although linking different CoPs is important in itself, the formation of an inclusive community that encompasses multiple communities, and an inclusive community based on proficiency, can promote boundary-crossing learning between communities and motivate participants to become more proficient.

Regarding the study limitations, we first acknowledge its limited validity as a single case study. Although the case study presented in this chapter is suggestive and contributes to single case studies, it is important to verify its implications with other case studies, quantitative studies, and so on. Further research and comparative studies of these CoPs are required.

## Nomenclature

| | |
|---|---|
| CoPs | communities of practice |

## Author details

Yuichi Matsumoto
Faculty of Business Administration, Kwansei Gakuin University, Nishinomiya, Japan

*Address all correspondence to: matsuyu@kwansei.ac.jp

## References

[1] Lave J, Wenger E. Situated Cognition: Legitimate Peripheral Participation. Cambridge: Cambridge University Press; 1991

[2] Brown JS, Duguid P. Organizational learning and communities-of-practice: Toward a unified view of working, learning, and innovation. Organizational Science. 1991;**2**(1):40-57

[3] Wenger E. Communities of Practice: Learning, Meaning, and Identity. Cambridge: Cambridge University Press; 1998

[4] Wenger E, McDermott R, Snyder WM. Cultivating Communities of Practice. Boston, MA: Harvard Business School Press; 2002

[5] Barley SR, Kunda G. Bringing work back in. Organization. Science. 2001;**12**(1):76-95

[6] Bogenreider I, Nooteboom B. Learning groups: What types are there? A theoretical analysis and an empirical study in a consultancy firm. Organization Studies. 2004;**25**(2):287-313

[7] Nicolini D, Pyrko I, Omidvar O, Spanellis A. Understanding communities of practice: Taking stock and moving forward. Academy of Management Annals. 2022;**16**(2):680-718

[8] Matsumoto Y. Jissenkyodotai no gakushu (Learning of Communities of Practice). Tokyo: Hakuto Shobo; 2019 (in Japanese)

[9] Boud D, Middleton H. Learning from others at work: Communities of practice and informal learning. Journal of Workplace Learning. 2003;**15**(5):194-202

[10] Singh P. Oral assessment: Preparing learners for discourse in communities of practice. Systemic Practice and Action Research. 2011;**24**:247-259

[11] Cook SDN, Brown JS. Bridging epistemologies: The generative dance between organizational knowledge and organizational knowing. Organization Science. 1999;**10**(4):381-400

[12] Borzillo S, Kaminska-Labbe R. Unravelling the dynamics of knowledge creation in communities of practice though complexity theory lenses. Knowledge Management Research & Practice. 2011;**9**:353-366

[13] Dingsøyr T, Moe NB. The impact of employee participation on the use of an electronic process guide: A longitudinal case study. IEEE Transactions on Software Engineering. 2008;**34**(2):212-225

[14] Argyris C, Schön DA. Organizational Learning: A Theory of Action Perspective. Reading, Mass: Addison-Wesley; 1978

[15] Fiol CM, Lyles MA. Organizational learning. Academy of Management Review. 1985;**10**(4):803-813

[16] Bateson G. Steps to an Ecology of Mind. New York: Ballantine Books; 1972

[17] Hanks W. Foreword. In: In: Lave J, Wenger E., editor. Situated Cognition: Legitimate Peripheral Participation. Cambridge: Cambridge University Press; 1991. pp. 13-24

[18] Mejirow J. Transformative Dimensions of Adult Learning. San Francisco: Jossey-Bass; 1991

[19] Gherardi S, Nicolini D. Learning in a constellation of interconnected practices: Canon or dissonance? Journal of Management Studies. 2002;**39**(4):419-436

[20] Ardichvili A, Maurer M, Li W, Wentling T, Reed S. Cultural influences on knowledge sharing through online communities of practice. Journal of Knowledge Management. 2006;**10**(1):94-107

[21] Styhre A, Josephson P-E, Knauseder I. Organization learning in non-writing communities: The case of construction workers. Management Learning. 2006;**37**:83-100

[22] Dörfler V, Eden C. Understanding "expert" scientists: Implications for management and organization research. Management Learning. 2019;**50**:534-555

[23] Furnari S. Interstitial spaces: Microinteraction settings and the genesis of new practices between institutional fields. Academy of Management Review. 2014;**39**(4):439-462

[24] Iedema R, Meyerkort S, White L. Emergent modes of work and communities of practice. Health Services Management Research. 2005;**18**(1):13-24

[25] Akoumianakis D. Practice-oriented toolkits for virtual communities of practice. Journal of Enterprise Information Management. 2009;**22**(3):317-345

[26] Schultze U, Leidner DE. Studying knowledge management in information systems research: Discourses and theoretical assumptions. MIS Quarterly. 2002;**26**(3):213-242

[27] George JF, Iaeono S, Kling R. Learning in context: Extensively computerized work groups as communities-of-practice. Accounting, Management and Information Technology. 1995;**5**(3/4):185-202

[28] Raz AE. Communities of practice or communities of coping? Employee compliance among CSRs in Israeli call centres. The Learning Organization. 2007;**14**(4):375-387

[29] Miner AS, Bassoff P, Moorman C. Organizational improvisation and learning: A field study. Administrative Science Quarterly. 2001;**46**(2):304-337

[30] Gau W. Public servants' workplace learning: A reflection on the concept of communities of practice. Quality & Quantity. 2013;**47**(3):1519-1530

[31] van der Velden M. From communities of practice to communities of resistance: Civil society and cognitive justice. Development. 2004;**47**(1):73-80

[32] Haas A. Crowding at the frontier: Boundary spanners, gatekeepers and knowledge brokers. Journal of Knowledge Management. 2015;**19**(5):1029-1047

[33] Cohen D, Prusak L. In Good Company - How Social Capital Makes Organizations Work. Boston, MA: Harvard Business School Press; 2001

[34] Irick ML. Managing tacit knowledge in organizations. Journal of Knowledge Management Practice. 2007;**8**(3):1-7

[35] Matsumoto Y, Kasamatsu H, Sakakibara M. Challenges in forming transdisciplinary communities of practice for solving environmental problems in developing countries. World Futures. 2022;**78**(8):546-565

[36] Jørgensen U, Lauridsen EH. Environmental professional competences:

The role of communities of practice and spaces for reflexive learning. Greener Management International. 2005;**49**:57-67

[37] Kelly L. Evaluation, research and communities of practice: Program evaluation in museums. Archival Science. 2004;**4**:45-69

[38] Swan J, Scarbrough H, Robertson M. The construction of 'communities of practice' in the management of innovation. Management Learning. 2002;**33**(4):477-496

[39] Ruikar K, Koskela L, Sexton M. Communities of practice in construction case study organisations: Questions and insights. Construction Innovation. 2009;**9**(4):434-448

[40] Parker P, Arthur MB, Kerr Inkson K. Career communities: A preliminary exploration of member-defined career support structures. Journal of Organizational Behavior. 2004;**25**(4):489-514

[41] Arthur MB, Khapova SN, Celeste PM, Wilderom CPM. Career success in a boundaryless career world. Journal of Organizational Behavior. 2005;**26**(2):177-202

[42] Stewart TA. Company values that add value. Fortune. 1996;**8**:99

[43] Buckley PJ, Carter MJ. A formal analysis of knowledge combination in multinational enterprises. Journal of International Business Studies. 2004;**35**(5):371-384

[44] Daniels C, Grove D, Mundt E. Command and communities of practice. Air & Space Power Journal. 2006;**20**(4):52-62

[45] Ishiyama N. Role of knowledge brokers in communities of practice in Japan. Journal of Knowledge Management. 2016;**20**(6):1302-1317

[46] Handley K, Sturdy A, Fincham R, Clark T. Within and beyond communities of practice: Making sense of learning through participation, identity and practice. Journal of Management Studies. 2006;**43**(3):641-653

[47] Yin RK. Case Study Research. 2nd ed. Thous and Oaks, CA: Sage Publications; 1994

[48] May T. Social Research. 3rd ed. Buckingham: Open University Press; 2001